Reflections of Grace

Jacob Harris

ISBN 979-8-89428-253-4 (paperback)
ISBN 979-8-89428-254-1 (digital)

Christian Faith Publishing
832 Park Avenue
Meadville, PA 16335
www.christianfaithpublishing.com

All biblical citations were derived from the King James Version of the Holy Bible.

Printed in the United States of America

1

Grace in Our Weakness

In 1899, a poem was written by Henry Coyle titled "Thankful Heart," that said the following about the grace of God. The poem states, "For we are human, weak and prone to wrong, and by Thy grace alone are we made strong."

Profoundly, Coyle articulates one of the many attributes of godly grace. We know that is true because, in Paul's second letter to the Corinthians, Paul writes about the sufficiency of grace in strengthening him throughout his afflictions. In 2 Corinthians 12:9–10, he writes, "And he said unto me, My grace is sufficient for thee: for my strength is made perfect in weakness. Most gladly therefore will I rather glory in my infirmities, that the power of Christ may rest upon me. Therefore I take pleasure in infirmities, in reproaches, in necessities, in persecutions, in distresses for Christ's sake: for when I am weak, then am I strong."

Biblical grace is a considerably inclusive term considering its many different functions highlighted in the Bible. It is in our weakness and depravity that Christ saves us (Romans 5:8), and it is in this weakness where the strength of His Gospel is made perfect and edifies and enriches the believer.

God is in the business of transforming weakness into strength and using the foolish things of this earth to confound the mighty (1 Corinthians 1:27). The grace of God operates through ways that seem contrary to man's schemes and the desires of the flesh. It operates in the mystery of Christ and in the riches of His glory that come through believing in His death, burial, and resurrection.

Enriching grace is abundant for the weak because Christ who is in you is strong.

2

Evel Knievel Faith

Evel Knievel. The name often brings various connotations to mind of a stuntman jumping high and far through the air over buses and obstacles, and of course, there's his famously failed attempt over the Snake River Canyon. Evel Knievel was truly a man who knew how to live his life thrill to thrill and experience to experience.

Interestingly enough, he is also a man characterized by his many injuries. During his lifetime, Knievel suffered 433 bone fractures and a spot in the Guinness World Records as the survivor of "most bones broken in a lifetime." He was a larger-than-life entertainer who thrived off the thrill of risky motorcycle acrobatics.

As much as I love watching these stunts, there is a reason that I mention this real-life legend of a man. In my short lifetime, I have found that it is often way more enticing to take the Evel Knievel model of faith than to live in the joy and peace that God offers. This model of life often makes the Christian live revival service to revival service, Sunday to Sunday, worship concert to worship concert, with the time in between confused and asking questions such as "Where is God?" or "Why don't I feel God like I used to?"

There came a point in my personal life where I had to come to understand that our relationship with Christ and the salvation He offers is not based upon my feelings, but rather my position. Let me explain.

When we first believe in the Gospel of Jesus Christ, which was revealed by the revelation of Jesus to the apostle Paul (Galatians 1:11–12), something rather marvelous occurs. At this point, we have a position change. We are placed and sealed by the Spirit in Christ Jesus and He in us. This is affirmed in 2 Corinthians 5:17, where it can be read, "Therefore if any man be in Christ, he is a new creature: old things are passed away; behold, all things are become new."

Likewise, Galatians 2:20 tells the Christian that as we are in Him, He abides in us. Paul states, "I am crucified with Christ: nevertheless I live; yet not I, but Christ liveth in me: and the life which I now live in the flesh I live by the faith of the Son of God, who loved me, and gave himself for me."

We are no longer in the position of the Israelites who relied on continuous sacrifices, and the Spirit does not waver within the Christian. It does not come and go, it does not need a prayer asking Jesus to show up, and Jesus is not found in an experience. His power is manifested in His Gospel, and He resides in the soul of every believer.

Let this be encouragement as you move throughout your days. Be encouraged that in your ups and your downs, in your excitement and boredom, in your peace and your anxiousness, God is with you. You do not need an exciting experience to ascertain God or an Evel Knievel faith. The Lord is with you.

3

Spiritual Endurance

The world is an absolutely cancerous place.

I intend for the word *cancerous* to stand out. I intend for this word to be prominent and for its many various meanings to come to the forefront of your mind. No meaning, to my knowledge, could bring about any semblance of anything positive. It is a harmful, mutated abnormality in any conceivable context, including the condition of the world that is, ever since the sin of Adam and Eve separated humanity from a right relationship with God the Father.

From this point onward, history has illuminated the depraved and corrupted earth, with an uncountable number of horrific events that continuously move our planet farther and farther away from the perfect canvas from which God first painted. Our own lives are a testimony of innumerable trials faced and often have the common individual searching through the Barnes & Noble self-help book section seeking an answer to the question "How can I endure?"

Dr. Roger Bannister once sought this answer under completely different circumstances. Roger Bannister was an incredible middle-distance track athlete who had many adorning achievements in his day. However, his legacy stands as a monument to endurance because of one notable achievement. In 1954, he became the first human being to run a sub-four-minute mile. Many track enthusiasts are bewildered by this procurement because he did this despite having a low-mileage training system and being virtually self-coached.

Saying this, my surprise was alleviated after examining some quotes by Roger Bannister. These quotes allowed me to look into the mindset of Roger Bannister and the mentality that he had developed to endure. Roger Bannister once stated, "The man who can drive himself further once the effort gets painful is the man who will win."

As a track runner myself, this quote sends chills down my spine as very rarely do I hear anything this true about the sport of track and field. As a Christian, the words of Paul resound even louder. In Philippians 3:13–14, Paul offers insight into what it means to endure as a Christian. He affirms, "Brethren, I count not myself to have apprehended: but this one thing I do, forgetting those things which are behind, and reaching forth unto those things which are before, I press toward the mark for the prize of the high calling of God in Christ Jesus."

To make it simpler. The key to spiritual endurance is "hope." Upon the reception of the Gospel of Jesus Christ, Christians inherit a very special hope. The apostle Paul often refers to this hope as a prize. In 1 Corinthians 9:24–25, Paul teaches, "Know ye not that they which run in a race run all, but one receiveth the prize? So run, that ye may obtain. And every man that striveth for the mastery is temperate in all things. Now they do it to obtain a corruptible crown; but we an incorruptible."

We, as Christians, have the hope of heaven eternal. An enriching hope that can constantly reassure us that no matter what this fleshly, rotten, corruptible world brings, we have the treasure of God's glory as our inheritance. He offers His peace and joy to sustain us on the journey home. This peace and joy are reflected upon by the psalmist himself when he writes, "I will both lay me down in peace, and sleep: for thou, Lord, only makest me dwell in safety" (Psalm 4:8). This inheritance I am referring to is not achieved by anything that we did, but by Christ alone, so that no man boasts.

Saying this, friends, as you move throughout your week, living in the grace of God, pray with a heart of thanksgiving for the hope that God has given to us freely. An enduring hope that carries us forward closer and closer to the Father through Christ Jesus.

To close, if any reader sees this devotion and does not know the hope of which I speak and has not believed in the Gospel of Jesus Christ, I encourage you to reach out to me through the email provided on my contact page and allow me to guide you through what the Bible says about this wonderful gift of Jesus.

4

Motivation from McDonald's

You ever have those days where you feel just…blaaah… You know, the days when you look in the mirror, and you're shocked to see Oscar the Grouch staring back? Just me?

Well, we all have days where our insecurities seem more obvious than usual. I recently had one of those days. I rolled out of bed surprised to find a glaring blemish glowing brightly on my forehead. My commute to work did my hair no favors as the wind and humidity transformed it into a giant puffball. Let's just say I wasn't feeling runway-ready. Sadly, something as vain as my appearance did affect my mood, and I remember having negative and gloomy feelings. That was until a fast-food employee transformed my whole day.

Feeling drained, I decided to make a quick stop at a McDonald's. Ready to bury my insecurities with a Big Mac, I pulled up to the cash register to pay. A young woman greeted me cheerily, and her tone was so upbeat it took me by surprise! What she then said made my day. As she took my card, she looked at me and said, "Wow! Your eyes are so pretty!" That little compliment warmed my heart. I grinned like an idiot and shyly replied "Thank you." And that's it. She gave me my food, and I drove off.

Except that wasn't just it. That small little interaction changed my whole mood, and I went from feeling down on myself to feeling special. That woman was able to affect my day for the better with just a few simple words. The point of this story is that you can do the same for others!

The First Epistle to the Thessalonians 5:11 says, "Therefore encourage one another and build each other up, just as in fact you are doing." God asks us to encourage each other and build each other up. This world is so full of negativity and pushes us to nitpick ourselves and one another. Let us push back by sharing God's love through the power of encouragement! Look for ways to compliment a stranger like that young lady did for me.

You could share with your friends why you love them or show your appreciation toward your coworkers or boss. You can simply give out a compliment to a stranger in the grocery store, at the bus stop, or wherever else! Remember to look for the positives, and don't be afraid to point them out! It makes all the difference!

I want to encourage you all by saying you are beautifully and wonderfully made. God is perfect and He doesn't make mistakes. Therefore, *you* are not a mistake, and don't you dare insult Him by thinking so! Share this good news with the people you love and maybe even a sweet fast-food cashier. It might just change someone's day for the better just like mine was.

5

Ad Activity

The other day, I was watching the National Pickleball Championship games while on the internet. Within the hour, I started receiving sales ads for everything pickleball: paddles, balls, shoes, lessons, and even pickle-ball glasses. I was being pursued from every side.

I began to think about how God through Jesus by the Holy Spirit has pursued me not for harm or brim (Ephesians 2:7) but for good. So now instead of being bombarded with all the wares and things of this present and evil world, I have set my affection on things above and not on things on the earth (Colossians 3:1–2).

So I can rest in my standing with Christ. I need nothing else, whether it be religious works or a sales pitch for things that will instantly make me play better. Let the right thing pursue you. We should rest assured that God pursues us. He loves us so much that He gave us the most precious gift of all time. He sacrificed His only begotten Son to pay our sin debt. He did not sin, and He did not owe the same wage of sin that every human owed (Romans 6:23).

Once we believe what Jesus did for us (1 Corinthians 15:3-4), our relationship is made personal; and no matter how far we fall away from Him, God still loves us and pursues us. He pursues while still teaching us the effects of sin on our lives. For we still have to deal with the consequences of sin, yet He never gives up on us. He never lets go of us because He is faithful (Romans 5:1–2).

6

Tough Feet

Feet. When I say it, everyone has a thought that springs to the forefront of their mind. We think of words such as *smelly*, *hairy*, *walk*, *run*, *big*, *small*, and so on. It is a body part, and like all body parts, it may need some maintenance.

For most people, feet are used so often that their importance to their owner is diminished. As you read, please allow me to reinstate them as a crucial implement for the journey that is often referred to as "the Christian Walk."

I once read a quote from the great philosopher Dr. Seuss that states, "Left foot. Right foot. Feet. Feet. Feet. How many, many feet do you meet."

When looking at this quote concerning the Body of Christ, I can make a few connections. The first connection is just how important feet are. Paul had a marvelous understanding of feet and their biblical position. In Romans 10:13–15, Paul exclaims:

> For whosoever shall call upon the name of the Lord shall be saved.
>
> How then shall they call on him in whom they have not believed? and how shall they believe in him of whom they have not heard? and how shall they hear without a preacher?

> And how shall they preach, except they be sent? as it is written, How beautiful are the feet of them that preach the gospel of peace, and bring glad tidings of good things!

He begins his exclamation by stating that whoever shall call upon the name of the Lord shall be saved. The Gospel is a very inclusive message. It has authority and has been endowed with the power to change lives. This power is in the name and finished work of Jesus Christ. Paul then asks a skillful barrage of questions that ultimately conclude with the question,

> And how shall they preach, except they be sent?

Paul affirms the power of the Gospel and what it can do; however, this begs the practical question of getting this power into the lost, broken, and powerless souls of unbelievers. The answer is to, quite literally, put feet to the Gospel.

This often seems to be a looming task, but when placed into the perspective that you are not alone in this duty, we begin to understand why exactly the Gospel is referred to as the "gospel of peace." As Christians, our feet carry us to where our words can glorify the work of God in our lives. As the Christian church, this is one of the reasons that unity is so important. Unified, all these feet moving in one accord and sound mind will make a significant impact. Unified, our joy is blanketed by the providence of God.

Another note that I would like to add is regarding the preparation for our sending. God graciously equips us through the Gospel. In Ephesians 6:15, Paul informs his reader that our feet are shod ("equipped with shoes") with the preparation of the gospel of peace. When Paul uses the term *shod*, he is not referring to the shoes that cover our feet. He is referring to the shoeing of horses' feet, which supports and increases the durability of horses while they work.

This is the kind of spiritual shoe that we need because the spreading of the Gospel will take us to all kinds of rocky places and terrains. We will find ourselves in valleys, mountaintops, hurt, and healing. Amid all the places that our feet take us for the furthering of the Gospel, we can rest assured that we can have joy and peace through it all.

In the power of the Gospel, we can relate to the words of the psalmist David when he proclaims, "Hold up my goings in thy paths, that my footsteps slip not" (Psalm 17:5). In the power of the Gospel, we can also relate to the words of the prophet Habakkuk when he proclaims, "The Lord God is my strength, and he will make my feet like hinds' feet, and he will make me to walk upon mine high places" (Habakkuk 3:19). In the power of the Gospel, we can relate to the words of Dr. Seuss and find out just how many more feet we can meet.

When in Christ, He gives us tough feet.

7

The Big Protest

Polls have estimated that roughly 15 million people in the United States participated in some sort of protest in the year 2020. But the purpose of this devotion is not about that.

I want to talk about the big protest. I am speaking about when God protested against sin. How did God do this, you may ask? It is when you look at Calvary. Jesus puts away sin by the sacrifice of Himself. The grace of God teaches you not to live in sin (Titus 2:11–12). The resurrection teaches you to live and to have life because sin has been dealt with. This is how Christ intended for us to live (1 John 3:14–15).

All sin begins in the heart. You cannot change the inside by fixing up the outside. Proverbs 15:16 affirms, "The thoughts of the wicked are an abomination to the Lord."

Even the word protest was not associated with marches and rallies until the early twentieth century and has never been associated with rioting and looting. I would like to leave you with the words of Paul in Ephesians 4:31–32:

> Let all bitterness, and wrath, and anger, and clamour, and evil speaking, be put away from you, with all malice:

> And be ye kind one to another, tender-hearted, forgiving one another, even as God for Christ's sake hath forgiven you.

Live in grace and peace, not protest and riot.

8

Happy Mother's Day

Have you all ever seen the movie *The Land Before Time*? I strongly recommend it! That is unless you have a strange aversion to bawling your eyes out. If you need a cathartic cry, this is the movie to watch.

This movie is about a group of young cartoon dinosaurs joining together as they are separated from their families. This occurs as they make their way to the luscious Great Valley. So obviously, this is a very complex story.

Anyway, the reason I bring up this movie is because of one particular scene. The character, Little Foot, is suddenly attacked and chased by the dinosaur Sharp Tooth. Little Foot's mother steps in, and thus commences a great battle. As Sharp Tooth falls, you can't help but sigh in relief as our beloved dinosaur friends are seemingly safe.

That is until you realize that Little Foot's mother is greatly injured and cannot complete their journey. As her baby Little Foot begs her to get up, she gently replies, "I'll be with you. Even if you can't see me. Little Foot, let your heart guide you. It whispers."

Isn't a mother's love just like that? It is like their love is imprinted on our hearts. It guides us even when we can't see it. It is a lot like God's love. In 1 John 3:16, the apostle John states, "By this we know love, that He laid down His life for us, and we ought to lay down our lives for the brothers."

It's almost like a cycle. The love that God instills in a mother is passed on to her child and then so on. God's love and a mother's love have something in common. It is a sacrificial love.

My mother spent many early mornings helping me finish last-minute school projects and late nights caring for me when my tummy hurt. Long days of work never stop her from asking about my life and being invested in my day. She is kind, smart, silly, caring, sweet, funny, and powerful. She has the gentleness of a sheep but the fury of a lioness. She is my confidante, my role model, my safe place, and most importantly, my mother. Because she wasn't just born a mother. Every day, she chooses to be my mother, and that is one of the greatest demonstrations of God's love.

So today and every day, thank your mother, biological or adopted. Thank you, Momma, for being the most wonderful woman in the world and for sharing God's love with me every day. Happy Mother's Day!

9

A Sincere Lie

I have once heard it said, "It doesn't matter what you believe just so long as you're sincere."

Scratch that.

I have heard an innumerable number of times that "it doesn't matter what you believe just so long as you're sincere." Each time this phrase slithers off a Christian's tongue, my ears ring as if a bomb has detonated nearby. The implications of that train of thought can derail a way of life quickly. R. C. Sproul once addressed this spiritually compromising quote, saying, "This little expression, 'It doesn't matter what you believe as long as you're sincere,' is a monstrous lie."

Notice, Sproul utilizes the phrase "little expression." This was a purposeful illustration of one of the scariest realities regarding this saying. It seems all too little; yet, the implications of sewing this mentality into Christian theology are earthshaking.

Sproul contrasts "little expression" and "monstrous lie" to show that God cares about the details. It is by this truth that the apostle Paul pleads "that we henceforth be no more children tossed to and from and carried about with every wind of doctrine by the sleight of men and cunning craftiness, whereby they lie in wait to deceive." There are many options of things to believe spiritually; however, the options are narrow. This sincere lie cannot be further from the truth. Nonetheless, if you have believed it, you are not far from grace. Most importantly, begin with salvation by Christ's death, burial, and resurrection alone and then study, study, and study. We are called to be people who live by each letter of the Word (2 Timothy 2:15)!

10

Comments from the Peanut Gallery

This phrase was first coined by the creator of *Peanuts*, Charles M. Schulz. It is an interesting quotation considering the devout Christian nature of Schulz that often resonated in his TV specials and comic strips. Although I admire many of his sayings and the contributions made by him to American culture, I would like to attempt to "stop the buck here." This comment is used way too often and often combats the Gospel of Jesus Christ instead of driving it forward to the many who need salvation.

When we believe in the Gospel, there is an inner work that is accomplished. We are placed in Christ and likewise, Christ is in us (Romans 8:10; 2 Corinthians 5:17). Paul explains that old things are passed away and that all things become new. The Gospel of Jesus is the first example of why what we believe matters. Anything apart from the pure, unsolicited Gospel that His Word provides (1 Corinthians 15:3-4) is a false hope and not a means for salvation.

Sincerity of heart is important, accompanying the belief in the finished work of Jesus Christ. What we believe matters. Jesus Himself lays an exclusive claim to this fact when He proclaims in John 14:6, "I am the way, the truth, and the life: no man cometh unto the Father, but by me." Jesus is pointing to His equivalence with God and pointing forward to the good news that He is making a way for all to come before God the Father and have intimacy with Him. The actuality is that He is the only way to Him. I further emphasize that what we believe matters.

11

Doctrine Isn't Important, Is It?

In the heading, I ask the question so that I can emphatically shout through your screen, "Yes! Doctrine is absolutely important!" In the Epistle of Titus, we find Paul giving the qualifications of the elders of the church in Crete. In listing the qualifications, Paul states in Titus 1:9 that an elder must be, "holding fast the faithful word as he hath been taught, that he may be able by sound doctrine both to exhort and to convince the gainsayers."

An interesting note that I feel is necessary to make is the importance of this qualification of the elders. Elders carry with them spiritual experience. One of them is that they have seen and experienced the malignant effects of people not adhering to godly wisdom. Continuing, Paul resumes in Titus 2:1 by stating, "But speak thou the things which become sound doctrine."

Following this, Paul illuminates and exemplifies how sound doctrine presents itself in our lives and that sound doctrine needs to be presented for the sake of the Gospel of Jesus Christ.

12

Whitewashed Tombs

> Woe unto you, scribes and Pharisees, hypocrites! for ye are like unto whited sepulchres, which indeed appear beautiful outward, but are within full of dead men's bones, and of all uncleanness. Even so ye also outwardly appear righteous unto men, but within ye are full of hypocrisy and iniquity.
>
> —Matthew 23:27–28

There comes a time in Scripture, toward the end of Christ's early ministry, after constantly being assaulted by the doubt and blasphemy of the Pharisees, that Jesus essentially preaches a sermon against the hypocrisy of the Pharisees. As this message progresses, Jesus addresses a common Jewish practice and likens it to the wicked actions of the religious leaders.

There came a time once a year when the Jews, out of respect for their dead and fear that the tombs of the dead would defile the population, would cover their tombs in white chalk and lime. It was a bit of superstition as the religious leaders were looking for every religious aspect to dominate and ensure that above all else, they made and were presented as holy. But Christ mocks their empty and vain religion by addressing them as chalky tombs that look beautiful on the outside, yet are dead as the bodies within their family tombs.

This is a vicious metaphor that ties perfectly to whom Jesus attributes as their father, Satan (John 8:44–46).

Years later, Paul addresses the Jews of Rome in a likewise manner by asking the question, "And thinkest thou this, O man, that judgest them which do such things, and doest the same, that thou shalt escape the judgment of God?" (Romans 2:3).

The trouble with such passages is that we are called to be blameless and holy in other passages, which seems almost contrary to what is preached in these passages. But the difference is this: the Pharisees of Jesus's time and the Jews of Paul's time had a disconnect between their inner being and their outer being. Their outer being had everything together and looked righteous, but as God looked at them, He saw a heart of filthy stone. They were hypocrites in every sense of the word, and Jesus disdains hypocrisy. Hypocrisy only seeks to please the flesh, while true faith pleases the Spirit.

Let this message be a subtle reminder to practice introspection. Day by day, are you putting on the new man and woman of Christ and suppressing the fleshly old man and woman who tries to rear his head up? Or are you a whitewashed tomb, dead from the get-go? If this is you, flee to Scripture and be renewed. Lay your life down as a living sacrifice and be transformed by the renewing of your mind (Romans 12:1–2).

Finale

I would like to conclude by offering this Scripture as a blessing, encouraging you to grow in sound doctrine found in the Word of God and to "speak the truth in love." And I would like to conclude with a warning against all the false teachers, unsound doctrine, and things contrary to sound doctrine that may be encountered.

Ephesians 4:14–15 urges that

> we henceforth be no more children, tossed to and fro, and carried about with every wind of doctrine, by the sleight of men, and cunning craftiness, whereby they lie in wait to deceive;
>
> But speaking the truth in love may grow up into him in all things, which is the head, even Christ.

Remember, sincerity is important when it accompanies the belief and acceptance of God's Word.

13

Bad Ankles

Blessed be God, even the Father of our Lord Jesus Christ, the Father of mercies, and the God of all comfort; Who comforteth us in all our tribulation, that we may be able to comfort them which are in any trouble, by the comfort wherewith we ourselves are comforted of God.

—2 Corinthians 1:3–4

I have been a runner for most of my life. It has been an enjoyable experience! Except for the pulls, the strains, the tears (from my eyes and muscles), the microfractures, and the rolled and possibly broken feet and ankles, which brings me today's focus—bad ankles. There is not a day that goes by where my ankles do not ache or swell. This is crazy considering I do not even run like I used to.

But I know the day it all began. When I was in my freshman year of high school, I had a good year running an event called the three hundred-intermediate hurdles. In our conference, I had worked my way as a freshman to second in the conference. Then one meet before regionals, where I was set to qualify, I lined up in the blocks. I had an absolutely beautiful start! Then on the first hurdles, my foot turned in and cracked, and as I fell, I saw the bottom of my spikes. Was my ankle broken? Probably. I tough-guyed it out.

From that point on, my ankle was never the same and has recurring injuries. When doing rigorous exercise, I have learned to trust ankle braces and ankle wraps. I do very little exercise without one on. Knowing my insufficiency, I feel so much more comfortable when something is hugging my ankle tight. When something is not on my ankles, I feel scared to live. Wrapped tight, I feel secure.

As I wrapped my ankle before a run the other day, I felt a pang of guilt. Whether I should have it or not, I do not know. But I thought about this. In some of life's hardest moments, I trust ankle wraps to hold me tight but often fall short of trusting God to hold me tight. My stress. My worry. I am a human. But God is always there (Romans 8:28). Jesus paid the ultimate price. He paid our ransom with His life, so we are able to freely speak with God and attain His comfort. Lean into His protective embrace (Psalm 23:4), for He loves you and is infinitely stronger than any ankle wrap. So fall on your knees and worship.

14

Redeeming the Time

In the prior devotional, a very subtle lie was evaluated. The quote said, "It doesn't matter what you believe, just so long as you're sincere." Well, it would be worthwhile to take a deeper look at this quote.

I once heard it said that "tomorrow is often the busiest day of the week."

When putting this anonymous quote into perspective, my anxieties often magnify at the prospect of having to put a duty off till the next day. I am inspired to work today, but only in response to a fear of the unknowns to come in the upcoming twenty-four hours.

Although I do not agree with religious perspectives, I find New Age author Wayne Dyer's definition of procrastination to be spot on. He diminishes procrastination to be nothing more than "the art of keeping up with yesterday and avoiding today."

As a college student, I am all too familiar with this term. As are many people at some point in their life. This art can very well become an injurious addiction if not habitually curbed. The Bible offers very practical insight into the art of time management.

In Ephesians 5:16–18, Paul addresses a pertinent time management strategy for followers of God, who are those who walk in the love of Jesus Christ. This time management strategy is to live, "redeeming the time." This essentially means to live according to

God's timeline for His will. This means serving the Lord and utilizing the time that is gifted to us. Utilizing this time may require changes to our schedules and stewardship of our time.

Ephesians 5:16–18 states

> See then that ye walk circumspectly, not as fools, but as wise, redeeming the time, because the days are evil. Wherefore be ye not unwise, but understanding what the will of the Lord is.

In this instruction, the apostle Paul instructs the Christian to redeem the time, "because the days are evil." You may ask (or this may just be my overcurious mind), how is a day evil? After all, a day is just a twenty-four-hour period, right?

The answer to this question is yes, a day is a twenty-four-hour period. However, this period can become evil with the exclusion of Christ's will in our lives. Days become evil when they are not spent living for God's will. When I carry this perspective, I no longer live out of fear of tomorrow but rather live in the opportunities of today.

In Ephesians 5:16–18, Paul gives a plan of action, firm details, and a goal to measure by. The goal for us, as we are living a lifestyle "redeeming the time," is based on the following question: Are we understanding the will of God (verse 18)?

The will of God is to "have all men to be saved, and to come unto the knowledge of the truth" (1 Timothy 2:4). This is a serious task that requires our time and spiritual discipline in the study of the Scriptures, prayer, and sharing the Gospel of Jesus Christ.

Saying this, I do not encourage undergoing this task of time management for the edification of the Body of Christ in reckless abandon. That is not biblical instruction, especially not in the context of the Scripture here. Paul states in Ephesians 5:16 to "see then that ye walk circumspectly, not as fools, but as wise." Walking "circumspectly" implies a level of cautiousness, weighing circumstances, and a desire to avoid mistakes.

One way to avoid critical mistakes is by following the pattern of godly wisdom ordained within the Scriptures. Apart from this, all men and women become fools (if not already are). Lastly, time management is an art that can carry over from biblical practices into many aspects of life and may organize our intentions organically. If time is being managed and we are truly attempting to reduce the vain and pointless rhythms of life for the glory of God and the furthering of His Gospel, then things that distract us from this task will dissipate in the effort.

15

Seasons of Change

Have you all noticed the weather lately? Personally, it has been so refreshing to me! Where I live, we are currently in the throes of spring weather. The grass is a fragrant green, the flowers are blooming in vibrant colors, and you can hear the sweet chatter of creatures waking up from their winter slumber.

Now, don't get me wrong… This time of year isn't all that it's cracked up to be. The smelly grass can be itchy to your nose, the pollen from the flowers irritates your eyes, and the constant chirping of the woodland creatures isn't always pleasant at six o'clock on Saturday mornings.

What do you think of spring? I honestly used to dislike the season. Something about all the changes in the environment stirred up anxiety about change in my own life. Change can be uncomfortable and even scary; however, it is also necessary. God at times requires change in our lives, just like He created nature to change.

Proverbs 16:9 says,

> In their hearts humans plan their course, but the Lord establishes their steps.

God has a plan for each and every one of us. Maybe your path has suddenly taken a sharp turn and you are afraid to keep moving.

I know I've been there many times. Why make a change in your life when everything is going just fine?

I want to encourage you by asking you to take a look at the world around you. You can see caterpillars transform into butterflies, daffodils sprout up in the midst of rocky terrain, and baby birds hesitantly hatch into the new world. There is a purpose for this season and change.

Sure, I guess the caterpillar was doing alright as a funny-looking green worm, but without its metamorphosis, we would never have the captivating butterfly! The same goes for the bright daffodils, the little hatchlings, and for *you*!

This season of change in your own life is a chance for beauty! God's plan for you may seem uncertain; however, He has wondrous things in your future. If God has such intricate plans for the ants and the plants, wouldn't you think His plans for you are even greater?!

Our lives and our world feel ever-changing, but remember, our God never changes and neither does His love for you! Hebrews 13:8 says, "Jesus Christ is the same yesterday and today and forever."

So go outside, take a deep breath, and embrace the change God has for you! But don't forget to take your allergy pills!

16

Taking Exams

Well, it's that time of year when I hear lots of friends and family say, "I'm taking exams." No one enjoys them, but they are useful. You don't want to spend all those days and nights studying and not knowing if you learned anything.

In life, we must all give ourselves an exam, and the subject is salvation. Do not worry though, it is a short exam.

Question 1: Do I need to be saved?

Answer: Yes. "What then? Are we better than they? No, in no wise: for we have before proved both Jews and Gentiles, that they are all under sin" (Romans 3:9). If we cannot understand how terrible sin is, we won't appreciate the greatness of salvation.

Question 2: Can I save myself?

Answer: No. "For He [God] hath made Him [Jesus] to be sin for us, who knew no sin; that we might be made the righteousness of God in Him [Christ]" (2 Corinthians 5:21). He took our hell down here, so we might have His heaven up yonder. He did that for us.

Question 3: How many things must I do?

Answer: One. Believe that Christ died for our sins (Acts 16:31), that He buried our sins with Him, and then He rose from the dead for our justification (1 Corinthians 15:3–4).

Well, that wasn't so bad of an exam. Let's go celebrate!

> Speaking to yourselves in psalms and hymns and spiritual songs, singing and making melody in your heart to the Lord. (Ephesians 5:19)

17

Called to Arms

Have you ever watched the movie *Hacksaw Ridge*? It is an inspiring yet harrowing tale of a soldier in the United States Army during World War II. This soldier was no ordinary soldier, however, because he was a staunch pacifist. This soldier refused to carry a weapon and, furthermore, refused to kill!

This was, and is, an oddity of a tale as this soldier lived out an extremely unpopular attitude toward the sanctity of life. Influenced by his unusual belief, the soldier saved seventy-five men's lives through his undying care for them in their battles. For his efforts on the Pacific island of Okinawa, he received the Presidential Medal of Honor, the highest honor achievable within the military.

This movie is an inspiring cinematic work that has received numerous awards from various film festivals and presenters. What inspires me most, however, is that this story is based on a true story, about a real soldier named Corporal Desmond Doss, who saved many men's lives in a truly dramatic fashion while injuring himself!

I am also inspired by Doss's bravery. For him to be used to his greatest potential, he had to deny orders to kill. He denied these orders and rather focused his efforts on the physical salvation of others. There is something to be learned from the life of Desmond Doss. Several things can be derived from our spiritual enrichment.

18

Unpopular Truth

The first lesson that I would like to note is that the popularity of something does not equal the truth of something. Poet Criss Jami once wrote, "When you're the only sane person, you look like the only insane person." The older that I get, the more I find truth in this remark.

Looking at modern culture in contrast to biblical statutes, we can find seemingly innumerable examples of this. Need a few examples? Try these:

- *John 14:6*. "Jesus saith unto him, I am the way, the truth, and the life: no man cometh unto the Father, but by me."
    - This is an easy illustration of unpopular truth, even in Christian circles. Jesus's life and finished work provide a way for us to the Father because Jesus is the way, truth, and life. We cannot buy, work, or hope our way to Christ. *The* truth is that you need to believe.
- *John 17:17*. "Sanctify them through thy truth: thy word is truth."
    - Once again, we find another easy example of unpopular truth. The Word of God is truth. As Jesus's time on earth neared an end, He affirmed this truth. This truly goes back to John 14:6 where Jesus claims that He is

the truth. This connects because God's Word is truth, Jesus is God, and the Word is God (John 1:1). This makes Jesus, the Word of Truth incarnate (in the flesh) (John 1:14). Despite clear evidence, the world often denies God's Word as truth, and many Christians deny God's Word as truth and rather follow doctrines of devils (1 Timothy 4:1).

- *Colossians 3:3*. "For ye are dead, and your life is hid with Christ in God."
    - Another unpopular truth is that when we believe and accept the Gospel of Jesus Christ, our identity is in Him. This is a truth that is often overlooked by secular culture and oftentimes not practically lived in the life of a Christian (thus being exchanged for a lesser truth, identifying ourselves with our past mistakes and current fears).

The Bible is full of unpopular truths! Because of this, I want to help point you in the right direction of where we should derive our truth, even at the cost of going against the grain.

19

God, Commander in Chief

One perspective that can help us remain centered on truth is to liken our Christian walk to an enlistment in a very special force: the army of God.

The apostle Paul makes this connection in 2 Timothy 2:3–4 when he states, "Thou therefore endure hardness, as a good soldier of Jesus Christ. No man that warreth entangleth himself with the affairs of this life; that he may please him who hath chosen him to be a soldier." As good soldiers in Christ, we are instructed to endure hardness (much like any soldier would).

We are also instructed to not entangle ourselves in the affairs of this life. Instead, our intentions and focus should be on what pleases our Commander in Chief, God. In Galatians 1:10, Paul warns against serving the latter option of pleasing man. He writes,

> For do I now persuade men, or God? or do I seek to please men? for if I yet pleased men, I should not be the servant of Christ.

In the military, leaving your post has two categories, things we must beware as good soldiers for Christ: absence without official leave (AWOL) and desertion. Do not get consumed with preaching the ever-popular truths of the culture over the unpopular truths of the Bible. As Christians, when we do this, we are going AWOL. Spiritually, this is leaving the Gospel and doctrine that God has called us to, to please people.

Like the military, there are very serious consequences to going AWOL or deserting. God, like the good Father and Commander He is, will simply leave you to yourself. It is in this position where people see just how insufficient they are without the grace of God. This is a scary place to be spiritually, considering that God and His ways are perfect (Psalm 18:30). This is a truth that no earthly commander can claim.

When we trust in God and His holy word (Hebrews 4:12), our Commander in Chief, we cannot go wrong and are safe. As a minister of God, I can assure you that serving men is an avoidable snare and a trap (Proverbs 29:25).

20

Armor of God

Lastly, some practical advice for you as a good soldier of Christ and standing firm in God's truth. In Ephesians 6:10–18, as Paul addresses our standing in Christ, he instructs the Christian to "be strong in the Lord, and the power of His might." Along with this, he says to put on the "whole armor of God" so that we can stand against the "wiles of the devil." Paul goes on to make it clear that the armor that we wear in the army of God is for our defense and our offense against spiritual attacks.

All the armor listed serves a purpose, from our head (the helmet of salvation, verse 17) to our feet (shoes with the preparation of the gospel of peace, verse 15), for our defense (the shield of faith, verse 16) and as an offensive charge (the sword of the Spirit, verse 17).

The component of the armor I would like to focus on is the action of having your "loins girt about with truth" (verse 14). Girding loins is a practice that would have been very common for soldiers within Paul's time. It essentially means to hike up your robes so that they do not restrict your movement. It is a practice that allows for better motion when taking an offensive.

Saying this, I would like to close by encouraging you, the reader, to gird your loins with the truth and knowledge of God's Word so that we can make moves against the evil tactics of our adversary, the devil. With God as our Commander in Chief, loins girded with His undefiled truth, we are ready to strike down unrighteousness with the sword of the Spirit, which is the Word of God.

21

A God-Owned Patent

At the end of an earlier post on Enriching Grace, the devotion ended with the verse Ephesians 5:19. I thought more about that verse and how one of the most precious things that God ever created was the human voice. The second part of the verse speaks of making a melody in your heart to the Lord. The definition of *melody* is "an agreeable succession of sounds."

God wants our behavior, prayers, and relationships to sing a song with one voice: His. Your voice holds the power to speak life or speak death. The voice has been used as medicine when a hymn of the Lord is sung at the bedside of one who is near death or to sing a lullaby to help a restless child. And when Jesus cried with a loud voice, it shook the world.

So amplify your voice. Even if you can't physically use your voice, we all have a voice within our hearts. Let it sing out.

> That if thou shalt confess with thy mouth the Lord Jesus, and shalt believe in thine heart that God hath raised him from the dead, thou shalt be saved.

> For with the heart man believeth unto righteousness; and with the mouth confession is made unto salvation.

Hallelujah!

22

A Celebrity Advocate

So I have a bit of a guilty pleasure. I'm just slightly obsessed with celebrity gossip. Please, no judgment, but I'm that person holding up the grocery line because I got distracted by some sleazy tabloid magazine.

As you probably know, celebrity news isn't often very wholesome, but today I want to share with you a story that inspired me. You may or may not know the actor Ashton Kutcher. He is best known for his roles in *That '70s Show*, *Jobs*, *Punk'd*, and a slew of romantic comedies. If you didn't know that, then you didn't know that Ashton Kutcher has a twin brother named Michael Kutcher.

Michael isn't an actor like his brother, and he isn't as well-known, but he has had a great impact on the disability community. Today, I read an article about how Michael's actor brother, Ashton, greatly affected his life through a simple interview. Around seventeen years ago, Ashton revealed in an interview that his twin brother Michael had cerebral palsy. Ashton, while only having good intentions, hurt Michael by revealing this information.

"I was very angry. Very angry. I remember speaking to him about it, I didn't want to be the face of CP. I never talked about it," Michael said of the incident. He felt that he didn't want the burden of being the representative of something that he hadn't even accepted in himself.

That was until Michael was reached out to by a mother, asking him to speak at a gala for cerebral palsy. His hesitation changed when he met the woman's young daughter named Bella. Bella also had cerebral palsy, and Michael realized that he wanted to accept himself so people like Bella could also find acceptance.

"I realized I needed to let go of the shame I felt and be a champion for people like Bella," Michael said. "I was finally ready to tell my story, and I knew because of my twin, I'd have a big reach." Michael Kutcher went on to become a spokesperson for the Cerebral Palsy Foundation and also an advisor for an app called Joshin, which helps families find caregivers for their loved ones with disabilities.

In other words, Michael became an advocate. What does it even mean to be an advocate? While discussing celebrities, you may think it's got something to do with promoting some product, politician, or ideology. I think the best way to define an advocate is to look at Jesus Christ.

The First Epistle of John 2:1 says, "My little children, I am writing these things to you so that you may not sin. But if anyone does sin, we have an advocate with the Father, Jesus Christ the righteous." Christ stands in our place for our sins. He is a spokesperson for us to God. Similar to what Michael said, Jesus is a champion for us.

Michael's story made me think about how Jesus is also an advocate for the small people in the world who may not be able to advocate for themselves. Jesus spoke to and loved lepers, prostitutes, tax collectors, and all the rejected in society.

If Jesus was alive today, who would be the "rejected" He would reach out to? Are we advocating for these people? Better yet, are we advocating for God? I know I don't do it like I should. Let us be like Michael, but more importantly like Jesus, and advocate for those around us. Let us stand up for those who can't stand up for themselves.

Not only that, let us empower them through God's love to advocate for themselves. Michael spoke about how shame and lack of acceptance kept him from being an advocate. What's holding you back? I know for myself, I'll admit I let my insecurities get in the way of sharing God's love. I become way too focused on myself rather than the Lord.

Michael's story and Jesus's love have inspired me today to put aside my insecurities and become an advocate. Like Michael, I am also very passionate about the community of individuals with disabilities. What and who are you passionate about? Who do you know that you can champion? Find out and become an advocate for them like Jesus was for you. Don't be afraid to be a champion and an advocate for God's love!

23

Remember the Time

The time of this writing is Memorial Day in the USA. The day is a somber reminder of the brave sacrifices men and women have made to keep the USA a free and just society. I find a wonderful similarity as we visit graves and place flowers or flags at gravestones. We thank them and let them know we remember them, much like in Joshua 4:19–24.

The memorial of twelve stones was to remind the people of God's miracles on their behalf. In the future, the parents could tell how God dried up the Jordan River just as He had dried up the Red Sea so they could cross. We should pass along stories of the protectors of our land and the people who made the ultimate sacrifice. Also, tell them of Jesus who made the ultimate sacrifice, not for land or people (Romans 5:8), but rather for the eternal soul of man (1 Timothy 2:6).

So let's pause and reflect on these things (Philippians 1:3).

24

This Is Just My Face

Once upon a time, I was a moody teenager. I walked around with the posture of a chimpanzee and an unintentional scowl that betrayed forlorn boredom. Although I am more aware now of my face's pitiful expression, I realize that the look on my face was not an indicator of my salvation. Although it could be a representation of my young faith.

A portion of this moody era was my freshman year of high school. Without getting too specific, this year was a time of excitement and fresh opportunity, while also holding moments of frightening, impending unhappiness.

Living in these moments, while I was sitting at dinner with my momma and stepfather, my stepfather asked, "What's wrong with your face?" Being the temperamental adolescent I was, I responded, "This is just my face!" I was dead serious, but my family burst into hearty laughter. Just like that, I had become a running joke in my family.

This is a lesson I look back on and reflect on often. It makes me laugh in my bad times and stands in the bowels of history as a time when I did not let my joy shine through. Joy is a steady, constant reminder of Christ's indwelling within the believer. Joy stands as a characteristic of the Christian. It stands alongside other necessary traits such as grace and peace, although it serves its special function.

In Romans 15:13, Paul reminds the believer of the source of joy. It is of the Lord. The Scripture reads, "May the God of hope fill you with all joy and peace in believing, so that by the power of the Holy Spirit you may abound in hope."

With this in mind, it is my hope that regardless of age or disposition, you can have a smile on your face!

25

To Live

To live is the rarest thing in the world. Most people exist, that is all.
—Oscar Wilde

When I was a younger Christian, I remember that many of my Bible studies were guided by the many questions that I had. A question would develop in my mind and then I would quickly refer to my Bible to find answers.

Some of these questions included "Where does God come from?" "Is there an unforgivable sin?" and "Are there more Christians or non-Christians?"

This last question eventually developed into the question "Are there more people in heaven or hell?" Now as a more mature Christian, this answer seems obvious, looking at the condition of the world. Scripture also affirms this often (John 3:36).

Saying this, although surely out of context, I find the above quote relatable. Life, that is real life, is provided by Jesus Christ's sacrifice on the cross and His victory over grace. Yet the beautiful free gift of grace is rejected more so than it is acceptable (2 Thessalonians 1:8–9). More people just exist, and very few live.

It is my prayer that these numbers flip-flop, but nevertheless, we can live on a mission to see more people live. This change will come through the work of the Holy Spirit and the consistent sharing of the truth. So many people exist and do not know the difference between being on earth and living on earth, and few more know what it means to live in heaven. Life is gifted to us by the life of the Son, Jesus Christ (1 Corinthians 15:3–4). Just believe and live.

"For the wages of sin is death, but the gift of God is eternal life through Jesus Christ our Lord" (Romans 6:23).

26

Joy Is a Constant Attribute

Late in the book of Nehemiah, Nehemiah finds himself offering consolation to the Jewish people who had good reason to displace their joy. They had a torn homeland and numerous adversaries (sound familiar with Israel today?). Yet in the midst of it all, Nehemiah states, "Neither be ye sorry; for the joy of the Lord is your strength" (Nehemiah 8:10).

Nehemiah had it right. Neglect the importance of happiness and uplift the sanctity of joy through it all. Joy is much more than happiness. Happiness is fleeting. The Lord is eternal. He is our source of joy. It is a constant, patient, rejoicing that abides in the Lord.

In Romans 12:12, Paul teaches what it means to be transformed in Christ's grace and what attributes Christians should possess. Paul describes the disposition of joy perfectly in his three-step guide to the undeterred Christian. He writes, "Rejoicing in hope; patient in tribulation; continuing instant in prayer."

Furthermore, joy is never a stand-alone trait; it is reinforced (as mentioned earlier) with other fruits. Galatians 5:22–23 teaches, "But the fruit of the Spirit is love, joy, peace, longsuffering, gentleness, goodness, faith, meekness, temperance: against such there is no law." Once again, we find joy paired with patience and peace. Joy truly is a beautiful constant attribute.

27

Smile! Your Face Can Share Your Joy!

Joy truly is contagious. This is a fact. Studies as recent as 2020 have shown that a person smiling causes other people around them to see the world in a more positive light. This secular study only reinforces what the Bible has taught for thousands of years.

Proverbs 15:13 offers this, "A merry heart maketh a cheerful countenance: but by sorrow of the heart the spirit is broken." Proverbs 17:22 uplifts us with, "A merry heart doeth good like a medicine: but a broken spirit drieth the bones." Do not take these proverbs lightly! Truth is truth.

As Christians, flaunt your joy and share the medicine of your spirit. Let the world know that Christ is the reason we smile through it all and that it is a free gift—a gift freely offered by Jesus Christ who paid the price for it on the cross (Romans 10:9–13).

28

Ever Changing, Never Changing

Have you ever been camping? It is a recreational time in nature that isolates individuals from the bustle of life to rejuvenate themselves. When camping, there is a beautiful thing that takes place early each morning. Once a person crawls into their nice, dry tent to lay their head at night, they wake up in the morning to a nearly extinguished fire; a wet, dewy tent; and a cool, crisp air that pierces deeper than the night prior.

I am always amazed by this change because I never catch it when it's happening. I go to sleep and I wake up to a world different. Reflecting on my camping experiences, I find it truly astounding that none of these elusive nights escape the eyes of God. Nothing in this world can ninja its way out of His gaze.

Hebrews 1:2–3 states in reference to God,

> Hath in these last days spoken unto us by His Son, whom He hath appointed heir of all things, by whom also He made the worlds;
>
> Who being the brightness of His glory, and the express image of His person, and upholding all things by the word of His power, when He had by Himself purged our sins, sat down on the right hand of the Majesty on high.

The very world that we see and don't see consists by the Word of God and can cease to exist by the very same tongue. As Christians, we should have no fear of tomorrow because while we are in God, the matter is controlled by His perfect will. Our souls are safe within the grasp of His Son, the Christ. The world may keep moving, but be encouraged that nothing catches God by surprise.

29

[D]ecision Day

D-Day. This day, June 6, 1944, was the turning point of WWII. Two thousand five hundred Americans were killed. A call to arms was made to the small community of Bedford, Virginia. There were twenty deaths, with nineteen deaths from one company. There were thirty-five total soldiers from Bedford in total, including the National Guard. Imagine the phone operator getting one telegram after another.

These young men had a cause to stop the spread of national socialism, also known as Nazism. This was a dark and evil time. However, the sacrifice of good prevailed. John 1:5 says,

> The light shineth in darkness; and the darkness comprehend it not.

As these men received a charge, we too have received a holy charge (Ephesians 4:1–3). Our fight is even more encompassing than Omaha Beach (see Ephesians 6:12). So may we be good soldiers of the cross, proclaiming the Gospel of Jesus Christ in all its power and truth to overcome evil with good.

The battle lines have been drawn. God has established the one true church, the Body of Christ. We are guardians of the faith, charged with defending and preserving righteousness "which is of

God by faith" (Philippians 3:9). We are not promised an easy victory, but God does give us the armor (Ephesians 6:11). In the end, God gives us victory (1 Corinthians 15:57).

So let us be steadfast and unmovable, always abounding in the work of the Lord. He has equipped us with His Word so may we rightly divide it (2 Timothy 2:15). This is the only way we will be able to stand and withstand in this evil day.

30

Slogans and Creeds

"Ba da ba ba ba, I'm lovin' it!"

Surely, you all are familiar with the famous McDonald's slogan. Or how about, "Have it your way"? I can appreciate a Whopper from Burger King. We have all kinds of slogans, jingles, and catchphrases that run rampant through our minds throughout the day.

How about this one? "Jesus is Lord." This simple slogan is often said idly without any true attention to the significance of the motto. "Jesus is Lord" is an ancient creed that is reaffirmed time and time again, especially in Pauline texts such as Romans, Philippians, and Colossians. Acceptance of this slogan has an eternal bearing on the direction of man. It is a saying that simply needs to become more than a saying and be incorporated into an unshakable foundation of truth in our lives.

In Romans 10:9, Paul shows that this truth is tightly woven into the essence of the Gospel and salvation. Paul proclaims, "That if thou shalt confess with thy mouth the Lord Jesus, and shalt believe in thine heart that God hath raised Him from the dead, thou shalt be saved."

When we live by the slogan "Jesus is Lord," we live in the acknowledgment that Jesus is 100 percent man, 100 percent God, and this truth is only evident by the Holy Spirit. The First Epistle to the Corinthians 12:3 states, "Wherefore I give you to understand, that no man speaking by the Spirit of God calleth Jesus accursed: and that no man can say that Jesus is the Lord, but by the Holy Ghost."

We also acknowledge Christ as Lord. "Duh," right? But what does this mean in a practical context? *Lord* is not just some archaic term used in medieval times to depict a noble. It describes a complete ruler over a domain with unquestionable authority. In our personal lives, that domain is our personal lives: our soul, spirit, mind, and body. No one or no other thing can be lord over this. Only Jesus our Lord is able to preserve us into eternity.

The First Letter to the Thessalonians 5:23 states,

> And the very God of peace sanctify you wholly; and I pray God your whole spirit and soul and body be preserved blameless unto the coming of our Lord Jesus Christ."

Only Christ can preserve us, and only Christ is worthy to be feared as Lord. He makes this evident in His earthly ministry when He claims in Matthew 10:28,

> And fear not them which kill the body, but are not able to kill the soul: but rather fear Him which is able to destroy both soul and body in Hell.

Considering this, take time and consider carefully the slogan "Jesus is Lord." Not only consider this lightheartedly, but apply this slogan with a matter of trust and belief.

31

Why Wait?

When I was a young boy in high school, riding home from school on the bus, I heard an older boy say to another boy in a conversation, "One day, after I live my life, I will become a Christian. I want to party. I want to have all the sex I can and do what I want, then I will become a Christian."

From a young age, I understood that this was a scary, risky gamble for several reasons. One basis for this being a frightening position is that when an individual thinks like this, they diminish Christianity to nothing more than a list of rules. Faith becomes religion and not (sorry for the cliché) relationship. Selective Christianity becomes legalistic rather than edified and enriched by the grace and Word of God.

I also found this boy's logic to be flawed in that the chances of truly understanding or having the desire to "be saved" is slim to none without the Holy Spirit. Saying this, I make the point that fleshly indulgences are enticing. They are not something that a person just decides to put aside after their body and mind are used up. One of the Spirit's roles before salvation is to convict. About the Holy Spirit, Jesus explains in John 16:8 that,

> when He is come, He will reprove the world of sin, and of righteousness, and of judgment: of sin, because they believe not on Me.

Conviction is not a self-inflicted cry for help to God. The flesh that we glorify before our placement into the Body of Christ is alluring. Don't believe me? Check out a biblical list of fleshly, worldly desires to beware of. In Galatians 5:19–21, Paul states,

> Now the works of the flesh are manifest, which are these; Adultery, fornication, uncleanness, lasciviousness,
>
> Idolatry, witchcraft, hatred, variance, emulations, wrath, strife, seditions, heresies,
>
> Envyings, murders, drunkenness, revellings, and such like: of the which I tell you before, as I have also told you in time past, that they which do such things shall not inherit the kingdom of God.

The work of the flesh is a list of all the things that our culture loves to watch, do, and promote. Without the power of the Holy Spirit, the plans of that boy will be foiled. In Proverbs 19:21, Solomon affirms this when teaching,

> There are many devices in man's heart; nevertheless the counsel of the Lord, that shall stand.

There are many more notes I can offer concerning these plans, but the last one that I would like to propose is this. Why wait? Do not be fooled by all the attractive deceptions! The Lord has so much in store for us. He has equipped us with all spiritual blessings in heavenly places (Ephesians 1:3) and has allotted us an amazing inheritance there as well (Ephesians 1:11–14). No need to wait to receive such a spectacular gift. The Bible says today is the day of salvation! So why wait?

> For He saith, I have heard thee in a time accepted, and in the day of salvation have I succoured thee: behold, now is the accepted time; behold, now is the day of salvation.

There is no guarantee of another day to make such a choice as Christ's rapture of the Church is impending. So why wait?

32

You Sunk My Battleship!

Have you ever played the board game Battleship? It is a brilliant strategy game that uses alternating turns to inflict damage on each other's battleships. The end goal is to, of course, sink all your opponent's ships. The game is a fun yet frustrating engagement that often leaves a person wondering if they are winning.

It was while I watched my fiancé and little cousin play this classic game that I realized an uncanny relationship with our day-to-day life. We may find ourselves in a monotonous, absent-minded exchange of hurtful interactions with the ones we love and interact with. So it goes, the rhythm of life is dictated by fleshly insecurities and squabbles instead of edifying and uplifting those around us.

I have been in this position, and I am sure there is a commonality between you and me. These situations are far too common. But let me offer a solution.

The First Epistle to the Thessalonians 5:11 says, "Wherefore comfort yourselves together, and edify one another, even as also ye do." Comfort one another. Focus your intentionality. Comfort and edification are not to be individual actions. When we comfort others, they are built up. When we are comforted, we are built up.

The relationship is a continuous, godly exchange that ultimately and undeniably edifies and enriches the Body of Christ. It may be time we step away from the harmful games we play before we regretfully say, "You sunk my battleship!"

33

Alone

There is a reality TV show called *Alone*. In this show, people are separated and spend a hundred days in the Arctic. They do have satellite phones and health checks; however, for all intents and purposes, they are alone. I do find it interesting that 2.5 million people come together to watch someone alone.

But what about your and my definition of *alone*? It is often associated with being without the presence of another. Lonesomeness is a state that belongs to no other. Sometimes, we will say, "I just want to be left alone." Nevertheless, we are not alone. We have the Holy Spirit. The walk of the believer is guided by the indwelling of the Spirit (Ephesians 4:30). Not only that, but we also have the Word of God, unlike Job. In his loneliness, Job cried (Job 31:35). Job did not have a Bible to comfort him like we do. We have the complete Word of God to comfort us in our loneliness.

So why is 22 percent of our population saying that they are lonely when 1 Thessalonians 5:16 instructs, "Rejoice evermore"? If you must get alone, get alone with God and His Word. You will find you are not alone after all. Do not despair, God is for us (Romans 8:31).

A group in 2009 called Diamond Rio wrote a song, and the chorus goes like this:

> God is there in the middle of your night
> In every single moment, in every single light
> He's reaching for you right where you are
> The God of the impossible is never very far
> Oh, imagine a place He would never be

So don't give up. God can heal loneliness. Remember the encouraging words of Romans 8:38–39:

> For I am persuaded, that neither death, nor life, nor angels, nor principalities, nor powers, nor things present, nor things to come, nor height, nor depth, nor any other creature, shall be able to separate us from the love of God, which is in Christ Jesus our Lord.

34

The Heat Is On

Have you ever stopped and thought about rock? No, not Pearl Jam or Aerosmith! Rocks, as in the gravel in a driveway or that of a beautiful granite countertop. You have little rocks, big rocks, pretty rocks, and not-so-pretty rocks. Rocks do a lot of things. They serve a lot of purposes.

Have you ever stopped to think about how a rock is made? Rocks can be made by processes such as melting, eroding, cooling, compacting, or deforming. Still, yet, another possibility is that rocks change into other rocks. This is called a metamorphic rock. How does a rock become another rock, you ask? Just apply heat, pressure, and time! These three elements change dull, seemingly useless rocks into something spectacular and desirable. These three elements turn limestone to marble, granite to gneiss, mudstone to schist, and slate to phyllite. A little bit of polish to those rocks and they are worth a pretty penny!

There is something to learn spiritually from this impromptu science lesson. When the heat of life is on and the pressure is crushing, give it some time because you will come out on the other side, brilliant. In Romans 5:3–5, Paul teaches,

> And not only so, but we glory in tribulations also: knowing that tribulation worketh patience;

> And patience, experience; and experience, hope:
>
> And hope maketh not ashamed; because the love of God is shed abroad in our hearts by the Holy Ghost which is given unto us.

Stand tall in moments that try our faith and join in the song of others who have had the privilege of struggle. Because when tribulation (which in Greek, *thlipsis*, literally means pressure) is added, patience is formed. Patience (time) crafts experience. In experience (heat), we begin to see the astounding plan and things that Christ has in store for us in heaven and in this life (Philippians 1:20–21), creating a shameless Christian, rejoicing in the love of God.

So do not be scared of elements and their crafting ability; God utilizes these tools to enrich the Body of Christ. It is a gracious after-effect of joining the family of God, a guarantee to build an absolutely beautiful personal ministry.

35

Measuring Faith

Measurement. It is an important concept that we all use to be successful in life. Carpenters and contractors utilize their skills to create the buildings we live and work in. People mentally measure the space it takes to cram all their luggage into the back of their car in order to take it all with them on vacation. We measure the temperature every time we check how hot or cold it is. Nearly every action we take requires a form of measurement. That includes our faith.

Oxford defines measurement as

> the act or the process of finding the size, quantity, or degree of something.

Measurement is built into the fabric of the Bible's composition. When someone refers to the Bible as "canon," they are affirming its power as a measuring unit. The word *canon* comes from the Greek word *kanon*, which is a straight reed (rod) that was used much like a yard or meter stick in ancient times. It is our rule of faith. It is by the canon that we can measure what is right and thus what is wrong.

By the canon (the Word of God), Christ's Gospel is revealed to us, and we see that God's ruler is the most reliable guide. The Second Letter to Timothy 3:16 affirms,

> All scripture is given by inspiration of God, and is profitable for doctrine, for reproof, for correction, for instruction in righteousness.

When we study Scripture, we are reading an accurate measurement that ultimately aligns us in our effort of producing spiritual fruits (Galatians 5:22–23).

When it comes to measurement, the canon also shows us that from the moment of salvation (Ephesians 4:7), we are all given a measure of faith. In Romans 12:3, this truth is unveiled when Paul teaches,

> For I say, through the grace given unto me, to every man that is among you, not to think of himself more highly than he ought to think, but to think soberly, according as God hath dealt to every man the measure of faith.

No matter where we are spiritually, our position does not change. The measurement reads that our position is in Christ. It reads that we are dead to sin (Romans 8:10) and hidden in Christ (Colossians 3:3). This is all done by the grace of God so no man can boast. Rather, we should turn our heads to heaven, offering thanksgiving to God for sharing His Word with humanity (Psalm 107:1).

God is the master contractor and the master builder. His Word is never off. His measurements are an accurate guide to pleasing Him and possess the perfect reading of salvation, written by Jesus Christ Himself.

36

Endure (with Some Help)

At the 1992 Olympics, in the four-hundred-meter semi-finals, renowned British sprinter Derek Redmond lined up as one of the top prospects and attractions of the race. This prospective attraction's hopes were quickly reduced to rubble after Redmond tore his hamstring early in the race. Although clearly in a lot of pain, Redmond continued limping around the track with the clear intention of finishing the race that he had begun. This limp could have ended early if it were not for Redmond's father racing himself onto the track to help his son finish the race. Redmond (and his father) received a standing ovation and was disqualified for accepting the assistance.

This is a touching display of humanity and shows the human capability to finish the races we begin, sometimes with the help of others. Ecclesiastes is often viewed as a relentlessly pessimistic book within the Bible. However, Ecclesiastes is chock full of beautiful proverbial wisdom that teaches about completing the work that we are called to.

Ecclesiastes 4:9–12 teaches,

> Two are better than one; because they have a good reward for their labour.

> For if they fall, the one will lift up his fellow: but woe to him that is alone when he falleth; for he hath not another to help him up.
>
> Again, if two lie together, then they have heat: but how can one be warm alone? And if one prevail against him, two shall withstand him; and a threefold cord is not quickly broken.

In our lives, support systems are often naturally implemented (family) or brought together (the Body of Christ). There are many functions for these institutions; however, as Christians, we all have a road to travel and a course to finish in faith. Sometimes, we fall. Sometimes, we endure hurt. In these times, lean into the encouragement of your support systems—of family, of the Body of Christ, of anything that will enrich and edify you in the truth. Bonding together will make a strong rope and will help carry us through.

It is a crucial facility on standby so that we can say like the apostle Paul,

> I have fought a good fight, I have finished my course, I have kept the faith" (2 Timothy 4:6–7).

37

Make 'Em Proud

"I just wanted my community and my family to be proud." I thought this to myself as I reflected on the past months and the unfortunate closing of our ministry's youth center and thrift store due to COVID-19. In my sulking, it was the small still voice that said, "Consider Me in your thoughts." Just as Elijah had expected God's voice in the strong wind, the earthquake, and the fire, it was in the fire and after the calm that he heard God (1 Kings 19:11–12).

I could hear God say to continue to serve even though it is not on a grand scale. Continue to preach, teach, and equip disciples at church. Continue telling your family, friends, and coworkers about ME. Continue to form meaningful relationships with those around you. That is what matters.

The Lord affirms in 2 Timothy 1:8–9,

> Be not thou therefore ashamed of the testimony of our Lord, nor of me his prisoner: but be thou partaker of the afflictions of the gospel according to the power of God;
>
> Who hath saved us, and called us with an holy calling, not according to our works, but according to his own purpose and grace, which was given us in Christ Jesus before the world began.

38

What Is Love?

Reading the title, you probably began singing the words, "Baby don't hurt me." Love. Globally, cultures are obsessed with defining the word. Most of history's top-selling songs are about it. For example, Whitney Houston's rendition of "I Will Always Love You." Love is an elusive concept that culture tries to pin down, meanwhile watering it down in the process.

I do not claim to be capable of fully and extensively explaining the ins and outs of love. However, I do know that the Bible tells me all that I ever would need to know. The First Epistle of John 4:16–18 teaches,

> And we have known and believed the love that God hath to us. God is love; and he that dwelleth in love dwelleth in God, and God in him.
>
> Herein is our love made perfect, that we may have boldness in the day of judgment: because as He is, so are we in this world.
>
> There is no fear in love; but perfect love casteth out fear: because fear hath torment. He that feareth is not made perfect in love.

God's Word tells the Christian that God is love. We learn that within the Christian, God abides. Therefore, if God is love and abides within the soul of Christians, true Christian love is a force exclusive to those within the Body of Christ. It dismisses fear and edifies the blameless Christians in their high calling and position.

Saying this, there is such a thing as fleshly love (1 John 2:15–16). Knowing what love dwells inside of us is an important tool within the Christian's spiritual toolkit. The vilest of criminals and abusers are capable of a form of love or at least a cheap imitation. Yet godly love has something different. It is pure, conducive to grace, and involves a desire to share in the love that Christ freely supplied when He laid His life down for us (Galatians 5:24).

Paul teaches that when we put on the new man (Colossians 3:10), love must be among high priorities. It is the "bond of perfectness" (Colossians 3:14), a bond and sealant so tight that no fear can be exhibited. God's love is unconditionally supplied, and it operates through unmerited grace (2 Corinthians 13:14). Access to His love and the wonderful benefits we preach, sing, and exemplify are only offered through the Gospel of Jesus Christ. Jesus Christ is love. God is love. The Holy Spirit is love. Knowing true, pure love is only possible when we are in Christ, and He abides in us.

> Let all your things be done with charity [love]. (1 Corinthians 16:14)

39

Complete or Complacent?

When you read Colossians 2:10, it says, "Ye are complete in him." At this, we seem to become complacent. But we must read on. In verse 12, you are buried and risen with Christ. Let's read on. In Colossians 3:1, we are to seek those things above, where Christ sits on the right hand of God. Seeking isn't complacency. Christ is sitting; however, He is not complacent. He is forever interceding on our behalf, for He is our great high priest.

When Jesus died for our sins, it was once and for all. Daily, a priest would go into the tabernacle for the daily offering sacrifices. Before this, God gave instructions on every item in the tabernacle (Exodus 25–30). But there was no chair to sit upon. This is summed up in two verses (Hebrews 10:11–12).

So yes, we are complete in Christ, but not complacent. We are commanded to strive toward the goal of perfection and the continual process of spiritual maturity (2 Corinthians 7:1). So what is our ultimate goal? It is to be in the will of God. It can be found in Romans 12:2 when Paul states,

> Be not conformed to this world: but be ye transformed by the renewing of your mind, that ye may prove what is that good, and acceptable, and perfect, will of God.

It is also in 1 Timothy 2:4. We know that God "will have all men to be saved, and to come unto the knowledge of the truth." Someone once said that many will go to hell unsaved, but not one will go unloved. God loves you, and Enriching Grace loves you. Be complete.

40

You're Overthinking It

"You're overthinking it!" We have all been told this. For some, you may have heard your father yell this at you as you join forces to solve a seemingly simple issue. Or maybe this was a situation you experienced with your significant other as they paced the floor battling a seemingly insurmountable problem. We have all been there.

When I was young, I had a seemingly insurmountable issue. My problem was tying my shoe. We have all been there; however, my young, childish mind had a limited perspective keeping me from reaching my goal. However, it was my uncle who reminded me that I was overthinking it. He stepped back, showed me again, and voila! With a different perspective in my grasp, I reached down, did my loops, and tied them. My perspective was forever changed.

Perspective is an important concept to learn control over. In a spiritual sense, perspective is just as important. To accomplish our God-given calling, we need to step back from the world and focus our attention on heaven. Colossians 3:2 reminds us to

> set your affection on things above, not on things on the earth.

Rely on faith in the glorious hope of Jesus Christ, instead of the illusory solutions that the world offers. The Word tells us,

> While we look not at the things which are seen, but at the things which are not seen. For the things which are seen are temporal, but the things which are not seen are eternal. (2 Corinthians 4:18)

Instead of being one-track minded, let us be three-track minded, deriving our perspective to be on the work of the Trinity, which is revealed in God's holy Word. When we live by faith, we stop over-thinking and start living in grace. For we know, "all things work together for good to those who love God, to those who are called according to His purpose" (Romans 8:28).

41

Christian Meditation

Meditation is a practice often shunned by Christian circles. I understand, nonetheless, as the common perception of meditation has been hijacked by various religions and practices. Claiming to be an expert on these religions' meditative practices would be an ignorant move on my part; however, I do know something. They are quite different from the meditation that the Bible discusses. An example of this would be when Buddha wrote,

> The mind is everything. What you think, you become.

I can assure you that this entire quote is a fallacy.

At one point in time, I heard that Christian meditation is not the emptying (or even the calming) of the mind. It is the filling of the soul with His Word. The mind is not everything. It is a tool. Honing it to its greatest capacity is impossible without the power of the Holy Spirit and God's Word. When our minds are renewed and we repent (change our minds) of our past thoughts and habits, we begin to see the will of God clearly laid out through His Scripture. Romans 12:2 tells the Christian,

> Be not conformed to this world: but be ye transformed by the renewing of your mind, that ye may prove what is that good, and acceptable, and perfect, will of God.

When it comes to meditation, the Scriptures (especially the psalmist) almost always align meditation with God's Word and reflection on His wonderful works. It calls for remembrance of the absolutes of our faith and the things that God has, is, and will do on earth and in heaven. It is in this heart that David writes, "I will meditate in thy precepts, and have respect unto thy ways" (Psalm 119:15). Similarly, Paul urges Timothy to focus and fill his mind and soul with sound doctrine. He states in 1 Timothy 4:13–15,

> Till I come, give attendance to reading, to exhortation, to doctrine.
>
> Neglect not the gift that is in thee, which was given thee by prophecy, with the laying on of the hands of the presbytery.

Saying this, meditation has inner benefits; however, its purpose comes alive when "profiting may appear to all." When we are built up in the Word of God, we have a responsibility to overflow and edify the Body of Christ through it. This is the intention when one refers to Christians as stewards of the Word. In 1 Corinthians 4:1, Paul exclaims,

> Let a man so account of us, as of the ministers of Christ, and stewards of the mysteries of God.

So let's be that! Stewards who meditate on the Word of God, day and night (Psalm 1:2), taking in all the things that edify our soul and the Body of Christ, instead of suppressing our minds in the hope that suppression will lead to revelation. We have all the revelation we ever need in the sixty-six-book love letter that God wrote for man.

42

Life's a Vacation

Every year, families work and toil away, saving up for a short period when they can rest. A day, weekend, week, or longer is set aside out of people's work schedules so that they can get away. They get away from the pressures of life, the monotony of its cycle, and often most importantly, work.

Logically, this is one of the many rhythms of life. There is a time to work and a time to play. Solomon writes in Ecclesiastes 3:13 that man should be able to cash in, so to speak, for all their labor. He writes,

> Every man should eat and drink, and enjoy the good of all his labour, it is the gift of God.

While defending his apostleship, Paul also defends this rhythm and cycle of life as an apostle. He asks the following:

> Have we not power to eat and to drink?
>
> Have we not power to lead about a sister, a wife, as well as other apostles, and as the brethren of the Lord, and Cephas?
>
> Or I only and Barnabas, have not we power to forbear working?

> Who goeth a warfare any time at his own charges? who planteth a vineyard, and eateth not of the fruit thereof? or who feedeth a flock, and eateth not of the milk of the flock?
>
> Say I these things as a man? or saith not the law the same also?" (1 Corinthians 9:4-8).

Paul goes on to say he does not glory in those things; rather, he lives to reap spiritual rewards through the finished Gospel of Jesus Christ. Nevertheless, logically, he has the power and freedom to take such a rest and indulgence if it were to be. Knowing that no man can judge (Colossians 2:16–17).

God has ordained rest following work throughout the Bible. In churches around the world, the same is true. Men and women toil and strive for the week with the hope of a coming 24-hour period coined Sabbath.

Saying this, let me ask some questions of you, the reader. What if I told you that you could take a rest every day? What if I told you that as the Body of Christ, you can have peace every day and in every way?

The apostle Paul suggests that this is not such a far-fetched idea. He informs us that God now gives us rest and peace regardless of our circumstances. Our faith is not based on earthly works to appease God. The only work that means anything in an eternal light is the work that Christ finished (Romans 4:5; Titus 3:5). And since our work is not of an earthly matter, neither should our rest be.

This is where we keep the Gospel at the center of our life and, like Paul, find our rest in it. When sealed within the Body of Christ (the Church), the "Lord of peace himself [will] give you peace always by all means. The Lord be with you all" (2 Thessalonians 3:14–16).

God gives us this constant vacation through His Son, Jesus Christ. Christ did not just come to "save us from hell" or any other of the true clichés we hear constantly. He also came to bring forth all the good and righteous things that God desires for man. Peace included.

Because of Christ, we do not have to be anxious about anything, and we can go directly to God with our concerns and exchange them for peace beyond anything the human mind can fathom. This unfathomable peace thus keeps our hearts secure (Philippians 4:6–7).

Life can be lived with peace. It can be lived beautifully vacationing with Jesus daily. We do not have to wait for the end of the week. God's power is not bound by time (Psalm 90:4).

Lastly, life is renewed daily in Christ Jesus. His Spirit keeps and preserves us. In 2 Corinthians 4:16–18, we are assured of this:

> For which cause we faint not; but though our outward man perish, yet the inward man is renewed day by day.
>
> For our light affliction, which is but for a moment, worketh for us a far more exceeding and eternal weight of glory;
>
> While we look not at the things which are seen, but at the things which are not seen: for the things which are seen are temporal; but the things which are not seen are eternal.

We can live renewed day by day, minute by minute. A lifelong vacation, free of charge, offered by the King of kings and Lord of lords.

43

What Is Your Craft?

The Bible contains real accounts of real people who lived real lives working real jobs. All the ins and outs of the lives of biblical characters are something that we do not often think about. Some biblical stories highlight these features of people's lives. Many people know that Jesus was a carpenter (Mark 6:3) and that Peter and John were fishermen (Luke 5:10).

In the Old Testament, there are plenty of jobs and crafts mentioned to give further insight into individuals' lives and the remarkable ways that God used them. As for Christians, some other occupations mentioned within the Bible include tent-makers (Acts 18:2–3), lawyers (Titus 3:13), and tanners (Acts 10:32), to name a few! All these "secular" jobs helped to fund spiritual endeavors and stand as a guide to Christian diligence and stewardship!

Nonetheless, I cannot leave out that the greatest craftsman is the God that we serve! He is the most versatile and skilled workman who makes no mistake. He has hung the stars and the moon. He made the earth from nothing, man from nothing, and created light where there was no light. I mean this physically (Genesis 1:3) and spiritually (1 John 1:5). Dark to light. Death to life. Mortality to eternity.

There is no craftsman like our God. He devised a way that humanity could be with Him. We are His workmanship, something the Lord takes pride in. Ephesians 2:8–10 states,

> For by grace are ye saved through faith; and that not of yourselves: it is the gift of God:
>
> Not of works, lest any man should boast.
>
> For we are his workmanship, created in Christ Jesus unto good works, which God hath before ordained that we should walk in them.

We are like a beautiful pot. We can be filled and utilized for good works. However, from our birth and creation, the dust, wear, and harmful factors of sin tarnished His craftsmanship. Still, God intends to restore and preserve His work. Therefore, He made a way through His Son, Jesus Christ. The death, burial, and resurrection are the polish and protective coating that gives humanity value. Only in Him is any service to God acceptable. By grace through faith.

Work does not save us. Christ does. However, in Christ, we are restored to the full capability of developing the ultimate craft: walking in the Word and edifying the Body of Christ. Saying this, come out and be restored, fellow journeyman! Be beautifully taught by the ultimate craftsman, Jesus Christ.

44

Order in His Court!

In the 1960s, there was a comedy TV show called *Get Smart*. This show was a parody of James Bond. In it, Agent 86 and 99 worked for CONTROL, and their nemesis was KAOS, an organization of evil. In the Bible, a lot is said about a sort of control called "order." You cannot have order and chaos.

The First Letter to the Corinthians 14:40 instructs,

> Let all things be done decently and in order.

There must be order in all things. Order in the Church for edifying, sanctifying, and serving. Without proper order, the Church becomes dysfunctional (chaos) and will never perform proper workmanship unto the Lord.

There is an order in life. Furthermore, we all start out crawling before we walk. Psalm 37:23 teaches the Christian that "the steps of a good man are ordered by the Lord: and he delighteth in His way." Then, we die.

> And as it is appointed unto men once to die, but after this the judgment. (Hebrews 9:27)

Following this, if you are in the Body of Christ, you have the resurrection. In this, we know that "if ye then be risen with Christ, seek those things which are above, where Christ sitteth on the right hand of God" (Colossians 3:1). Clearly, there is an order to be born again (Romans 12:2). We are to die (Colossians 3:3) and then live again (Romans 6:4).

So let's keep step in order of God's plan, looking for that blessed hope (Titus 2:13). That is to be forever with the one who died for our sins and has prepared a place in heaven for us. May we continue to look to Him, the author and finisher of our faith (Hebrews 12:2). As you go throughout this week, cherish order over chaos and be enriched by the holy Word.

45

That's a Good Recipe!

For most, good cooking requires a good recipe. A good recipe delivers an excellent dish. English chef Mary Berry once noted that she thinks "baking is very rewarding, and if you follow a good recipe, you will get success." Although a very simple observation, I find this quote to be very profitable when we understand exactly what a recipe is.

Webster's Dictionary defines a recipe as a "set of instructions for making something from various ingredients." Within the Bible, there are many recipes for individuals to follow to obtain success. However, there is no greater success than what comes from following the recipe for salvation. It has one simple step for three simple ingredients found in the pantry of God's loving word.

Here is the recipe (1 Corinthians 15:3–4; Romans 10:9):

The New Man

Ingredients (Christ's):

- Death
- Burial
- Resurrection

Steps:

- Believe

You see? This recipe is not so hard to follow and it brings eternal success. The recipe is God-ordained and does not require any work or experimentation. It is a perfect gift.

Following this recipe brings some extraordinary flavors and reactions to the new man. I am not just referring to some of the common ones that we cite (going to heaven, for example); although, they are still brilliant. My reference is to CRIBS. CRIBS is an acronym for some reactions that occur in the making of the new man.

It stands for the following:

- Circumcised

  "In whom also ye are circumcised with the circumcision made without hands, in putting off the body of the sins of the flesh by the circumcision of Christ" (Colossians 2:11).
- Regenerated

  "I am crucified with Christ: nevertheless I live; yet not I, but Christ liveth in me: and the life which I now live in the flesh I live by the faith of the Son of God, who loved me, and gave himself for me" (Galatians 2:20).
- Indwelt

  "But if the Spirit of him that raised up Jesus from the dead dwell in you, he that raised up Christ from the dead shall also quicken your mortal bodies by his Spirit that dwelleth in you" (Romans 8:11).
- Baptized

  "Know ye not, that so many of us as were baptized into Jesus Christ were baptized into his death?" (Romans 6:3).
- Sealed

  "In whom ye also trusted, after that ye heard the word of truth, the gospel of your salvation: in whom also after

> that ye believed, ye were sealed with that holy Spirit of promise" (Ephesians 1:13).

When God makes the new man, He sets into motion the ingredients that make the man rise (leavening) and keeps his flavor.

Isn't our Father a great cook?

46

Mine!

Anyone who has met a small child (nearly everyone) knows that children can be feisty and a bit selfish. It is human nature. From birth, humanity's ambition is set on sustaining itself and getting the things that we need to survive. Often, from the age of two, when a child spots something they like or want from another person, you may notice they exclaim, "Mine!" Whether it is or not, their heart is set on something, and that something reflects self.

It reflects a fleshly struggle that wants love and satisfaction above dealing it out. Reflecting on selfishness, God does not call us to neglect ourselves. He simply calls us to esteem Him high and value the importance of others for the movement of the Body of Christ. This may mean esteeming ourselves below others so that love can have an effectual working within the Body of Christ (Ephesians 4:15–16).

Reducing selfishness is a product of living within what many call the Golden Rule (Romans 13:9–10). The Golden Rule is part of a bigger set of regulations known to many as the "great commandments" (Matthew 22:36–40). Jesus and Paul were providing their listeners with timeless knowledge from the Law (Leviticus 19:18; Deuteronomy 6:4–5). With this instruction being a doctrinal staple through all dispensations, it holds a powerful place within the Christian lifestyle.

When contrasting selfishness and love, John Piper states,

> Selfishness seeks its own private happiness at the expense of others. Love seeks its happiness in the happiness of the beloved. It will even suffer and die for the beloved in order that its joy might be full in the life and purity of the beloved.

Putting aside selfishness and putting on love does not require a self-help book or mental gymnastics. We need to simply put on the new man that we are called to equip from the moment we are saved (Ephesians 4:24). Putting on the new man allows us to live graciously within Christ's righteousness, which He covers us in. With this new mindset, we can live in "lowliness of mind" as described in Philippians 2:3–4.

The apostle Paul gives practical advice when instructing that we,

> Let nothing be done through strife or vainglory; but in lowliness of mind let each esteem other better than themselves.
>
> Look not every man on his own things, but every man also on the things of others.

Moreover, put on the new man today and allow Christ's righteousness and grace to work within your heart. Look to esteem others above ourselves and as fellow heirs to His heavenly kingdom.

47

Healthy Prayer Life

Within Christian circles, the phrase *prayer life* is often used to describe the condition of our meeting times with God. Whenever the term is used, it often refers to questions such as "How many times do you pray a day?" or "Are your prayers fulfilling?" Although, in some cases, such questions have an applicable position in our lives, many times they are trivial in comparison to the question "What is the content of our prayer?"

I am not writing this to be the questioner; however, I do want to share my experience of a moment when my prayer life (for lack of a better word) was shifted. It shifted in a time of what I would deem "satisfying prayer." Concepts such as prayer without ceasing (1 Thessalonians 5:17) and this heavy charge's possibility through constant fellowship with the Spirit (2 Corinthians 13:14) remained continually in mind. Nonetheless, there was a problem.

My prayer was full of pleading for God to do things; however, this centered my prayer as a talk at God instead of a talk with God. These prayers strayed from a biblical formula prevalent throughout the entirety of the Bible. Supplication with thanksgiving. Thanksgiving with adoration. For the apostle Paul urges,

> Be careful for nothing; but in every thing by prayer and supplication with thanksgiving let

> your requests be made known unto God. (Philippians 4:6)

In the same light, the psalmist notes that thanksgiving is complete when coupled with adoration and praise for the Supplier who is worthy of thanksgiving: God. Psalm 100:4 states,

> Enter into His gates with thanksgiving, and into His courts with praise: be thankful unto Him, and bless His name.

These are not the only examples of reminders to do such. It is in the many scriptural reminders that thanksgiving and adoration were placed on my spiritual radar. These reminders are the basis for the acronym ACTS. During a church service, I had heard of this powerful acronym.

Before sharing, I want to note that I do not hold rigidly to this acronym; however, it did serve as a powerful reminder of the comprehensive nature of a simple conversation with God in the Spirit. ACTS stands for

- adoration,
- confession,
- thanksgiving,
- supplication.

Its creator ordered it with the intention of importance, first to last. However, I simply want it to be a reminder to position the God of glory first within our prayers as we cast our burdens upon Him (Psalm 55:22). He cares for each one.

48

Magna Carta

In America, we have a written list of rights that protect certain liberties as free Americans. This would be our Constitution. This document is strongly influenced by another document known as the Magna Carta.

The Magna Carta (Medieval Latin for "Great Charter of Freedoms") was a document that English barons forced King John to sign in June 1215. This document guaranteed their fundamental rights as people and protection. This document is fundamental to world history, and because of its significance, the term *magna carta* can be used as a generic term for a list of rights and emancipation.

When we as Christians look to Galatians 1, we find something of a magna carta, emphasizing the beautiful liberties provided by the Gospel of Jesus Christ. In Galatians 1:3–4, Paul describes who gives liberty and deliverance from this evil world that we live in. He describes not only the source but the action that occurs within the life of a Christian. The Scripture reads:

> Grace be to you and peace from God the Father, and from our Lord Jesus Christ,
>
> Who gave himself for our sins, that he might deliver us from this present evil world, according to the will of God and our Father.

The Greek word that Paul uses to describe "deliver" within verse 4 is *exaireo*. This word describes an active and continuous tearing out of something. In a literal sense, according to Strong's lexicon, verse 4 depicts God as actively "tearing [us] out" of this "present evil world."

We are freed by the Gospel and torn from the evilness of the world by Christ Jesus so that we can live freely within His righteousness as free people. This is all according to God's will. Luckily, this is clearly stated within the Bible so that we do not have to ponder and seek wildly what His will is!

The Gospel does not just deliver us and leave us to our own demise. It does much more than what we could ever hope for. Whereas we are saved by it, the Gospel delivers and transforms (Galatians 1:4; 2 Corinthians 5:17). When believing in it, we become a new creation. We are torn out from this world and transformed by the renewing of our minds.

Paul writes in Romans 12:2,

> Be not conformed to this world: but be ye transformed by the renewing of your mind, that ye may prove what is that good, and acceptable, and perfect, will of God.

Once again, this is all in the perfect will of the Father.

So this liberty is a free gift to us, although it was not free. Jesus Christ died for our sins, was buried, and rose again (1 Corinthians 15:3–4) so that we can be justified (Romans 4:25). Whenever a man is justified by the Gospel, he becomes free (John 8:36). Therefore, if you have not taken this magna carta for your life, take this opportunity to consider. Believe in the Gospel and what Christ has done for you. Liberty is that close.

49

Emergency!

A visit to an emergency room can be symbolic of your soul care. Let me present you with some comparisons.

1. *Do you need the emergency room?* The answer is yes. Romans 3:23: "For all have sinned, and come short of the glory of God."
2. *Check-in.* Romans 12:1 teaches us to "present your bodies a living sacrifice."
3. *Wait.* The paperwork is reading the Word, rightly divided (1 Timothy 2:15).
4. *Triage.* Numbers 32:23 tells us to "be sure your sin will find you out." What needs priority?
5. *Wait again.* Take time to meditate and recognize your condition (1 John 1:8–10).
6. *Treatment room.* "The Lord is nigh unto them that are of a broken heart" (Psalm 34:18).
7. *Exam/test.* Your state is the way you are, but your standing is your goal to be the way God looks at you in Christ (Romans 6:13).
8. *X-ray.* The Word of God pierces our inner soul, spirit, and inner being (Hebrews 4:12).

9. *Wait again.* While we wait, be watching for Christ's return and the Church's rapture! (1 Thessalonians 4:16–18).
10. *Release instructions.* "Ye are complete" (Colossians 2:10), and our release will be to heaven! (Philippians 3:20–21).
11. *Home to heal.* God "hath blessed us with all spiritual blessings" (Ephesians 1:3) and "Christ has set us free" (Galatians 5:1).
12. *Get bill.* Fortunately, Christ paid it all! (Isaiah 53:5; 2 Corinthians 5:21).

Now get well soon!

50

Go for a Walk!

Poet W. H. Davies once wrote a dialogue between Pleasure and Joy. In this dialogue, he writes:

> Now shall I walk or shall I ride?
> "Ride," Pleasure said;
> "Walk," Joy replied.

It is important and interesting to know that the man who wrote this dialogue was a hobo. A hobo is a traveling worker who often could be seen, particularly during the Great Depression, riding a train, town to town looking for work. This hobo's choice of travel is an interesting one. He opts for the difficult one and not the easiest one.

As Christians, this is asked of us. When we accept Christ's invitation of salvation and peace, ironically, we choose a path contrary to the logic of the world. We choose to continuously fight fleshly desires and carnality. With this, we choose to live spiritually minded and walk by the Spirit of Christ. By His Spirit, we no longer have to gratify the desires of the flesh (Galatians 5:16–25).

Saying this, when abiding in Him and He abides in us (1 John 2:6; 1 John 2:27), it would be hard to consider us spiritual hobos;

although, the world might just see it that way. We are grounded and positioned in the family of God (Ephesians 2:19–22), taking the scenic walk home.

51

Cut and Polish

As a stone fabricator, I have the privilege of transforming raw stone into not only beautiful but useful creations. These creations include granite, quartz, and other stone countertops, backsplashes, etc. How are these gorgeous products made? The easy answer: cut and polish!

There is generally a very large slab of stone that is the base from which a countertop is made. The process all begins by cutting the shape from the rest of the slab. By itself, that slab offers nothing creative. It may be pretty but lacks purpose. At this moment, it lacks any practical value, although the fabricator has purchased it at a cost (1 Corinthians 6:20).

Secondly, once the shape of a countertop has been pulled from the mass, its sides are polished, and its full potential becomes obvious. Moreover, it is effective to serve the patrons whose homes it inhabits. I simplified this beautiful process to make this point. Christ, at the cross, paid the ultimate price so that we can have life abundantly (John 10:10). He reconciled the slab of humanity and He made it possible to be cut out from the uselessness and weathering that is due to the heap of stone.

That may be the most important part, but it is just the beginning of our Savior's intention. Jesus does not just want to cut us from the slab and save us, He wants to refine us, by the handiwork of His flawless hands (Ephesians 2:10). However, the question that is asked to humanity is, "Will you let Me?" After all, the Word states that God's will is to "have all men to be saved, and to come unto the knowledge of the truth" (1 Timothy 2:4).

Following salvation comes sanctification. By sanctification, Christ imputes His righteousness upon us and allows us to be set apart for the purpose of God. With His justification and sanctifying power, He gives us true worth. We can grow and, for lack of better words, be polished. Serving God more beautifully each day as we are refined by His Word (2 Timothy 3:16–17). Continually growing in the knowledge of the truth. Never stop allowing Christ to polish your edges.

52

Christmas in July

Peace and joy. Add in *love*, and the three words can be found displayed on practically every Christmas card. Christian or secular, that is. Alongside these words, you may see the word *believe*. As if believing in a holiday can bring these great attributes into an American's troubled life for a short season.

For a Christian, we celebrate the birth of Christ, but we know (hopefully) that we are saved by believing in the Gospel accomplished at the end of His earthly ministry. Certainly, it is by believing in this that we ascertain joy and peace. In Romans 15:13, Paul explains,

> Now the God of hope fill you with all joy and peace in believing, that ye may abound in hope, through the power of the Holy Ghost.

In believing, God Himself fills us with all joy and peace!

Therefore, the cheesy Hallmark cards do not have it wrong necessarily; they just need to point a little further to the God who is in heaven! For those who are math-oriented, I have even noticed that the Bible made a bit of a formula.

Believing = (Joy and Peace) Hope

Notice how hope is tacked to the end of the formula? Experiencing the rest of the formula allows hope to abound and be multiplied within our life! Hope from our past, hope for today, and hope that ushers us into eternity. Because, after all, "hope maketh not ashamed" (Romans 5:5). I hope this was an encouraging word. Merry Christmas.

53

Christ Ablaze

Infinite God, nothing outlasts your throne.
Through times past, but now and ages to come,
You preserve the gathered righteous alum.
By Your sure Word, the hungry soul You hone.
Bewildered, I live to make Your name known.
To Thy Gospel, I willingly succumb.
Sanctified under the cloud of Your thumb.
Understanding the will that You have shown.
What is man that You are mindful of him?
How could your Spirit devise to save me?
What on earth could deserve your sacred gaze?
Questions with answers, too bright for me dim.
Necessary rebuttals evident in Scripture I see,
Faith leads to hope of glory, Christ ablaze.

54

Cool and Refreshing

A cold drink on a hot day. That is what we have been needing a lot this summer of 2021. If you do any activity at all outside, you'll soon thirst like Samson did after slaying 1,000 Philistines (Judges 15:18–19). Now we may not do it to that extent; however, with the Lord, you can have times of refreshment, both physically and spiritually.

As Paul was describing his walk and testimony as a good soldier of Christ, some had turned away from him and his doctrine. Nonetheless, one house where he could find refreshment was the house of Onesiphorus (2 Timothy 1:16). Again, when we read Romans 15:1–3, it speaks of pleasing or refreshing one another, for even Christ pleased not Himself like He did with the woman at the well (John 4:14).

Saying this, it refreshes the soul to share the living water that only flows from the throne of God. It is everlasting, so you may say the following with Paul:

> That I may come unto you with joy by the will of God, and may with you be refreshed. Now the God of Peace be with you all. (Romans 15:32–33)

Amen.

55

Deliver Me!

Protection. What comes to mind when you hear the word? A shield? Armor, perhaps? These are just a couple of clichés. For Christians, often we claim God as our fortress, shield, strength, high tower, and our deliverer (Psalm 18:2).

Paul regarded God as his deliverer in 2 Timothy 4:18. Paul states,

> The Lord shall deliver me from every evil work,
> and will preserve me unto his heavenly kingdom:
> to whom be glory for ever and ever. Amen.

Contextually, 2 Timothy is Paul's last letter before he was beheaded, according to primary sources. He knew of his imminent death by the hands of the Romans; yet, in boldness, he proclaimed that the Lord will deliver him from every evil work. He stated this despite knowing that an evil work was going to be commenced to him. Why? Because he understood that deliverance is not always a physical attribute.

In fact, spiritual deliverance offered by Jesus is of much more importance! This is why Christ stated,

> Fear not them which kill the body, but are not able to kill the soul: but rather fear him which is able to destroy both soul and body in hell. (Matthew 10:28)

Paul also understood that preservation is a matter of deliverance. The body may endure harm; however, our soul is sealed and preserved unto heaven regardless of circumstances. Amen!

56

Providence—You Mean Rhode Island?

Providence, Rhode Island. The capital of Rhode Island was founded in 1636 by Roger Williams, a reformed Baptist exile from Massachusetts Bay Colony. In finding the beautiful land, he named it in honor of "God's merciful providence." Which begs the question: What is this familiar but still yet foreign word?

Webster's Dictionary defines it as "divine guidance or care" or God's "power sustaining and guiding human destiny." Those few words generate a topic with a large amount of breadth to explore within a small devotion! So we won't. But we will explore the limitations of our enemy.

Job 1:12 is one of the common Scriptures that Christians turn to when defending providence as a characteristic of God. In the book of Job, we see that the many awful things that transpire are not a work of God, but simply an allowance of God. Satan has no power above or against God and is an opportunist who prowls the earth waiting for an opportunity to administer evilness (Job 1:7; 1 Peter 5:8).

Nothing happens that God does not see. Nothing happens that God does not know. Although there is sin in the world, from the original sin of Adam, there is nothing that God cannot work to the good of those who love Him and are called according to His purpose (Romans 8:28). Be sure that God's will and plans are higher than ours. And like Job, no matter the storms of our lives, we can stand firm and glorify God through it all.

Like Paul, we can fight the good fight, finish the course, and receive our heavenly reward. The apostle Paul proclaims in the face of his imminent death that,

> I have fought a good fight, I have finished my course, I have kept the faith:
>
> Henceforth there is laid up for me a crown of righteousness, which the Lord, the righteous judge, shall give me at that day: and not to me only, but unto all them also that love his appearing. (2 Timothy 4:7–8)

God cares for each and every one of us. Do not be dismayed when life's trials present themselves. Our names may be cursed, our bodies may be broken; nonetheless, by God's providence and sealing of our soul, we will stand firm to see the light of His heavenly gates (2 Timothy 4:18).

57

God's Palace, Not His Prison

It was once said by the famous Puritan preacher, Thomas Brooks, that "though Heaven be God's palace, yet it is not His prison." John Arrowsmith is recorded saying, "A heathen philosopher once asked, 'Where is God?' The Christian answered: 'Let me first ask you, where is He not?'"

The Bible says, "The eyes of the Lord are in every place, beholding the evil and the good" (Proverbs 15:3). God is omnipresent. Omnipresent is an attribute of the Lord. It describes His ability and constantly present state everywhere at once. There is nowhere that we can escape His eye. Not in the deepest valley or the crevice of the highest peak.

The psalmist once contemplated the following:

> Whither shall I go from thy spirit? or whither shall I flee from thy presence? If I ascend up into heaven, thou art there: if I make my bed in hell, behold, thou art there. If I take the wings of the morning, and dwell in the uttermost parts of the sea; even there shall thy hand lead me, and thy right hand shall hold me. (Psalm 139:7–10)

Humanity would be foolish to believe that anything could possibly be hidden from God! In fact, God was present yesterday, today, and our future days! Colossians 1:17 states,

> And He is before all things, and by Him all things consist.

The Father's Holy Spirit is the power by which Christians exist, and His presence is never to leave us. Continuing in Colossians, we find Paul going as far as to say that "the riches of the glory of this mystery among the Gentiles" is "Christ in you, the hope of glory" (1:27).

His presence is a rich treasure. Christ's internal indwelling in each and every believer is a brilliant gem and a grand wealth of grace. Be aware! God is not only omnipresent; He is here, functioning individually and collectively through His body, the Church.

How can we be aware? Read His Word that tells us of His attributes and pray ceaselessly to the Spirit of Him who lives in you (1 Thessalonians 5:17; 1 Corinthians 6:19). Live today aware of God's presence in and around you! After all, "Where is He not?"

58

The Good, the Bad, and the Spirit

I recently read an insightful, yet secular, article that offered a good bit of life advice. It proposed the idea that if we stop constantly rating our life experiences as good and bad, we could live meaningfully "in the moment." This is a fascinating concept; although, it can develop into a very frightening reality real quick.

Christians have a much more in-depth truth needed to gauge life while meanwhile "living in the moment." Good and bad are important considerations. But what are the roots when they present themselves practically? Simple answer: Spirit versus flesh.

When in Christ, we are to walk in Spirit, putting on the new man (Ephesians 4:24)! Walking is an active word. We need to live considering the things of God which are found in His Word, applying them and honoring God in the process! Walking in the Spirit negates walking in the flesh. In Galatians 5:16, Paul teaches that,

> This I say then, Walk in the Spirit, and ye shall not fulfill the lust of the flesh.

Walking in the flesh is a lustful existence, which is not possible to break without the resurrection power of Christ's Gospel! It plagues humanity from the moment we are born and has been a destructive reality since the fall of man in the garden of Eden (Romans 5:12).

Secular culture waters this down. This is what secular culture would call "bad." Ignoring the effects of Spirit and flesh in order to feel as if life is "meaningful" is not a healthy position for Christians. Because those whose position is in Christ are positioned in the Spirit! So yeah, forget "good" and "bad." Live in the "Spirit" and put off the "flesh."

59

Foggy Mornings

As I travel up the Coalfield Expressway in West Virginia this morning, it is very foggy, as it is most mornings. Through the dense fog, I always get nervous because, although I have traveled this road often, I cannot see or remember the curves of the road.

This morning, God spoke to my heart and reminded me that our lives are like fog sometimes. We cannot see, and it feels unending, as if we will never get through it. However, as quickly as it comes, the fog lifts, and we find our way. Isn't it wonderful to know that our God sees us through the fog of life even when we cannot find our way? Then the light is revealed and our fears relieved! Amen!

> The Lord is my light and my salvation; whom shall I fear? the Lord is the strength of my life; of whom shall I be afraid? (Psalm 27:1)

60

We Can Go On!

Recently, I was reading from the classic devotional *My Utmost for His Highest*, and I read an installment titled "This Experience Must Come." In this writing, Oswald Chambers recounts the story of how Elijah was taken up to heaven, leaving the prophet Elisha alone to himself (2 Kings 2:11–12). From this moment, he had to carry on without Elijah. Much like this story, we must live ultimately trusting in God, rather than our fellow workers. Chambers writes, "'I cannot continue without my 'Elijah.' Yet God says you must continue."

In Philippians 4:19, the apostle Paul shows his full trust in God when stating,

> My God shall supply all your need according to
> his riches in glory by Christ Jesus.

This is not to neglect the edification that the Body of Christ is instructed to provide by the Word of God (Ephesians 4:29). Although, realize that the source is once again the Word of God, not man. We must go on and we can thrive spiritually in the riches of Christ Jesus. We can trust God.

61

Where Wealth Accumulates, Men Decay

Wealth. There is a hefty emphasis placed upon the topic of wealth, regardless of cultural background. From the beginning of time, man has begun a vain pursuit of accumulating "stuff." It is an endless pursuit, which although has its place in everyday life, can sap the very essence of humanity out of people. The Irish novelist Oliver Goldsmith once wrote,

> Where wealth accumulates, men decay.

Another wise man by the name of John Locke once penned,

> All wealth is the product of labor.

These points, within their original context, stand firm as solid reminders of where our intentions should be as we strive for wealth. Although, be assured the Word of God has plenty to say about it as well. In the pursuit of wealth, many have opted for service to funds rather than the God who has funded our eternity. Paul administers a strong warning in 1 Timothy 6:10 when he teaches that

> the love of money is the root of all evil: which while some coveted after, they have erred from the faith, and pierced themselves through with many sorrows.

As Christians, eternal wealth is what is perpetually guaranteed unto us. It is guaranteed and is, as John Locke put it, a product of labor. No, we do not work for our faith. Yet Christ has already put in the work and it is finished. By His finished Gospel and labor of love, we are saved, and prescribed a heavenly inheritance with wealth beyond imagination. It is a free gift of God. Romans 6:23 shows this when it is written,

> For the wages of sin is death; but the gift of God is eternal life through Jesus Christ our Lord.

When considering physical wealth over the spiritual wealth of God, I think of the classic charge laid by Joshua:

> Choose you this day whom ye will serve. (Joshua 24:15)

The strive for wealth often comes from the innate fear that humans have regarding a lack of security. God instills this within humanity. Rather than turning to the bondage of prosperity gospels, we have assurance that God will take care of us! In Hebrews 13:5, the writer notes,

> Let your conversation be without covetousness; and be content with such things as ye have: for he hath said, I will never leave thee, nor forsake thee.

We can have assurance that the Lord has dominion over our souls and that nothing can separate us from the love of Christ (Romans 8:39). His promises stand, and we will see the riches of the glory of His inheritance (Ephesians 1:18), where moths and rust have no claim (Matthew 6:19–21). So trust in the wealth of Christ, and lay down the burden of earthly pursuit!

62

God Is Our Refuge

God is our refuge and strength, a very present help in trouble.
Therefore will not we fear, though the earth be removed, and
though the mountains be carried into the midst of the sea;
Though the waters thereof roar and be troubled,
though the mountains shake with the swelling thereof. Selah
—Psalm 46:1–3

Psalm 46 is a beautifully written reminder from King David to the Israelite people of God's providence. Their position was in God as His chosen people, regardless of the external circumstances. He was calling them to rest within the refuge of His all-powerful being.

God's character does not change. How He may deal with humanity might; however, His character is unwavering. The Lord is a refuge. He is our strength. God is always present in the heart of each and every believer.

In fact, much like when a day is too strong and our first reaction is to run home to our bed and lie under our comforter, we never could outrun our beloved Savior. His Spirit is the promised Comforter (John 14:26). By His Gospel, the same God of refuge to the Israelites indwells in you and our souls are anchored. Indeed, we are secured in hope (Hebrews 6:18-19), growing in His ever-enriching grace and by the knowledge of His Word (2 Corinthians 12:9; Colossians 1:10).

63

Gifts and Grace

Christians who seek power, an experience, or a purpose often desire supernatural gifts of the Holy Spirit. Yet the knowledge of God's grace is the greatest gift God gives us today. Now I know what some are already saying: "What about 1 Corinthians 12:1?"

In the membership of the Corinthian church, unfortunately, the members were grieving the Holy Spirit by the carnal ways that they were using spiritual gifts. They were like children with toys instead of adults with valuable tools and they needed to mature. Spiritual gifts are not "God-given talents," natural aptitudes, practiced skills, or even spirituality.

People want supernatural powers as seen in Acts 2. Spirit gifts appeal to people who seek power, an experience, or a purpose. In 1 Corinthians 12:31, Paul teaches, "And yet shew I unto you a more excellent way." Gifts are good, but only if ministered in love. God never tells you to seek a gift. If you had to seek it, it wasn't a gift.

Starting at the end of 1 Corinthians 13:8, we read that gifts shall vanish away. Then in 1 Corinthians 13:10, it is stated, "But when that which is perfect [the Word] is come, then that which is in part [gifts] shall be done away." Paul later affirms in Colossians 1:25,

> Wherefore I [Paul] am made a minister, according to the dispensation of God which is given to me for you, to fulfill the Word of God.

Grace excels the gifts you see (Philippians 1:9–10). The Word praises,

> Thanks be unto God for His unspeakable gift.

This grace is not what you say before meals. It is the power of God (Romans 1:16). Grace in you produces faith, hope, and charity.

Spiritual gifts were given because grace given to the Body of Christ had not yet been established. The knowledge of God's grace is greater than anything that they had at Pentecost. Your gift is to edify, to give rise to faith, hope, and to put on charity (Colossians 3:14). Your role is not limited to one "power" anymore, but a Son fully equipped by grace. When you minister, you are using God's gift to you—grace. We as a body can all have it so that no one's "spiritual gifts" are better than another person's. Each member serves a vital role.

So what was the purpose of the ministry gifts? The answer can be found in Ephesians 4:12–13. The child of God has been "blessed [us] with all spiritual blessing in the heavenly places in Christ" (Ephesians 1:3).

64

Prayer of Comfort

Father, I am going off script. I know that You are not the author of confusion, but God, I am confused, and I don't know where that leaves me. Nowhere can I run to escape You, nor would I ever, yet as life rolls on like waves in high tide, I am lost. The devil and his handy tool of the flesh rattle me to my core, and God, I feel frail.

You see me and You know me intimately. You know the desires of my heart and You have spoken Your will abundantly clear. So God, I will always give You thanks. I will stand firm in awe and adoration. Equipped in Your armor, I will fight the darkness that swarms around like bees to a nest.

Yet, God, I must ask for discernment, mighty enough to present order in and despite the world's confusion. I plead for the waves to come but not overcome me. Keep my head above the water and fixated on Your truth. Abba, Father, most importantly, as Your child I ask for comfort. Let my flesh try in vain as Your righteousness usurps it. Take my frailty and strengthen the bones of my soul so that through it all, the world may say, "Wow! There is the true God. Deserving of all praise and glory!"

I ask this all in the undefiled, righteous name of Jesus Christ, who was, and is, and is to come. Amen.

In honor of my dearest mother. Lift her up in prayer.

65

How to Keep Running (A Spiritual Guide)

> But they that wait upon the Lord shall renew their strength; they shall mount up with wings as eagles; they shall run, and not be weary; and they shall walk, and not faint.
>
> —Isaiah 40:31

Track and field is such a raw sport that does an excellent job showcasing qualities such as grit, determination, and the limitless work of God in the lives of individuals. For many years now, I have been a runner who has striven to be an example of all of the above attributes. Through many years of training, I have developed enough experience to say,

> running is an honest sport. Liars are forced to show the truth by performance. The title of hard worker is tested in each race, and if you stop, you lose. How you started means nothing if you do not finish well.

It takes a lot of faith to cut countless hours of work from the limited length of life's cloth for a relatively much shorter length of race. Track icon Usain Bolt was once recorded saying,

> I trained four years to run nine seconds, and people give up when they don't see results in two months.

Ethiopian long-distance standout Haile Gebrselassie understands Bolt's statement all too well. He once laid a formula for the runner's ambition to finish their race when he stated,

> All athletes need three things: commitment, discipline, and hard work. Without that, it's hard to keep running.

Much like the runner's drive to continuously build endurance, the apostle Paul stands as a coach to all who are struggling to stay within the run. This is for all who are discouraged in their faith. The Church is the pillar of truth, pointing back to the race plan and correcting form to avoid injury. We train all our lives for the moment we step into eternity. This is a prize far greater than any gold.

66

Comfort—Where's the Source?

When I was young, I found much comfort in a good book. I was an oddball. My comfort was in sitting down and reading a good, non-fiction, historical analysis of some period's misfortunes. The World Wars, the Spanish Influenza, presidential assassination attempts—these were all things I enjoyed reading to escape from my own time in history.

There is much irony in my dorky pastime, I now realize. I oddly found comfort in things that broke the hearts of many. However, this is not uncommon. Many find comfort in watching horror films depicting brutal murders or are expert mass murderers, padding the kill-death ratio on Call of Duty.

But the topic of this devotional is not to admonish the pastimes of these individuals, as I often am one. It preps the reader for my primary question: When we retreat to our comforting pastimes, do we find hope?

Not many of the activities I listed above offer hope; although, they do present temporary pleasure. Sometimes, reading a good book may offer temporary hope. Yet my point is this: Only the Good Book can offer a hope of a lifetime into eternity.

67

Addicted to the Ministry

Addiction. The very word makes many Americans feel a shudder. It brings about painful memories and vivid imagery of someone with an addiction, if not themselves. Often, our mind displays connotations of alcohol, cigarettes, and illicit drug use. These thoughts are reasonable.

Nearly 21 million Americans possess at least one addiction, and only 10 percent of Americans ever receive treatments of some kind. Since 1990, American drug overdoses have tripled. Twenty percent of Americans who have depression or an anxiety disorder also have a substance abuse disorder. Statistics align with the Bible in this way. They show just how depraved the world is.

I want you, the reader, to be aware of how frequently we observe addiction worldwide, so that I can suggest this: What if Jesus Christ is more than just a healer of addiction? What if Christ caused an addiction so fervent that it could hijack the stigma of addiction as solely evil? Dream with me for a moment if you would.

Get Addicted

In 1 Corinthians 16, Paul is coming to the end of an excellent letter of doctrine to the Corinthian church. Addressing the local bodies, he gives his final anecdotes and notes, when he addresses the household of Stephanas. In his brief address, he attributes them to have become addicted to the ministry of the saints (1 Corinthians 16:15).

Stephanas and his household were people who Paul had ministered to and possibly converted during his work in Corinth (1 Corinthians 1:16). Often, we hear of people who have become "on fire for Christ." It has become somewhat of a cliché within Christian circles and represents essentially "addicts to the Gospel." Stephanas and his household were common people who are only briefly mentioned; however, Paul was thankful for their ministry and that they "refreshed [his] spirit." They were submitted to the faith and did all things with charity (1 Corinthians 16:13–14). Because of this, they were described as addicted to the ministry of the saints.

The word translated in English as *addicted* is *tasso* in the original Greek. This word essentially denotes an orderly appointment. Like an addiction that creates orders and rhythms of unhealthy and systematic alleviations, this household ordered their life for the furthering and edification of the Body of Christ. They were sold-out, focused, and determined to live their life according to ministry.

This family may not have been your stereotypical minister as we see them today (pastors, evangelists, etc.); nonetheless, you would not be able to see a difference. They were addicts. Addicted to God's work. Addicted to their high calling. Addicted to His word. If it was good and of God, they were fiending. They needed it.

The attributes they displayed, Paul tells the Christian to "submit yourselves unto such" (1 Corinthians 16:16). Paul gives practical advice, and practical advice has practical implications. So what would be the practical implications of a Christian addict?

Needing It

I do not intend to make light of addiction in this writing. However, biblically the topic has a place. So bear with me. If we have fellowship with the light (God) through Jesus Christ and we are universally, as a Church, lifting true, unadulterated doctrine in the world above the darkness, there will be an effect. Addiction to the ministry is powerful and able to bring healing to those with addiction to depravity. God's Word and grace are sufficient (2 Corinthians 12:9).

We can be sealed in the Body of Christ but not be addicted to the ministry and calling that is laid upon our lives. This is a scary position to be in. I beg for us, the Church, to live otherwise and cling to the Scriptures, praying for supplication with thanksgiving, and preaching the truth that Jesus saves.

68

I Fear No Monster

Monsters. Fear tantalizes. It is something that no one wants to experience on a personal level; however, it excites them second-hand. This is increasingly obvious with the world's saturated market depicting trivialized figures of horror and demise: zombies, vampires, demons, and lately (one a bit more personal) terrorists. We often describe these creatures and beings as monsters and villains. This judgment is rightfully so.

But as Christians, how are we supposed to respond stepping into the world of real monsters called reality? The author of the critically acclaimed fiction series *Percy Jackson and the Olympians* once wrote,

> The real world is where the monsters are.

We know this to be true. One of *Oxford Dictionary's* definitions of *monster* is "an inhumanly cruel or wicked person."

History is riddled with them, and all I can think of lately is the recent slaughter of thirteen soldiers in Afghanistan. They were murdered by monsters. As Christians, we view these crimes and we know that because of Adam and Eve's original sin, man's character is naturally depraved. Humanity is born sinful. Apart from Christ, no one is "good" and intentions are muddled (Psalm 51:1–3; Romans

3:10–18). The world tries to deceive by preaching the humanistic lie that men and women are "inherently good." The Bible teaches that humanity is "inherently sinful."

Two Paths

If we choose to follow the truth, it takes us on a separate trek from the world. We walk side by side with those who remain on the pathway to destruction; meanwhile, pleading for them to join this new family—a new family heading to abundant, eternal life. The path to destruction is conducted by the Prince of Darkness, Satan. When something evil is carried out, the first thing that one may assume is that the transgressor is our enemy.

This may be true, and all fault is on that person as an enemy to our flesh. But, Christians, let me ask you this: If from the moment of our salvation, we have crucified the flesh with Christ, then what do these monsters truly have to hold against us (Galatians 5:24)? Life in the kingdom and the family of God is found in the Spirit of Christ, not earth where moths and rust destroy (Matthew 6:19–21). Furthermore, because our flesh is not a priority, neither should our focus be on fleshly enemies. Rather the father of such evilness.

The War

In Ephesians 2:2, Paul teaches that these "monsters" are children of a much more devious being. He states, "Wherein in time past ye walked according to the course of this world, according to the prince of the power of the air, the spirit that now worketh in the children of disobedience." Later in Ephesians 6:12, Paul elaborates more by saying,

> We wrestle not against flesh and blood, but against principalities, against powers, against the rulers of the darkness of this world, against spiritual wickedness in high places.

He goes on to empower the Christian with the Spiritual Armor of God. In this armor, there is no weak spot or place to infiltrate. Satan and his subordinates will only receive gashes from the sword of truth, God's Word.

The longest wars on earth are not the Hundred Years' War, the Vietnam War, or the War in Afghanistan. It is the spiritual war waged for the souls of each and every person on earth.

The Answer

Little does the enemy know that the battle has already been won and death has been defeated. The Savior of the world, Jesus Christ, has defeated death. He has defeated the devil (Hebrews 2:14). Christ Himself died but now is alive forevermore, holding the keys to death and Hades (Revelation 1:18). How can fear tantalize us any longer?

If you do not have this assurance of a war already won, I want to offer you this piece of Scripture. We all are sinners who are in need of a Savior. No longer do you have to live as a child of disobedience; rather, join the love of a newfound heavenly Father. Simply know

> that if thou shalt confess with thy mouth the Lord Jesus, and shalt believe in thine heart that God hath raised Him from the dead, thou shalt be saved. For with the heart man believeth unto righteousness; and with the mouth confession is made unto salvation. (Romans 10:9–10)

69

Man by Eternity's Cliffside

Once a child, yet evolved into a man.
Looking over the cliffs, I see the sky.
In my soul, delighting that You are nigh.
That Your eye can see across such great span.
Across the fields and above blue seas.
Composing essence by power of Word.
By nature, paper, and by paper heard
Thy refined, righteous voice beckon unto me.
Teach my soul and reprove to understand.
Despite season I ought to be ready.
Forlorn souls rely on Thine truth steady.
For you always leave room for ampersand.
Pleading for man to join me by the edge.
That they may gaze and lift You all prestige.
For glory and Hades, your Son did siege.
By belief, their will and being to pledge.
Not for bread but each Word from hallowed lips.
Neither sights nor elating conditions.
The Body lives for Gospel fruition.
Peer in awe, the work of Your fingertips.
I pray, a man by eternity's cliffside.

70

My Redeemer Lives

My Redeemer lives. We often hear this in songs of praise and adoration of God. But biblically, is there such a beautiful proclamation? To no surprise, this is a biblical proclamation; however, it may not be where you would expect. Job 19:25 reads,

> I know that my redeemer liveth, and that he shall stand at the latter day upon the earth.

Surprised? It was not shouted in a fiery sermon by John, Peter, Paul, or any other of the persecuted in Christ. It was proclaimed by Job within deep anguish thousands of years before Christ's death and resurrection. Continue on past this proclamation and we see that he affirms this truth after a series of plagues has left his body rancid. This would not distract him from the truth that he served a God who is alive.

He continues,

> And though after my skin worms destroy this body, yet in my flesh shall I see God:

> Whom I shall see for myself, and mine eyes shall behold, and not another; though my reins be consumed within me.

This makes me ponder the question for myself. What circumstances in my life may distract from the focal point of our faith, which is that our Redeemer lives? Is it physical ailments? Family strife? Sheer unbelief? I know our circumstances are not the same as Job; however, let us join together in unity and have a perspective that proclaims, "And though." Because though the world may fall apart, our Redeemer still lives and is on the throne. Our precious hope of glory.

> But for us also, to whom it shall be imputed, if we believe on him that raised up Jesus our Lord from the dead;
>
> Who was delivered for our offences, and was raised again for our justification. (Romans 4:24–25)

71

Cold Pillow, Warm Bed

Sometimes life's greatest comforts come only from being in life's most uncomfortable positions. Like being snuggled up in bed on a really cold day. There is no sensation like it. Our focus on the cold (cold being an absence of heat) makes us appreciate the heat all the more.

Spiritually, this is true as well. As Christians, we do not lose the presence of the Holy Spirit in our lives. He indwells within us, sealed as a letter. Nonetheless, moments prevail in life because tragedy strikes or our sin leaves us with regrets we wish we never had. Be encouraged! These moments are where we appreciate the joy and grace of Christ Jesus even more. We are reminded in these situations that Jesus Christ is an active God, heavily involved in our lives.

Paul knows full well what this means as he reflects on the great Comforter in 2 Corinthians 1:3–4. The Scripture reads, "Blessed be God, even the Father of our Lord Jesus Christ, the Father of mercies, and the God of all comfort; Who comforteth us in all our tribulation, that we may be able to comfort them which are in any trouble, by the comfort wherewith we ourselves are comforted of God."

Another church leader who had a grasp on the spiritual temperatures of our souls is James. In James 1:2–3, James teaches his congregation of the benefits of the "cold" and pressure. He encourages them by saying,

> My brethren, count it all joy when ye fall into divers temptations; knowing this, that the trying of your faith worketh patience.

So be encouraged! There is much to gain in our cold days. Furthermore, our cold days are not only an opportunity for a warm blanket. They are a reminder that there will be warmer days. The most temperate of these days, however, being the day we are able to see our Savior face to face.

> For I reckon that the sufferings of this present time are not worthy to be compared with the glory which shall be revealed in us. (Romans 8:18)

———

72

Take Your Vitamins

The great philosopher Hulk Hogan once told his students, "To all my little Hulkamaniacs, say your prayers, take your vitamins, and you will never go wrong." In the same way, famed gospel singer Mahalia Jackson is quoted as saying, "Faith and prayer are the vitamins of the soul; man cannot live in health without them."

Interestingly enough, I found these quotes soon after I took my daily vitamin. For years, I have taken Men's One-A-Day vitamins because I recognized just how many healthy elements are packed into one small capsule. As curiosity overcame me, I was presented with a question that I believe should be addressed in the life of a believer. What makes a spiritual vitamin?

To answer this, I looked at my daily vitamin for comparison.

Spiritual Vitamin

The majority of a Men's One-A-Day is vitamin B-12. The human body utilizes B-12 for many purposes, but essentially energizes the body because of its crucial role in red blood cell formation. For the church (the body), our B-12 is the Gospel of Jesus Christ. From the earliest days of Levitical law, it was understood that life is in the blood (Leviticus 17:11). As Christians this is exceedingly true. Our life is in the precious blood of Jesus Christ, and we are energized by His resurrection. Without the Gospel, this mighty spiritual multivitamin is essentially worthless.

The next largest vitamin group in the Men's One-A-Day is vitamin D. Many know this vitamin as the vitamin that strengthens bones because it absorbs calcium. Vitamin D makes our bones strong. Our bones are the foundation of the body. All things are supported by them. The bones of the Body of Christ must be the word of Christ. In Ephesians 2:20–21, Paul articulates that Christians

> are built upon the foundation of the apostles and prophets, Jesus Christ himself being the chief cornerstone;
>
> In whom all the building fitly framed together groweth unto an holy temple in the Lord.

Our foundation can be in no other Word (1 Timothy 6:3–4). So take your vitamin D(octrine)!

Coming in third place for percent vitamin content is vitamin B-5. This vitamin serves the interesting function of breaking down fats and wastes, so that the body can rebuild. When we are broken down and in need of waste management, this is where our spiritual vitamin B-5 comes alive. Our vitamin B-5 is prayer. In prayer, we go to the Holy Spirit to intercede for us and we can rest in assurance that God can carry our infirmities and weakness (Romans 8:26).

As for the many other elements in the spiritual multivitamin, these are the good things that we as Christians are called to dwell on, such as the honest and true things we are called to in Philippians 4:8. These things include the many sequential benefits of our tribulations as mentioned in Romans 5:3–4 which produces "patience, experience, and hope."

Bring It Together

All these components work together to improve the spiritual health of the believer. They have far-reaching benefits within each member of the body! These elements are encapsulated by faith, and by faith we receive them. The Gospel we receive by faith (Ephesians 2:8–9), doctrine we receive by faith (Romans 10:17), prayer is conducted by faith (1 John 5:14), and in faith we face the tribulations of the world!

So take your vitamins, fellow saints. Join me in the venture to strengthen the body and serve our God fully nourished!

73

Are You Working Out with God Today?

Lifting has always been a recreational activity for me. However, as I developed more athletically, I found a greater need for lifting heavier. And heavier. And then heavier. Recently, while lifting, I received advice to adjust my form to lift more efficiently for my sport. Upon taking this advice, I lifted the weight from the rack, and as I squatted, the weight (to my surprise) nearly threw me to the ground. Fortunately, I caught the weight and was able to save myself from a very scary near-miss injury. I did not utilize this form correctly.

It was then that I realized that I still needed to do the rep! The stance that I had put myself in had caused poor weight distribution and leverage. My posture caused me to nearly be crushed under the weight. Upon redirecting my posture, I was able to lift the weight and ultimately get stronger. The truth is that the hearts of men and women are the same way. Poor posture equals excessive force caused by heaviness.

In Proverbs 12:25, we are taught that

> heaviness in the heart of man maketh it stoop:
> but a good word maketh it glad.

Anxieties of life are going to try and overtake us. Our adversary is still trying to steal the joy that is in Christ Jesus. But be encouraged, oh ye of little faith, there is hope! A good word maketh the heart glad! The Good Word maketh it glad (Romans 15:4).

When we redirect our posture, looking to the Word of God, our stance becomes stronger to lift the heaviness off our hearts. This is not of our own strength, however. The Word of God is our posture. It props us up and is sufficient to lift the burdens of our souls. God is a willing workout instructor if you are willing to trust His routines. Work out with God. You will not regret it.

74

I Ain't Lazy

There are many ways to insult someone. You could attack them personally by making light of their socioeconomic status. One may insult another's political affiliation. If someone really wants to get under the skin of another, they will offer a backhanded compliment that will act as a slow burn throughout the mind of the receiver.

Insulting me is a bit easier, though. All one has to do is call me lazy. This word stings as if it were salt to an open wound. Claiming that I am anything resembling lazy unnerves me. As Christians, if we are okay with being identified as lazy, whether spiritually or physically, there needs to be a reevaluation of self.

Our position in Christ does so much more than merely give us the illuminated title of "Christian." Another title we may proudly boast is "workman." We are Christ's workmanship and called to walk unto good works (Ephesians 2:10). This walk should be conducted heartily as this pleases the Lord (Colossians 3:23). The Lord should be the priority and destination of our walk.

We are to be workmen in our day-to-day lives, our relationships, and even as studious Christians within our study of the Word—be a workman! Scripturally, we are called to be workmen who rightly divide the Word of Truth.

The Second Epistle to Timothy 2:15 states,

> Study to shew thyself approved unto God, a workman that needeth not to be ashamed, rightly dividing the word of truth.

No matter what we do, because of what Christ has done, our intentions should be set upon Him! We are merely mirrors reflecting the glory of God, and if your mirror is dirty, I pray this is a call to pull out the spiritual Windex, which is the Word of God (1 Corinthians 10:31)!

75

Grace for Grace

And of his fulness have all we received, and grace for grace.
—John 1:16

The phrase *grace for grace* is a relatively well-known phrase that has made its way into many aspects of a Christian's life. Music, decorative signs, and T-shirts may be seen or heard in the thralls of mainstream Christian culture.

Interestingly enough, the phrase rarely has the same translation across interpreters, which may lead to confusion in the concept that the apostle John was presenting in John 1:16.

To make my point, let us take a look:

- King James Version: "Grace for grace"
- New American Standard Bible: "Grace upon grace"
- English Standard Version: "Grace upon grace"
- New International Version: "Grace in place of grace"
- New Living Translation: "One gracious blessing after another"

The ambiguity of understanding seemingly can be remedied with a look into the Greek preposition that divided the terms for grace. We are familiar with the term *anti*. In its context, it has been translated as "for," "upon," "in place of," and "after another."

Truthfully, these all correlate strongly with *anti*. Thayer's Greek lexicon defines the term as "of succession to the place of another," literally placing the concept of the grace that Christ brings as something that is perpetually replaced.

A more plain way of saying this is that the grace of God is never exhausted! And why? Because the wrath of God was satisfied in the fullness of Christ and His finished work! One verse down, John states, "For the law was given by Moses, but grace and truth came by Jesus Christ." Furthermore, by Jesus Christ, this endless grace is what satisfies us. It is all-sufficient grace!

In the apostle Paul's affliction, he called out to God yet was met with the answer,

> My grace is sufficient for thee: for my strength is made perfect in weakness. Most gladly therefore will I rather glory in my infirmities, that the power of Christ may rest upon me. (2 Corinthians 12:9)

There is so much that can be said regarding the sufficiency of Christ; however, one of the many reasons it is so sufficient is because it is unending. Humanity in itself is an end to itself. But a person of God has no end as they take part and identify with the infinite grace of God, offered in His Son (Ephesians 2:8). There is no end to God's grace.

76

The Battle Is Already Won!

Therefore, my beloved brethren, be ye steadfast, unmovable, always abounding in the work of the Lord, forasmuch as ye know that your labor is not in vain in the Lord.
—1 Corinthians 15:58

Many ministers are familiar with the saying, "Whenever you see a 'therefore,' you need to go back and see what it is 'there for.'" Chapter 15 has major doctrinal implications pertaining to the Gospel, resurrection, and eternity. Just prior to verse 58, Paul explains that death no longer has any dominion over humanity:

> O death, where is thy sting? O grave, where is thy victory? (1 Corinthians 15:55)

Death has no power because Christ came and has fulfilled the Law! The Law was the strength of sin; but now, the strength of a Christian is the Holy Spirit (2 Timothy 1:7). Because Christ had the victory when rising from the grave many years ago, we are living testimonies of victory.

But this is not anything we can boast of in ourselves. The battle is won by the work of the Cross, and as our identity is now in Christ, we boast of Christ (Galatians 6:14). God gave us the victory, so it is little comparably to simply give thanks in all that we do (Romans 12:1; 1 Corinthians 15:57). Therefore, do not worry. We are strengthened in Christ Jesus. Live alive. He has made a way, and the labor we toil is not in vain (1 Corinthians 15:51–54).

77

Last Words

People always have a fascination with the last words of celebrities, actors, and well-known people. When General John Sedgwick was sitting on his horse looking toward the Confederate Army, he said, "They couldn't hit an elephant at this distan—" He was killed by a sharpshooter at the Battle of Spotsylvania Court House. You never know if your last words will make an impact.

In the last words of Paul to Timothy in 2 Timothy 4:5, he wrote,

> Watch thou in all things, endure afflictions, do the work of an evangelist, make full proof of thy ministry.

He was telling him, as he tells us, to fulfill whatever God wants us to do. No God-directed ministry is small or unimportant.

Timothy wasn't only a preacher; he was also a soldier who would have to endure afflictions. Most of these afflictions would come from the religious crowd. Some don't want to hear the truth or even the Gospel. But our ministry must have soul-winning at heart along with soul feeding. Paul's last were encouraging but also straightforward.

So words do matter, whether they are the first or last to a lost and dying world. Paul later in verse 7 said those famous words,

> I have fought a good fight, I have finished my course, I have kept the faith.

This is how you quit like men. The First Epistle to the Corinthians 16:13 teaches us to be strong, carry out the Gospel, and you will finish well.

78

Remodeling

Remodeling. It may be a joy or a drudgery. This all depends on the person and the project. Sometimes, it may just be a matter of finances. Big projects demand big cash. Other times, it could just be a matter of energy expenditure. Remodeling is usually a side venture to the normal strains of life. And still yet, for some, you have everything in place to start a project; however, you just do not know where to start.

Take a room for example. There is an empty room within your home. Almost literally, a blank canvas. It could be a home theater, a workout room, a study, or just another bedroom. Where do you start?

From a background in construction and remodeling, I would suggest taking care of the big things first. If it needs cleaning, clean the walls and the floors first before you dust the corners. Painting? Paint the majority of the walls first and then touch the intricate details.

It may come as a surprise to you that this is how our faith operates as well. No believer's faith begins in the fine-tuning and details. Biblically, the only way it can begin is at the end of self. Christ's Gospel is our beginning, and ultimately, it should be the most seen aspect in the finish as well.

From here, we add. We grow. There comes some subtraction of ungodliness that would ultimately make our room tacky or out of sorts. But nonetheless, the Gospel is shining bright and displayed at the forefront. As Christians, the room of our soul is primed by the Holy Spirit and covered by Christ's redemptive grace. He is our foundation, and the finished product consists of His work.

In 1 Corinthians 3:11, Paul teaches that

> other foundation can no man lay than that is laid, which is Jesus Christ.

Furthermore, the new creation formed through our salvation remains forever transformed as a suitable dwelling for the Holy Spirit! Later in 1 Corinthians, we find that the "body is the temple of the Holy Ghost which is in you, which ye have of God, and ye are not your own" (6:19).

As Christians, this signifies that our soul is not merely primed and formed for and by Christ, but we also find that we release the property title back to God, our creator and sustainer. So allow God to sustain you today, remodeling you inside and out with a fresh soul that carries over gracefully in eternity with God.

In closing, we read 2 Corinthians 5:1–2; 6–8,

> For we know that if our earthly house of this tabernacle were dissolved, we have a building of God, an house not made with hands, eternal in the heavens.
>
> For in this we groan, earnestly desiring to be clothed upon with our house which is from heaven…
>
> Therefore we are always confident, knowing that, whilst we are at home in the body, we are absent from the Lord:
>
> (For we walk by faith, not by sight:)
>
> We are confident, I say, and willing rather to be absent from the body, and to be present with the Lord.

79

I'll Fly Away, Oh Glory

There is a famous hymn in which many people, Christian and secular, are familiar with. "I'll fly away" is sung at nearly every country, bluegrass, folk, homecoming, (sometimes) rock outings, and movies.

The song has an amazingly biblical principle. Surely, we will fly away and be preserved into the heavenly kingdom of our great God (2 Timothy 4:18).

This song was penned by a man named Albert Brumley in reflection on his days of picking cotton on his father's Oklahoma farm. This song compares the world to a prison where our soul can escape upon death.

The skeleton of this song can be found in an old ballad that Brumley would hum on the farm named "The Prisoner's Song." In reference to a prison, we find Moses describing his desire to fly away from the prison of life's wandering in Psalm 90.

It is interesting to note that this is the only Psalm attributed to Moses within the Psalms and therefore the oldest of the Psalms. Scholars believe that this Psalm was written toward the end of wandering for the Israelite generation barred from the promised land (Deuteronomy 1:35). Moses himself being within this group, is seeing the generation die out and the mortality of man.

Despite the circumstances and realization of life's brevity, Moses affirms that his time on earth must still be used for God's purpose, even in the light of eternity.

With this tidbit in mind, check out the words of the psalmist Moses in Psalm 90:9–12,

> For all our days are passed away in thy wrath: We spend our years as a tale that is told.
>
> The days of our years are threescore years and ten; and if by reason of strength they be fourscore years, yet is their strength labour and sorrow; for it is soon cut off, and we fly away.
>
> Who knoweth the power of thine anger? Even according to thy fear, so is thy wrath.
>
> So teach us to number our days, that we may apply our hearts unto wisdom.

Moses speaks of numbering our days so that we may apply the God-given wisdom we obtained because our days are numbered.

In regards to New Testament language, this is what it means to "redeem the time" (Ephesians 5:16–18).

It is worth noting that Ephesians 5:17 Paul also is teaching the Christian to not be "unwise." Understanding the will of God will teach us to number our days and make the most of each one for the Gospel, despite the circumstances.

We will constantly be immersed in non-ideal circumstances. The "days are evil" (Ephesians 5:16) so we should not expect anything less. In the truest sense, the world is like a prison since we are not home yet.

Yet while everyone is here, make the most of the opportunities God gives us each day until that glorious day when our souls are released and we see our Savior face to face!

And yes, I say *our*. There is only one Gospel able to breach the prison walls and strongholds. Share it! And on that fateful day, the sky will be full of soul's taking flight unto heaven.

When the shadows of this life are gone,
I'll fly away.
Like a bird from prison bars has flown
I'll fly away.

80

Another Coat

Painting calmed the chaos that shook my soul.
—Niki de St. Phalle

Unlike the above quote, painting does not calm my soul. I hate painting. I am not someone who enjoys the tediousness of it and I especially do not like having to apply second coats when painting homes.

I hate working so hard—only to have to do it again as soon as it dries. This would be when the whole choir shouts, "Amen!"

But this action is necessary. Every coat of paint laid onto the wall covers a prior layer of filth and varying color. The beautiful truth is, though, that our outward man is perishing every day; yet as believers, our inner man is renewed day by day (2 Corinthians 4:14–16).

The undercoat will never fade away. It will never grow filthy. It will never get beyond repair. Because Christ, like the diligent painter, renews the walls of our heart daily (Romans 12:1–2). This means we are made new every day we open our eyes. This pattern continues into eternity (2 Corinthians 4:14).

Coat after coat. Our hearts are renewed by the loving blood of Christ which is shed abroad in our hearts (Romans 5:5). Aren't you glad God never gets tired of making a new creation (2 Corinthians 5:17)?

81

Misinformation

Every year, the *Oxford Dictionary* campaigns to find the word of the year. This year, the word of the year will probably be *misinformation*. We have all heard this word a lot this past year; however, it is open for debate as to whose claims of misinformation is correct.

This is not anything new. In 2 Timothy 17–18 we read of Hymenaeus and Philetus. Paul compares their misinformation to a canker. Like gangrene, it spreads, infects, and kills other tissue.

So false doctrine too infects the body of believers, the Church. It must be exposed, removed, and replaced with healthy doctrine.

They had wandered from the truth by teaching that salvation is resurrection in a spiritual sense, so the believer must not expect a physical resurrection. This is misinformation and a serious matter. Read 1 Corinthians 15:12–19. No wonder these false teachers were able to "overthrow the faith of some" with misinformation. The resurrection is a foundational truth of the Gospel. Notice in 1 Corinthians 15:1 when Paul says, "moreover" and what follows is of first importance for all. We must all hinge on that, and that, my friend, is true information.

82

Sitting on a Bench

When I was much younger, I considered myself quite the poet. I still like to write poetry, although God's grace has revealed to me that it is not as good as I once thought.

Saying this, have you ever had a work of art that you were proud of as a kid? This can be a poem, a picture, a macaroni sculpture, etc. I know I did. In my sixth-grade English class, I wrote a poem called "Sitting on a Bench." It was a masterpiece in my mind. The work was absolutely the greatest piece of poetry in the human mind that would have my teacher's heart enraptured with thoughts of God's glory.

The one problem however: it was hot trash.

"Sitting on a Bench" made no sense at all to anyone who read it—except for me. For a poem about heaven, its theology was self-constructed. Its form was sloppy. The thought that I had invested into it did not translate into anything coherent. When it was not favored above my classmates, I was crushed.

I say all this to make a point. As we live with the title "ambassadors for Christ," we must faithfully present the Gospel of Jesus Christ. In our lives, Christians might hold it high as the crowning achievement, yet disregard what it is biblically and saturate it with our personality instead of allowing the person of Jesus Christ to speak by His Holy Spirit.

"Overdoing" the presentation of the gospel is a very real reality. We are not to preach ourselves but, rather, preach the foundation that is already laid (1 Corinthians 3:11; 2 Corinthians 4:5). Do not boast in your eloquence, boast in Christ's excellence (1 Corinthians 2:1–5; 2 Corinthians 10:17).

Lastly, do not get discouraged in rejection. As Christians, we are to present the Gospel, and it will be rejected by many. After all Paul teaches that

> the preaching of the cross is to them that perish foolishness; but unto us which are saved it is the power of God. (1 Corinthians 1:18)

Our job is to simply present the masterpiece of our faith, the Gospel of Jesus Christ, and rest assured in the saving grace and power of it.

In fact it is not only a masterpiece, it is the standard and level of our faith!

So put aside our own glory and lean in the beauty of God's Word!

83

Rainbow Faith Bracelets

North Carolina residents mark their calendars yearly for the opening of the North Carolina State Fair. This was the first year however that I was able to make it to this large event and share in the fun that many state fairs experience each year!

These fairs are filled with oddities of food, rides, attractions, and vendors from within and outside of the state. This is where people can boast that they ate deep-fried Oreos, deep-fried chocolate-covered bacon, and deep-fried butter sticks. For a tamer crowd, some could simply hang around the farm portion of the fair and see beautiful animals and vegetables!

Despite the many wild things and people that I saw, as a Christian, there was one simple thing that really stood out to me. At one of the vendor tables, there was a Christian organization handing out "Rainbow Faith Bracelets." Upon receiving mine, a wave of nostalgia rolled over me as I remember making these wonderful illustrations of faith when I was considerably younger.

The bracelet consists of five different-colored beads on a leather string. These beads stand for the following:

- *Gold or yellow.* Our heavenly destination and home (1 Corinthians 2:9)
- *Black.* Our sin that separates us from God (Romans 6:23)

- *Red.* The blood of Christ and His resurrection by which we are saved (1 Corinthians 15:3–4)
- *White.* The effect of the blood that washes us white as snow (Isaiah 1:18; Romans 4:22–25)
- *Green.* Growth in Christ (a.k.a. "Enriching Grace") (Colossians 1:10)

This bracelet is an excellent way to minister and begin spiritual conversations that lead to spiritual conversion. But regardless of what we wear on our outside, always minister of what went on inside of you when Christ saved you.

Christ's Gospel is the only thing that saves broken humanity, and people notice the change when you are a new creation! (2 Corinthians 5:17)

Let's get colorful and get the Word out!

84

The Immutable Infinite

Many Christians are familiar with Jesus's assertion of being the "Alpha and Omega," the beginning and end of the Greek alphabet. It is a powerful declaration that promotes many of the incommunicable attributes of God. Some of these attributes that we can observe at face value are God's immutability and His infinitude. God doesn't change. He has always been. Forever will He reign. He was in the beginning and before the beginning, and His qualities have never changed (John 1:1; Hebrews 13:8).

In response to this declaration, there may be some who have no problem believing this yet, with a skeptical heart, ask the question, "So what? What do God's unchanging, infinite qualities have to do with my ever-changing, finite life?" To God's inquisitor, I would have to reply simply and precisely: everything!

French Romantic Victor Hugo once wrote,

> Change your opinions, keep to your principles;
> change your leaves, keep intact your roots.

As humans, we are prone to changing. Although fleshly progress is made, without God, it is at the cost of an eroding soul. If you do not believe me, look at the journals of the father of modern psychological progress, Sigmund Freud. His perception of success tormented him. His world and opinions were constantly changing, but never did he have an anchor for his soul. The flesh and soul will constantly rub together, causing friction, unsettling the spirit of humanity.

You see, Christian progress needs to be equivalent to spiritual growth (Colossians 1:10). Growth is only possible when we are rooted, when we are anchored. In a plant, for example, the root supplies the nutrients that nourish growth and guard against upheaval. Knowing this, the eternal God supplies growth. Paul teaches this in the following illustration:

> So then neither is he that planteth any thing, neither he that watereth; but God that giveth the increase.
>
> Now he that planteth and he that watereth are one: and every man shall receive his own reward according to his own labour. (1 Corinthians 3:7–8)

As for being anchored, the skeptic's question would be, "Anchored in what?" I once again have the answer: hope (Hebrews 6:19). We hope in the Gospel of Jesus Christ, which was the plan of God before the foundation of the world (Ephesians 1:4). We hope that God does not change, our salvation is eternally secure, and that God is the A to Z that He says He is.

As you strive for progress, allow the anchor and root of hope in an immutable God to progress deeper into your foundation.

85

Say His Name

Within the Bible, God is known by nearly three hundred different titles! Is this surprising to you? It shouldn't be. Considering how magnificent, holy, and righteous our God is, it makes sense that humanity is not capable of singling out a title or that God simply offers humanity a one-dimensional aspect of Himself within His name. Names mean something. It is more than just an address.

For example, my name is Jacob. It derives from the Hebrew word *ya'aqov*. The name's origin can be found in Genesis 25:26 when Jacob grabs the heel of his brother Esau during the birthing process. The name commonly means "supplanter," "grabbed by the heel," or in some cases, "deceiver." All three of these names describe an aspect of the biblical character Jacob and his life. In the same way, God's name has a meaning and often depicts a dimension of His character and being.

Below are a few common examples out of the exhaustive list:

- *Elohim* (Genesis 1:1). "God"
- *Yahweh* (Exodus 3:13–14). "The Lord" or "I Am"
- *Abba* (Romans 8:15). "Father"
- *El Elyon* (Psalm 7:17). "God Most High"
- *El Roi* (Genesis 16:13). "The God Who Sees"

- *El Shaddai* (Psalm 91:1). "God Almighty"
- *Yahweh Yireh* (Genesis 22:14). "The Lord Will Provide"

As amazing as these names are and what attributes depict about God, none of these attributes can be experienced without first believing in the name Jesus.

This is the name that connects us to the "most high," "all-seeing," "all-providing," "almighty Father."

Actually, allow me to be more specific: this is the God who graciously allowed His children to know and connect with Him, to join His Body and be able to proudly proclaim that our God is who He says He is.

Join me as I lift His holy name on high!

86

Bless Their Heart!

Bless them that curse you, and pray for them which despitefully use you.

—Luke 6:28

Jesus in His earthly ministry had a way of pointing out the conduct expected within the Kingdom program. Here in Luke 6:28, Jesus teaches a principle that, in a simpler form, is well-known.

The Jewish population knew well that loving others as yourself was commanded by the Law. Examining Leviticus 19:18 affirms that not only is God a God of justice, but of love as well.

The Scripture speaks,

> Thou shalt not avenge, nor bear any grudge against the children of thy people, but thou shalt love thy neighbour as thyself: I am the Lord.

The Jewish population were a people who lived by the letter. Down to the letter, we would see that the Scripture says not to "bear any grudge against the children of thy people" (emphasis added). So of course, they would live by this code and love their people as themselves.

When Paul made the statement that in the Body of Christ there is no longer Jew or Gentile, this broke a multigenerational division that was long maintained by Jewish leadership.

As Christ being the Word incarnate (John 1:1), in His perfect timing, He is able to take a step further and call the Jew to pray for the man that curses them and spitefully uses them. He says this despite that person possibly being Roman, their nation's enemies, and or another Jew.

Flash forward to Christ's revelation to Paul. In Romans 12:14, we find that this action of blessing those who oppose is reciprocated within the teachings of Paul.

You may ask why there is such an uncanny resemblance. Well, think of it this way.

The Great Commission is often pontificated as the last words of Christ. But fast-forward, and we see that Christ kept speaking to His apostles. Paul directly received his words (or should I say Christ's words) from Jesus (Galatians 1:12).

"Bless them which persecute you: bless, and curse not" is what Paul wrote.

Blessing those who are deemed undeserving, is not just what God calls us to do. It is in His being to do it. In fact, He did do it. We do not deserve God's grace or the sacrifice of His Son. Yet freely, He gave (Ephesians 2:8) so that we can be restored and conformed to the image of His Son (Romans 8:29).

So cling to this cross-dispensational truth of God to love those that seem impossible or undeserving. Follow Paul's example (1 Corinthians 11:1) when he teaches to "bless, and curse not," for this is right before the sight of God.

In doing this, we are not negating justice either. We simply take God at His word when He proclaims, "Vengeance is mine; I will repay" (Romans 12:19).

We are simply called to love as Christ loved the Church.

87

A Simple and Ordinary Life

> Ivan Ilych's life had been most simple and most ordinary and therefore most terrible.

Some may recognize this quote as a Leo Tolstoy construction from his work *The Death of Ivan Ilych*. This novella presents an allegorical confrontation of death and the fear thereof.

Infamous religious skeptic Cesare Borgia exclaimed as his life slipped from him on his deathbed,

> While I lived, I provided for everything but death; now I must die, and am unprepared to die.

These two quotes paralleled speak volumes about why people fear death. Before I continue, I must confess that I understand the hesitancy and consistent plague of reality that says one day your mortal body will die. There is a fear of dying ordinary, unprepared, and longing for an absolute answer of "what's next?"

Famous Puritan theologian Richard Baxter seemed to know the answer as he stated in his last words,

> I have pain—but I have peace, I have peace.

He had peace in eternity. It was reconciled in his mind that death is more than blackness and absence of consciousness. He knew that he was not going to be consumed by unending flames. Baxter was convinced that his life had meaning.

But how could he be sure? How can we be sure? We all feel a longing and calling to eternity (Ecclesiastes 3:11). This God-instilled longing is often recklessly ignored or rejected for the span of an individual's life. Know this, however: it also often has the last space vacant in the mind of an unbeliever. For the Christian, believing in the Gospel of Jesus Christ is where this possibly frightening reality is reconciled in mind *and* heart.

> For the wages of sin is death; but the gift of God is eternal life through Jesus Christ our Lord. (Romans 6:23)

Be encouraged! Not only do we have eternal life, but we also have comfort in the truth that Christ gives value to life here on earth until the redemption of our glorified bodies. You can be a "new" creation (2 Corinthians 5:17). Lean into this truth today and believe in Christ's finished work (1 Corinthians 15:3–4). And if you believe, praise God. You can share in the words of Richard Baxter:

> I have peace, I have peace.

88

Serve to Lead

You don't have to hold a position in order to be a leader.
—Henry Ford

How does this resonate with you? Does it sound…wrong? It may be worth noting that sometimes leadership requires a person to expel their view of authority in a position to wear the true fabric of a leader. A Christian leader may need to strive for the godly attribute of impartiality blanketed in humility (Romans 2:11; Philippians 2:4). Leaders are first servants—servants who influence others to serve. This can be in multiple capacities.

This model can be used in business, family, etc., but the process derives from the Scriptures and is encompassed simply by what we call "Christian fellowship." Follow along with me, if you would, in Paul's address to the church in Philippi. Philippians 2:2–4 states,

> Fulfil ye my joy, that ye be likeminded, having the same love, being of one accord, of one mind.
>
> Let nothing be done through strife or vainglory; but in lowliness of mind let each esteem other better than themselves. Look not every man on his own things, but every man also on the things of others.

> Look not every man on his own things, but every man also on the things of others.

Jesus, the Servant. Jesus, the King. Paul furthers his discourse by offering the beauty of Christ's earthly ministry as the perfect servant and the authority that He holds eternally from the Father. No, we cannot be Jesus, who illustrated leadership and humility in all perfection. However, we can practice leadership with a purpose like Paul states in verses 16–18. He writes,

> Holding forth the word of life; that I may rejoice in the day of Christ, that I have not run in vain, neither laboured in vain.
>
> Yea, and if I be offered upon the sacrifice and service of your faith, I joy, and rejoice with you all.
>
> For the same cause also do ye joy, and rejoice with me."

Pure godly leadership is sacrifice, service, and joy. Hold forth the word of life, who is Jesus, Lord of all (Romans 10:9–10). He was the servant King on earth and is the ruling King of heaven, whom we are predestined to conform to His image (Romans 8:29). Therefore, He justified us and called us out unto Himself (Romans 8:30). This is for His glory. We are a part of the Body of Christ. Each of us is a functioning component with a leading role to fill (Romans 12:4–5). For example, a hand leads the procession to grasp an object, but it is useless if it doesn't serve the Body to pick it up. So once again, I plead: Serve to lead.

Do not conform to the world but instead be transformed by the renewing of your minds. Only then can we "prove what is that good, and acceptable, and perfect, will of God" (Romans 12:1–2). Serve God. Serve others. Lead in servanthood. Any other form of leadership will surely have its root in pride and its fall in misplaced authority that truly never was ours to wield (Romans 13:1; Philippians 2:9).

89

I'm Just Shy

Have any of you ever felt a sense of apprehension or nervousness when approaching people? I can testify that I have (and do) quite often. Many people are familiar with shyness. One of the biggest first decisions of my life was originally hindered by being shy.

In early high school, I was young and in love with my now fiancée, Hallie. We had hung out, we were great friends, and I wanted to commence the next big thing. So I decided in my mind that after math class one day, I would ask her to meet me outside, and I was going to ask her on a date. So in math class, I said, "Hey, will you meet me outside after class?" And she said, "Sure!"

When the bell rang, I rushed out of class to wait for her. But then, as I stood there waiting for her to come out, my anxiety overcame me. I ran around the corner and watched from there as she came out of the room confused. I repeated this process for an entire week. How embarrassing!

Saying this, I would like to tell you that I finally "manned up" and asked Hallie. But I didn't. She eventually grabbed me and forced me to face my fear of rejection. The question is, though, "What if she didn't?" My shy nature could have radically altered my life and the godly relationship that was to be. But this godly woman had something that was still developing in me: a nonanxious spirit of love, power, and of a sound mind (2 Timothy 1:7).

The believer's walk has some uncanny similarities to my story of young, blossoming love. God did not set in us a spirit of fear that shies away from opportunities to be effective ministers. Justified and sanctified by Jesus Christ, we can be unashamed to carry the Gospel to the unbeliever. Paul states in Romans 1:16 that this is our power! He proclaims in himself,

> I am not ashamed of the gospel of Christ: for it is the power of God unto salvation to every one that believeth; to the Jew first, and also to the Greek.

With the Gospel as the power of God unto salvation, we should and can boldly live our life with Christ's finished work as our mantra. Do not miss out on opportunities to proclaim this wonderful truth. Shyness can have endless consequences, good and bad. So let's get to it!

90

One Small Word, One Big Difference

William R. Newell was an evangelist Bible teacher and assistant superintendent at Moody Bible Institute. One day, on his way to teach a class, he started meditating on Christ's suffering at Calvary and all that it meant. So he stepped into an empty classroom and scribbled a hymn on the back of an envelope. On that day in 1895, minutes later, he showed this hymn to the music director, Daniel B. Towner. One hour later, they had the hymn titled "At Calvary."

It is a wonderful hymn, but if you think about it, maybe one small word would make a big difference. Replace *at* with *by*. Our salvation today comes by Christ's work on Calvary's cross; however, salvation was not made known at the time of Calvary's cross, as Paul later revealed in 1 Corinthians 2:7–8. So now when you sing the chorus of this wonderful hymn, it has much more meaning with the change of one word:

> Merry there was great and grace was free
> Pardon there was multiplied to me
> There my burdened soul found liberty
> By Calvary.

Sing it today with Ephesians 1:7–8 in mind. Sing as unto the Lord (Psalm 104:31–35).

91

The Cynical Realist

Many have once heard in some form or another, "I am not cynical, I am a realist." Often, I found it true that many people cannot distinguish between the two. So what does that leave them with? A disappointing reality to live in? Comedian George Carlin once stated,

> Scratch any cynic and you will find a disappointed idealist.

Our fleshly desires make cynicism an easy resort instead of its counterpart—optimistic hope. As Christians, we can take a subjective view of a broken world and then say, "There is a solution." God sent His Son into a broken world to overcome the world, which most assuredly He did (John 16:33). By His Gospel, He saves us and preserves us from death and unto heaven (Galatians 1:4–5). This finished work does more than just save us from death. It makes living for tomorrow possible. It makes life vibrant.

Our entire outlook on life can be radically transformed to where we "rejoice in hope, [are] patient in tribulation, and continue instant in prayer" (Romans 12:12). There is an old hymn titled "Because He Lives," in which the chorus proclaims:

> Because He lives, I can face tomorrow.

Because He lives, all fear is gone.
Because I know He holds the future,
And life is worth the living just because He lives.

Cynicism is a reasonable answer to an unfulfilled life without Christ because truly, such a reality is depressing. But it does not need to be that way. Christ has come and He offers a new, better reality. It all begins simply with belief (1 Corinthians 15:3–4).

92

Jesus Loves the Little Children

The world is a dark place, with this darkness seemingly evolving each day. Although we know that we do not wrestle with flesh and blood, it often seems as if the battleground between darkness and light rests upon the shoulders of children. The battleground for contrasting ideologies erupts within the desks of young ones. Fifty percent of American marriages end in divorce, thus leaving children with deep-seated internal turmoil from such a dramatic life change.

Abuse, feelings of smallness, and seeing a world constantly evolving with no feeling of control or anything to grasp—this is just a glimpse of the calamity a child may face in the twenty-first century. It may be easy to write these small people's concerns off as a result of a depraved world. Although accurate, it does not answer the five-year-old who is oh-so good at asking the question, "Why?"

Even if we cannot fabricate a practical answer to such a good inquiry, we could offer something possibly more valuable: hope, grace, and love. These are godly characteristics and all things that Christ desires for children. God made children, and He loves children. That is why many, many, many times, God makes provisions for children and the conduct He expects adults to adhere to for them (Psalm 127:3–5; Proverbs 17:6; Matthew 18:10; Ephesians 6:4).

So my request is this: whatever child or children are in your life today, give them grace. Train them up and gracefully instruct them so they may know how they ought to respond to transition and ungodliness. Raise them to understand the truth found in an old song. The truth is that Jesus loves the little children of the world and that Jesus died on the cross, was buried, and rose again for them just as much as He did for adults (1 Timothy 2:6; 1 John 2:2). I hope this message is a challenge to all who may see a child today.

93

What a Day!

Eliza Hewitt, a schoolteacher in Philadelphia in 1898, wanted to reach her students with the Gospel and wrote the classic hymn, "When We All Get to Heaven." The music was written by Emily Wilson, who was also the wife of a Methodist district superintendent. The anticipation of heaven has often been described as the oxygen of the human soul (1 John 3:3). Allow your imagination to anticipate that day in heaven.

The original first verse of this hymn describes "mansions bright and blessed" and states "He'll prepare for us a place." This description comes from John 14:2, when Jesus comforts the disciples by telling them about His coming in the earthly kingdom. This line may be changed to reflect our different destinations in this dispensation. The change is reflected as "In the air we'll rise to meet Him, then we'll see Him face to face" (1 Thessalonians 4:17).

So sing it with joy to the same tune!

1. Sing the wondrous love of Jesus, sing His mercy and grace:
   In the air we'll rise to meet Him, then we'll see Him face to face.
2. Pressing t'ward the prize before us, soon this glory we'll behold
   We'll redeem our heavenly bodies, leave behind our flesh of old.

3. He which raised up the Lord Jesus, shall raise us up in that day;
   Then we'll be with Him in glory, ever with the Lord to stay.

   Chorus:
   When we all get to heaven, what a day of rejoicing that will be!
   When we all see Jesus, we'll sing and shout the victory!

May you enjoy this afresh and anew. Sing as unto the Lord (Psalm 104:31–35).

94

Soul! FM

Have you ever been driving and, while flipping through radio stations, found that there was nothing good to hear? I do not mean anything good as in positive, I mean there is just nothing worthwhile to listen to. If yes, as most have had this happen, what station do you eventually give up and stop on? For most, it will be the station that is playing the most familiar song. It may not be a good song, just a tolerable one. And we all know that by this point, the ride has become increasingly less enjoyable and dull.

Life, in a similar regard, can portray a dull tint when settling on a drab, familiar station. When you turn off seeking and no longer expect something great, then you become desensitized to the hope that is set in the heart of the believer from salvation. The Christian walk that we are called to should be directed by the hope and prize of our high calling. Paul affirms this in Philippians 3:14 when proclaiming,

> I press toward the mark for the prize of the high calling of God in Christ Jesus.

Paul never turned off "seek," and he was always listening and living for the good grace that proceeds only from the Father by the Holy Spirit. Paul was quick to proclaim the author of such grace (1

Corinthians 15:10). Be like Paul (1 Corinthians 11:1–2). Never settle and always seek godliness in your life (Philippians 4:8).

In Him, we know that the ride may not always be smooth. It may be bumpy, and it may get hot. But by Jesus Christ, we may have joy through it and sing in Him a new song daily (Psalm 98:1; Romans 15:13).

95

The Fountainhead

For God is good—or rather, of all goodness He is the Fountainhead.
—Athanasius of Alexandria

This statement was penned by early church father Athanasius of Alexandria in a work discussing the incarnation of Jesus Christ. He states the phrase, "For God is good."

We hear this all the time but in a variety of ways. For instance, many hear it often in the following rehearsed prayer.

> God is great, God is good;
> Let us thank Him for our food.
> By His hands we all are fed,
> Give us Lord our daily bread.
> Amen.

Do you find it interesting that God's goodness and praise precede the request? Or that by God's goodness the request is filled? Or that every line of this beautiful prayer is sewn together by the very fiber of God's omnibenevolence (all-goodness)?

God is not merely good—He is all-good. Everything that is truly good is of His beautiful authorship. That is one reason He desires for us to dwell on good things (Philippians 4:8). Good things reflect the glory of the good God. Therefore, when we pray for good things, it should be done appropriately with thanksgiving (Philippians 4:6; Psalm 107:1). We are reporting to God, who is good and already looking to tend to our needs (Philippians 4:19).

But it is senseless to only praise God as good because of what He does; we need to praise Him simply because He is good. In Psalm 145:1–13, the psalmist reflects on God's great and abundant goodness, showing that God's works are not what make Him good. Instead, they showcase the all-good quality of His being.

There is a trend in modern society that will begin an argument against God in this manner: "If God is good, then why…" God's goodness is not bound to humanity's frustrations and quarrels about life. It is not bound to anything. The fact is that God is good. Another fact is this: we can experience God's goodness through God's Gospel (literally meaning, "good news"). Even though we were bad (an understatement), Christ came to die, be buried, and rise again so that we can be known by His goodness. His righteousness may be imputed to us so that when God sees us, He sees the goodness of His Son over us. This is God's work, and because of this, we may reflect His goodness by boasting that such a good gift came from Him—the Fountainhead (Ephesians 2:8–9).

My point? Nothing is truly good apart from God. He is the author and maintainer of goodness. So, Christians, boast that your God, Jesus Christ, is the good God. Unbelievers, know that this good God is apt to begin and finish good work in you, unparalleled to any other mortal relationship or hope (Philippians 1:6). Just believe (Romans 10:9–13).

96

Jesus Saves

Priscilla J. Owens, a Baltimore public school teacher for forty-nine years, wrote these stirring soul-winning words for a missionary service in the Sunday school of Union Square Methodist Church. Music was not added until some fourteen years later by William Kirkpatrick. All of this hymn is sound except for one small verse in the second stanza. It states, "Earth shall keep her jubilee." A better rendering for the dispensation we are now in would be, "Now we have salvation free."

You see, the original second verse comes from the Mosaic law, where God commanded Israel to "hallow the fiftieth year, and proclaim liberty throughout all the land… It shall be a jubilee unto you" (Leviticus 25:10). This was a picture of Christ's reign on the earth as king, still yet future. Using such a reference would be inappropriate for spiritual application for us today. Among other reasons, we are not concerned with earthly things but are to set our affections on things heavenly (Colossians 3:2).

The rest of the hymn is good in announcing that Jesus saves "for there is one God, and one mediator between God and man, the man Christ Jesus" (1 Timothy 2:5). This is the heart of the Gospel, that man would be saved (1 Corinthians 15:3–4). Try to speak to someone about trusting Jesus and Him alone for salvation from sin and the satisfaction of every need.

Carry this musical message:

> Bear the news to every land, climb the steeps and cross the waves;
> Onward! 'Tis our Lord's command; Jesus saves! Jesus saves!

Psalm 96:2–3 urges us to

> sing unto the Lord, bless His name;
> Shew forth His salvation from day to day.
> Declare His glory among the heathen,
> His wonders among all people.

97

Operator! Operator!

> Who is he that condemneth? It is Christ that died, yea rather, that is risen again, who is even at the right hand of God, who also maketh intercession for us.
>
> —Romans 8:34

With the invention of the telephone, communication was revolutionized. People could bypass telegraphing or, even worse, snail mail. Until the midtwentieth century, to connect a call, an individual would have to first speak into the phone and connect to an operator. Although much simpler now, communication was as easy as exclaiming, "Operator! Operator!" The operator would then connect your call.

This concept was not foreign to Paul when he set out to write the epistle to the Romans. "Calling" God was the work of the priests and prophets. Through Christ's finished work on the Cross, He provided a way for all men to approach the Father and speak. Jesus revolutionized communication. Christ is the mediator who makes connecting with God possible. He is unique in that He does not have to plug in a wire for us because He is the wire. His position is at the right hand of God, and because He is near to Him, so are we.

98

A Faithful Foreigner

And Ittai answered the king, and said, As the Lord liveth, and as my lord the king liveth, surely in what place my lord the king shall be, whether in death or life, even there also will thy servant be.
—2 Samuel 15:21

The adoption process is such a long but beautiful process. Through a series of steps, a family bond is created between two people foreign to each other. Loyalty is established without a series of troubling trials testing the mettle of parents and a child. In 2 Samuel 15, King David is in the midst of a trial. His son has developed a coup and is attempting to usurp David's kingship. Within this captivating story, we see a foreigner, Ittai the Gittite, pledge his loyalty to David despite David's plea for him to leave.

Likewise, God pledges faithfulness and goodness to those who call upon His name and believe in His Gospel (Ephesians 2:19–22). This is an undeserved faithfulness that surpasses human logic and understanding. This faithfulness should incite us, His adopted children, to a pledge of loyalty and obedience to Him as well—a loyalty that is not broken, in death or life.

99

A Mighty Fortress

I will say of the Lord, He is my refuge and my fortress: my God; in Him will I trust.

—Psalm 91:2

On March 17, 2003, due to multiple diplomatic tensions between NATO countries and Iraq, diplomatic relations between Iraq and the United States ended. With them, thousands of NATO troops were deployed to confront the Iraqi regime headed by Saddam Hussein. With these soldiers, wallet-sized cards containing Psalm 91 were deployed as well. Whether Christian or not, these were carried by many soldiers as a reminder of God's protection.

Psalm 91 was believed to be written by Moses and carries strong admiration for the faithfulness of God to sustain him. Within it, we see Moses proclaiming that God is his protection and that, despite dreadful circumstances, God is near. As soldiers within the army of God, we can be assured through this captivating Psalm that God likewise will preserve us in times of difficulty (2 Timothy 2:3–4). Snares, pestilence, and wickedness have no power in the refuge of the Almighty. He secures our soul steadfast in Him and is mighty enough to thwart the arrows of our soul's adversary (Ephesians 6:16). In Him, we can possess an immovable faith.

100

Victory in Jesus!

But thanks be to God, which giveth us the
victory through our Lord Jesus Christ.
—1 Corinthians 15:57

The hymn "Victory in Jesus" was written by Eugene M. Bartlett (December 24, 1885–January 25, 1941). Two years before his death from complications of a stroke, the song first appeared in a paperback songbook called *Gospel Choruses*. He also published a monthly song magazine called *Herald of Song*. He also wrote two other well-known songs titled "Just a Little While" and "Everybody Will Be Happy over There."

Now "Victory in Jesus" is a well-known song, but dispensationally, a few things need to be pointed out and changed. The second stanza says, "I heard about His healing, of His cleansing power revealing, how He made the lame to walk again and caused the blind to see." This is true, but not related to our victory. It comes from Israel's kingdom and prophecy (Revelation 4:6). Also, the last line in the first stanza says, "Then I repented of my sin and won the victory." Whereas a correct verse for the Body of Christ would be, "Then I was forgiven of my sins and won the victory" (Romans 8:3; Colossians 2:13).

Finally, the last verse of the chorus is too suggestive of water baptism as it sings, "He plunged me to victory beneath the cleansing flood." A better verse would be, "He placed me in Christ Jesus the Son."

Selah (Psalm 96:2–3).

101

The Fish Bowl

Fish. They come in many shapes, sizes, colors, types, functions, and so on and so on. Saying this, I need to ask if you have been to an aquarium. Have you owned or seen a fishbowl filled with a beautiful diversity of fish? It is a fascinating sight that, if you are not careful, may absorb an unprecedented amount of time. This sightseeing becomes addictive. Before long, you may start to pick your favorite fish or give them names based on their traits and personalities. But why?

Standing from the outside of the tank looking in, what within the glass box is able to mesmerize you? Flip the question. Why do the fish ignore you as you gawk endlessly at them? The fish tank may be filled with a large number of fish, but notice it is the brilliant attributes of a particular fish that may catch your eye. Even amid the normal, large pool of drab fish in which they live, the fish is different. It presents a different color. The fish moves differently from the pack. There may be a scent of humility as they wait for the other fish to get their fill of food before they eat. Note whatever it is that catches your eye.

Now think of Christian life. Think of your sanctification. Living in the world, Christians and non-Christians alike are being viewed. They are being watched from outside the tank. God is omniscient (Psalm 147:5). He sees us here on earth pooled together. God is omnipresent (Colossians 1:16). He is Emmanuel, God with us (Matthew 1:23). Presently, by His Holy Spirit (1 Corinthians 6:19–20).

Every illustration has its limitations, but let the point be this: God sees all in the fishbowl. Take the illustration further: in the pool of fish, we, the Church, live among all in the habitat. But we are different. The Greek word for church, *ecclesia*, literally means "the called-out ones." And that means that we are a brilliant creation when we identify ourselves with Christ.

So what makes us different? The list is enormous! But let's look at this critically for a moment. What makes the Church of Christ different from any other secular charity project that gives out food and meets social needs? I can affirm this. The Church sets itself apart in the fishbowl as new creations by standing as the Pillar and Ground of the Truth (1 Timothy 3:15). We have the Truth, and we know the Truth, and therefore, as the Body of Christ, we hold the Head and the Truth, Jesus Christ, up.

That is the difference. Works are essentially meaningless without Christ, and humanity's self-created "righteousness" is the equivalent of filthy rags without the Truth to purify and cover in true righteousness (Isaiah 64:6–8; 2 Corinthians 5:21). The Truth, Jesus Christ, makes us swim differently, be different, and be seen in this drab fishbowl. Simply being seen is important. Because when seen, the striking feature we carry, Jesus Christ's finished Gospel, points to the Creator who is worthy to be glorified (1 Corinthians 6:20).

102

How's Your Christmas Going?

Christmas is often recognized as a time to come together—a time for peace, harmony, unity, goodwill to men, and all the many great things that are sung about from October to the beginning of January. How is it going? Think about it, and answer to yourself. I ask that question for you to identify it and now throw it to some far-off winter wonderland, far from you. Leave it behind, at least for a moment. Look with me at what Christmas time is supposed to look like and what joyful times Christmas should stimulate for the rest of the year.

Many people are familiar with the term, the "reason for the season." Even though many people constantly reiterate this phrase, many may leave the phrase as some mystical revelation without ever revisiting it again, thus leaving Jesus as a baby. The two need to remain hand in hand. You may ask how I can make such an assertion. My answer would simply be that the Bible never separated the two, so why would we?

The news of Jesus to Mary in Luke 2 was quickly announced to be "good tidings of great joy, which shall be to all people." What are these good tidings? You do not have to look to the Greek to put context clues together, but I think it may be worth the time to do it. The original word for "good tidings" that will be to all people is *euangelizō*. It is a verb form of the word *euaggelion*, or *gospel. Euangelizō* means to evangelize or proclaim the Gospel! In Greek translations of the Old Testament, the word is used for any form of messianic good news as well! To divide the story is to take an unbiblical look at Emmanuel's coming and therefore lighten what it means for Christ our Lord to be "God with us" (Isaiah 7:14; Matthew 1:23).

So allow me to reiterate the story and get back to the first question: how is your Christmas season going? Jesus was prophesied to come (Isaiah 7:14). He came, born of a virgin (Luke 1:27). Then, He grew up in stature and godly wisdom (Luke 2:52). Jesus lived a sinless life (1 John 3:5). He performed many miracles and was obedient to the Father up to (Matthew 19:2) His unjust sentencing, death, burial, and soon resurrection (1 Corinthians 15:3–4)—a resurrection that gave power to our justification (Romans 4:25). He was seen by the disciples and many others (1 Corinthians 15:5–8).

Emmanuel ascended, but Emmanuel did not leave man to themselves (Acts 1:9). Christ's Holy Spirit descended at Pentecost and then (Acts 2:4), Jesus revealed Himself and spoke continually again to the apostle Paul (Acts 9; Galatians 1:12). The apostle Paul went out and spread the Gospel to the Gentiles (Acts 22:21). This ushered in the beautiful age of grace we live in now, where we can speak expressly to the Father through Jesus forever and ever. Amen (Ephesians 3:2–4). Jesus is coming back through the Rapture to take His Church and eventually to reign a thousand years on earth where, following, He will right every wrong and eternally (1 Thessalonians 4:16–17; Revelation 20:4), He shall receive our praise. For He is worthy (1 Timothy 1:17).

So again I ask, how is your Christmas season going? Christ came to give hope, joy, and Noel not for a couple of months each year, but rather each second of every day eternally. Join me as we entertain this perspective and the life-changing implications it may bring. That Christ is Emmanuel, forever.

103

A Christmas Candle

There is a beautiful quote by a little-known wordsmith named Eva K. Logue that states,

> A Christmas candle is a lovely thing;
> It makes no noise at all,
> But softly gives itself away;
> While quite unselfish, it grows small.

This quote has a fascinating connection to the action taken by our Savior Jesus some two thousand years ago. As the Lord came down from heaven in all His splendor, He humbled Himself and gave Himself away while simultaneously being obedient unto the Father. A baby born to a man crucified. When we tell the full story, we realize that regardless of the life phase, Christ was and is highly exalted (Matthew 3:17; Philippians 2:9).

Philippians 2:5–11 defends this when Paul teaches,

> Let this mind be in you, which was also in Christ Jesus:
>
> Who, being in the form of God, thought it not robbery to be equal with God:

> But made himself of no reputation, and took upon him the form of a servant, and was made in the likeness of men:
>
> And being found in fashion as a man, he humbled himself, and became obedient unto death, even the death of the cross.
>
> Wherefore God also hath highly exalted him, and given him a name which is above every name:
>
> That at the name of Jesus every knee should bow, of things in heaven, and things in earth, and things under the earth;
>
> And that every tongue should confess that Jesus Christ is Lord, to the glory of God the Father.

Nonetheless, if we liken Christ to this illustrative candle above, I can reason that Christ did not stay noiseless and unnoticed (Isaiah 53:2). Christ's humble act made a big impact and provided us with the Good News that institutes Jesus as our mediator (1 Timothy 2:5). From birth, we see His humility. Come the Rapture, where the Church meets Him in the sky, we will see humility as well. Humility is an absence of arrogance. This is not to say we will not see Him in all might because it is impossible for Christ to be arrogant when despite a timeline, He is worthy of all glory.

God's nature does not change; how He deals with humanity may (Hebrews 13:8). The small babe, Jesus, is the same Jesus who holds the keys of hell and death, and who reigns eternally! Let us hold our Christmas candle high. Jesus we hold high, the Light of the world who now abides and lights our way (John 8:12; Ephesians 5:8).

104

Christmas Eve in the Bible

I hope that you found the title suitable and that it drew your attention to this writing. Now that I have you here, I want to begin by saying that the Bible says nothing definitively about a Christmas Eve. There is a lot of emphasis on Christmas Eve, but the Bible does not specifically detail the events of Christmas Eve. Even the angels who appear to shepherds affirm in Luke 2:11 that

> unto you [shepherds] is born this day in the city
> of David a Savior, which is Christ the Lord.

Nonetheless, do not be dismayed! As a teacher of the Bible, I often warn people against assuming or "reading into" the Bible. But be sure of this: there was once the Christmas Eve.

Merriam-Webster dictionary defines an *eve* as

1. the evening or the day before a special day,
2. the period immediately preceding.

There was an evening before Christ our Savior was born. Believe me, as I also assure you that heaven was as prepared as an American sipping eggnog and looking satisfied gazing at their stack of presents under the tree. This was the last evening before the Savior of humanity came into the world to reconcile God's wrath so that we could receive His grace.

In Psalm 30:5, the psalmist states that "weeping may endure for a night, but joy cometh in the morning." An eve precedes joyful mornings. Later in Psalm 118:24, we see that Eve comes before what we now often refer to as our day of salvation. In reference to our Savior Jesus Christ, the psalmist proclaims, "This is the day which the Lord hath made; we will rejoice and be glad in it."

It is right that we celebrate Christmas Eve as this eve preceded the rest of history and the coming of the hope in the morning. So rejoice and be glad in it! Jesus is coming, Jesus is come, Jesus came, Jesus is coming again!

105

Abner and the Discerning Journey

Following the holiday season, people need many things. Practically, two that come to mind immediately are money and more sleep. But beyond the practicalities, there is so much more that we need! In the infamous work *Jane Eyre* by Charlotte Brontë, we are reassured,

> You are human and fallible.

Throughout the holidays and the Christmas season, we all pool together to try our best to appear strong and neatly pulled together when there are things within that just are not so.

Another quote to be aware of is derived from Robert Louis Stevenson as he emphatically penned,

> Alas! In the clothes of the greatest potentate,
> what is there but a man?

Saying this, some other things required for a successful transition into a new year are extra: grace, love, and perhaps…discernment?

Discernment is spoken of often within leadership seminars, TED Talks, and churches, but practically, it may be reasonable to ask questions such as, "What does it look like?" A lot of people know what discernment is. Nonetheless, many people do not realize that acquiring discernment practically is much messier than the cookie-cutter methods preached on.

If you would like a biblical example, stick with me as I discuss the tantalizing story and character of Abner. Some incorrectly misdiagnose Abner's story as if he were some kind of villain at times, but this would be a poor review of him. The story of Abner shows a man who was living role to role and shows realistic progression as a man navigates an ever-changing situation, much like ours today.

In 1 Samuel and early 2 Samuel, the reader will see that Abner is a skilled warrior and passionate commander of King Saul's army. He could also be described as loyal and patient, although not a fool for loyalty's sake. Abner was an important character in the life of Saul and David. He played a mediating role between Saul and David following David's slaying of Goliath (1 Samuel 17:55–58; 1 Samuel 20:25).

Later, in this large narrative, Saul (although he loved David like a son) pursued David in order to kill him. King Saul realized that David was to be ordained as king by God over him and, in a maniacal rage, attempted to kill David to maintain his authority. In this turn of events, Abner, Saul's military commander, was caught on the wrong side of things. This essentially created an internal conflict within Abner. Abner was loyal to Saul, his king, but soon realized that God had called David to rule. The question became whom to serve: God or man?

Here now, as much as then, we should carry the apostle Paul's sentiment when he prods in the book of Galatians,

> For do I now persuade men, or God? Or do I seek to please men? For if I yet pleased men, I should not be the servant of Christ. (1:10)

Abner's story shows the messy overlap and process behind resolving conflicts of interest. In this challenging time, Abner continued to do what he felt called to do—serve Saul faithfully. He served

Saul until his death and even after, instead of submitting to David, he served Ish-Bosheth, Saul's son.

Meanwhile, at this time, there was a gradual but sure transition of power in Israel from Ish-Bosheth to David. Abner's shortcomings were great, much like many of the fathers of the faith that we esteem, including David. Abner was a mighty warrior, and during this illegitimate reign of Ish-Bosheth, no doubt Abner was the one with true power. Despite this power, he humbled himself because of an infuriating accusation from Ish-Bosheth. It was from this accusation that Abner's calling was affirmed. He knew what he must do.

In 2 Samuel 3:9–12, he pledged loyalty and all his might to David and was sold on God's appointing of David. Abner then faithfully served David, and because of him, Israel was further united, and Abner served as an instrument of God Himself. Discernment does not always come immediately or swiftly. It is God-given and strengthened by training in righteousness. Discernment is God-given in the Scriptures, and application is where we show the fruits of God's glorious work in our lives.

The Bible teaches that good discernment comes in an appropriate amount of time. The apostles have much to say about it. John the Beloved wrote to "try the spirits" (1 John 4:1). In Hebrews, it is taught that mature discernment of good and evil comes by training and experience, particularly in the Scriptures, mind you (Hebrews 4:12; 5:14). Paul reaffirms that by the renewing of our mind, we may prove what the will of God is (Romans 12:2; Philippians 1:9–10).

To paint Abner as a villain, although God was working in his life to show him the appropriate decision, which he ultimately obeyed and did great things because of, would be hypocritical. God was patient with the great man Abner, just as much as He is with all Christians! We lived lawless lives before we accepted His Son, Jesus Christ, as our Lord and Savior (2 Peter 3:9). Despite our evil nature, God is faithful and just. His will be done.

The great warrior Abner teaches us of God's patience. Abner teaches us about human nature. He teaches us what true, biblical discernment looks like and how to achieve the winning side—God's side. Abner's character was consistent while alongside it, God's mercy and will are mighty! This is a formula for an amazing story of God.

Continuing, it is also worth noting how Abner's story ends. The reader will find, as the story progresses, that in a fit of rage, another general of David's named Joab tragically murders Abner because of a past situation where Abner had killed Joab's brother in combat (2 Samuel 3:30).

Now you may ask why I would end this lesson with this addition. The truth is that without it, the story is not complete, and we would not see the beauty of Abner's wise discernment! In Abner's death, King David was grieved, and Joab was cursed by David. Abner's journey of discernment left him known as a man who made great decisions. David's lament has it recorded that Abner was "a prince and a great man" (2 Samuel 3:38).

As Christians, we are known as "heirs of God" and "joint-heirs with Christ," made into "great men (and women)" because of Christ's imputed righteousness (Romans 8:16–17). We are known by our greatest discernment—when we discern Christ as Lord of our lives! Now we rely on His discernment and, like Abner, can rest knowing that in Christ, we are royalty and great like Him.

106

Anno Domini

As a new year approaches, many people make resolutions to give up this or to stop that. A classic hymn was written by Judson W. Vandeventer (1855–1936), with the tune composed by Winfield S. Weeden (1847–1908). Weeden was a song leader at a New York YMCA. The name of the hymn was "I Surrender All."

But "Nay, in all these things we are more than conquerors through Him that loved us" (Romans 8:37). Many think that if they just surrender their heart's greatest desires, God will accept their sacrifice and grant them love and salvation. Romans 5:8 explains it is not about our surrender, but His surrender at the cross:

> But God commendeth his love toward us, in that, while we were yet sinners, Christ died for us.

So as we modify the lyrics to this old hymn, declare the victory we now have through Christ.

1. All through Jesus, I can conquer, all my sins He doe's forgive;

   I will ever love and trust Him, for His purpose daily live.

2. All through Jesus, I can conquer, thankful for the grace I've found;
   Victory over worldly sorrows, thank You, Jesus, praise You now!
3. All through Jesus, I can conquer by the cross, my works resign;
   Praying for me, Holy Spirit, truly Thou has made me thine.
4. All through Jesus, I can conquer, You surrendered all for me;
   Sin and death are all defeated, over all the victory!
5. All through Jesus, I can conquer justified I now can claim;
   O, the joy of full salvation! Glory, glory, to His name!

Chorus: I can conquer all—I can conquer all through Thee, my blessed Savior, I can conquer all.

May you be able to sing this in the New Year and throughout all eternity.

Selah (Psalm 96:2–3).

107

Word of the Day

Would you like to widen your vocabulary? Maybe impress your friends with a new, intelligent-sounding, and profound word? Try this one: *gainsaying*. It is a good word to use for your smarty-pants children. Example: "Don't you dare gainsay me!"

Or maybe a work acquaintance who continually undermines you and needs to be confronted! Example: "I really wish you would not gainsay me in front of the boss."

And of course, we need a biblical example. Example: "But to Israel He saith, All day long I have stretched forth my hands unto a disobedient and gainsaying people" (Romans 10:21).

What does this interesting Scrabble word mean? *Merriam-Webster* lists the word *gainsay* to mean

1. to declare to be untrue or invalid,
2. to contradict.

The words translated as "gainsaying" in Scripture are *antilego* (as in Romans 10:21) and *antilogia* (as in Jude 11). Both variants are intriguing as they indicate opposition to logic or fact. In the case of Romans 10:21 (and Jude in a similar fashion), Paul describes Israel as a gainsaying nation as they had the truth in their midst but did not accept. In the following chapter, we see that by their gainsaying, the Gospel came unto Gentiles!

This could be an example of how God works all things to the good of those who love Him and are called according to His purpose (Romans 8:28). God had a plan, and the ignorance of humanity could not hinder it. In fact, despite it and regardless of it, God's will was done.

The apostle Paul states,

> According as he hath chosen us in him before the foundation of the world, that we should be holy and without blame before him in love:
>
> Having predestinated us unto the adoption of children by Jesus Christ to himself, according to the good pleasure of his will,
>
> To the praise of the glory of his grace, wherein he hath made us accepted in the beloved. (Ephesians 1:4–6)

Therefore, we can learn from the biblical examples of gainsaying, primarily through the Israelite people and false teachers confronted by the apostles. We should learn that the opposite of gainsaying is holding firm. We are to hold firm to the sound, healthy doctrine that has been given to us in the Scriptures (Titus 1:9). In doing so, we pursue righteousness and align with what God is doing and has done for us (1 Corinthians 15:3—4; 2 Timothy 3:16). Also, by holding firm, we can gainsay the false truth and false doctrine warring against the Gospel of Jesus Christ. Needless to say, we, as Christians, know who wins that battle (2 Corinthians 2:14).

108

Soap Bubbles

Vanity of vanities, saith the Preacher, vanity of vanities; all is vanity.
—Ecclesiastes 1:2

Does this verse ring with utter positivity and make you excited to read on?! I sure hope so… As you read on, mentally tag the word *vanity*. Moving on, the writer Solomon begins to depict the many things that humanity prizes and esteems. But he often circles back and depicts it all as—you guessed it—*vanity*!

Solomon in all his wisdom mirrored the words of his father David in Psalm 94:11 when David states,

> The Lord knoweth the thoughts of man, that they are vanity.

Both writings use the same word for vanity. The Hebrew word transliterated is *hebel*. You may be interested to know (I sure was) that this word literally rendered has multiple meanings including: "breath," "vapor," or in some usages, perhaps "a soap bubble."

But why is this important? I will answer my question with the following statement: these three things depict quickly disappearing and ineptly meaningless things. They are there one moment and then gone as soon as they come! In context, the soap bubbles used to illustrate vanity were bubbles that were when soapy scum bubbles burst against a surface. Not only were they quickly vanishing, but they were nothing but remnants of filth. The things of this world have no value and are just remnants of things that once were and have been.

What hope does this leave for us lowly humans who live in the remains of filthy scum bubbles? I cannot ask this question apart from the fact that Jesus Christ, our God, has given us a new hope. He has elevated us above scum and loved us despite our sinful nature that was contrary to His holiness. The things of this world are vanity, but in Christ, we are pulled out of the vain flesh and now live by His Spirit.

The Second Letter to the Corinthians 5:16–18 has the breakdown. The apostle Paul proclaims,

> Wherefore henceforth know we no man after the flesh: yea, though we have known Christ after the flesh, yet now henceforth know we him no more.
>
> Therefore if any man be in Christ, he is a new creature: old things are passed away; behold, all things are become new.
>
> And all things are of God, who hath reconciled us to himself by Jesus Christ, and hath given to us the ministry of reconciliation.

In Christ, we live in the Spirit, and in the Spirit where we are reconciled to God, we find that "all things are of God." We who have "all spiritual blessings in heavenly places in Christ" are elevated above all else that is vanity. By Christ's righteousness, we (who were once filthy bubbles fixing to pop) can be found pleasing to God, living on mission according to His will, with the hope of our eternal residence (Romans 8:24–25). We praise God and His wonderful plan to give a higher calling. Praise His Son who made this possible, and the Holy Spirit, who elevates us in this life and the next to be more than a soapy bubble.

109

Level of Effort

In project management, there is a scale used by managers called the "level of effort" scale. It does not necessarily measure how much work is done, but it can gauge the work performance and quality of the work conducted.

It would appear that Hall of Fame quarterback Joe Namath would approve of this scale as he once begged the question, "If you're not gonna go all the way, why go at all?" There are many versions of the level of effort scale, often with the lowest portion showcasing little effort and the top of the scale presenting the maximum effort and performance.

This is worth noting, as the Bible has much to say about effort and performance. The number 1 thing to understand about performance is this:

1. Our salvation is not based on works (Ephesians 2:8–9).

   Salvation comes from Christ's finished Gospel and nothing else. We could never work to earn favor in God's eyes. His Son did the work for us, and now we are to simply believe!

With our salvation secure, we can rest easy as we explore other biblical aspects of effort and performance! Moving on, we see this:

2. Work is good in the sight of God (Genesis 2:15; Proverbs 16:3; 2 Thessalonians 3:10).

   It is good in the sight of God, despite the common misconception that humanity is entitled to life free of it. Even from the world's earliest days, humanity tended to God's earthly creation (Genesis 2:15). Even when work was included in the punishment of Adam and Eve, work was not cursed but rather the ground. Following this, humanity's attitude toward the now difficult action was tainted (Genesis 3:17–19).

Because of Adam's sin, humanity inherited a tainted nature and disposition, and men and women stood separated from God. With this state, we can see the following:

3. There can be ungodly work done (Psalm 6:8; Matthew 7:21–23).

   Apart from God, we are "workers of iniquity" who serve the wrong side.

But referring back to point 1, there is something more for those who are in Christ. Our salvation is paid for by Christ's finished work, and He enables our service to be acceptable unto God. In the Body of Christ, we know this:

4. We can be workers who are unashamed by rightly dividing His truth (2 Timothy 2:15).

   There is a standard for godly work. As we pursue godly work, it must be conducted in the very nature of Christ—in grace and truth (John 1:17). The two exist only together and need to remain tethered.

   In a work by doctors Richard Fowler and Natalie Ford, titled *Grace-Based Counseling*, it is stated,

   > Grace ceases to be grace apart from truth. Jesus was full of both grace and truth (John 1:14). Grace

> and truth are not opposing principles in need of balance; instead, they are united as one. Both are equally necessary for abundant living (19).

Now living in His grace and truth, there is something good to know:

5. Unashamed, we are called to work heartily (Ecclesiastes 9:10; Colossians 3:23–24).

   In grace and truth, empowered by the Holy Spirit, we are not only called to work heartily—we are able to work heartily! Spiritually, working heartily means we work "as to the Lord," knowing that we have hope when it all ends (Philippians 3:14; Colossians 3:23–24).

Live Heartily

Working heartily should not have an off switch. It is to be done in the most basic moments of our life and the largest, most extravagant moments too (1 Corinthians 10:31). When we work heartily for the Lord, we are living earnestly to say, "Christ, be glorified."

So as you go throughout your days, live as to the Lord as if someone were to hold up a "level of effort" chart in front of you. You could point to the very top and say,

> There I am. I am living maximally to reflect the glory of God who considers me worthy by His Son, Jesus Christ.

Let this be your prayer today.

110

Like a Boss

Like a boss.

What comes to mind when you read these words? For me, it brings back memories of the late 2000s and early 2010s when the "Like a Boss" trend was in full swing. Merchandise and entertainment were defined by these three words. There was the "#likeaboss," the "Like a Boss" button, "Like a Boss" T-shirts, movies, and music all reflecting the nature of the phrase.

Exactly where and when this trend originated, I am not sure. One thing I do know, that remains to this day, is that everyone wants to be a boss. It became culturally obvious as people everywhere flaunted that the life and actions they presented were that of a boss.

But what does it mean to be a boss? During his presidency, Ronald Reagan had a sign in his office that stated the following:

> It's amazing what can be accomplished by any person if he doesn't care who gets the credit.

In simple terms, a good boss delegates.

I stress the word *good* because a delegate is not entirely a boss. A boss is simply someone who is in charge of overseeing. But a good boss delegates and is not afraid of allowing someone to have their due credit while also not afraid of taking responsibility for their shortcomings when necessary.

Politician Byron Dorgan knew this all too well when he stated,

> You can delegate authority, but you cannot delegate responsibility.

Biblically, this overseer model is followed. In Acts 6, the reader would find that God's church was growing, and as it grew, the apostles began to neglect the needs of Grecian widows. As a response, the apostles delegated positions to honorable and capable people so that they could dedicate their time to prayer and the ministry of the Word. The twelve apostles collectively agreed that "it is not reason that we should leave the word of God, and serve tables" (Acts 6:2).

This model continued as a cross-dispensational truth as we see Paul utilize this model in the age of grace as well. In 1 Timothy 3, Paul lists the qualifications of a bishop and the deacons. Later in writing, Paul reaffirms that the things that he taught must be delegated down to maximize the efficiency of teaching and replication in the lives of others. Paul tells Timothy (whom he has already delegated teaching) in the epistle,

> The things that thou hast heard of me among many witnesses, the same commit thou to faithful men, who shall be able to teach others also. (2 Timothy 2:2)

Pastor and writer John Maxwell understood the power of delegation well as he wrote,

> If you want to do a few small things right, do them yourself. If you want to do great things and make a big impact, learn to delegate.

The greatest businesses and the most powerful armies understand this well. In the United States military, delegation begins with the commander in chief and then branches down to the generals, colonels, majors, and so on.

Therefore, it should be no surprise that Paul continues by stating,

> Thou therefore endure hardness, as a good soldier of Jesus Christ.
>
> No man that warreth entangleth himself with the affairs of this life; that he may please him who hath chosen him to be a soldier. (2 Timothy 2:3–4)

God Himself has already delegated a mission to us: to glorify Him and proclaim the Gospel of His Son, Jesus Christ. He even equipped us with the necessary utilities to get the job done: His Word and His Spirit (John 16:7; 2 Timothy 3:16–17).

So as Paul leaves this amazing example, follow him as he follows Christ (1 Corinthians 1:1). Whether in a church position or day-to-day responsibilities, it is important to humble yourself and allow others to help bear the load you carry, which is never meant to be carried alone. I stress humility here. As you let go and let God work through those in your life, you build relationships and increase longevity in that occupation.

Let us close with the words of former secretary of defense, George C. Marshall:

> If you want someone to be for you, never let him feel he is dependent upon you; rather, in some way, make him feel that you are dependent upon him.

Let this word encourage you as you go through your day today—like a boss.

111

The Old Rugged Cross

George Bennard was born on February 4, 1873, in the coal mining town of Youngstown, Ohio. He aspired to be a Christian evangelist, but his father died, so he stayed to support his mother and sister. Later, he became involved with the Salvation Army and then an ordained minister in the Methodist Episcopal Church. Bennard died on October 10, 1958, at eighty-five years old.

When he was forty years old, during some spiritual struggle, he spent long hours in study, prayer, and meditation. He became convinced the cross was far more than just a religious symbol; it was the very heart of the Gospel. Philippians 2:8 says,

> Being found in fashion as a man, He humbled Himself, and became obedient unto death, even death of the cross.

Notice that God *humbles* Himself, not *empties* Himself. Father God humbled Himself to behold His creation (Psalm 113:6). Jesus humbled Himself to become His creation in the likeness of man (Philippians 2:6–8). The Spirit humbled Himself to be in His creation in the Church (Ephesians 1:13). In Christ, by His grace, God became humble to give grace to those who were not humble. Our life in Christ involves humbling ourselves and reckoning ourselves dead for others.

Christ could only die if He was a man, and He could only die for our sins if He was God. So yes, the cross is much more than a religious symbol. As you sing "The Old Rugged Cross," remember how it speaks of salvation through Jesus's death on the cross as a glorious and cherished event.

As for this writer, I especially like the fourth stanza:

> To the old, rugged cross, I will ever be true,
> Its shame and reproach gladly bear.
> Then He'll call me someday to my home far away,
> Where His glory forever I'll share.
>
> Chorus:
> So I'll cherish the old rugged cross,
> Till my trophies at last I lay down.
> I will cling to the old rugged cross,
> And exchange it someday for a crown.

Sing as unto the Lord (Psalm 104:31–35).

112

I Can Face Tomorrow

There are particular moments from early childhood that many remember vividly. These moments may be good or bad, big or small, but for some reason, they stick out to us.

One moment that often comes to mind randomly but always providentially is when I was a kid, in church, singing along with the choir and congregation. In this memory, the air is warm and the sanctuary is bright with color as we sing the words:

> Because He lives, I can face tomorrow,
> Because He lives, all fear is gone,
> Because I know He holds the future,
> And life is worth the living,
> Just because He lives!

The memory is splendid, and I used to wonder why this seemingly small clip of my life constantly plays over and over in my mind. I am consistently reminded—by the Lord, I am sure—of the assurance that used to wash over me as I sang the lyrics, looking around at the people singing the Gaither classic. Their faces are joyful along with mine as we all recall the power of Christ's resurrection and present-day position in the throne room of God.

"Because He Lives" was written in 1969 by Bill and Gloria Gaither during the height of the Vietnam War, racial tensions, and large-scale change in the United States. Despite it all, the song called the nation to not look around at the madness but rather up to the resurrected, ascended Christ.

Is this not the very same message that a hurt, confused nation needs to embrace today? That because Jesus is alive, we can be made alive as well? That because Jesus is alive, we can live with no fear?

Read with me for a moment these verses of encouragement:

- *Romans 6:4*. "Therefore we are buried with him by baptism into death: that like as Christ was raised up from the dead by the glory of the Father, even so we also should walk in newness of life."
- *Romans 8:11*. "But if the Spirit of him that raised up Jesus from the dead dwell in you, he that raised up Christ from the dead shall also quicken your mortal bodies by his Spirit that dwelleth in you."
- *Romans 8:34*. "Who is he that condemneth? It is Christ that died, yea rather, that is risen again, who is even at the right hand of God, who also maketh intercession for us."

As Christ is alive, by belief, we can be made alive as well! Being alive in Christ, we are given the Holy Spirit. With the Holy Spirit of the resurrected Christ, we have hope. Paul teaches in Romans 5:1–5:

> Therefore being justified by faith, we have peace with God through our Lord Jesus Christ:
>
> By whom also we have access by faith into this grace wherein we stand, and rejoice in hope of the glory of God.
>
> And not only so, but we glory in tribulations also: knowing that tribulation worketh patience;
>
> And patience, experience; and experience, hope:

> And hope maketh not ashamed; because the love of God is shed abroad in our hearts by the Holy Ghost which is given unto us.

Here is where the trickle-down effect takes place, and we see why we have nothing to fear: because He lives! Because of the love of God made accessible through Christ's death and resurrection, we have hope and peace. God's love drives out fear, and we can know true peace because He lives. John proclaims,

> There is no fear in love; but perfect love casteth out fear: because fear hath torment. He that feareth is not made perfect in love. (1 John 4:18)

In Christ, we can confidently sing the words of the song "Because He Lives." We can because we serve a risen, living God, and "greater is He that is in you, than he that is in the world" (1 John 4:4). Jesus Himself affirms this when He tells His disciples to "be of good cheer; I have overcome the world" (John 16:33).

So if you agree with me when I say that all the things of this world to fear have been overcome and our heavenly inheritance is the only thing awaiting us, then let your heart sing with mine these words:

> Because He lives, I can face tomorrow,
> Because He lives, all fear is gone,
> Because I know He holds the future,
> And life is worth the living,
> Just because He lives!

113

Do I Dare?

"Amazing Grace, how sweet the sound!"

The composer of the beloved hymn, John Newton (1725–1807), had this hymn first published in what is called the *Olney Hymns* book. It was an illustration of the potent ideologies of the evangelical movement in England at the time. The "Amazing Grace" tune as we know it was composed by E. D. Excell, who wrote, composed, or arranged more than two thousand published songs. Shortly before John Newton's death at age eighty-two, he is quoted as proclaiming with a loud voice, "My memory is nearly gone, but I remember two things: that I am a great sinner, and that Christ is a great Saviour!" What amazing grace.

When John Newton wrote this hymn, he expressed well the limitlessness of God's grace beyond our scope of comprehension. The apostle of grace and revelator of the mystery, Paul, has given us a very full testimony of the wonders of His grace. Paul writes to the Thessalonian saints, "Now our Lord Jesus Christ Himself, and God, even our Father, which hath loved us, and hath given us everlasting consolation and good hope through grace, comfort your hearts, and stablish you in every good word and work" (2 Thessalonians 2:16–17).

What treasures we possess by God's marvelous grace! Not only that, but in Ephesians 2:13 it is said,

> Now in Christ Jesus, ye who sometimes were far off are made nigh by the blood of Christ.

You see, nothing in this wonderful hymn needs to be altered, but it is interesting to note that the song neither mentions the blood nor the cross of Christ. We sing of God's amazing grace, acknowledging that we receive that grace only by believing in the blood of Christ shed on the cross that saved a wretch like me!

Sing as unto the Lord (Psalm 104:31–35).

114

The 5 Ps of Accomplishing Godly Goals

Many models claim to navigate people to success and the completion of their goals. But here, we take a look at a spiritual model whose goal is to assist in molding the inner and outer person in Christ Jesus.

Join us as we explore this list!

1. Pray (Psalm 145:18; Philippians 4:6–7; Colossians 4:2)

   Prayer prepares the Christian to not only accomplish godly goals, but first and foremost, ascertain godly goals to strive for.

   It is communication with God that not only forms transactive dialogue, but prepares the heart to ultimately prepare to pursue.
2. Prepare (Proverbs 24:27; Ephesians 6:15; Philippians 4:8)

   Blanketed in God's peace, we now prepare to meet these goals by filling ourselves with the good things of God and the things necessary to accomplish goals promptly.

   Preparation requires a good, godly headspace and establishing a foundation for success.
3. Practice (Proverbs 12:1; Philippians 4:9; 2 Timothy 2:15)

   Good practice requires knowledge (godly knowledge) and corrective practices that align you to ultimately move in step with God's higher calling for your life. This requires the right division of the Word for a complete and godly walk.

4. Patience (Psalm 27:14; Galatians 5:22; Philippians 4:11)

   Most goals worth setting do not occur instantaneously overnight. It involves a continuous reproval process that molds the inner and outer man to abound in more wisdom and knowledge.

5. Praise (Isaiah 25:1; Philippians 4:10; Jude 25)

   This proponent truly does not belong to only one portion of this grand formula. They all overlap! Praise should be a lifestyle, for God is worthy and nothing sincere can be accomplished without Him.

As you complete your goal; however, be sure to understand the source and strength by which you made it. Jesus Christ!

115

Learn to Live

When I was younger, I remember how saturated the Christian media was with questions such as "Would you die for Christ?" and "If the situation were to arise, would you deny Jesus in your last moments?" There are hundreds of variations to these questions, and upon reflection, I believe I know why these questions were so prevalent.

On April 20, 1999, two high school students shot and murdered twelve students and one teacher at Columbine High School in Columbine, Colorado. Up to that time, it was the deadliest high school shooting in American history, and the nation stood baffled that something so horrendous could be devised within the minds of these students.

More noteworthy than their evil deed, however, is a story that arose regarding one of the murdered—or as we will see, martyred. The story goes that in the weeks before her murder, the killers mocked her for Christian values, and on the lawn of the school, it is believed that they asked her to confirm her belief in God. Following her affirmative reply, the report goes that Eric Harris, the killer, said, "Then go be with Him." Following this was a barrage of fatal shots.

There is speculation regarding this report, which frankly matters little to me considering that it is confirmed that Scott was often harassed by the killers for her belief in Jesus Christ. My point is this:

following this account, numerous movies, foundations, studies, and material were created, essentially romanticizing and diminishing martyrdom.

Growing up, my peers and I were frequently asked, "Would you die for your faith?" To this question, smiling and elated, we would all cheer, "Yeah!" Little did we know that all of us would struggle to live for it. Little did we know the pressures, trials, and temptations that would barrage us daily for the rest of our adolescence. Little did we know that our faith would be tried in other ways, such as through experiencing divorce, poverty, death of family members, and all the other things that make or break a child.

Our focus possibly should have pinned to living for Christ first and fulfilling His will for our life, not fantasizing about when and how it would end. We could reflect on verses such as Matthew 10:33, where Jesus warns His students about disowning Him, but look to where we are now and realize just how out of place and out of context that people stitch that verse.

Paul understands this dilemma of being caught in between two worlds. In Philippians 1:20–24, he states the following:

> According to my earnest expectation and my hope, that in nothing I shall be ashamed, but that with all boldness, as always, so now also Christ shall be magnified in my body, whether it be by life, or by death.
>
> For to me to live is Christ, and to die is gain.
>
> But if I live in the flesh, this is the fruit of my labour: yet what I shall choose I wot not.
>
> For I am in a strait betwixt two, having a desire to depart, and to be with Christ; which is far better:
>
> Nevertheless to abide in the flesh is more needful for you.

Some important context to these verses is that Paul was in a filthy Roman prison. Truly, Paul had good reason to want to depart, as do we, to go and be with Christ in glory. But he understood that there were people who could not confidently say that was their destination. He understood that Christ still had a purpose, life, and role to play for His heavenly kingdom here on earth.

So my challenge is this: Keep your hope before you, for this is godly (Romans 8:24–25). But do not neglect Paul's truth that to "live is Christ." Take life, one phase at a time, addressing the edification of the Body and promotion of the Gospel step by step.

My challenge is this: learn to live for the faith first, and let the rest be dealt with in Christ's timing.

116

Jesus's Currency

Yesterday's price is not today's price.

—Fat Joe

No, I am not promoting the philosophy and ethics of rapper Fat Joe, but in passing, I once heard this quote. I can affirm, however, that this quote reflects culture and society briefly with one short sentence.

> This is the way the world operates—
> Supply and demand.
> Inflation.
> Currency value.

Of these three things, many people are aware, and it affects our day-to-day lives. People also often note it because, as Fat Joe is aware, it is constantly changing. Now juxtapose that to the following Bible verse:

> Jesus Christ the same yesterday, and to day, and for ever (Hebrews 13:8)

Would it surprise you if I told you that this verse was given in the context of the writer speaking on contentment? I hope this won't, because this truth should be the cornerstone of our personal contentment.

The world is changing, and indeed, yesterday's price is not today's price. Although this often determines our contentment, consider the truth of Hebrews 13:8. Jesus truly possesses the only stable currency, and it never inflates. He bought humanity at a price and has redeemed us at the cost of His death. The receipt is His resurrection and proof of purchase.

Peter beautifully describes this transaction when he writes,

> Forasmuch as ye know that ye were not redeemed with corruptible things, as silver and gold, from your vain conversation received by tradition from your fathers;
>
> But with the precious blood of Christ, as of a lamb without blemish and without spot" (1 Peter 1:18-19).

And how did He do this, you may ask? Well, we were redeemed from the curse of the law by Him becoming a curse for us. If that sounds odd, I understand, but it is true! In Galatians 3:13, it is stated,

> Christ hath redeemed us from the curse of the law, being made a curse for us: for it is written, Cursed is every one that hangeth on a tree.

It was not a cheap purchase; in fact, it was the costliest purchase. But the bill is paid, and we proudly boast God's riches of grace in our life on earth and the next (Ephesians 1:7).

Being bought at a price, it is also important to realize that being bought means now that we are not our own. Being not our own and under the Lordship of Jesus Christ, we reside within an anomaly of freedom with the simple condition that we glorify Him who made such a costly purchase (1 Corinthians 6:19–20).

Being bought, we have communion with the Holy God by His Holy Spirit, and where the Spirit of God is, there is freedom (2 Corinthians 3:17). This freedom does not change either, being from an unchanging God.

Do you see why Christians are different from the world? Because truly, in Christ, in all things important, we have nothing in common with the ever-changing world. We are bought and secured by an unchanging God!

So therefore, glorify God today and thank Him for this beautiful truth.

117

The Sticking Point

A few may have once heard of this principle or idea. They know that the sticking point is the point at which their obstacle or challenge is the greatest. In weightlifting, this is a prominent idea. The sticking point occurs during a lifting movement, and simply put for brevity; it is the most difficult point of a movement. It is the place where the difficulty of a resistance movement is greatly disproportionate to the difficulty of the beginning and end of a movement. For example, while doing bicep curls, this would be the middle of the movement. This is the place in a lift that "makes or breaks" success.

One could think of a sticking point in spectrums. For the curl, the spectrum would be easy, very hard, easy. This idea has translated well into other arenas of life, such as habit making, planning, and business. Economist Jay Abraham wrote a critically acclaimed book on the topic titled *The Sticking Point Solution*. In this book, he stated the following:

> As soon as you open your mind to doing things differently, the doors of opportunity practically fly off their hinges.

He offers fascinating insights that I completely agree with but may not be helpful in some arenas. Case in point: weightlifting. The sticking point will be there regardless, and the only solution is to get stronger and get past it to the easier stage in the movement.

Often, this is how the spiritual life of a Christian works. Innovation unlikely will hinder persecution. It must be endured. Innovation will not make God answer your prayers faster; endurance sees God's timing through.

Biblical proof of this concept can be found within Paul's early epistles to the Thessalonians. In Thessalonians 1:4–5, Paul writes:

> So that we ourselves glory in you in the churches of God for your patience and faith in all your persecutions and tribulations that ye endure:
>
> Which is a manifest token of the righteous judgment of God, that ye may be counted worthy of the kingdom of God, for which ye also suffer.

My heart breaks for the Thessalonian people within this passage. They were under severe persecution, not by a government entity, but by their own fellow citizens. Being a young Gentile church, they suffered the wrath of Jewish citizens within Thessalonica, which was spurred from Paul's promotion of the Gospel (Acts 17).

So what were they to do? Innovate and adapt the Gospel to match the Jews' belief? Water down their belief in hopes that they would somehow magically coexist?

Surely not! They had to push through the sticking point with patience and faith. Paul encourages the Thessalonians by sharing that their endurance is evidence that reflects the Spirit within them. Innovation could not save them, only God's power, which equipped them to endure.

A characteristic of the Christian is the profound ability to be able to "glory in tribulations." Christians live in the paradigm of God's reality. Troubles that are intended to break humanity, God redirects to build the spiritual muscles of those that love Him—in this case: patience, experience, and hope (Romans 5:3–5; Romans 8:28).

Whatever is tasking you and wherever you are in this spiritual workout that we call life, endure. Keep pressing past your sticking point, building up until you have ascertained the prize of this high calling in Christ Jesus (Philippians 3:14). The end of this lift and human spectrum is the reward of eternity with God.

118

I Knew Not

Daniel Webster Whittle (1840–1901) was a gospel song lyricist, evangelist, and Bible teacher. He marched with Sherman and was wounded at the Battle of Vicksburg. He mostly wrote under the pseudonym "El Nathan." He was widely known for the hymn "Moment by Moment" and today's topic, "I Know Whom I Have Believed."

It is wonderful to have a song whose entire chorus is a quote from Pauline Scripture—in this case, 2 Timothy 1:12. Yet in contrast to Paul's statement of "knowing" who he had believed, the author Mr. Whittle writes the preceding verse as "not knowing." God tells us that He would not have us to be ignorant (Romans 11:25) and has made known His manifold wisdom (Ephesians 3:10). A single letter change makes a major doctrinal difference. Instead of "I know not," it now reads, "I knew not" and "but now I know," as well as some other doctrinal changes made, as you will see.

We will keep the wonderful tune by James McGranahan (1840–1907) written with Whittle in 1883.

I Know Whom I Have Believed

1. I knew not why God's wondrous grace to all
   He hath made known, nor how, unworthy

Christ in love—Redeemed us for His own.

2. I knew not how His righteousness to me,
He did impart, nor how through faith in God's shed blood,
Wrought peace with-in my heart.
3. I knew not how the Spirit places us in Christ's death for sin,
Nor how I could be crucified with Him,
Never my works to build again.
4. I knew not how my Lord may come to meet us in the air,
Nor where I could spend eternity,
Forever reigning with Him there.

Chorus: But I know whom I have believed,
And am persuaded that He is able,
To keep that which I've committed
Unto Him against that day.

You can know too (Acts 16:30–31)!
Sing as unto the Lord (Psalm 104:31–35).

119

Live, Life, Laugh

The wonder of a small child. A babe will cry and then seconds later, smile and giggle uncontrollably. Vice versa. A baby will go from uncontrollable happiness to inconsolable distress. I, for one, can relate. In our faith, at one moment we will be at the top of the mountain, glorying in Jesus as if we are the disciples at the Transfiguration (Matthew 17:1–17). Then, without realizing it, suddenly we are at the bottom of the mountain, confused as to how we got down or why we ever needed to come down.

It was once preached to me—in what some would call a spiritual drought—that if I would just pray more, read more Scripture, and volunteer more, then I would feel closer to God. But the reality is that Christ did not save us to do more but to be more. Emotions can be indicators of many things in life. They can lead to great things. But emotions do not determine our position and state, which is in Jesus Christ. Whether one feels happy, sad, filled with emotion, or completely empty—if you are in Christ, you are sealed until the day of your redemption (Ephesians 4:30).

I want to encourage you by saying this:

> Live in what you know to be true and not what you feel.

I learned this lesson from my stepfather, Darrell, who in decision-making would quote to me Jeremiah 17:9,

> The heart is deceitful above all things, and desperately wicked: who can know it?

Contrast this verse with just a couple prior where God offered Jeremiah the solution,

> Blessed is the man that trusteth in the Lord, and whose hope the Lord is. (verse 7)

We live above the bondage of feelings in our walk with Christ and simply know what is true and prescribed within God's Word. This is part of the process of "renewing the mind." Paul states that the old man (the old "us") is corrupt. Yet the Spirit which dwells within us constantly and ceaselessly renews our mind with truth and not subjective feeling (Ephesians 4:22–24).

Live life assured, despite internal struggles. God has got you, friends.

120

My Savior 'Tis of Thee

The tune "God Save the King/Queen" is popular in sheet music and was used by many nations. In America, its history can be traced to Samuel F. Smith (1808–1895). In 1832, he put words to what is now known as "My Country, 'Tis of Thee," which has become an unofficial American anthem. There are many wonderful, positive aspects of our great land, and we give praise to God for all His past blessings.

Combined with a general doctrinal aspect, there is now a stronger orientation in our churches on "defending freedom." Through flag-waving and military memorials, rather than our ministry in Christ, the Bible says that the source of our freedom comes from our deliverance in Christ, not from a country.

Now, I am proud to live in the greatest country on earth, but like Jesus said in Luke 2:49,

> Wist ye not that I must be about my Father's business?

So let the Church be the Church and the government be the government (Matthew 22:21).

Saying this, the focus of these new lyrics to the same popular tune of "My Country 'Tis of Thee" is on the "liberty wherewith

Christ hath made us free" (Galatians 5:1). Our liberty in Christ made us free from the Law, sin, and death. As ye have received Him, walk in Him (Colossians 2:6). Carry this musical message as you go.

My Savior, 'Tis of Thee

1. My Savior, 'tis of Thee, our God of liberty, of Thee I sing,
   Hand whereby Jesus died, planned to be crucified;
   There every man was tried,
   Let freedom ring!
2. By nature sin in me; man's blood can't set me free,
   I look above; my faults became the chain;
   Thy Law was made therein; His death was made my gain,
   Commend His love!
3. I stand in liberty; no army captures me;
   The work is done;
   Great men of old have fought against what pride has wrought;
   Not knowing what You bought;
   Freedom is won!
4. All nationalities, in bonds or poverty, can be set free;
   "God, help us to be bold," our souls to You are sold;
   Thy Gospel must be told;
   Make all men see!

Sing as unto the Lord (Psalm 104:31–35).

121

The Die Is Cast

"Alea iacta est!"

To many, this may appear merely gibberish or some form of mad gab. But I assure you, these words carry meaning. The words were proclaimed as world history as we know it was altered. On January 10, 49 BC, Julius Caesar spoke these words as he crossed a narrow stream known as the Rubicon, officially making him an enemy of the powers of Rome and sparking a civil war that would end the Roman Republic.

From Latin to English, this means "The die is cast." In stepping across the Rubicon, he made his intentions known and therefore, he was past the point of no return. I find it funny that this once-popular saying did not stand the test of time. Rather, his action is what is remembered. This is where we get the phrase "crossing the Rubicon." This phrase signifies a crucial moment in the life of a person and a landmark action.

The implications of his action far superseded the lot he was dealing with. Talk alone often cannot stand. If we talk about action but never act, our talk is void.

We serve a Savior not familiar with bluffing. He had a saying Himself signifying a point of no return. On the cross when He cried, "It is finished" (John 19:30)!

Now as a result of His words and action, we can have our Rubicon moment. A defining moment is when we believe in Christ's finished Gospel, and enter a war with the flesh with the victory assured. A Rubicon moment that is like Caesar's—changes everything.

It changes our internal government, and we are no longer slaves to sin but servants of God (Romans 6:17–18). Our nourishment is fed no longer with the empty calories society provides, but rather with the Bread of Life (John 6:35). Like never before, His imputed righteousness brings value to once-void words and deeds (2 Corinthians 5:21).

This is the God we serve. No die could catch Him off guard. He splits the waters we dread, and He finishes what He begins (Philippians 1:6).

Amen.

122

There Is a Better Way to My Heart

But one of the soldiers with a spear pierced his side,
and forthwith came there out blood and water.
—John 19:34

Have you ever wondered about the thoughts that ran through Jesus's mind in His earthly ministry? I know it is speculation, and is something I am not fond of but really—just imagine with me for a moment. With Christ being fully human and fully God, what thoughts did Jesus possess as He asked Judas Iscariot to follow Him, knowing full well that he would betray Him?

One could only speculate on the exacts, but I know exactly by what nature the thoughts were. They possessed grace and truth (John 1:14). They could be characterized by a love unseen to those who walked with Him then, and those who walk by His Spirit now (John 15:13; Romans 5:5).

And as He was dying on the cross, the thoughts that raced through His mind, I'm sure human words could not portray. Agony reconciled by love for those whom He came to save. In retrospect, we look back to the character of Christ on the cross to define the character we embody now.

Dwight L. Moody once preached a sermon depicting the love that Christ has for humanity. In it, he illustrates the fact that Jesus even loved those who carried out the desires of the Jewish population against Him—the Romans. Once again, dealing with hypotheticals, Moody states the following in a narrative of the story:

> Go hunt up that man that put a spear in my side and tell him there is a better way to get near to my heart.

Isn't that beautiful?

Even when we were enemies to God and far from His beautiful heart—He loved us (Romans 5:8). He settled the debt we owed in one final swoop so that we no longer had to pursue Christ as if we were spear fishers, but rather sons and daughters free to address Him as Father (John 1:12; Romans 8:14–17).

We are as near as near can be. Christ is near, as near can be. We abide in His body, and He abides in us (1 Corinthians 6:19–20; 1 John 2:6).

This is because we came to God's heart, on His terms, by the blood of Christ. We are able to receive His very Spirit.

123

I Can't Make Sense of It

I once heard it preached,

> You're saved! Stop trying to make sense of the Bible, and let the Bible make sense of you!

For the rational and logical intellectual, this quote is a slap to the things they hold dear. For those who would not self-prescribe into this category, it seems like an impossible task. To the word and letter, this may not be 100 percent the best way to approach every Bible study, but the point stands.

In our humanity, what and how is the best way to approach the holy Word? Is it merely a coagulated clot of words or as alive as the most animate, organic matter? Examine this verse and see how graciously the Bible operates on the depravity of humanity.

> For the word of God is quick, and powerful, and sharper than any two edged sword, piercing even to the dividing asunder of soul and spirit, and of the joints and marrow, and is a discerner of the thoughts and intents of the heart. (Hebrews 4:12)

What does this popular verse in Hebrews illustrate? The Word of God is alive (quick), powerful, and knowledgeable of your spiritual anatomy. Delving beyond the knowledge of your condition, the author of Hebrews states the Word takes action and discerns the thoughts and intents of the heart!

In other words, it makes sense of you.

In reading, the Spirit works hand in hand with the holy Word of God as He had when He delivered it to the original writer and can make sense of your spiritual condition, your shortcomings, your confusion, and your flippancy to God's will.

Therefore, relinquish control. Put aside prior biases that interpret for you. Lay down your hesitancy to confront the hard verses. Open your Bible and converse with the Word, with an emphasis on listening.

The Word of God is alive; it'll speak.

124

Shut Up About the Sun!

Copernicus is a man characterized by persistence regarding ideas that went against the grain of his contemporaries' thinking. He introduced the idea of a heliocentric solar system, which states that the sun, not Earth, is the center of the universe and that the planets revolve around the sun.

This was contrary to the popular belief of the day that Earth was the center of the universe. This was an idea heavily propagated by the Catholic Church. It would be inaccurate to say that the Catholic Church immediately opposed this belief, as Copernicus himself was a Catholic, but history shows that eventually, many efforts were taken to mute Copernicus and, later, bring about Galileo's conviction.

The Church stated that the notion of a heliocentric universe not only refuted basic physics but also biblical teaching, so by their logic, Copernicus, his teachings, and later scholars like Galileo were considered heretical. To be fair, this opposition was by the Catholic and Protestant churches. Martin Luther opposed this view on the grounds of verses such as Joshua 10:10–15.

This truly caused a stale digression in the scientific realm, as what later was proven to be true was outlawed anywhere the Catholic Church held authority. Copernicus first introduced this idea in 1543. The Catholic Church's repeal of the prohibition on Copernicanism was not issued until the years 1820 to 1835, with full reinstatement in the late twentieth century.

Copernicus and Galileo continued to promote their belief and observations at every opportunity. Now what is deemed as common knowledge was opposed at every chance by churches of that day. Truth is not popular. For those who embrace wrong thinking, it may appear offensive to offer correction, even in a loving manner. This does not make the truth any more unnecessary or need to be shared.

When you promote that the Son, Jesus Christ, needs to be the center of the universe and not our own, earthly flesh, it may be opposed. Nonetheless, the truth remains. It is Christ who lives in us and empowers us (Galatians 2:20; 2 Timothy 1:7). But then again, we know that the Gospel is powerful and, by the grace of God, able to alter the course of the recipient's history, just like Copernicus altered the history of the world by sharing the truth.

Do not grow weary in doing good and remain persistent in all situations, never doubting what you know to be true (Galatians 6:9; 1 Corinthians 9:22). Never allow shame to creep in as opposition grows. The truth will not change (Romans 1:16).

In the end, like Copernicus, the truth will be revealed (1 Corinthians 15:50–54).

125

All the World's a Stage!

William Shakespeare once wrote in the comedy *As You Like It* that "all the world's a stage." Personally, I have never disagreed with this statement; however, I do relate this verse to an entire context. Humanity notoriously holds this view that indeed the world is a stage. Different scenes hold focus on comedy, while other scenes of life are indeed tragedy.

Also familiar, humanity carries this trend of confusing just who the director is (Acts 5:29). God is the author of life's script, although as the saying goes, the devil loves to be in the details (Genesis 1:1; Romans 1:20). Satan loves to draw from the glory of the true genius of brilliance while he is a confused actor, costumed as an angel of light (2 Corinthians 11:14).

So the question then becomes, Who do we, on the world's stage, regard as the director? God, author of creation and our salvation, or Satan, just another jealous improviser who seeks to pull you further and further from the will of the Director?

The world's a stage. The Lord knows the actors who have submitted to His script, and He knows who has not (2 Timothy 2:19). He loves them regardless, and His Word and loving Spirit urge their return to the beauty of His glory. Our wonderful Director even stepped onto the stage and showed just how to stay in step. He made a way with His Son, Jesus Christ (1 Corinthians 15:3–4).

I understand this illustration has its limitations, as all of them do. Nonetheless, it can bring you close enough to my point for me to ask,

On the world stage, who is your director?

126

Asleep at the Wheel

Therefore let us not sleep, as do others;
but let us watch and be sober.
—1 Thessalonians 5:6

There have been moments in my life that have provoked drastic change, usually for the better. One of those times was late one night while I was living in southern West Virginia. In high school, I lived in a rural mountain town called Mullens. Finding work often required a commute. So while juggling school, athletics, and a personal life, I decided to pick up a job in one of the closest towns—Beckley.

For those unfamiliar or rusty on their West Virginia geography, at the time, this was over a half-hour drive. Many times I worked around forty-five hours a week and had to work the closing shift in order to get any kind of work and maintain some semblance of a private life.

Now the stage is set. I was driving home one night (or technically morning) over a rather mountainous area of West Virginia. I had the windows up, the heat on, tired out of my mind, and the radio off. The ride was going well, nothing was different than normal—then I woke up.

At the last part of a windy road known locally as Slab Fork, I was heading up a hill and for a cliff. It was nearly the end. Half of my

Jeep was off the road and in gravel, and it took a good effort to steer my car back to the safety of the road.

Recalling this experience, there were a few habits (whether I realized it or not) that changed. It was around this time that on my wrestling team, I stopped cutting weight as much and wrestled in a healthier weight class. Unless it was raining, I kept my windows down at night so the wind could restore my tiredness. Shamefully, this began my energy drink addiction.

I say all this to say this: there are times when your rhythms will cause you to sleepwalk through life. You will seemingly be alert and sound, then confused about what steps you took to get where you are. Just know, I understand.

Through the centuries, people have come up with different formulas and ideas for removing these periods of comatose; however, let me suggest this: focus on getting home. In a physical sense, this was my problem. I had lost sight of my loved ones waiting for me at home.

In a spiritual sense, it's a problem all Christians face. The world battles for the Christian's attention and sometimes succeeds in subconsciously telling them that this world is their home. But it is not.

The apostle Paul constantly confronted those who were growing weary of the heavenly destination and therefore encouraged them with instructions such as the following:

> Teaching us that, denying ungodliness and worldly lusts, we should live soberly, righteously, and godly, in this present world;
>
> Looking for that blessed hope, and the glorious appearing of the great God and our Saviour Jesus Christ;
>
> Who gave himself for us, that he might redeem us from all iniquity, and purify unto himself a peculiar people, zealous of good works. (Titus 2:12–14)

Or

> But ye, brethren, are not in darkness, that that day should overtake you as a thief.
>
> Ye are all the children of light, and the children of the day: we are not of the night, nor of darkness.
>
> Therefore let us not sleep, as do others; but let us watch and be sober. (1 Thessalonians 5:4-6)

It is often heard to "live in the moment." I will not deny that we should. But let me take this phrase further:

> Live in the moment, keep heaven in sight.

Much like driving, when you forget where you are going, the drive becomes much longer and prone to problems.

We are children of light and children of the day, living in the radiance of God's glory and grace (John 1:14; 2 Corinthians 3:18). So let's be alert. Stay awake, make your pit stops, and speak with those who do not share your hope and have nowhere to go (Titus 2:14).

127

If You Can Dodge a Wrench...

In 2004, actors Ben Stiller and Vince Vaughn starred in what soon became an instant classic. The comedy is *Dodgeball: A True Underdog Story*. In this movie, a successful gym owner aims to take over a failing gym named Average Joe's. To save their gym, the owner of Average Joe's gathers a team of average Joes to compete in a Las Vegas dodgeball tournament and secure enough money to ward off a hostile takeover of their gym.

In one scene, Average Joe's gym owner, Peter LaFleur, recruits a quirky ex-dodgeball legend to train his team. They soon discover that this legend has some unique methods required to bring desired results. One of these methods is where we get the quote, "If you can dodge a wrench, you can dodge a ball."

Generally, this saying would seem nonsensical when applying it to a real-life setting, as he did. But philosophically, this quote may hold a surprising quantity of truth. Some hard trials will come in life. Whether physical, spiritual, mental, etc., they are bound to come.

It'd be wrong to say that hard trials directly make future trials "easier." They do not. When you have hard things coming at you and attacking you in life, you develop discerning attributes. One of these important attributes first and foremost is patience (Romans 5:3; James 1:3).

Having tough obstacles that challenge your faith points us to the fact that we must rely on God because we in ourselves are frail. Therefore, when we rely on God, this means that we must rely on His timing as well. As a result, we grow patient. In patience, we allow God to refine us into purer vessels of gold and silver, uprooting us from being vessels of wood and earth (2 Timothy 2:20).

When we rely on God, the next attribute we grow in is experience. We experience that as we wait on God's timing, live in His faithfulness, and experience God's grace daily. Consequently, we have experienced seeing how He works all things to the good of those who love Him and are called according to His purpose (Romans 8:28). The emphasis here is on what God deems good, not what we may deem good. It takes experience and reflection on His holy Word to know.

If we know that God is going to see us through, ultimately in a heavenly inheritance, then naturally we would develop an unashamed hope as a result of the above attributes (Romans 5:5; Romans 8:18).

I say all this to say this: Life may be hard now or may soon test your faith. Perspective is key. Know that wrenches in your plans prepare you for the latter obstacles to come, and God in His goodness allows these things—ultimately for a better purpose.

128

Mine Eyes Have Read the Glory

Julia Ward Howe's lyrics to the traditional American melody "Mine Eyes Have Seen the Glory" are fraught with error. Now before you get upset about changing an age-old song, you must know she indeed changed the words to this tune that was called "John Brown's Body" herself. Howe's lyrics spiritualizing prophetic references after prophetic reference reflect the political events of her time, in Northern America during the American Civil War.

What's more, the chorus repeats only two words that serve very little to teach or admonish. We have reconstructed the lyrics to reflect how God dealt differently with man at different times throughout history, and it would be wrong to take verses out of context to describe current events and wars.

The tune to this song was composed by William Steffe (1830–1890), who lived in Philadelphia and wrote camp-meeting songs. There would be a lot of Scripture to direct to in this reconstructed version, so just sing along and study the verse.

1. Mine eyes have read the glory of when God created earth;
   And then by one sin entered, and it entered us by birth;
   So God chose one man to give his seed the promises of worth;
   His faith in things not seen! God gave promises to Abram;

God gave promises to Abram; God gave promises to Abram;
His faith in things not seen!

2. I've read about the chosen tribes who walked across the sea;
God said, "If you will obey my laws, you will be bless'd by me,"
And so when they broke the law of God, for sins they paid a fee;
Their faith in sacrifice! God gave covenants to Moses;
God gave covenants to Moses; God gave covenants to Moses;
Their faith in sacrifice!

3. Then to His own came Jesus to confirm the promises,
Preached "A kingdom come, sell all you have, repent of all your sins;
And when I return I'll judge the earth, keep watch and lift your chins!"
Their faith would come with pow'r. God have to Pentecost to Peter;
God gave Pentecost to Peter; God gave Pentecost to Peter;
Their faith was in God's pow'r!

4. Before he came again to judge, He came to save one man;
Christ revealed through him the mystery of God's eternal plan;
'Twas for all that Christ had died, and for our life He rose again!
Our faith in Christ alone! God gave Paul a dispensation;
God gave Paul a dispensation; God gave a Paul a dispensation;
Our faith in Christ alone!

(Psalm 104:31–35.)

129

A Thing Largely Ignored

To the Fahaeans, the rain them, both implausible
and prehistoric in that valley where the fields were in
love with the river, was a thing largely ignored.

In the novel *This Is Happiness* by Niall Williams, there is a quaint village by the name of Faha. This was a village characterized by constant rain and little sunshine in a beautiful Irish location. Nonetheless, because it always rained, no longer did anyone pay it (or the sunshine, for that matter) any mind. The beauty of their homeland was largely ignored because of the rhythms of life.

Williams has a way of painting imagery and putting the reader into the story. I could feel the misty rain and the plush, green grass underneath my feet as I read. And then it struck me. Do I recognize the "ordinary" beauties around me and the daily, simple graces that God has, is, and will give me? Many people who would undertake this introspection would likely come to a similar conclusion as me—not at all.

God is active in making us new each day. He does not save us and then leave us to our own wicked devices. The apostle Paul makes it clear that God renews that inner man "day by day" (2 Corinthians 4:16). We live by His saving grace and we live in daily graces. Theologians for years have termed these daily graces as "common graces." But there lies the problem.

God's endless, frequent blessing should never be deemed common. Whether we see them new each time or not, any dispersion of grace by God is unique in that it is totally undeserved—yet freely given. They are not common. As a matter of fact, everything truly unique and beautiful is of God. Therefore, I find fault in humans' tendency to disqualify that every good thing is of God (Ecclesiastes 3:11; James 1:17). Every good thing of God is a gift, by which we have access because of His gift of grace through the Gospel of His Son, Jesus Christ (Psalm 84:11–12; Ephesians 2:8).

Saying this, I want to encourage you, the reader, to look around and inward today. What gift of God has become common to you today? Start this introspective journey with thanksgiving for the indescribable gift of your salvation (2 Corinthians 9:14–15). Then work down and count your blessings. Who knows what God is doing or has done in your midst today?

130

Let Thy Words Be Few

Have you ever had to speak publicly and did not say exactly what you wanted to say? Scratch that. Have you ever spoken to your crush, friend, or loved ones, and when the words come out, well, they cause less than favorable reactions?

I know how it goes. We as humans are prone to mess up when it comes to speaking! This is why it always baffles me when I hear self and truth preached above the Word of God. For those within Christian circles, we know how it goes. Prayer's opening services sound something like this:

> "God, allow my words today to be your words."
> "Let my words today, be your words, not mine."
> "Lord, speak through me."

Churches across the United States hear this prayer. Then within particular contexts, you will hear fifteen to forty-five minutes of stories, jokes, tear jerkers, and then if the congregation is lucky, a breadcrumb or smidgen of Scripture.

If this resonates in any way, then please ponder the following question with me: "How did it get to this?"

In the lives of Christians, when did experiences and self-exaltation become more comfortable to preach the Word of God *already* spoken? People will "rely" on the Spirit but ignore the complete volume He has already authored for us. Without the substance of Scripture, speakers turn unto empty talk and what Paul refers to as "vain jangling" (1 Timothy 1:6).

Therefore, let us take the wisdom of Solomon in Ecclesiastes 5:2–3, and in the truest sense, let the Spirit speak what He has spoken through us. It says, "Be not rash with thy mouth and let not thine heart be hasty to utter anything before God: for God is in heaven, and thou upon earth: therefore let thy words be few. For a dream cometh through the multitude of business; and a fool's voice is known by multitude of words."

The Lord *has* divinely revealed His attributes, His love, His truth, and His glorious redemptive plan for humanity through His Son, Jesus Christ. He did so in His sixty-sixth book, which is a love letter to humanity, the object of His love. Why look anywhere else or minimize His words under a blanket of foolishness?

Paul aims to reduce confusion around his intentions in ministry by proclaiming the following: "For we preach not ourselves, but Christ Jesus the Lord; and ourselves your servants for Jesus' sake" (2 Corinthians 4:5). It was in Christ *alone* as revealed by God that Paul, a few verses down, can assure that "we are troubled on every side, yet not distressed; we are perplexed, but not in despair; persecuted, but not forsaken; cast down, but not destroyed" (verses 8 and 9).

One cannot get that assurance from the five-step programs of men's philosophy but only from the one-step program of the Gospel—believe (1 Corinthians 15:3–4). Let me summarize and flat-out state my intentions. Get your truth from God's truth.

Going to the Word will show you what is true *and* will illuminate what is of human devices. Only one is destined to enrich.

131

Enriching Grace

enrich[ing]: (1) To make rich or richer, especially by the addition or increase of some desirable quality, attribute, or ingredient (2) To add beauty to (3) To enhance the taste of (4) To make (a soil) more fertile (5) To process so as to add or increase the proportion of a desirable ingredient

grace: (1a) Unmerited divine assistance given to humans for their regeneration or sanctification (1b) A virtue coming from God (1c) A state of sanctification enjoyed through divine assistance (2a) Approval; favor (2b) Mercy; pardon

For the faithful participant of Enriching Grace Ministries, one may wonder: Why do we have the name Enriching Grace?

It is a fair question. Grace is a popular word thrown around without any true understanding, and the word enriching? Well… you wouldn't hear it much unless on a nutrition label or you were a nuclear physicist looking to enrich materials such as uranium. Nonetheless, the words put together illustrate a beautiful, divine disclosure to humanity by God. The word enriching itself, as the above definitions from *Merriam-Webster Dictionary* illustrate, is something desirable and that adds value to its partaker.

Simple enough? Grace may prove a bit more elusive for concrete definition; however, these definitions have some things in common. Specifically, God's grace is "unmerited" and "divine." Pastor Justin Johnson characterizes grace as having three elements:

1. You did not do the work.
2. You benefit from it.
3. You do not deserve it.

By these definitions, anyone can give grace. But no one's graces can even remotely match the effects of God's grace. Theologians divide God's grace into different purposes at different times, such as salvific grace, prevenient grace, sanctifying grace, and so on.

In the search to name our ministry, the original name was shaping up to be "Edifying Grace." But alas and earnestly truthful, this ministry name was taken. We were aiming for a mission word that encompassed the nature of God's grace. It was by a glance that we ran across the word enriching. And the truth is, no matter how humanity systematizes the unmerited favor of God, if God provides this favor, it will make you spiritually rich. No amount of grace supplied by God will reduce or stagnate your value. By God's grace, you are able to intimately know the God of the universe and ascertain all spiritual blessings in heavenly places (Ephesians 1:3, 8–9).

God chose humanity, who is undeserving of any merit from Him, to pour out spiritual prosperity and the riches of His love in Christ Jesus by the riches of His grace (Ephesians 1:6–7). His grace accepts, redeems, and transforms (Ephesians 1:4, 7, 18). All processes that in the truest sense, enrich. He gave us the blessing of His Word to guide us, His Spirit to comfort and empower us, and a Savior who in every sense brings us into His beautiful body to co-heir with Him for eternity. And believe me, although these examples are some of the most notable, God's grace permeates every portion of the believer's life and draws the skeptic near to Him.

So that's why our mission is to be an outlet pointing you, the reader, to the knowledge of God's truth (1 Timothy 2:4). Because by grace through faith, the truth will set you free, enrich, and carry you through and up to the throne of God when that glorious day comes.

> Immerse yourself in the curriculum of grace. (Max Lucado)
>
> Grow in the root of all grace, which is faith. Believe God's promises more firmly than ever. Allow your faith to increase in its fullness, firmness, and simplicity. (Charles Spurgeon)
>
> Grace means undeserved kindness. It is the gift of God to man the moment he sees he is unworthy of God's favor. (Dwight L. Moody)
>
> Grace can neither be bought, earned, or won by the creature. If it could be, it would cease to be grace. (Arthur W. Pink)
>
> Grace is sufficient even though we huff and puff with all our might to try and find something or someone that it cannot cover. Grace is enough. (Brennan Manning)

132

God's Will, Day by Day

What is the will of God for my life? This is a common question that is often asked in contemporary Christian settings and, on occasion, within the secular realm. Many times this question is a form of code language that is really begging the questions: "What kind of job am I going to have?" or "Who am I supposed to marry?" I pray I am not overgeneralizing, but in ministry, I know from experience that the question asker expects a spiritual leader to point them to the end results of five-year plans and year-long ambitions.

But my question is often, "When does the Bible address God's will for the Christian's life as something so…rudimentary?" Yes, the Bible does address the will of God. And yes, God does address how we are to live for Him. However, rarely is His will addressed to a yearly organizing calendar; rather, He provides an intended result for the product of our day-to-day living. God's will always leads to His glory. It is not a plan that is intended to merely parallel the direction we are going. Rather, it is more likened to a GPS-led transport, guiding humanity to God's glory and intentions.

In an age of fact-checkers, I am encouraging the reader to prove me wrong with Scripture. The will of God was always for the advancement of His glory and to bring those whom He loves into a relationship and salvation (Romans 8:29; Ephesians 1:4–5). At what point has God's will changed to accommodate humanity by focusing on secondary matters and gratifying human desires? The answer to this question, I am sure, is it hasn't (Ephesians 5:15–17).

The question is, "What is God's will for yourself day by day to advance His heavenly kingdom and grow in godliness, ultimately glorifying Him?" This sounds harsh; nonetheless, as we are in God, truly we are privileged. Functionally, in fulfilling His will, He will take care of us (2 Corinthians 12:9; Philippians 4:19; 1 Peter 5:7). As the accompanying verses exemplify and the testimonies of the martyred saints show, this is not always a physical meeting of needs. Beautifully, this would show us that God has grander plans for the spiritual than the physical prosperity of humanity. From physical (and spiritual anguish, for that matter), He did not even spare His own Son. Rather, the Trinity worked and fulfilled the Gospel in this way so that we could freely receive Him and all the glorious treasures that He has stored for us in heavenly places (Romans 8:32; Ephesians 1:3).

As we align with God's will of salvation and become a component of His Body, we have hope. Hope and comfort of the Spirit can be likened to fuel to present the Gospel and be used as vessels for others to align with God's will as well (Romans 15:13; 1 Timothy 2:4). Saying this, allow the hope of Christ's coming and the richness of God's love shed abroad in our hearts to drive our life. Christian culture would be better off to break from replacing the hope of God with the hope of a job, spouse, instant healing, or whatever our hope is mistakenly staked on. If this resonates, uproot that rusty, weightless, dragging anchor and replace it with the secure anchor of Jesus Christ (Hebrews 6:18–19).

Stop asking, "God, what is your plan and will for my life?" and ask the more appropriate question of "What are we doing today, Abba [Father]?" God resides outside of time but works in the day to day. Scripturally, prophets like David and Jeremiah had a firm understanding not only of how God works but also His understanding of a human's pace and frailty (Psalm 19:2; Lamentations 3:20–26). But praise be to God that He made a way and provided us with the discerning power and strength of His Holy Spirit (1 Corinthians 2:14; Romans 8:11).

133

Jesus Loves Me

Anna B. Warner (1820–1915) wrote a hymn that, without doubt, has been sung by more children than any other hymn. Written in 1860, it came from a novel that Ms. Warner and her sister had written called *Say and Seal.* The composer of the music, William Bradbury (1816–1868), also composed "Sweet Hour of Prayer," "Savior, Like a Shepherd Lead Us," "Angel Band," and the very familiar "Just as I Am."

In the third verse of "Jesus Loves Me," this classic children's song teaches a future salvation with the words, "He will wash away my sin." But we stand in a present possession of salvation (Romans 5:2). The new and revised verses have been provided to reflect this fact along with a clearer explanation of humanity's sin problem (Romans 3:23), how God has reconciled that problem (Romans 5:8), and even makes a distinction between prophecy and mystery (Ephesians 2:11). May as you sing this revised version, see just how much Jesus loves you!

1. Jesus loves me, this I know, for the Bible tells me so;
   Little ones to Him belong, they are weak, but He is strong;
2. None are righteous, this I know, for the Bible tells me so;
   We can know Romans 3:10: We're all guilty of our sin;
3. At one time I had been lost, He died for me on the cross,
   He commends His love for me, by His death on Calvary;

4. In time past was prophecy, but now it's the mystery.
Was not known in ages past, grace through faith is here at last!

Chorus:
Yes, Jesus loves me! Yes, Jesus loves me!
Yes, Jesus loves me! The Bible tells me so!

134

Do Be, Be Do

> The main thing between you and God is not so much your sins; it's your damnable good works.
>
> —John Gerstner

Truly, I wish Christianity would be as intended when written in the Scriptures—simple. Nonetheless, the philosophies of man continue to assault simplicity and rearrange truth to suit themselves and vainly attempt to minimize Christ (Colossians 2:8–10). They put makeup on it and therefore put on it a new face, degrading it.

In the process, philosophy plus theology will lead us to base our identity on what we do instead of the things we do being based itself on who we are, which is in Christ (2 Corinthians 5:17; Galatians 3:26). Be on guard. Not all of these assaults are from "nonbelievers." Know this: we do "things" because of who we are. Who we are is not what we do. I intend to use the word *things* in a facetious manner because apart from a sound and healthy identity, that is what they remain—things.

The Gospel requires belief. The Word says it is "not of yourselves" but "it is [a] gift" (Ephesians 2:8–9). *Merriam-Webster* defines *gift* in this way:

> Something voluntarily transferred by one person to another without compensation.

The Bible defines it in this way:

> It was the third hour, and they crucified him. (Mark 15:25)

Talk about paid in full! Jesus was a ransom for all, and we can add nothing to the price He paid with His death and secured with His resurrection. Nothing else will suffice for our salvation (1 Timothy 2:9; Psalm 49:7). Many are familiar with the classic song, "Jesus Paid It All." The words ring true: "Jesus paid it all, all to Him I owe…"

I could never deny that this is true, but functionally, how is the Church doing with embracing the fact that Jesus paid it all? What are our works but filthy rags if not bathed in the righteousness of our Redeemer (Isaiah 64:6; Ephesians 2:10; Philippians 3:9–21)? They are merely "things" until life is lived in the beauty of the Holy Spirit's saving, regenerative, and renewing power (Titus 3:4–6).

Owing our lives to God does not imply that it is feasible to repay the debt that we owe (Romans 12:1). Christ took care of the debt as a gift. Believing His Gospel relinquishes humanity's phony grip on eternity, allowing the lost to now abide in the Holy Spirit and earnestly cry, "Abba, Father" in celebration of our newfound adoption (Romans 8:15; Galatians 4:6).

Doing does not equate to being. A member of the Body of Christ is your being and your identification when you are saved. This state of being is your reality, and the accompanying "doing" is merely the by-product of the Holy Spirit's righteous indwelling and discernment of Scripture (2 Timothy 3:16–17; Titus 3).

135

Polar Opposites

Trump/Biden. North/South. Rural/urban. Conservative/progressive. McDonald's/Wendy's. Poverty/wealth. Traditional/modern. Young/old.

Do you recognize what these are? They are polarities, opposites, and ends of spectrums that culture designates identity as. None of which I am endorsing in this devotional, these are merely examples. But I want you to think about these. Do you fall on any end of this spectrum? If not the end of a spectrum, I guarantee you are in the middle ground of some.

Now think of your life and beliefs regarding your Christian faith. Let's examine a few spectrums. Legalistic/relativist. Catholic/Protestant. Perseverance ("Once saved, always saved") / conditional security. Hymns / contemporary music. You may think that I am now going to suggest finding the middle-ground or a win-win situation to where your faith can accommodate both ends of the spectrum. But I'm not. That is called compromise.

Doctrine is not supposed to be a compromise, although this is often how Christians circle-divvy it up. Christians are called to jump from the spectrums devised of the world, and walk in and by His light, therefore worshiping accordingly: in Spirit and in Truth (Psalm 119:105; John 4:24; Ephesians 5:8–13). Truth is not subjective. God's Word is truth, and Jesus is His Word incarnate (John 14:6; 2

Timothy 2:15). In fact, truth has an objective place in the life of the believer. Functionally, it becomes ineffective when we allow external influences and biases to interpret God's Word, instead of God's Word interpreting itself (2 Peter 3:15–18).

These external influences and vain ideas attempt to carve up truth into spectrums and still call the spectrum truth. In 1 Corinthians 1, Paul refers to unity in truth. He reasons to the Corinthian church that there can be unity and consensus in truth, despite this not seeming to be an option today.

> Now I beseech you, brethren, by the name of our Lord Jesus Christ, that ye all speak the *same* thing, and that there be *no divisions* among you; but that ye be perfectly joined together in the *same* mind and in the *same* judgment. (1 Corinthians 1:10, emphasis added)

This example, among many others, shows ideally what fellowship within the Body should be like as we worship God in Spirit and in truth. Practically, if this is the intention, this should cause an evaluation of self. Where have the members of the Church split truth and where might repair be necessary in order to make the Church more effective in spreading the Gospel? What spectrums have we constructed outside the biblical view of life and outside the parameters of the Gospel and God's grace?

136

Left Behind...?

On December 31, 1995, Tim LaHaye and Jerry Jenkins kicked off the *Left Behind* series with its first book of the same name. Since then, the series has been critically acclaimed and has made multiple appearances on the *New York Times* Bestseller List. When I was younger, these books fascinated me, and the movies that ensued were sensational! They highlighted what reality was to look like when the Church was raptured, and people were—*gasp!*—left behind.

But looking back, I wonder how these books impacted Christian culture. Because yes, it is true that the Rapture will take the Church away and will begin an age of tribulation. However, for many, this truth has been used to alter and or subvert the gospel of assurance by Jesus Christ, with a form of a gospel that plummets the human spirit into turmoil and fear, always asking the question—"Am I a *true* believer?"

Granted, the Bible does have ways to gauge this question, but in matters of eternity, fear should not overcome God's desire for a *watchful spirit*. When the fear is in being left behind, we place more stock in the things that happen during tribulation than the God who institutes it to draw those whom He loves back to Himself.

Jesus has a rule of thumb regarding this. He preaches,

> Fear not them which kill the body, but are not able to kill the soul: but rather fear him which is able to destroy both soul and body in hell. (Matthew 10:28)

To the Church, I say this: do not fear. We will not be there in the trial; we will be with our Savior. If you believe in the Gospel of Jesus Christ, you are sealed and can have assurance, for the Spirit of God bears witness (Romans 8:16–19; 1 Corinthians 15:3–4; Ephesians 1:13–14). From the moment of your belief, your responsibility is now to keep watch. To reach out while looking up.

As for the timing of Jesus's coming to take His Church, it is uncertain. Nonetheless, uncertainty of timing should not equal uncertainty of His coming. God is certain of the timing and therefore He is coming (1 Thessalonians 4:16–17). Have faith (2 Corinthians 5:7). Augustine of Hippo once wrote,

> Uncertainty then as to the time of the Lord's return is to promote the watchful spirit.

Paul wrote to Titus that

> for the grace of God that bringeth salvation hath appeared to all men,
>
> Teaching us that, denying ungodliness and worldly lusts, we should live soberly, righteously, and godly, in this present world;
>
> Looking for that blessed hope, and the glorious appearing of the great God and our Saviour Jesus Christ.

Notice a pattern here: saved (on earth), live, look, saved (to heaven).

Moving on, I have another word to Christians. Preach salvation for all today and not salvation for tomorrow. The *Left Behind* series is told from the perspective of people who were, well…left behind. The Church had gone to glory. Share the glory of God, for God desires a relationship with all and heaven's population to increase more than He desires to pour out wrath. A healthy relationship is centered in love, grace, and truth.

Entering this relationship with God and maintaining it out of crippling fear is not ideal or healthy for the maturation of new believers. Therefore, share grace (Ephesians 2:8–9).

137

Memory Problems

Memory is the scribe of the soul.

—Aristotle

Memory. What comes to mind when you hear the word? Possibly an unforgettable vacation? For some, it is the moment they and their spouse said, "I do." For others, this word could carry a sadder weight as they remember the death of a loved one. For others, when they read the term, they think of the unfortunate reality that they are getting older and that they can never seem to remember what they ate for lunch or what day it is.

I do not think the famous philosopher Aristotle would take offense to either thought process because, in all of these examples, *something* was engraved into your mind or etched onto the heart. In moments of trouble and doubt, there are two words that should wiggle their way to the forefront of your mind: remember and hope.

When we remember what the Lord has done for us, we can be affirmed in our hope of what He has promised He will do. This is a model that transcends history. It was applicable to the Jews, and it is applicable to us today. God often called the Israelites to remember their deliverance from captivity by other nations (Deuteronomy 6:12; Psalm 77:11). In the Body of Christ, the scribe of our soul also reminds us of our deliverance, but rather it is our deliverance from the bondage of sin (Galatians 5:1).

We remember and esteem the finished work of Christ that secured our soul's salvation (Ephesians 2:8–9). In hope, we remember and esteem the fact that Christ is coming back to secure our heavenly salvation (1 Corinthians 15:52–55). Experience. Our past experiences of God's goodness in the midst of trials, coupled with our current state of joy, is bound to illustrate a life defined by hope (Romans 5:1–6).

Remember and Hope

God has given us all spiritual blessings in heavenly places, and He has provided access to a beautiful eternity with Him (Romans 8:18; Ephesians 1:3). There is nothing that we cannot face in light of His graces that is beneath, above, beside, and inside of us (Romans 6:14; 1 Corinthians 12:9). Therefore, set your mind on things above (Colossians 3:1–4). Let your memory serve you well, by the power of the Spirit (Proverbs 10:7; John 14:26).

138

Many Waters Cannot Quench Love

"Set me as a seal upon thine heart, as a seal upon thine arm: for love is strong as death; jealousy is cruel as the grave: the coals thereof are coals of fire, which hath a most vehement flame. Many waters cannot quench love, neither can the floods drown it: if a man would give all the substance of his house for love, it would utterly be contemned."

—Song of Solomon 8:6–7

Love. We, as people, "love" many things. Often, we emphasize the beauty of God's love for us and therefore, our love for Him. Our ministry is also prone to emphasize love for our neighbors and love for "good" things. Nonetheless, something not often addressed in many Christian arenas is romantic love. I say this to the detriment of the Church, our nation, and countries abroad. The Bible talks about it, but the Church does not go beyond the cultural battleground of same-sex marriage and discuss what true, biblical romance is characterized by.

Some might call this an incongruence. I learn more and more every day that as a man engaged to my beautiful soon-to-be bride, Hallie, I need to learn to "love better" every day. We live in a delightful tapestry of give and take, but when reflecting upon myself, I know that unidentified self-interests are often a harmful trip-wire that has me falling, mangled time and time again, landing with my foot in my mouth. Oh, the joys of love. I'd have it no other way!

But I often ask myself, what are the guardrails in biblically maintaining my God-ordained love with Hallie? King Solomon understood a thing or two about the dying art of romance. As biblical narratives suggest, sometimes he got too enamored in the artistry (1 Kings 11:1–4). He pursued what the Bible terms "strange women," and he had a lot of them. It is interesting to note that Solomon knew the warnings from God to the Israelites to not marry these women, for they will "turn your heart after their gods." Despite this warning, Solomon "clave unto these in love," and as a result, the Bible says that "his heart was not perfect with the Lord his God."

We often hear of people giving their heart away to those they love. Interestingly enough, the Hebrew word in 1 Kings 11 for "heart" is *lēḇāḇ*. This word can be defined as "the inner man" or "will," along with other similar synonyms. You see, God expected even Solomon's romance to be postured to Him. As Americans, one's love life is the precarious portion of their heart that we expect no one, not even God, to have access to. But we'd be foolish to assume that God does not already know (Proverbs 21:2). The place where we invest romantically within ourselves is the same place that Christ came to save.

Our soul. Yet so often we displace the two into two different parts of our life. True, biblical romance begins with a true, biblical posture toward God. Luckily, Solomon's shortcomings are not the only example of his life that we are offered. In his biblical work, the Song of Solomon, we are offered an example of a developing (courtship, marriage, and growing relationship) love between the king and his bride. One large thing that a reader will note, whether reading deeply or not, is that language is careful, intentful, and spoken only to build each other up. They valued each other as prized treasures, one to another. The bride spoke these words in Song of Solomon 2:16:

> My beloved is mine, and I am his: he feedeth among the lilies.

Where has culture gone so wrong? Although people pay lip service to "giving their heart away," dating relationships and marriages end so often because both are not "feeling it anymore." You do not just stop feeling like you have a treasure. You have it or you don't. What really happens is that people may stop recognizing the treasure they possess (Proverbs 31:10). Unless God wills it otherwise, this is where romance dies. Truly, when posture is turned from God, one could not possibly esteem a God-given treasure. This does not require a PhD in theology. This is logic.

When the king's bride is ultimately moved to exclaim the famous words, "Many waters cannot quench love," this was in contrast to her depiction of love as "coals of fire." Biblical romance and marriage are designed to be unquenchable, indistinguishable, and maintained by the flood wall of God's Spirit (Mark 10:8–9; Ephesians 5:25). As you live and love, do not compartmentalize your life and love. It all simmers down to the abundance or lack of abundance of godly love in your innermost places. Growing in godliness is to grow in love for all humanity, in this case, especially your romantic interest. Edify them. Build them. Treasure them. Rest assured that many waters cannot quench love.

139

Perspective>Experience

From middle school all the way up to my collegiate track career, I remember the feelings of anticipation and apprehension that preceded the coming Track and Field season. I also remember that the feeling did not dissipate at the arrival of the track season, but rather was amplified prior to every meet. But nothing compares to the feelings of expectation that reside within you until the firing of the starter's pistol, where a sudden vacancy is replaced with feelings of engagement to the adrenaline of competition. I have found no *emotion* to be even remotely similar.

However, that all changed. Halfway through my senior year of college, I was plagued with injury and illness. Now, my attention remained strictly sideline. It was also during this time that I was able to supplement my love for track and field with a volunteer coaching position at a local high school. In this season, there was a drastic shift of perspective. I was able to see things that prior, I could only feel. My experience had to be assessed and transferred to other people who now were where I was, not so long ago.

Perspective. Now I stood trackside and felt the wind of runners instead of the direct wind on my face. Despite this, I still felt so alive. So what am I getting at? I blabbered all about this portion of my life to say that perspective affects experience.

In the Christian walk, we undergo a wide variety of situations. Sometimes, Christians are in the middle of it, and sometimes they are trackside to our spiritual family. In both areas of life, you have something to offer, whether in word or deed. Experience is usually and rightfully attributed to age (Proverbs 7:7). But in the Body of Christ, the paradigm is that earthly age and spiritual age do not always correlate (Hebrews 5:12–14). Therefore, Christians of all ages have something to edify other believers, with the primary responsibility being on seasoned Christians (Galatians 6:1–6; 2 Timothy 2:2).

You can be engaged regardless of position because you stand in Christ. We have fellowship by the Spirit and, as a member of the Body of Christ and children of the Almighty, this makes you a member of the most powerful assembly on earth (2 Corinthians 13:14). Therefore, ensure your words and deeds reflect the words and deeds of the Assembly Head, Jesus Christ. In our creation, He created us unto good works (Ephesians 2:10). In His Word, He instructs us to gracefully give wisdom to those who are without (Colossians 4:5–6).

Know that perspective on a situation will affect your experience, but do not allow an experience to shift your perspective, which ought to remain in Christ Jesus.

140

Grace Greater than Our Sin

Julia H. Johnston (1849–1919) wrote the lyrics to this great hymn along with Daniel B. Towner (1850–1919) arranging the music. The song was published in a hymn book called *Hymns Tried and True*. The song comes from Romans 5:1–2, 18, and 20.

This grace that we sing of here is not just sufficient grace; it is abounding grace as is depicted in 2 Corinthians 9:8 and Ephesians 1:7. Only a few word changes are to be made in this wonderful hymn. We substituted the title of "Lord" where the song refers to Christ as the "Lamb" (a title only given to Christ in reference to Israel's program). There is no question that anyone who believes solely on the Cross work of Christ can be saved (Titus 2:11). The original lyrics suggest a person "may" be saved, allowing room for doubt of a person's salvation. Changing the word to "can" more accurately describes the surety of free salvation available today. Will you receive this grace today (2 Timothy 1:9)?

1. Marvelous grace of our loving Lord, grace that exceeds our sin and our guilt;

   Yonder on Calvary's mount outpoured, there where the blood of the Lord was spilt;
2. Sinned and despair like the sea waves cold, threaten the soul with infinite loss;

Grace that is greater, yes, grace untold, points to the refuge the mighty Cross.

3. Dark is the stain that we cannot hide, what can avail to wash it away?

   Look! There is flowing a crimson tide; Whiter than snow you can be today.

4. Marvelous, infinite, matchless grace, freely bestowed on all who believe;

   All who are longing to see His face, will you this moment His grace receive?

Chorus: Grace, grace, God's grace, grace that will and clean within;

Grace, grace, God's grace, grace that is greater than all our sin.

141

Sleeping on Gold

Have you ever heard of the Treaty of Tordesillas? If you have, you probably know that it is one of the worst land deals of all time between two countries. This treaty also inaugurated the stark cultural differences between Brazil and the rest of South America. In 1494, two years after Christopher Columbus's famous expedition, Portugal and Spain were engaged in a competitive conquest for land and resources in the New World. In this feud, there was a lot of overlap in the land that they claimed.

This dispute caused the two nations, who were the only two in the New World at this time, to take their disagreements on land to a neutral source to mediate a solution. Being two Catholic nations, the pope was their *obvious* geopolitical expert and arbitrator (note my sarcasm). The pope's solution was to slap a line down on the map of the known New World and call it a day. This line is known as the line of demarcation. Little did Portugal know that there was still much to discover in South America and ended up with only the far eastern tip of Brazil. This left the rest of South America, Central America, and any other land in North America protected for Spanish conquest. Both countries abided by this decree despite them both eventually seeing how lopsided it was. In the truest sense, this is an example of someone ignorant of what they have or what could be.

In the same breath, there is a story of an Australian landowner who lived in poverty near Queensland, Australia. He sold his land to prospectors not realizing that this land would turn into a profitable gold mine and could have lifted him from his situation. In studying these stories and the many like them, I wonder to myself. Could the spiritual lives of Christians be hindered by ignorance of their spiritual wealth as well?

Each member of the Body of Christ, literally, has the Spirit of God residing in them, but they neglect or dismiss the blessing that this is (1 Corinthians 6:19–20). The Holy Spirit saves, seals, delivers, intercedes, convicts, encourages, and resides as power in the believer! It is not uncommon for these truths in themselves to be neglected or diminished, but practically? The lives of many Christians will appear void of His inner working.

Furthermore, a Christian's ignorance is not made complete without neglect of the Word. The Holy Bible is not merely a book. It is a sixty-six-book love letter, compiled of God's literal and inspired revelation. Nevertheless, it is utilized as a mere ethics textbook, if that. My grandfather has said on numerous occasions that a verse a day is not going to cut it (Psalm 1:1–6).

Scripture is, among many things, a living Word that is able to coach and train the Christian in righteousness (Hebrews 4:12–13; 2 Timothy 3:16–17). Much like one push-up a day will not prepare an athlete for competition, a quick glance at Scripture will not build the spiritual muscles of the inner man. It requires diligent study and the Holy Spirit's discerning power (1 Timothy 4:7–9).

Do not neglect the wealth of these two mines, waiting to be dug into. Entrench yourselves within the richness of God's divinity. Join yourself with how His Spirit moves and be blessed with the message that the Lord has for you, in His Word (Ephesians 4:22–24). Otherwise, you will be like the fool who does not know just how rich they are. These people have land but do not know it. They have gold but sleep unknowingly on top of it at night.

Live in the wealth of God's grace and in the acknowledgment that you *are* blessed (2 Corinthians 12:9; Ephesians 1:3). Do not leave it as head knowledge but allow it to be lived out as wisdom.

142

It's My Prayer, and I Need It Now!

God's silences are His answers. If we only take as answers those that are visible to our senses, we are in a very elementary condition of grace.

—Oswald Chambers

Instant gratification. This phrase is thrown around a *lot.* I am not going to pretend that many of you readers do not know what this means because, well…we are a bit too acquainted with the term. We know that it means we receive something without having to wait. Even if by chance the definition is not known culturally, the American lifestyle reflects it.

When you go to a "fast" food restaurant, how quickly do you expect to get your food? Fast, right? If you open your pantries and you desperately need a food item, not many Americans look out back at a garden or farm and say, "Shoot, only two more weeks till it's ripe!" Typically, we drive to a store and buy it. Instantly.

Or what about money? Iconically, J. G. Wentworth financial services coined the phrase, "It's my money, and I need it now!" Now if you think that I am suggesting that these expectations are inherently bad, you would be mistaken. Nonetheless, my point is this. Living in this atmosphere, more times than not, will move you to impose cultural standards onto an eternal God. To this I say, you will not get the same results.

Henry David Thoreau once suggested that "Things do not change, we change." To Christianize this quote, I would claim this:

> God does not change, He changes us. (Malachi 3:6; Hebrews 13:8; 2 Timothy 2:21)

As humanity trended downward to this state of instant gratification and broken patience, God never changed. He remained and remains perfectly patient (Psalm 86:15).

Being perfectly patient also means that He will patiently wait to answer prayers when they accord with His will. However, do not mistake this as Him not giving an answer. Waiting is a verb and conscious response (Ephesians 6:18). Maybe, when we pray a righteous prayer and we hear silence, we should allow the Spirit to interpret this in a way we can understand—"Not yet" (1 John 5:14–15).

Truly, these types of responses are a trial of faith, but even more than that, they are a workout for spiritual maturity (Romans 5:3–5; Colossians 1:27–28). It could be taking you from what Chambers calls an "elementary condition of grace" to a "lifestyle of grace" (2 Corinthians 9:8–15; 12:9).

143

Don't Judge Those Cows!

I was driving back from work a while ago on the same roads I always drive, at the same time I usually drive them, and looking at the same scenery I always see. But this time, I noted that in this beautiful field on the right-hand side of my car, there were cows. I had never noticed this group of cattle before nor had I noticed how seemingly absurd the thoughts and actions of a cow could be. There was a group of cattle with their heads through the barbed wire fence that contained them, eating the grass positioned at the side of the road.

I have heard of cows doing this and it always has me baffled. However, I had never seen a whole group of them doing this before! It was then that I attempted to think like a cow. For the rest of the drive, I wondered what made that grass so appealing that all the cattle felt the urge to ignore the large acreage of grass offered to them for that little bit of tasty delicacy.

Then, in an odd form of spiritual epiphany, I thought, *I am a cow*. No, I do not say "Moo," and I do not eat that much… Well, maybe I do overindulge sometimes, but that is beside the point. I am such a spiritual cow. God has abundantly blessed me and provided me with everything needed for spiritual sustenance, yet there are moments when I find myself yearning for the grass on the other side of the fence (Romans 7:15).

That being the things of the world, my own flesh, and vain wisdom of men. I felt the Holy Spirit begging this question deep within my soul: *How can you judge those cows?* This experience was a call back to a strict diet and caloric regimen consisting only of God's Word and the seasonings of edification by His Church (Ephesians 4:29; 2 Timothy 3:16; 1 Thessalonians 5:11).

This brings me to my closing remarks. What in your life are you sticking your head through the fence for? Through a quick or tasking introspection, I believe all believers can easily find their shortcomings. To them, I plead for you not to dwell on them (Romans 8:1)! Simply pull yourself to the pasture of God's Word and grow in that which He has given to you. He has purchased you with a mighty cost and that which He has purchased for so much, He would not allow you to starve (1 Corinthians 6:20).

So grab a Bible and eat up! That which is on the other side of the fence is not for you!

144

Soul Friend

I would rather walk with a friend in the
dark, than alone in the light.

—Helen Keller

In the Church, there is often an astonishing value imposed on community, fellowship, and the like. Rightfully so, may I add. But when do we ever break from the "bigger picture" and focus on the element that makes God's ideal image of community and the Church so grand? Here, I am referring to friends.

Everybody *likes* having friends, but what of the *love* for a friend? In this specific context, I am referring to good friends. This is not a message discussing what makes a good or bad friend but simply the godly ideal of cherishing one another.

In his work *Spiritual Direction*, author Henri Nouwen refers to spiritual companions as "soul friends." This is a work that I have read recently, and a phrase that at first had me conflicted but grew on me. Reason being, good friendships and connections go beyond physical enrichment. This is often how it is manifested, but Christians are to grow inside (spirit, meditation of the Word), out (fruits of the Spirit). No longer do we have to grow outside (messages from the world), in (corruption of the heart). Good friendships edify the inner man and speak those things that uplift (1 Thessalonians 5:11–13)!

Giving real perspective, this is why I believe my relationship with my fiancée has been so solid. Our friendship was molded firstly around the things that God loves: His Word and His creation. We bonded first off, in middle school through a Christian club we found called Children of Light (Ephesians 5:8). My dear Hallie became my "soul friend" before she doubled her role as my "soul mate."

In friendship, strive to be more than an acquaintance masquerading behind the title of friend. Let's do what friends are called to do and build each other up (Romans 14:19).

145

Finish the Story

It is not an uncommon occurrence among many people to be telling a story, and someone feels at liberty to interrupt and interject, only to find out that they did not hear the full story! Sometimes, that interrupter might just be you. It is okay to admit! Most people do this at some point in their life, but when you find yourself in this situation—make it right and *finish* the story.

As Christians, this ignorance of the full story plagues the way that we minister to others. We need to tell the whole story because Jesus completed the whole story. Jesus Christ came as a babe, lived a sinless life, was wrongly accused, and was killed on one of the most brutal torture devices known to history—the Roman Cross (Luke 23:33). And yearly on Good Friday, we share this brutal story of Christ's death as good—I mean, great news!

It may seem like as Christians, we live in a paradox by calling the death of our God good, but it was on the Cross that He was delivered for our offenses. But in ministering, I so often hear people talking about the death of Christ for our sins but disregard His resurrection on the third day. Finish the story. Shortchanging your listener is comparable to a parent who tells an inspiring bedtime story about a grand hero but right at the climax says, "The end."

No! No! No! Finish the story! Christ was delivered for our offenses *and* raised again for our justification (Romans 4:25). There is no power in a dead God. Our God is alive (Luke 24:6–7)! Christians divide this grand story of redemption into over a month of Lent and then a seven-day Holy Week of anticipation. But we are not anticipating His death and we are not anticipating His resurrection. It is a done deal. As believers, we are daily participants in this *finished* work (Romans 6; Romans 10:9–13).

So finish the story. Because *Good Friday* is not good news without *Resurrection Sunday.*

146

Christ Arose!

Robert Lowry (1826–1899) was a Philadelphia Baptist preacher and hymn writer. In 1874, he wrote the popular hymn "Christ Arose!" He also arranged the tune. While having devotions one evening, he was impressed with the events associated with Christ's resurrection when he read Luke 24:6–7.

We read in 1 Corinthians 15:4, 13–14, that our hope lies in the resurrection of Jesus Christ. And so we love to sing about it every chance we get. While this song does not necessarily address doctrine unique to this dispensation of grace, it does a great job of reminding us of and rejoicing in Christ's death, burial, and resurrection without placing believers under wrong teachings from Jesus's earthly ministry to Israel.

1. Low in the grave He lay, Jesus my Savior;
   Waiting the coming day; Jesus my Lord!
2. Vainly they watched His bed, Jesus my Savior;
   Vainly they sealed the dead; Jesus my Lord!
3. Death cannot keep his prey, Jesus my Savior;
   He tore the bars away; Jesus my Lord!

Chorus:

Up from the grave, He arose! With mighty triumph o'er His foes.

He arose a victor from the dark domain, and He lives forever with the saints to reign!

He arose! He arose! Hallelujah! Christ arose!

(Psalm 104:31–35.)

147

Stream of Christ

This is the Lord's doing; it is marvelous in our eyes (Psalm 118:23)
Though I have all spiritual blessings, they
appear to multiply (Ephesians 1:3)
No longer constrained by the grip of mortal flesh (Romans 8:6)
In this life and continuum, I have unutterable
rest (2 Thessalonians 3:16)
No height. What depth? I disregard all
monstrosities (Romans 8:39)!
They have no bearing as my anchor holds in Thee (Hebrews 6:19)!
My God, you are unfailing love; an all-consuming light (1 John 4:8)
I am a tree nurtured by the stream of Jesus Christ (Psalm 1:3)
Selah.

148

Does Anybody Have a Testimony?

If the focus of our testimony is our changed life, we as well as our hearers are bound to be disappointed. Focus instead on Jesus and His grace.

—Michael S. Horton

"Does anybody have a testimony?!" This line used to be a staple inquiry from the pulpit of small to medium-sized church settings across America. Following, there may be a number of church members recollecting just how terrible they used to be ending in or similar to "But thank God, He saved me."

When I was younger, there were times I would drown these moments out. As I got older, truthfully, I could not help but notice an emphasis with many on self, and affirmation of this truth every time I heard the word *I*. Upon noticing that I was not in an optometrist's office, this at times would be very frustrating. Upon maturity, this is my response.

Jesus Christ, who was before time, sustainer of eternity, and purchaser of our salvation, should be the subject of our testimony. Not merely a period and much more than a comma as we gloat about our human depravity and sinfulness. In everything a Christian does, we should be the reflection of His grace, His mercy, His truth, His love, and His righteousness. Our testimony is really not about us. It is not cheap entertainment as Christians gathered, and Christ's testimony of Himself (the Gospel), was not cheap. What is often shared as an icebreaker in greeting is what ripped our eternal soul from hell's grasp.

But if it is not what we think it is, then what is it? I will answer my own question and offer an example of how to tell your testimony biblically. In 1 Timothy 1:12–17, the apostle Paul writes the following:

> And I thank Christ Jesus our Lord, who hath enabled me, for that he counted me faithful, putting me into the ministry;
>
> Who was before a blasphemer, and a persecutor, and injurious: but I obtained mercy, because I did it ignorantly in unbelief.
>
> And the grace of our Lord was exceeding abundant with faith and love which is in Christ Jesus.
>
> This is a faithful saying, and worthy of all acceptation, that Christ Jesus came into the world to save sinners; of whom I am chief.
>
> Howbeit for this cause I obtained mercy, that in me first Jesus Christ might shew forth all longsuffering, for a pattern to them which should hereafter believe on him to life everlasting.
>
> Now unto the King eternal, immortal, invisible, the only wise God, be honour and glory for ever and ever. Amen.

Check the content. He quilts together words such as: mercy, grace, faith, love, save, longsuffering (patience), life, eternal, immortal, invisible, wise, honor, and glory. These are all attributes and actions of God. He is the subject. There was only one line where Paul refers to his depravity, but it is not apart from the saving grace of Jesus Christ. As Christians, let us move away from self. Believe me, you will get tired of it. Let us practice flipping the center of our faith from self to Christ. Just as Paul opened his testimony with, "And I thank Christ Jesus our Lord…," let it be so in our testimony.

> Come and hear, all ye that fear God, and I will declare what he hath done for my soul.
>
> I cried unto him with my mouth, and he was extolled with my tongue.
>
> If I regard iniquity in my heart, the Lord will not hear me:
>
> But verily God hath heard me; he hath attended to the voice of my prayer.
>
> Blessed be God, which hath not turned away my prayer, nor his mercy from me. (Psalm 66:16–20)

149

To God Be the Glory

The writer of this beloved hymn hardly needs an introduction. Fanny Crosby, whose actual name was Frances Jane van Alstyne, was born on March 24, 1820, and wrote more than eight thousand hymns. She lived a fascinating ninety-four years of life, well worth reading about.

But we are focusing on one hymn today, "To God Be the Glory." This hymn was written around 1872, with the tune composed by William Howard Doane (1832–1915). Doane was a choir director and a successful wood-making machinery inventor. Together, they composed this hymn, which was more popular in Europe than in America at that time.

This song of praise glorifies our redemption and pardon of sin, freely received through the blood of Christ. The last phrase of the first verse originally mentioned God opening "the life-gate that all may go in." This is a reference to Matthew 7:14, when Jesus taught about the kingdom gospel. Here we describe a future works-based salvation as part of a covenant with the nation of Israel. We replaced the original line with a true statement for today's dispensation in the spirit of Romans 5:8:

> But God commendeth His love toward us, in that, while we were yet sinners, Christ died for us.

Only Christ could die for us; no other man could (Ephesians 1:22)!

1. To God be the glory, great things He hath done,
   Commendeth His love that He spared not His Son,
   Who yielded His life an atonement for sin,
   And offered salvation that's free to all men.
2. O perfect redemption, the purchase of blood,
   To every believer the promise of God;
   The vilest offender who truly believes,
   That moment from Jesus a pardon receives.

Chorus:

Praise the Lord! Let the earth hear His voice.
Praise the Lord! Praise the Lord! Let the earth hear His voice!
Praise the Lord! Praise the Lord! Let the people rejoice.
O come to the Father through Jesus the Son,
And give Him the glory, great things He hath done.

150

A Big, Big Wall

Constantinople, now known as Istanbul, Turkey, held a lot of political weight in the ancient world. The city acted as a continental gateway, sitting at the geographical crux of Europe and Asia. Its fall was to the infamous Ottoman Empire, but its origin dates all the way back to the thirteenth century BC. It was a magnificent place.

Throughout its history, it boasted incredible walls that offered state-of-the-art defense. The greatest, however, were those built by the Roman emperor Theodosius II. After a massive defeat that resulted in a large number of deaths, he knew something had to be done. So in the fourth century BC, this double set of walls was constructed.

These walls stood century after century and withstood siege after siege. *But* something changed. It did not change drastically, but it did change and ultimately led to Constantinople's demise. With the increasing usage of gunpowder and the invention of the cannon, the defensive effectiveness of walls got lower and lower. Meanwhile, cannons got bigger, and invaders were able to load them faster. Nonetheless, these innovations were not overnight marvels. But as the weapons changed, the defense remained the same.

The wiles of the devil are much like Constantinople's invaders. They do not stay the same; they constantly attempt to attack the integrity of God's Word and, therefore, the integrity of Christians. Do not become stagnant defenders. Build your defense and fight back!

We build our defense first by equipping the armor of God. It is in His armor that we make our stand (Ephesians 6:10). Next, you identify who your enemy is, and no, it is not that pretentious person that comes to mind; it is the evil forces led by Satan himself (Ephesians 6:11). Only then can you take a stand (Ephesians 6:12).

This armor consists of loins girt in truth and a heart covered in the breastplate of righteousness. Your feet must be swift, shod with the preparation of the gospel of peace. A shield is only useful when it is maintained and repaired. Do not allow your shield, your faith, to be dented. For your defensive arsenal, if this factor is compromised, then you may fall in your faith, just as the Byzantines fell to the Ottoman Empire. Be alert; the Devil is crafty. He is renovating cannons to compromise your shielding, but do not let him get close enough. Shortly, we will view our offensive!

The helmet of salvation completes an armor defined with the very word *peace* (Ephesians 6:13–17; Philippians 4:6–7). We can be confident that we will hold, unwavering, as we abide in Christ, despite the great offensive (Hebrews 6:19).

But what is *our* offense? It is a sword! The sword of truth, God's very word! It holds a dual purpose. It may thwart the blow of an attack but is also a very intimate weapon of attack itself. Our weapon is not a bow and arrow to strike invaders from afar; God calls us to be intimate and fight face to face, confident that Christ goes before us!

The enemy is crafty indeed. But we can take presumptive action and stand. Do you believe this? Is your shield strong and your sword raised? If so, let us watch and be ready for sieges!

151

You Are on the Fastest Route

Modern technology is amazing. We have refrigerators that can play movies, speakers that can keep better conversations than your friends, and up-to-the-second travel updates. It is music to my ears to hear my Google Assistant say, "You are on the fastest route to your destination."

But it isn't always this way, and spoiler alert—I am not just referring to a navigation app. As people, we are all on the way to one of two places. I do not want to sugarcoat this truth. It is heaven or hell. Whether you are a believer or not, dark forces attempt to control the flow of traffic (Ephesians 6:11–12). For the non-believer, these forces want to keep the spiritual interstate southbound clear for you to fly 120 miles per hour to hell. For the believer, he will congest traffic and use slow-downs to make you a slow and ineffective Christian (1 Peter 5:8–9).

But catch this: the biggest, most accessible roads are not always the fastest or smoothest. Still, a lot of people travel them. For the nonbeliever, God has opened a detour that truly is the only way you will ever make it to a heavenly destination (Romans 10:9–10; 1 Corinthians 15:3–4). To the believer, you may be going northbound, but don't get content with the congestion of the interstate and loud music during the stops (1 Corinthians 2:9). This metaphor reflects a passive faith. Be proactive and take the better route (2 Corinthians

5:7)! Avoid the slowdowns and lead your fellow life-drivers (1 Corinthians 2:5)!

This is the way of holiness and righteousness, paved by the blood of Jesus and signed by His resurrection (Galatians 3:13; 1 Corinthians 3). Now I understand, you may be heading northbound, but God offers a way of power, love, and a sound mind as you travel (2 Timothy 1:7). So why settle?

152

You Want a Bloodless Gospel Story?

Inspired by 1 Corinthians 15…

You want a bloodless Gospel story?
Well, I cannot oblige.
It was by the death of Christ,
That freedom was applied.

Hung Him up and suffered high,
For the cost of man, I tell you why.
Laid down below in borrowed tomb.
Yet rose again with death consumed.

You want a bloodless Gospel story?
Well, my God cannot oblige.
It was by the death of His Son,
That freedom was applied.

This was planned, from ages past.
Though we fell, His love steadfast.
Ascending high, sending Spirit low.
Equipping saints for all to go!

You want a bloodless Gospel story?
Well, the Trinity cannot oblige.
It was by the death of One of Them,
That freedom was applied.

153

Safe and Sound

It seems the word of the year has become *safe*. The irony is that here on earth, nothing is 100 percent safe. The hymn we're discussing today assures us of sure safety, being in Christ. The chorus of this song exclaims:

> I've anchored my soul in the haven of rest.
> I'll sail the wide seas no more.
> The tempest may sweep o'er the wild, stormy deep:
> In Jesus I'm safe ever more.

We do not have exemptions from storms in this life. As the Word says in Job 5:7, "Yet man is born unto trouble, as the sparks fly upward." As also affirmed in Titus 2:13, we who are in the Body of Christ have a blessed hope:

> Looking for that blessed hope, and glorious appearing of the great God, and our Savior Jesus Christ.

Today's hymn was written by Henry L. Gilmour (1836–1920), who came to the USA from Ireland, so he knew a little about a ship in stormy water. The music was composed by George D. Moore (1800–1900), an evangelist from Pennsylvania. The song was written in 1890. As you sing this hymn, keep in remembrance Philippians 4:7 as it states,

> And the peace of God, which passeth all understanding, shall keep your hearts and minds through Christ Jesus.

The Haven of Rest

1. My soul in sad exile was out on life's sea, so burdened with sin and distressed,
   Till I heard a sweet voice saying, "Make Me your choice," and I entered the haven of rest.
2. I yielded myself to His tender embrace, and faith taking hold of the Word,
   My fetters fell off, and I anchored my soul. The haven of rest is my Lord.
3. The song of my soul, since the Lord made me whole, has been the old story so blest,
   Of Jesus, who'll save whosoever will have a home in the haven of rest.
4. O come to the Savior. He patiently waits to save by His power divine.
   Come, anchor your soul in the haven of rest, and say, "My Beloved is mine."

Chorus:
I've anchored my soul in the haven of rest.
I'll sail the wide seas no more.
The tempest may sweep o'er the wild, stormy deep: In Jesus I'm safe evermore.

(Psalm 104:31–35.)

154

My Response to Social Issues

Look around, and ask, "What topics are trending right now?" Actually, you do not even have to look. Just listen. What words are being pumped into your eardrums? Abortion, LGBTQ+, insurrection, war, immigration, voting, etc. I was recently asked why I don't address topics such as abortion and immigration. The angle in which this question was asked made me curious about the intentions behind the question. So here I am to address it.

My goal is to point you to the answer already written and published by the direction of the Holy Spirit. The news that you hear now is merely biased, secondary commentary. They do not have an answer. Christians are not called to answer the world in response to the news station; rather, they are called to answer the world in response to the inerrant Word of God.

If you want my answer on abortion, here it is:

> Thou shalt not kill. (Exodus 20:13)

Typically, the response is, "But what about ___ [insert situation]," or "Science says that life begins at ___ [insert irrelevant tidbit]." Although I could shower you with Scripture that indicates abortion is wrong and provide a bar of grace to help scrub, that one verse shows what God desires. God desires life.

Nonetheless, I am not writing to specifically address abortion or any of these topics. I am here to redirect you. Respond to Scripture, not to the world. As a minister, my job is to point you to Scripture that you may be built up. In Acts 20:28, Paul proclaims regarding ministry,

> Take heed therefore unto yourselves, and to all the flock, over the which the Holy Ghost hath made you overseers, to feed the church of God, which he hath purchased with his own blood.

Everything that a Christian studies in Scripture builds what "educated" people call your "theology" and what the Bible calls the "renewing of your mind" (Romans 12:1–2). When your mind is renewed by the Word and Spirit of God, Scripture says that you will be able to "prove what is that good, and acceptable, and perfect, will of God."

You want to know if abortion is good? Allow God to renew your mind through His Word and find out. We here at Enriching Grace will travel alongside you, living out our mission statement with you:

> To enrich and edify, in Jesus's name.

Oh, and one more thing. Right after Paul teaches about ministry in Acts 20:28, he writes this:

> For I know this, that after my departing shall grievous wolves enter in among you, not sparing the flock.
>
> Also of your own selves shall men arise, speaking perverse things, to draw away disciples after them. (Acts 20:29–30)

God is not the only one warring for your attention, because satanic opposition follows suit. Nonetheless, it cannot hold a flame to the might of God's inspired Word. Therefore, I will pray and commission you, the reader, with the following words of Paul to stand ready against such opposition:

> And now, brethren, I commend you to God, and to the word of his grace, which is able to build you up, and to give you an inheritance among all them which are sanctified. (Acts 20:32)

155

Be a Traveler, Not a Tourist

The traveler sees what he sees. The tourist
sees what he has come to see.

—G. K. Chesterton

Our life is but a splinter on a tree of time that never ceases to grow. As a believer, one should come early to the realization that this world is not our home. Therefore, if this world is not our home, then it would be much easier to relax our grip on possessions that are not ours to keep (Matthew 6:20)! Relationships would be richer! Ministry would be simpler! And love might just be fuller, as a traveler sees things that are previously unseen in their lives and their normal rhythms.

In contrast, a tourist comes for the attractions. If you travel to New York City, of course, you see the Statue of Liberty, the Empire State Building, and wild individuals on many city sidewalks. Now take this traveling mindset and apply it to your Christian walk. From the moment you believe, your residency address is in heaven, and you are simply a journeyer through this world.

As the famed Charles Dickens writes in *A Christmas Carol,* in reflection on the Christmas season, let us think of others "as if they really were fellow passengers to the grave, and not another race of creatures bound on other journeys."

It is in the realization that the craziness of the world is not our eternal lodging that we have hope. The apostle Paul defends this truth in writing,

> Therefore we are always confident, knowing that, whilst we are at home in the body, we are absent from the Lord:
>
> (For we walk by faith, not by sight:)
>
> We are confident, I say, and willing rather to be absent from the body, and to be present with the Lord.
>
> Wherefore we labour, that, whether present or absent, we may be accepted of him. (2 Corinthians 5:6–9)

Whether we are presently away from home or nearing it, our standing is in Christ, and therefore, we can be confident and have hope that the future, ultimately, will be better. When walking by sight, there is only so much we can see. Oh, but in faith, our confidence is overwhelming, and our hope is steadfast. So take heart! Travel together and travel light, for all shall be unpacked (Psalm 34:3; Philippians 3:20–21). Attractions here pale in comparison to that which shall be revealed (1 Corinthians 2:9).

156

The Perfect Christian

Christians are always seeking to "be better." The proof is in the pudding. The contemporary Christian book market is flooded, and frankly, oversaturated, with "Christian" self-help books. If you don't believe me, allow me to name a few of the best-selling Christian books this week according to Audible, an app many enjoy:

- *Balance: Positioning Yourself to Do All Things Well*
- *Winning the War in Your Mind: Change Your Thinking, Change Your Life*
- *Undistracted: Capture Your Purpose. Rediscover Your Joy.*

This list is not exhaustive. These are just three of the best sellers. Looking at the market, it makes me wonder just how many Christians would consider themselves "complete." In fact, it makes me wonder… Do you? Would it be likened to a curse word to even suggest it? The apostle Paul did not think so. In fact, he offers a very blunt answer to the curious question:

> Ye are complete in him, which is the head of all principality and power.

Saying this, allow me to be careful of being overly critical. Nonetheless, it would appear that many Christian authors capitalize on everyone's fear of falling short. But the truth is, we did fall short, but Christ rose high (Romans 3:23; 1 Corinthians 15:3–4). There is no money in a complete person; therefore, many writings sell the idea of never-ending renovations.

This fear can be alleviated in knowing that being complete does not mean that you do not sin, but rather you are blameless from the sin. Read Paul's explanation of being complete:

> In whom also ye are circumcised with the circumcision made without hands, in putting off the body of the sins of the flesh by the circumcision of Christ:
>
> Buried with him in baptism, wherein also ye are risen with him through the faith of the operation of God, who hath raised him from the dead.
>
> And you, being dead in your sins and the uncircumcision of your flesh, hath he quickened together with him, having forgiven you all trespasses;
>
> Blotting out the handwriting of ordinances that was against us, which was contrary to us, and took it out of the way, nailing it to his cross;
>
> And having spoiled principalities and powers, he made a shew of them openly, triumphing over them in it. (Colossians 2:11–15)

Salvation really means that you are saved. You are not partly saved. Christ's work on the Cross and His resurrection mean that such sins are blotted out. They are: zilch, gonzo, and done. You are justified, sanctified, and now living for your reward in heaven, received when you are glorified (1 Corinthians 3). Yes, there are areas in life that need to be addressed. But no number of things you do can affect your standing provided by what Christ did.

You are complete. Therefore, live completely free of fear in the light of God's grace (2 Timothy 1:7)! You really are a perfect Christian!

157

The Dismal World That Jesus Overcame

For whatsoever is born of God overcometh the world: and this is the victory that overcometh the world, even our faith. Who is he that overcometh the world, but he that believeth that Jesus is the Son of God?

—1 John 5:4–5

Right now, the world looks pretty dismal. The world is obviously overcoming many people. Turn on the news. Look out the window. Call your loved ones and ask, "How are you?" What will their answer be? At the moment, even in our "high" moments, the culture will not allow flight without turbulence. At the tip of our fingers, we are alerted of every possible tragedy occurring globally. The world is composed of many evil strongholds.

But (which can be such a beautiful word) in the mere shadow of Christ's victory, God shakes them to rubble (1 Corinthians 15:57). Our salvation identifies us with Christ, who suffered and paid the ultimate price (1 Corinthians 12:27). But (there's that beautiful word again) he was victorious!

Jesus Christ overcame the world and all its evil and filth, and it is by this victory that our faith stands, our comfort lies, and tragedy has no ultimate jurisdiction over the soul of the believer (1 John 5:19; Romans 5:8). King David writes that "The Lord is nigh unto them that are of a broken heart; and saveth such as be of a contrite spirit" (Psalm 34:18). David lived before the indwelling of the Holy Spirit. We, who live now, have a unique opportunity and may experience comfort intimately (2 Corinthians 1:3–4)! No nearer can the Lord be than establishing a temple in you and graciously allowing His Holy Spirit to live there (1 Corinthians 3:16; 6:19).

In this position, we can have hope. We can be consoled when life sucker punches our gut, because the problems of life cannot overcome our Head, Jesus Christ (Colossians 1:18). Cling to God and hold firm as the world goes crazy (Romans 5:1; 12:9). Peace He brings, and peace He leaves with you (John 14:27).

> Yesterday is history, tomorrow is a mystery, today is a gift of God, which is why we call it the present. (Bill Keane)

158

Blessed Assurance

We are going to explore another wonderful Fanny Crosby (1820–1915) hymn written in 1873 with composer Phoebe Knapp (1839–1908), who was one of the most widely known women of the 19th century. This hymn, "Blessed Assurance," was so loved by Fanny Crosby that the first verse is inscribed on her headstone.

The Scriptures teach us that we can know with absolute confidence, or assurance if you will, of our salvation (2 Timothy 1:12). Scripture tells us, "For which cause I also suffer these things: Nevertheless I am not ashamed: For I know whom I have believed, and am persuaded that He is able to keep that which I have committed unto Him against that day."

We did not need to change any of the lyrics for this popular hymn. However, the second verse has been omitted, for it refers to the fulfillment of Israel's prophetic program in John 1:51. In this dispensation, we can sing of assurance of salvation because we know we are sealed by the Spirit (2 Corinthians 1:22; Ephesians 1:13).

The end of the first verse is a reference to Titus 3:5–7 and Galatians 4:1–7.

1. Blessed assurance, Jesus is mine! O, what a foretaste of glory divine!

Heir of salvation, purchase of God, born of His Spirit, washed in His blood.

2. Perfect submission, all is at rest, I in my Savior am happy and blest;

   Watching and waiting, looking above, filled with His goodness, lost in His love.

Chorus:

This is my story, this is my song, praising
my Savior all the day long;
This is my story, this is my song, praising
my Savior all the day long!

Sing as unto the Lord (Psalm 104:31–35).

159

Worry from the Pulpit

Sometimes, pastors get asked questions like, "Is it okay to preach on something that you haven't quite gotten over yourself?" I used to think the same as the inquisitor. But now, in a position where people may sometimes seek my counsel, I think this: The qualifications of an overseer are quite specific (1 Timothy 3). Indeed, a pastor must remain above reproach. Nonetheless, some topics need to be addressed that few have overcome. Specifically, I mean the topic of worry.

We worry about this, and we worry about that. Brothers and sisters, we can encourage others in the midst of worry because we are not their solution. Present hope according to the Scriptures. So "Is it okay to preach on something that you haven't quite gotten over yourself?" In this case, yes! Why? Because you preach the Scripture, rightly divided, Christ glorified and not yourself. In fact, Paul states to the Corinthian church that he preaches "Christ Jesus the Lord" and therefore himself, their servant, for "Jesus' sake" (2 Corinthians 4:5–7).

It should be no surprise that some of the most popular Scriptures memorized are about worry. Here are two examples:

> Be careful for nothing; but in everything by prayer and supplication with thanksgiving let

> your requests be made known unto God. And the peace of God, which passeth all understanding, shall keep your hearts and minds through Christ Jesus. (Philippians 4:6–7)

Or

> Casting all your care upon Him; for He careth for you. (1 Peter 5:7)

Notice how in both of these verses, we are to take our worries to God. Have you ever critically thought about why we take our worries to God? Well, it should also not come as a surprise that God wants to do something with your worry because He cares for you. He wants and will replace it with peace because Christ's sacrifice made you and me at peace with Him (Romans 5:1–11).

So as I pardon your annoyance with me for asking once more, "Is it okay to preach on something that you haven't quite gotten over yourself?" I'll leave it as a maybe. Sometimes, they might just be preaching hope to themselves.

160

Wildfires and Life

Many agree that for humans, wildfires are disastrous. The immediate effect of these natural phenomena can be property loss, health complications, and Lord forbid, death.

I acknowledge the tragic reality of wildfires first because, as many ecologists will acknowledge, wildfires also can find themselves being vital to the health of certain biomes. It seems contrary to logic (e.g., how wildfires affect us); however, wildfires can spark new true growth by causing seeds to spring forth from cones. Nutrients trapped on forest floors are also released and assisted by ash, and natural diversity is fortified. Fires are necessary in healthy forests.

So what does this have to do with us?

Well, I did not mention that it takes nearly thirty to forty years for most trees to be restored to their original glory.

The Bible ensures believers that trials are going to come (John 16:33). Our faith is going to tried. Nevertheless, we know that God uses trials, hard times, and struggles for His glory and to better us (Romans 8:28). Christ's power is magnified when we are in a state of graceful humility (2 Corinthians 12:1–9). Know this though: struggles may not instantly mature you in Christ. Maturation and experience come with time (1 Corinthians 3:1–3)! Like a forest goes through the process of succession, beginning from ash until filled with large, healthy trees, so goes the believer who studies and grows in the faith, unshaken by the madness of the world around.

And remember, the wildfires around you are not fiercer than the God who overcame the world (Ephesians 6:10).

161

This Is My Father's World

We are constantly reminded of the violence, tragedy, and ugliness in today's world, but we can still rejoice in the beauty of nature and give praise to God for all the beauty of His world that our five senses can freely enjoy.

Maltbie D. Babcock (1858–1901) wrote "This Is My Father's World," though the exact year it was penned is unknown. Shortly after his death at age 42, his wife Katherine published it. It was set to music in 1915 by Franklin L. Shepphard (1852–1930), a close friend of Babcock.

We only sing three verses, and for some reason, the last verse changed in hymn books. The original lyrics sang:

> This is my Father's world: Why should my heart
> be sad?
> The Lord is King: Let the heavens ring!
> God reigns: Let the earth be glad.

Much of it refers to Jacob's exclamation, "The Lord is in this place" (Genesis 28:16) and the still small voice in 1 Kings 19:12. The final stanza paraphrases Psalm 96:10–11 and is summed up in Psalm 24:1–10.

Verse 1: This is my Father's world, and to my list'ning ears,

all nature sings, and round me rings the music of the spheres.

This is my Father's world. I rest me in the thought

of rocks and trees, of skies and seas—His hand the wonders wrought.

Verse 2: This is my Father's world. The birds their carols raise.

The morning light, the lily white declare their Maker's praise.

This is my Father's world. He shines in all that's fair.

In the rustling grass, I hear Him pass; He speaks to me ev'rywhere.

Verse 3: This is my Father's world. O let me ne'er forget

that tho' the wrong seems oft so strong, God is the Ruler yet.

This is my Father's world. The battle is not done;

Jesus, who died, shall be satisfied, and earth and heav'n be one.

Selah (Psalm 104:31–35).

162

Nonetheless

Over-spiritualization is a thing. A thing that happens way more than it should. It is always a danger that looms when we read the Holy Bible.

One may over-spiritualize in big things (e.g., insisting that child sacrifice should be done because of God's interaction with Abraham and Isaac) or in little things (e.g., insisting that because we can do all things through Christ who gives us strength, God ordained a victory for your sports championship). Application matters.

If I am honest, my urge to want to over-spiritualize comes when I am reading, primarily the Old Testament, and I see miraculous things happen such as with Elijah and the widow's son (1 Kings 17:17–24) or Elisha and Naaman (2 Kings 5). I read these stories and I think to myself, "I want that for my family and me. Why does sickness fail to discriminate? Where do I fit into these stories of great healing?"

But the truth is—I don't. You don't. We don't. Nonetheless, there is Someone who does: God. We don't fit into these great narratives. Nonetheless, God does. We worship the same God who healed these people in amazing ways. Even more amazingly, He went so much further than healing our physical ailments. God sent His Son, Jesus Christ, to come and save our spiritual ailment that led no other place than eternal death and separation from Him (1 Corinthians 15:3–4; Titus 3:5).

He did not make sickness obsolete, but Jesus Christ made sickness ultimately irrelevant because its end is not our end. It has no bearing. It is by this truth that when Paul begged God for relief from his ailment, God responded, "My grace is sufficient for thee," and therefore God's strength was made perfect in weakness (2 Corinthians 12:9).

We worship the same God on a new day (Psalm 104:33–34). In sickness, He may heal, or He may not. Nonetheless, His grace is always sufficient for thee.

Take heart, be of good cheer. Our God, our Christ, has overcome the world (John 16:33).

163

Weed Eating

Mowing is a reality of life in the summer months for many. You mow one Saturday, and then give it a week or two, and your yard has returned to its original disheveled state, begging to be trodden again with a mower.

I know you know what I am talking about. Sometimes, mowing goes smoothly. Other times, it is frustrating to no end.

Recently, while mowing my new home's yard, I had one of these experiences. I had finished mowing without much complication, but then, I ran upon a group of strings lying coiled on the ground.

In my laziness, I decided not to pick up the string but rather to trim as close to it as I could. I got close. But that wasn't close enough. Then I got closer. I still wasn't close enough. And then my Weed Eater ground to a halt.

Before I could realize what happened, I had wound up all the strings around the head of my Weed Eater and locked it up. I knew what I should have done. Yet I ignored it. Now I was caught.

Sin works in the same way. As humans, we like to get as close to sin as possible while still staying clean. Nonetheless, the very mindset is what begins to wind the coil. Like my laziness, our flesh moves us to avoid stopping a sinful tirade, but as believers in the Body of Christ, we are strengthened by the might of the Holy Spirit to walk according to the Scriptures.

This strengthening begins from the moment of our redemption—our regeneration. We acknowledge that there is no condemnation in Christ Jesus (Romans 8:1–2). Now, we walk by the Spirit, not by the flesh. God has made us aware of the dangers of such "harmless strings" and has called us to efficiency—to holiness in His Son, Jesus Christ (2 Corinthians 7:1).

Our Spirit is new and strong and does not consist of fear (2 Corinthians 5:17; 2 Timothy 1:7). Therefore, walk in the Spirit of newness! Put on the new man and put off the old man (Ephesians 4:22–25). The string of sin and flesh looms, but it could never be nearer than the Holy Spirit who resides in you.

164

That's a Good Cup of Joe

As of 2020, seven out of ten Americans drink coffee every week, with 62 percent of Americans drinking it daily. The average American coffee consumer drinks three cups a day. Coffee really is a phenomenon. There are fast-food chains to support the habit, maintain preferences in style, and countless ways to serve it.

Though many like an espresso concoction or a slow-drip cup of joe, I prefer mine from a French press. With a French press, you can control the flavor in a timely manner and in an easily portable carafe. However, my reasoning for introducing this method is not necessarily to teach you a new method of brewing but rather a new method of perspective.

I particularly like the French press because its method centers around the "press." If you have never noticed, let me enlighten you. Good things happen when pressed. Diamonds are made, money is fabricated, and excellent, strong coffee is acquired. The apostle Paul understood this.

Read what pressure has done for him. He writes:

> We are troubled on every side, yet not distressed;
> we are perplexed, but not in despair;
> Persecuted, but not forsaken; cast down, but not destroyed;

> Always bearing about in the body the dying of the Lord Jesus, that the life also of Jesus might be made manifest in our body.
>
> For we which live are always delivered unto death for Jesus' sake, that the life also of Jesus might be made manifest in our mortal flesh.
>
> So then death worketh in us, but life in you....
>
> For which cause we faint not; but though our outward man perish, yet the inward man is renewed day by day.
>
> For our light affliction, which is but for a moment, worketh for us a far more exceeding and eternal weight of glory;
>
> While we look not at the things which are seen, but at the things which are not seen: for the things which are seen are temporal; but the things which are not seen are eternal. (2 Corinthians 4:8–12; 16–18)

Paul understood that pressure may truly break the outward man, and we all know that pressure does not discriminate in breaking a person's spirit either. Yet day by day, God's grace is often illustrated in these experiences if we are acute enough to spot the sinews of His mercy. There is always hope. If we understand that the pressures of today do not always lead to the hopes of tomorrow. They point to the hope of eternity, where our focus should stay grounded.

Like coffee, pressure makes you strong, or rather, the power of Christ strong in you (2 Corinthians 12:9). It is hard to consider pressure joyfully and even harder to fathom that something good can come of them (Romans 5:3–4; James 1:2–3). Nonetheless, tried and true, God's Word is true (2 Timothy 3:16). Have faith (Romans 10:17).

When under pressure, remember:

> O taste and see that the Lord is good: blessed is the man that trusteth in Him. (Psalm 34:8)

165

Hit the Nest, Hit the Bee Too

"If you are going to hit a bee's nest, hit the bee too."

Recently, I have established this as a personal and practical proverb for myself. In the midst of a North Carolina summer, keeping this saying fresh on your mind will guard you from the onslaught of irritated bees. It came to my mind after I attacked an obvious enemy. A large wasp's nest was situated on a trailer that I needed to access. It appeared empty, so I went in for the kill.

Unfortunately, it was not the obvious target that suddenly began to blitz my neck and arms. My unseen enemy, the wasps who watched from a distance as I destroyed their home, swarmed me. I escaped with six bullet marks and much frustration.

Later on, I pondered the experience. I thought about the many obstacles I have faced in my life and some that I may anticipate. The culmination of these experiences, I realized, were the things that blindsided me. We do not realize, or at least think of, how long we truly have with loved ones. Sometimes, they leave this world very quickly. We do not expect a stupid decision to come back from the past and plague us, but sometimes, it does.

What people say to us, about us, and to spite us is out of control. Even more so, the consequences to follow. In our personal and corporate ministries, there are devices that our enemy, Satan, is plotting against us to hinder us from sharing the eternity-altering news of the Gospel of Jesus Christ. Not everything that happens to us is because of this, but never think these things are not taken advantage of.

As I thought of the many unseen enemies dispersed throughout our timeline, I thought of the struggles of the apostle Paul. He writes in 2 Thessalonians 3:1–5:

> Finally, brethren, pray for us, that the word of the Lord may have free course, and be glorified, even as it is with you:
>
> And that we may be delivered from unreasonable and wicked men: for all men have not faith.
>
> But the Lord is faithful, who shall stablish you, and keep you from evil.
>
> And we have confidence in the Lord touching you, that ye both do and will do the things which we command you.
>
> And the Lord direct your hearts into the love of God, and into the patient waiting for Christ.

In conclusion to his letter of comfort and assurance to the Thessalonians regarding the Coming of the Lord, Paul asks for prayer. What does he ask for prayer? The Word of God to be spread and deliverance from wicked men without faith. This is a very noble prayer, with the priority being first and foremost the spread of the Gospel then protection.

Notice also that both prayers are rather passive. God does both. He allows a free course of the Gospel, and He protects. The most active part of these prayers is—well—the prayer. Petitions of the Body of Christ!

Some may call this action faith. It is trusting that God has your blind spots and that, as verse 3 teaches, "the Lord is faithful." Regardless of what happens, the Lord is faithful and shall (that's a definite) stablish you and keep you from evil.

The end is already established: Jesus wins and is coming for you (5). Until then, like Paul, have confidence and allow God to direct your hearts into the love of God. Pray and request prayer. And if you do not know how to start, pray with me below:

> God, I adore you. All glory and power to Your holy name. The world is opposed to You and therefore opposed to me; nonetheless, I know that all who live godly lives shall suffer persecution (2 Timothy 3:12). Therefore, be my Rock and be my Shield (Psalm 18:2). Allow Your Gospel to have free course in my life and protect me from wicked people without faith. Protect Your children with little faith and who do not know how they ought to pray (Romans 14). I will glorify You despite my troubles and give thanks (1 Thessalonians 5:18). Not only for what You do but also for who You are. I humbly offer this prayer in the name of the Father, the Son, and the Holy Spirit. Amen.

166

I Need Thee Every Hour

Annie S. Hawks (1836–1918) and Robert Lowry (1826–1899) together published the hymn "I Need Thee Every Hour" in 1872. This song is a testament to constant devotion to the Lord and praising Him for all spiritual blessings. Paul spoke of these blessings in Ephesians 1:3 when stating:

> Blessed be the God and Father of our Lord Jesus Christ, who hath blessed us with all spiritual blessings in heavenly places in Christ.

This popular hymn just needed a few adjustments, several of which concerned Christ's presence in us. For example, the original lyric of the second stanza said, "Stay thou nearby." This implies that God might leave you, but we know that being sealed with the Holy Spirit (Ephesians 1:13), this is not possible. The song continues to say that "temptations lose their power when thou art nigh," but we also know that the way to render temptations powerless is to put on the mind of Christ (Philippians 2:5). We changed *voice* to *words* in the first verse to emphasize that it is through the Bible that God speaks to us.

The third verse is sound; we should be able to follow along with Paul in Philippians 4:11–12. So we will finish up with Ephesians 6:10:

> Finally, my brethren, be strong in the Lord, and in the power of His might.

1. I need Thee ev'ry hour, Most gracious Lord
   No tender words like Thine can peace afford.
2. I need Thee ev'ry hour, Though I am made nigh
   Temptations lose their pow'r, With Thou in mind.
3. I need Thee ev'ry hour, In loss or gain
   In me Thou dost abide, Or life is vain.

Chorus: I need Thee, O, I need Thee
Ev'ry hour I need Thee!
I praise Thee now, my Saviour, I come to Thee.

(Psalm 104:31–35.)

167

We All Make Mistakes

> Mistakes are the portals of discovery.
>
> —James Joyce

Mistakes are an inevitable part of life. Some may think contrary, but this would be to their own detriment. Biblical authors are quick to point humanity to their inability to overcome failures and mistakes, something that often characterizes human nature. The apostle James discusses this nature in chapter 3 of his letter:

> For in many things we offend all. If any man offend not in word, the same is a perfect man, and able also to bridle the whole body. (2)

Notice, James includes himself in discussing the shortcomings of the human tongue. Likewise, Paul made a sobering statement in Romans 3:23:

> For all have sinned, and come short of the glory of God.

That's the problem, right? Falling short? From my experience, I find this to be one of the most frustrating situations to be in. Words like *unqualified*, *failure*, and *regrets* sting like salt water in an open wound. Nonetheless, I do not expect this guilt to constantly bear down on everyone. The natural human response to these problems is to suppress them! My urge, however, is this: avoid that urge.

Because truly, mistakes are portals to discovery. It is by mistakes that innovation is birthed to avoid mistakes. Some of the world's greatest inventions were molded out of the skeleton of a mistake. This list includes penicillin, pacemakers, superglue, and… popsicles?

I do not say this to glorify mistakes; rather the opposite. Mistakes elicit responses! For instance, humanity's fallen nature elicited a gracious response from God. By the grace of God, He did not want to leave us drowning as we reached upward to Him and therefore His glory.

Continuing on from Romans 3:23, we read that:

> Being justified freely by His grace through the redemption that is in Christ Jesus:
>
> Whom God hath set forth to be a propitiation through faith in his blood, to declare His righteousness for the remission of sins that are past, through the forbearance of God;
>
> To declare, I say, at this time his righteousness: that he might be just, and the justifier of him which believeth in Jesus" (Romans 3:24–26).

Simply put, God redeemed us from the bondage of sin by the sacrifice of His Son, Jesus Christ. *Now* by identifying with His righteousness, we have access to the throne room of God and His glory, which formerly we had none (Romans 3:23).

With this in mind, words like *unqualified*, *failure*, and *regrets* have no bearing on us. They are replaced with words like *love*, *forgiven*, and *justified*. So for the person seeking these kinds of words to define their life, begin with a word found in Romans 3:25: *faith*.

Believe in Christ and His finished, reconciling work on the Cross and His resurrection, and you will be saved (1 Corinthians

15:3–4). For the believer dwelling on mistakes of the past, turn to His Word, for there is freedom there and instruction for righteousness (2 Timothy 3:16–17). And remember, mistakes are portals of discovery!

168

Jesus and Economics

Economics is usually a concerning topic. When we hear the word, we may think of negative trends regarding inflation, the housing market, gas prices, and so on. These terms are just words, but what they represent carries a very real weight in the lives of the typical consumer. Saying this, economics is such a tricky topic with some straightforward and more elusive solutions. Not because money is hard to manage, but because economics is not necessarily about the money.

Economics is about quality of life. Upon listening to a series of lectures by Professor Edward Stuart of Northeastern Illinois University, I took a look into the works by famed free-trade enthusiasts such as Adam Smith and Milton Friedman. The term and idea of economics, in a modern sense, derive from two Greek words: οἶκος, "household"; and νέμω "management, distribution." It pertains to the intimate ins and outs of a nation or groups of people and their well-being. Money is simply a conduit to improve the quality of life of these people.

With this in mind, I couldn't help but wonder about my own spiritual economy. By this, I mean, how am I investing the currency of Scripture into my soul, therefore improving the quality of my inner man? Am I suffering from an episode of inflation? Being puffed up beyond what the state of my faith shows, therefore discrediting my love (1 Corinthians 13:4)? God forbid. Am I carefully watching my housing value? Not disregarding the temple for the Spirit making my testimony a sellable asset for the Gospel (1 Corinthians 6:19)? Surely not, I pray the Lord forbid. Am I in poverty, lacking in much? Not at all. God has paid everything for me, and I am rich in blessing (Ephesians 1:3, 7–8). Although I live to increase the GDP of souls unto heaven, I know God's GDP of grace to me as I fail is unlimited. Join me in this evaluation.

169

Scoping Dishonest Questions

Answer not a fool according to his folly,
lest thou also be like unto him.
—Proverbs 26:4

In the "enlightened" world we live in, there appear to be more questions than answers. Questions, even more so, seem to be more accepted and sought after than answers. In a world where questions were limited and answers were once guarded by a select few in a feudal hierarchy, the Enlightenment opened a floodgate of questions. The only problem is the number of questions far surpasses the number of answers that human wisdom can offer or accept in our sinful nature.

In his book *Expository Apologetics*, Voddie Baucham Jr. discusses questions because the point of apologetics is to give an answer for your hope (1 Peter 3:15). Questions require answers. Even rhetorical questions have an answer; it is just not expected to be answered out loud.

But in order to give an answer for your hope, there must be a question. In this world laced with questions, anything grounded in sureness concerns the skeptical spirit of the age. So the skeptic's response is to question. Why Jesus? Was He a real man? How can you trust the Bible when there is not one original manuscript? Why does God allow "bad" things to happen to "good" people?

And the list goes on and on, with more and more being added to the exhaustive list. But then Baucham addresses an unfortunate reality in the world of questions, although this topic spans beyond the Age of Enlightenment. Dishonest questions.

Dishonest questions are questions characterized by their intention. They are questions phrased in a manner that ensnares a person in order to label them with something malicious and are birthed out of genuine curiosity. If you want a cultural example, look at scraps and disagreements between politicians. Public policy is often manufactured on the premise of dishonest questions and lopsided answers.

Jesus was asked dishonest questions often by the religious authorities of His day. One example of this can be found in Luke 20:27–40. I have the exchange below:

> Then came to him certain of the Sadducees, which deny that there is any resurrection; and they asked him,
>
> Saying, Master, Moses wrote unto us, If any man's brother die, having a wife, and he die without children, that his brother should take his wife, and raise up seed unto his brother.
>
> There were therefore seven brethren: and the first took a wife, and died without children.
>
> And the second took her to wife, and he died childless.
>
> And the third took her; and in like manner the seven also: and they left no children, and died.
>
> Last of all the woman died also.
>
> Therefore in the resurrection whose wife of them is she? for seven had her to wife.
>
> And Jesus answering said unto them, The children of this world marry, and are given in marriage:

> But they which shall be accounted worthy to obtain that world, and the resurrection from the dead, neither marry, nor are given in marriage:
>
> Neither can they die any more: for they are equal unto the angels; and are the children of God, being the children of the resurrection.
>
> Now that the dead are raised, even Moses shewed at the bush, when he calleth the Lord the God of Abraham, and the God of Isaac, and the God of Jacob.
>
> For he is not a God of the dead, but of the living: for all live unto him.
>
> Then certain of the scribes answering said, Master, thou hast well said.
>
> And after that they durst not ask him any question at all.

Men who did not believe in the resurrection asked Jesus a question about the resurrection. It is the epitome of dishonesty and malicious intent. Nonetheless, Jesus knew the Scriptures, the standard of truth, and He knew the proverb,

> Answer not a fool according to his folly, lest thou also be like unto him. (Proverbs 26:4)

Baucham states it this way: "Don't answer a fool until you answer his folly." Jesus took a question about worldly relationships and made it into a spiritual matter. There were many follies and fallacies within their convoluted question, so Jesus did not answer their question. He addressed the hole in the argument.

God is not a God of the dead, but of the living. Likewise, as you witness to this lost world, you will have similar situations. People who despise you because of the One living within you. They will confront you and ask questions, with an answer already situated within themselves.

Paul addresses these lofty arguments in this way:

> For though we walk in the flesh, we do not war after the flesh:
>
> (For the weapons of our warfare are not carnal, but mighty through God to the pulling down of strong holds;)
>
> Casting down imaginations, and every high thing that exalteth itself against the knowledge of God, and bringing into captivity every thought to the obedience of Christ;
>
> And having in a readiness to revenge all disobedience, when your obedience is fulfilled (2 Corinthians 10:3–6).

Fighting not with the flesh, our weapon of warfare is none other than the Word of God, a double-edged Sword of the Spirit (Ephesians 6:17; Hebrews 4:12). Never argue on a false premise and give credit to evil; rather, combat darkness with light and give your answer on the basis and root of the assault (Psalm 18:28).

170

From North to South

I am from the South. We talk slow, we walk slow, and we live slow. That's just the pace of life. As I reflect on Southern United States culture, I find it baffling how much a simple latitude change can affect our pace of life.

Recently, I had the opportunity to visit New York City and its surrounding suburbs. Oh, what a latitude change can do. Here, our Northern brethren and sisters live fast. Fast traffic, quick interactions, and something my southern friends would find unbelievable—fast grocery store lines.

As I reflect on this difference, I also cannot help but think of the practical applications to the believer. Christians are not to be of this world, but until our glorified bodies are received, we surely are in this world. To be more specific, the apostle Paul tells us to "be not conformed to this world" (Romans 12:2). Finishing his instruction, he says to be transformed by the "renewing of your mind."

In a world that demands conformity, it is your mind that needs security from this demand. Different places require different paces. But different paces provide different opportunities for the uniform and solitary Gospel. Paul addresses the difference between carnal seeds and spiritual seeds (1 Corinthians 9). Paul, who was constantly immersed in various cultures, proclaimed that he "suffer[ed] all things, lest we should hinder the Gospel of Christ" and those "which preach the Gospel should live of the Gospel" (1 Corinthians 9:12–14).

What does this "suffering" look like? It looks like a labor of love. Moving on, Paul states that he is a "servant unto all" (19). This means being "weak" unto the weak and temperate in all things. Constantly renewing your mind by Scripture's charge, but keeping your body in subjection. Bearing with the ebbs and flows of life's constant flux. Whether you are a witness to New York City or small town, USA, live unto the Gospel, a servant unto all for Christ's sake.

171

The Chemistry of Salvation

It is a passion of mine to find new and innovative ways of illustrating the same, powerful Gospel of Jesus Christ. Sometimes my approaches involve science. Other times, I will refer to history. Still, yet, I have also found ways to incorporate everyday mundane things such as cooking or a doctor's visit.

However, today I appeal to the science and artistic qualities of chemistry. Journey back with me to your high school chemistry course and recall your emotions as an equation such as the one below was brought to you:

$$6CO_2 + 6H_2O \rightarrow C_6H_{12}O_6 + 6O_2 + 6H_2O$$

Unless organic chemistry is a strong interest of yours, many people would not recognize that this is an equation for the process of photosynthesis. A necessary process for most of life to function. If this process all of a sudden stopped functioning in all the plants on earth, other organic beings, like you and I, would be struggling, to say the least. Life hinges on the reality of this equation and the subsequent reaction in nature.

Nonetheless, do not despair. Even if the constants of the world, including plant life, were to fail, there is one equation powerful enough to overcome the detriments. I call it the "Gospel equation." The Gospel equation is:

$$B(1L+3D+1R) \rightarrow E$$

In order to solve this equation, we need to know what property is needed to solve it and what the variables represent. We already have the coefficients (numbers). Let's look at the variables first.

B—belief
L—life
D—days
R—resurrection
E—eternity

This equation will not work without the variables. Next, we must look at the property used to solve it. This problem would be solved with the distributive property. Therefore, you distribute belief into the life of Christ (given for you on the cross), His burial of three days, and His resurrection from the dead. When belief is distributed into all three of these components, the product is eternity. Those variables combined change the entire molecular structure of the soul and make a new creation (2 Corinthians 5:17) (or compound to continue the analogy)!

It is a simple equation and, frankly, very difficult to get wrong, unless you believe that there is a better way. This is the only equation for eternal life, clearly defined by the perfect textbook—the Holy Bible (1 Corinthians 15:3–4)! Now that I have taught you, you give it a try!

172

Lean into and Boldly Proclaim

Everywhere is walking distance if you have the time.
—Steven Wright

Ministry is opportunity. An opportunity to introduce others to eternity and a glimpse of it in the meantime. For, "to live is Christ, and to die is gain" (Philippians 1:21). In living, we are able to magnify Christ and glorify God! This is ministry. It consists of the opportunity to glorify God by how one lives and brings others unto the realization that they were created, ultimately, for the same purpose.

We have the victory of life! But the victory of mortal life is the foreshadowing of the victory in store in the next life (1 Corinthians 2:9). The opportunities are ripe to live for Christ! Opportunity is not just local. For ministry, unlike the quote by Steven Wright, it is not about time; it is about the will to act on scriptural principles. To lean into opportunity and boldly proclaim the Gospel (Colossians 4:3–6).

173

Hypertension

In America, there are many troubles lurking that may lead to death. Crime, cancer, car accidents, diabetes, and much more. Death does not discriminate. But the top killer has been and still is heart disease. This term encompasses a large variety of illnesses surrounding the heart, but one killer still holds a certain fear in most Americans. That killer is hypertension, better known as high blood pressure.

Hypertension is often caused by constriction of the blood vessels for different reasons, usually determined by genetics and poor diets. High blood pressure is often called "the silent killer" because of its ability to silently deteriorate the health of an individual. Once diagnosed (preferably prior), high blood pressure needs to be addressed. Nothing good comes from high blood pressure. A common sign is called angina. This is a tightness of the chest that often makes the victim feel as if they are dying. Another issue that causes this pain is panic attacks.

Spiritually, we too may have spiritual hypertension. We are born with sin constricting our freedom and joy (Romans 3:23). The result too is often angina. Angina may also occur when we think of the treatment necessary for this heart condition to be alleviated (John 19:30; 2 Corinthians 7:9–10).

Jesus Christ, the great physician, noticed our condition (Psalm 147:3; John 3:16). He knew of the suffering the world was destined for. The treatment necessary anguished our good God as well (Matthew 26:39). But He loved us enough to meet us in that condition and treat us (Romans 5:8). When I realized the depth of what Jesus Christ did for me, it caused me chest pain as well. But unlike the angina that accompanies heart disease, something good came of this sorrow. My conviction quickly was replaced with gladness when I accepted this beautiful truth and accepted the treatment He suffered and died to prescribe.

His resurrection is the prescription. That we too shall rise again (Romans 6:4; 1 Thessalonians 4:14). So reflect on Christ, the great physician. He loves you more than you could ever imagine and understands the suffering. Nonetheless, He made a way to clear your spiritual hypertension. Respond with simple belief and thanksgiving.

174

Praise Him! Praise Him!

Today, we will explore another Fanny Crosby (1820–1915) hymn with the music of Chester G. Allen (1838–1879). This joyful tune was published in 1889 in a hymnal called "Bright Jewels." The original title was "Praise, Give Thanks." This we certainly should do each and every day (1 Thessalonians 5:18).

However, the original hymn contains the words *hosanna*, *prophet*, *priest*, and *shepherd*, as well as quotes from Isaiah 53. We have replaced these verses to sing of His current position as Head of the Body (Romans 12:5; Ephesians 4:4)! We kept much of the hymn, which allows the hymn to retain its flow. With just a few alterations, we were able to include some great theological terms that rarely make the cut in hymnody such as *reconciliation* (Romans 5:10), *resurrection* (Romans 1:4), and *mystery revealed* (Ephesians 1:9–10). So take this song and sing of the gospel of grace and praise Him!

Praise Him!

1. Praise Him! Praise Him! Jesus, our blessed Redeemer
   For our sins He suffered and bled and died.
   Christ, our Saviour, hope of eternal salvation
   Hail Him! Hail Him! Jesus, the crucified.

2. Praise Him! Praise Him! Jesus, our Lord and our Saviour
   For the myst'ry He has revealed today.
   Hail Him! Hail Him! He is the Head of the Body
   One new creature, old things are passed away!
3. Praise Him! Praise Him! Jesus, who reigneth forever
   Sing, ye saints, His gospel of grace proclaim.
   Hail Him! Hail Him! Whom God has highly exalted
   Jesus Christ, the name above ev'ry name.

Psalm 104:31–35

175

In Awe, to the Holy Trinity

I could praise You with my lips unending, for the entirety of my life, yet it would still fall infinitely short of what is due to You. *Adoration* is a word that comes to mind when I think of Your holiness (Philippians 2:10). Nonetheless, no mortal word could quite exact Your splendor (Psalm 145:5).

But to me, what You say is enough. Gracefully, You deal with me and it is blissfully sufficient (2 Corinthians 12:9). In this statement, there is a sinew of confession. I acknowledge my carnal desires, but as I acknowledge Your truth, the old man is suppressed, and rather this new man basks in the righteousness of the Son (Ephesians 4:24).

Brilliant and right are Your ways. Straight is the path You set before me (Proverbs 3:6). In You, there is not one crumb or a mere particle of darkness (1 John 1:5). In fact, I know that one speck of Your light illuminates innumerable expanses.

Now, I thank You. Even in Your sacred perfection, You looked from heaven, came from heaven, and now dwell with us in Spirit and truth (Ephesians 5:18). My sincere appreciation I lay at Your feet with my life as a sacrifice.

Often, I seek supplication, but now, my only plea is to know of Your grace more and more (Philippians 4:6). To all this, I pray in the name of the Father, the Son, and the Holy Ghost.

176

The Persistence of Hungry Ant!

Lately, my wife and I have noticed a sudden influx of ants surrounding our kitchen sink. Mind you, we try our hardest to keep a clean kitchen, so you can imagine the frustration as we wage war on these tiny vermin, seeking out their main headquarters so we can flank them!

But then, one day, as I ran surveillance in this household game of search and destroy, I spotted it. A single line of ants marching from the back door, through the dining room, into our kitchen to plant their flag. I had not thought to look there. They were not coming in from the kitchen or anywhere even remotely close. Their hunger drove them to drastic measures. It drove them to march across the cold, tile floor and brave our footsteps, so that they could provide for their colony.

Oh, what faith would be like, to be like that of an ant! To know what must be done and persistently pursue it.

It brought to mind the words of the apostle Paul after he discussed the fruit by which we must bear in the Spirit.

That we must strive to sow in the Spirit and not the flesh. But then he writes,

> And let us not be weary in well doing: for in due season we shall reap, if we faint not.

> As we have therefore opportunity, let us do good unto all men, especially unto them who are of the household of faith. (Galatians 6:9–10)

With that I say, God give me the persistent faith of a hungry ant!

177

Bitter, Sweet

Patience is bitter, but its fruit is sweet.

—Aristotle

I love this quote because it is permeated with deep, experienced wisdom. Unfortunately, it was spoken by the same guy who wrote:

> It is the mark of an educated mind to be able to entertain a thought without accepting it.

It is easy to entertain the thought of patience, but in this regard, it would be better to accept it.

Patience is a godly virtue. We are to be patient with others, patient with ourselves, and maintain patience as we wait on the Lord (Ecclesiastes 7:8–9; Romans 8:25; Ephesians 4:2). Patience is learned. It is not inherited like land or wealth, although those who learn it have wealth indeed. This is that prosperous fruit that the ancient thinker recalls.

Therefore, as you recall this wisdom, remember that young fruit is bitter. Apples do not start out delectable. They are tried by weather and nourished by the sun. Our patience will also be tried and nourished by the Son, Jesus Christ. It may appear bitter, but know this: God will work it to the good and make it sweet (Romans 8:28).

178

By Grace, I Stand

C. Austin Miles (1868–1946) in 1911 wrote the words and music to the familiar hymn "Dwelling in Beulah Land." He was prolific in his writing of 398 hymns, including the music to eight. We have retained the tune with the entire chorus, although the title and much of the song were written to reflect doctrine for the church today. The original hymn would have you living on a mountain, drinking from a fountain, and eating manna all while dwelling beneath the sky in "Beulah Land," which is a term found in Isaiah 62:4, describing a literal land on the earth that God promised to Israel.

Whereas the Body of Christ was promised an eternal hope in heavenly places, as we read in Titus 1:2,

> In hope of eternal life, which God, that cannot lie, promised before the world began.

Along with this verse, we see this hope in Ephesians 2:6 when it is spoken, "And hath raised us together and made us sit together in heavenly places in Christ Jesus."

God has quickened you in Christ, made you sit in Christ, will inherit you through Christ, and your place is in heaven (in Christ). It is not our job to keep our resurrection because God will see it through. Nothing separates your place because of God's grace and

His love. Romans 8:32 states, "He spared not His own Son, but delivered Him up for us all, how shall He not with Him also freely give us all things?"

1. Far away the noise of strife upon my ear is falling,
   then I know the sins of earth beset on every hand;
   Doubt and fear and things of earth in vain to me are calling,
   none of these shall move me,
   By grace I stand!
2. Through the tribulations grow, and men may come to hate me,
   I am safely sheltered by the love of just one man;
   Since He spared not His own Son, then who can separate me,
   I am saved forever,
   By grace I stand!
3. Life on earth is but a shadow, evil days are needy,
   few good things will ever last while enemies withstand;
   Wealth is empty, pain is plenty, death is always greedy,
   But I live rejoicing,
   By grace I stand!

Chorus: I'm living in the Spirit, with a place up in the sky,
I'm walking with a power that never shall run dry;
O yes, I'm singing of the glory that's waiting when I die where I'll be dwelling,
By grace I stand!

(Psalm 104:31-35.)

179

An Honest Advocate

Sometimes, the word *advocate* is used to represent someone who stands up and in the place of another person when faced with a difficult situation. But if you are asked to describe precisely what an advocate is and does, it is sometimes easy to forget that an advocate is someone defined by their public support.

It is amazing to me how often Christianity is seen as a secret faith. We sometimes encounter people and leave asking the question, "I wonder if they are a Christian?" We see their kindness and their upbeat disposition, and curiosity overcomes us. Not all nice people are Christians. Furthermore, not all Christians are nice people. Shame.

But Christians are not called to be a brand of spiritual double agents. A Christian's life should not be a two-way mirror, with two contrasting views. A transparent glass pane is much more preferred, allowing the viewer to see that God is on the other side!

In being a new creation (which all believers are), honesty is an important attribute. Being honest is more than words said, but also a fiber of the character we hold (Proverbs 12:22). The apostle Paul addresses the standard when stating,

> And that ye put on the new man, which after God is created in righteousness and true holiness.

> Wherefore putting away lying, speak every man truth with his neighbour: for we are members one of another. (Ephesians 4:24–25)

Now, what does this have to do with being an advocate? Strong public support of anything requires honesty in life. Without it, you are like a house of cards waiting for a gust of wind to carry it away. There are many public advocates who have fallen prey to this situation. Politicians, pastors, teachers, medical workers, etc. These fields and so many more are full of people who have advocated for the needs of others, while their need for healthy, self-nourishment falls short. We are called to personal honesty and scriptural holiness provided by Christ alone.

From here, we can advocate and publicly support the lost, advocate for the hopeless, and bring the Gospel to a world that needs it. Live blameless and shoot big when you share the Gospel (1 Thessalonians 2:4; 2 Timothy 4:5)!

180

How's Your Hygiene?

Speak thou the things which become sound doctrine.
—Titus 2:1

How's your hygiene? You may hear this question asked by your dentist, your doctor, or perhaps, your mom. It's a sincere question. It is an important question. Your hygiene can say a lot about your lifestyle and a lot about where you are going. With poor hygiene, your health is to follow. Poor hygiene may cost you a job. Hygiene reflects life and your life reflects your hygiene.

In Titus 2, the apostle Paul is teaching on things which correspond with sound doctrine. The Greek term for *sound* is *hygiainō*. Looks familiar, doesn't it? *Hygiainō* literally means "to be of health," "uncorrupt," and "wholesome." He is not only teaching this life to Titus, he is telling Titus to speak and replicate hygienic doctrine in his ministry!

Hygienic doctrine desires holiness and is a reflection of the God who gave it all to bring us into His family. It is charitable, temperate, holy, patient, and all the good things that God elicits for Christians in this age! So with this in mind, ask yourself: How's your hygiene? Are you brushing those spiritual teeth? And are you cleaned by the blood of Christ? Are your hygiene products supplied by the wonderful store of Scripture? How is your spiritual health?

181

Misinformation

The buzzword nowadays is *misinformation. Misinformation* is defined as "N. Wrong information; false account or intelligence received." Also, *disinformation* is used as in prior times, as it was first recorded in 1965. It was a translation of a Russian word that means "deception."

But really, these are not new. In Genesis 3:3, Eve said, "But of the fruit of the tree which is in the midst of the garden, God hath said, 'Ye shall not eat of it, *neither shall ye touch it*, lest ye die.'" But in the prior chapter, God clearly said in Genesis 2:17, "Thou shalt not eat of it. For in that day that thou eatest thereof thou shalt surely die [spiritually]."

In recent years, I believed that Christ died for my sins and He saved me. But at this point, then the misinformation began. I was told the following:

1. *I must join a church.* The Bible never says to become a church member, yet Acts 2:41; 47, and Hebrews 10:25 are used to justify this. Also, I remember being told to attend every time the doors open.
2. *I must be baptized in water* (Acts 2:38). But Paul, the apostle to the Gentiles, in speaking to Gentiles states from what he had learned from revelation of Christ that "for by one

Spirit are we all baptized into one body (1 Corinthians 12:13)" and there is "one Lord, one faith, one baptism" (Ephesians 4:5).

3. *I must pay a tithe plus offering to be blessed.* If you don't, you will be cursed. Here come the familiar verses of Malachi 3:9–10. But we see by the direction of Romans 6:14 and Galatians that we are no longer under it. Today we abide by the spirit of 2 Corinthians 9:7.
4. *I must go up to the altar and turn it all loose and hold on at the same time.* Sometimes, this is justified with Matthew 5:23–24. But we know that Christ died for all sins, once and for all (Romans 5:8).
5. *I must repeat the sinner's prayer, which is not in the Bible.* Nonetheless, many will try to justify it with James 5:16 and 1 John 1:7–9.
6. *I must repent of sins for remission.* This is justified once again by Acts 2:38. Salvation is not an action; it is belief. We are told to change our mind and attitude with grief toward our behavior (2 Corinthians 7:10). We are to agree with God that we are all sinners (Romans 3:23)!
7. *I must invite Jesus to be our Lord.* We must understand, as Christians Jesus is already Lord of your life and He is Lord of all.
8. *I must build God's kingdom here and now on earth.* This is coming from Matthew 6:10. This verse is found in what's commonly known as "the Lord's prayer," but notice Jesus never prayed it Himself. Our home, along with all the saints in this dispensation, will be the new heavens (1 Corinthians 15:51–58) for those that don't pass first in the glorious rapture of the Body of Christ.
9. *I can "lose" my gift of salvation.* Most commonly cite Hebrews 10:26 as evidence. But we must understand that the moment we were saved, we were sealed (Ephesians 1:13; Ephesians 4:30).
10. *Finally, I must receive all that God has to say through the pastor.* Hebrews 13:17 is the reasoning. We do need pastors

> (Acts 20:28), but most importantly, we must study God's Word and rightly divide it ourselves (2 Timothy 2:15). Like a shepherd, pastors protect and lead the church to the grazing area, but the sheep must put their heads down and eat the good green grass! Still yet, we are not sheep but members of the Body of Christ, although the application still works the same!

So study, read, believe, and be saved (1 Corinthians 15:3–4)!

182

Pray with a Sense of Urgency!

I remember being younger. We all do, I would imagine and I would hope. In recalling your younger self, think upon your work ethic. Hopefully, it has matured. As humbly as I can say it, I believe that mine has. I know this because sometimes I can hear the words of my elders exclaiming, "Let's move with a sense of urgency!"

Now, as if caught in a cycle of responsibility, I catch myself telling those younger than me, "Let's move with a sense of urgency!"

For the Christian, we are often preached that urgency for the Gospel is important. This I know is true. But little do I ever hear of a quickness to pray. It may be said that we need to pray as different situations arise, but when is it ever said, "Let's pray with a sense of urgency!"

This is strange considering Christendom's legacy of prayer, particularly that which is found in the life of the apostle Paul. In Romans 15:30–32, we see an illustration of urgent prayer as Paul beseeches the church in Rome to pray for him to God, for deliverance and for the gospel of grace to have its way. No different of a prayer is prayed in 2 Thessalonians 3:1. And oh what beautiful and humble words proceed in the prayer of Ephesians 6:19–20:

> And for me, that utterance may be given unto me, that I may open my mouth boldly, to make known the mystery of the gospel,
>
> For which I am an ambassador in bonds: that therein I may speak boldly, as I ought to speak.

Prayer to God is a work of faith, no lesser in service unto fellow Christians. So now I encourage you the same as myself,

> Let's move with a sense of urgency!

Urgency coupled with the purpose of the Gospel is an indispensable power that we all are richly blessed in carrying by the Holy Spirit. Pray for one another.

183

007 Christians

Spies. Many are infatuated with them. Some fear that they are among us at all times. American culture usually idolizes them as the heroes that we never see or dread them as incognito menaces.

Spies come in many forms. Some are more brazen, and some simply live amongst the enemy, collecting intelligence while working for the interests of another. In popular culture, the most popular agent would probably be James Bond. He is a British secret agent who works for the interests of the British government but lives among his enemy as a suave, yet casual passerby. Truly, an undercover ambassador.

Bond has always piqued my interest because he never uses an alias. If you were to ask him who he is, he'd reply, "The name's Bond. James Bond." He is a secret agent who is not scared of his identity because his identity is safe within himself. A secret agent is someone who lives in a country but works on behalf of their true citizenship.

To me, this sounds like the life of a Christian. We possess a heavenly citizenship and live for the mission of God's message of hope, although assigned to a land contrary to all that we believe (Ephesians 2:19). I think every Christian can take notes from Bond. Never hide from who you are to Christ and live faithfully unto His purpose, no matter where you are assigned (Colossians 3:23–24). We live with a certain amount of tact, but never sell out Him who began a good work in us (Colossians 4:6).

In doing so, you'll be like Bond and other brands of double agents, living on a mission for Christ, if you choose to accept it.

184

Chemistry in the Bible 1: God over All

The God of the world is the God of science. He created the earth in all its brilliance. His design sustains life. Who here looks down and tells their heart to beat or their lungs to process air? The planets and stars are placed perfectly. This design is far from mere coincidence.

It is suggested that life began from a coincidental explosion of one minute particle and that since that particle, the universe continues to expand! Nonetheless, as physicists and astronomers excitedly talk about the possibilities of someday "proving" the big bang theory, they seem to disregard something. Or rather many things.

First of all, the law of conservation of mass. This law (not a theory, mind you) states that mass (everything that has matter and occupies space) cannot be created nor destroyed. The Bible supports this law, with only one exception (Ecclesiastes 1:9). God did (Genesis 1:1), He is in the business of making the believer new (2 Corinthians 5:17), and God will defy the law of conservation of mass again (Revelation 21:1). Only God is able to make something from nothing; therefore, God's divine power is the exception to the law of conservation of mass. The big bang holds no divinity and holds no exception.

God is the God of the world, science, and the elements in which the world and universe are composed. As we embark on this series and explore what the Bible says about the elements on the periodic table, I encourage you to evaluate God and science. I am sure that you will see that God is sovereign above all. He set the scientific laws in motion and only He can unzip the fibers of reality and intervene.

Continue with us as we journey through the wonders of science from a biblical perspective!

185

Chemistry in the Bible 2: Tin

Tin. Not *ten*, as in the number, but *tin*, the metal. Metals make up nearly 75 percent of the periodic table. With 118 elements, 75 percent of them are metals. Saying this, most of the elements—the things that compose Earth—mentioned in their purest forms in the Bible are metals.

Tin has special mentions within the Word of God. Tin was a means of currency (Ezekiel 27:12), much like gold, silver, and copper (all of which are also found in the Bible). It had value. It has value today. If you don't believe me, run by your local hardware store and look at how much a sheet of it costs. The Hebrew word *bᵊḏîl* denoted tin as a precious metal. In a more figurative sense, tin was regarded as the material purged away when Israel was under judgment (Ezekiel 22:18; Isaiah 1:25). Tin was obtained by smelting.

Smelting is defined as a process used to remove metal by adding heat and or melting out other metals. And like all things precious, God requires that it be purified (Numbers 31:22). We too are like tin. We are first made pure by the blood of Christ, justified by His resurrection. But we are tried many times over by the trials of life (Romans 5:3–5; 2 Timothy 2:20–21). Likewise, tin, when refined, becomes a beautiful metal and, despite the processes applied, becomes extremely functional. It is malleable, moldable, and strong!

Christians, through trials, become "a vessel unto honour, sanctified, and meet for the master's use, and prepared unto every good work" (2 Timothy 2:21). Oh, to be like tin! To look into the face of a furnace and relish the beauty to be! Christ makes us even more precious than a precious metal, and trials, functionally turn up the heat, making us strong and pure.

186

Humbly Admitting Lack of Humility (Pride)

I find joy in the Word of God. In a proper reading, grace abounds, and one exits this conversation with God inspired. God in all His glory made His glory evident. Not only in Word but also in deed. Look around you in nature and by the blessing of life—this is true. The Old Testament is quick to illustrate God's glory, personality, and traits. It also highlights His desire for the love and faith of humanity.

In one prophetic message, the book of Micah, God made His disdain for faithless offerings known. As a consequence, Micah justified the right sacrifice by teaching God's personality.

> He hath shewed thee, O man, what is good; and what doth the Lord require of thee, but to do justly, and to love mercy, and to walk humbly with thy God? (Micah 6:8)

God is a God who desires justice, mercy, and humility. How we manifest this truth today may be different from Israel, but know that

God's traits do not change (Malachi 3:6; Hebrews 13:8). These all are reflections of His character. So we must ask ourselves the following:

- How do we live humbly today, in light of God's humble character?
- What is justice to a God who is the standard of justice?
- Can we practice mercy in similitude to the One who loves mercy the most?

These and similar questions are what I have wrestled with often lately. But it keeps coming back to this question, at least for me: How do I subdue the power of pride? You want to be "the man/woman." But in striving to hold on to this title, your grip is so tight, only vain conceit and pride ooze out. We all know the consequences of this.

If you struggle with pride, only start striving for resolution in light of resolute Scripture. I'll give you a good, heart-wrenching starting place:

- "When pride cometh, then cometh shame: but with the lowly is wisdom" (Proverbs 11:2).
- "Pride goeth before destruction, and an haughty spirit before a fall" (Proverbs 16:8).
- "A man's pride shall bring him low: but honour shall uphold the humble in spirit" (Proverbs 29:23).

Notice that pride is a spiritual problem, and lowliness is the answer. I can give numerous reasons why pride is so wrong, including seeing its corrosive properties in my own life, but let me save you a lecture and say—God hates it. He hates pride. Hear it for yourself.

> The fear of the Lord is to hate evil: pride, and arrogancy, and the evil way, and the froward mouth, do I hate. (Proverbs 8:11)

Pride and arrogance appear to be part of a collection of spiritual illnesses called "the evil way." God hates evilness. Therefore, for something God hates, we should be on our toes to seek the things that He loves. Pinpointing what exactly pride is can be difficult. It has been defined as an "overindulgence in one's own achievement" and "consciousness of one's own dignity." But both of these bring consequences, and all but the pridefully seared mind can identify pride. This is the first difficult step of ascertaining a solution—knowing you are a prideful person. Many times, by the time you realize this truth, you have already been overtaken.

But God knew this as He unveiled wisdom through the apostle Paul when it was written,

> Brethren, *if a man be overtaken in a fault*, ye which are spiritual, *restore such an one in the spirit of meekness*; considering thyself, lest thou also be tempted. Bear ye one another's burdens, and so fulfil the law of Christ. For if a man think himself to be something, when he is nothing, he deceiveth himself. (Galatians 6:1–3)

God, in all His foresight, has a multi-fold purpose for the Body of Christ. One beautiful purpose is simply to be. Be there. One will be overtaken in a fault. Once this is identified, be there. Bear each other's burdens and point them back scripturally to the Spirit of Meekness. Identify, be, point. Some problems can only be solved by "being." Pride is likewise. Be restored by the Spirit. Move on and point others to Christ's redemptive power. Do not swallow your pride, spit it up. Give it no longer place in your life.

187

Gobblefunk

Don't gobblefunk around with words.
—Roald Dahl

Stop it! Don't do it. If you do not speak gobblefunk, stop trying! It sounds like nonsense because it is! Well, unless you are a twenty-four-foot giant who speaks the language of gobblefunk. If that's you, I will cut you some slack. Otherwise, zip it! For those of you who have not the foggiest idea of what words I speak, perhaps I should admit I may struggle with gobblefunk as well.

Roald Dahl originally made the world aware of gobblefunk in his famous book *The BFG* (Big Friendly Giant). Gobblefunk is a language of nonsense spoken by the giant, which took logical words and…well… made them nonsensical. Don't do it to your words and please, I beg you, don't do it with your theology (views of God).

> For God is not the author of confusion, but of peace, as in all churches of the saints. (1 Corinthians 14:33)

Before you speak on the holy things of God, it is best to align yourself with what His Word says! Otherwise, your language is just rommytot, and you let everyone know you are jumbly and muggled! I mean your language is just nonsensical, mixed up, and confused.

As a man who enjoys a good scientific reading, I often read of people who find the love of God to be frivolous or of little concern. That is a sad way to live and the ultimate example of a fluent gobblefunk speaker! God loves me and God loves you. He sent His Son, Jesus Christ, to this earth to carry a sinner's cross and die a sinner's death (which He did not deserve) for the sins of you and me (1 Corinthians 15:3–4)! He rose again and offered a way to ditch our gobblefunk and swigpill lives! What do you say? Believe His Gospel, and let Him make sense of your life.

188

Banned

Banned books. There have been many throughout history and continue to be. For Americans, the very idea of having something banned seems revolting. As a matter of fact, freedom of speech is included in the First Amendment of the National Constitution! So why would a book be censored?

To answer your question, I say—that's not important right now. Not for this conversation, at least. I am merely going to suggest to the Christian—perhaps there are times we should censor ourselves. This thought has popped into my head as I read a book titled *Banned Books* from Dorling Kindersley Publishing. It was early in the work that there was discussion on the famed banned book *The Decameron*. This work was written in the 1370s and was frequently condemned for its innuendos, sexual references, and irreverent content.

Nonetheless, its author Giovanni Boccaccio defended his writing by saying,

> Nothing is so indecent that it cannot be said to another person if the proper words are used to convey it.

Now let us play a comparison game with a book that many have tried to ban and censor for thousands of years. Catch the difference in this quote:

> Let your speech be always with grace, seasoned with salt, that ye may know how ye ought to answer every man.

Have you seen this quote before? For many, many, many years this book has been scrutinized as well but still remains flawless! It's called the Holy Bible and was written by inspiration of the Holy Spirit! This quote is penned by the apostle Paul in Colossians 4:6.

Upon comparing the quotes, you may notice that they say two vastly different things. Boccaccio desires justification for the indecent, and Paul desires graceful, restrained speech uplifting to every person! As a Christian, I can confidently say your preferred view should be that of Paul. Because yes, speech matters.

Need an example? Let us look at 1 Timothy 1:18–20:

> This charge I commit unto thee, son Timothy, according to the prophecies which went before on thee, that thou by them mightest war a good warfare;
>
> Holding faith, and a good conscience; which some having put away concerning faith have made shipwreck:
>
> Of whom is Hymenaeus and Alexander; whom I have delivered unto Satan, that they may learn not to blaspheme.

Godly faith comes with a good conscience and controlled tongue. Many have heard, "Loose lips sink ships." Truly, these men's loose lips shipwrecked their faith. We should not live in tactful vileness but rather edifying faithfulness. Consider this as you journey through this life!

Let your speech be always with grace, seasoned with salt, that ye may know how ye ought to answer every man. (Colossians 4:6)

189

To the Only Wise God
Desire

Never be afraid to trust an unknown future to a known God.
—Corrie ten Boom

Who is your god/God? Notice when reading, I wrote a lowercase *g* and an uppercase *G*. I want to be very broad in this question. Whoever reads this, I am asking for honesty. Honesty is the foundation of a fair trial.

Are you an atheist? Very well. Think precisely what that means. Agnostic? What exactly are you searching for? The point of the agnostic is to find something. Perhaps the known God? Or maybe, just maybe, you tell yourself, "I care nothing of a god." I understand. Life is preoccupying. But what do you think about when it is not?

Every person lives their day-to-day lives as a quilt. A quilt of desires. At least one of these quilted fibers is seen at every moment of life. What do you desire? Famed lay theologian C. S. Lewis was an atheist notable for denying the things of God. Until God showed him how undeniable His case was. And C. S. Lewis desired the undeniable! Reflecting on his salvation he claims,

> If we find ourselves with a desire that nothing in this world can satisfy, the most probable explanation is that we were made for another world.

I ask once again, "What do you desire?" A desire usually is something we want to ascertain. So what of God? We can make gods of many things, but only one God can keep us from falling and preserve us blameless until eternity meets us in a sudden moment (Jude 24). Assuming one believes in eternity. What if they don't believe? I would suggest this person recognizes "the only wise God" (Jude 25). Who stands outside of time and has made Himself abundantly obvious to humankind, with never one contradiction (Isaiah 57:15).

Who else can say the same? Your desires speak abundantly clear to the "something more" that Jesus Christ provides (Romans 1:16; Romans 8:16–17; 1 Corinthians 15:3–4). You can find a lot in what you desire.

> Yea, if thou criest after knowledge, and liftest up thy voice for understanding;
>
> If thou seekest her as silver, and searchest for her as for hid treasures;
>
> Then shalt thou understand the fear of the Lord, and find the knowledge of God. (Proverbs 2:3–5)

190

Do You Trust Your Bank?

Moreover it is required in stewards, that a man be found faithful,
—1 Corinthians 4:2

Banking has not always been banking as we know it. The history of banking is one of shakiness and mistrust that has extended even up to this day. You may still hear the occasional, "I don't trust the bank." These people usually have a good reason based on experience and an even better reason if they know the history of banking shortcomings.

I, on the other hand, have placed my trust in my bank to be faithful stewards of my money. Modern banking as we know it comes from Italian vendors such as merchants and goldsmiths, who would make payments on behalf of other people. (Sound familiar? For example, debit cards.) But what makes a steward a steward? What more is required than to simply be found faithful? Otherwise, not much responsibility or possessions would be entrusted. The key word is entrusted.

There is much to be said about a good steward, but instead of speaking deeply to the quality of a steward, we must first understand that a steward is not merely a man or woman of money. It is a person of diligence, faithfulness, and discernment (Proverbs 10:4; 14:23). A good steward understands that there is a profit in everything under their watch. Money is not the only commercial quantity. Patience is cultivated under a watchful eye and experience is a valuable quality in which the greatest of stewards exhibits. In fact, a steward in its original and purest sense is someone who manages household affairs. It is even a requirement of the church leadership (1 Timothy 3:4).

So I say all this to ask, what is under your care? Is it a household? Is it finances? Or maybe something a bit more abstract such as the "temple of your body" (1 Corinthians 6:19–20)? Did you know that as a Christian, God has entrusted you with the glorious message of salvation (1 Thessalonians 2:4)? It is a free gift, but one that is far too great to sit within the vault of your heart (Ephesians 2:8–9).

Sometimes, stewards have to disperse what is in their care! Examples include banks giving money, parents allowing kids to go to school, and the church going on a mission. Stewards do not hoard; they discern how to allocate. Allocate the Gospel boldly.

191

Trophies of Grace

trophy (n.)

1. a cup or other decorative object awarded as a prize for a victory or success.
2. (in ancient Greece or Rome) the weapons and other spoils of a defeated army set up as a memorial of victory.

There are two types of sports families. One type carries a strong disdain for "participation trophies," while the other sees the beauty in congratulating everyone for their best effort. If you are within a sports family, know that I appreciate both ends of the spectrum! We can all agree that a trophy is something special. It is significant—a symbol of something that has been accomplished.

I recently heard Pastor Steven Lawson addressing Paul's list of "trophies of grace" in Romans 16. In the last chapter of Romans, Paul warmly greets a diverse population of people in the Roman church who were men, women, free people, slaves, Gentiles, and Jews alike. The common connection, however, was not their socioeconomic position, race, gender, or anything of the like. Their connection is that "there is neither Jew nor Greek, there is neither bond nor free, there is neither male nor female: for ye are all one in Christ Jesus" (Galatians 3:28).

Christ is the great equalizer. By His stripes, all of us become co-heirs with Him (Romans 8:17)! Co-heirs who are trophies of His grace. Each believer exemplifies and represents victory achieved one morning, many years ago, when Christ rose from the grave victorious. The victory is not ours to claim; nonetheless, it is ours to receive by faith. An abundant gift of grace indeed (Ephesians 2:8–10).

How can we deny such a prize? It has the best of both sides of the spectrum. It was achieved through a holy effort, and everyone gets to participate. It's a win-win!

192

You Preach Unity?

Unity. You hear of it often nowadays. There is much discussion about what it requires.

At a recent festival our church attended, we were in the community offering hope and attempting to meet fellow Christians. It was during this experience that many Christians brushed us off as I reached to shake their hands to say "Hello" and some kept me from even taking a breath.

We heard these snarks much of the day: "We have a church!" or "I know the Bible." Furthermore, some "Christians" even refused to speak to me and resorted to glaring at me until they were out of sight, thinking that I was looking to "steal church members." As a church, we had no interest in doing such a thing. Our goal was to speak the Gospel and fellowship with those who believe, and give a message of hope to those who do not believe.

Instead, I saw people pulling at the arms of loved ones saying, "Get away from there! You have a church! It's [insert *Baptist*, *Methodist*, *Presbyterian*, or *Pentecostal*] church!" After these experiences, I saw a collection of bodies and not one ounce of love for a Christian outside of their club.

Another time, when promoting an event recently, we have had local churches staple flyers above our own as if our flyers had leprosy and needed to be covered. These are merely a few of the recent experiences that have given me a sick feeling when looking at the local church, which has an ungodly disdain for us as we attempt to uphold love for them.

Where is the unity? Ask many people, and they will claim unity comes by accepting each other's differences. Perhaps. There is beauty in diversity. But know this: acceptance brings Christian unity as well, but also forces the hand of rejection.

Accepting differences is not the fabric of a healthy church and should not be the exterior fabric paraded. The Body of Christ accepts that the name and person of Jesus Christ is superior and reigns as Lord, by His Gospel manifested in His death, burial, and resurrection. There is so much confusion on this topic itself when Jesus ensured that it be presented simply (1 Corinthians 15:3–4).

With this being our foundation, still we are not called to acceptance of doctrinal differences; we are called to be "perfectly together in the same mind and in the same judgment" (1 Corinthians 1:10).

Read this verse to many a spiritual leader and this would be (directly or indirectly) reasoned as a lost cause. How sad a predicament? The Body of Christ is called to be of the same mind, but the Church continues to live separately, unanimously lying to ourselves, calling it unified. On one occasion, in frustration, Paul asks the Corinthian church in their quarreling, "Is Christ divided? Was Paul crucified for you? Or were ye baptized in the name of Paul?" (1 Corinthians 1:13).

Now what solutions do I have practically for the chasm in love and truth that stands between fellow Christians? Nothing immediate. But let me point you to the place that has the answers. The Word of God calls us to eagerly agree on truth (2 Corinthians 13:11; Ephesians 4:3). Not differences. What true unity can come from agreeing on differences?

Christianity is exclusively composed of right belief and wrong belief. If the true Body agreed on what is right, then ultimately, they would agree on what is wrong as well. As Christians, we are to contend for truth. The Biblical Church, although known for unfailing hospitality, is told to curb hospitable actions toward those who bring false doctrine.

The Second Epistle of John 1:10 states, "If there come any unto you, and bring not this doctrine, receive him not into your house, neither bid him God speed." John makes no delineation here. The apostle Paul uses some of the strongest language in the New Testament when defending the primacy of truth. He proclaims, "But though we, or an angel from heaven, preach any other gospel unto you than that which we have preached unto you, let him be accursed" (Galatians 1:8).

Yet too often, we make light of such tall orders, knowing full well that unity is in truth, and we are glued together in the bonds of love (Colossians 3:14). Disunity presents itself as unity, until unity requires disunity from evil.

> Therefore to him that knoweth to do good, and doeth it not, to him it is sin. (James 4:17)

Be on high alert. Guard your hearts and guard the truth. True godly, unified fellowship is worth the fight.

193

Counting the Cost

Advice my daddy always gave me with any major decision of my life was, "Did you count the cost?" As I have had many major life changes including moving and job changes, I have pondered the cost of it all both monetarily and figuratively. But most importantly, I reflect on counting cost spiritually as my Savior, Jesus Christ, teaches, "For which of you, intending to build a tower, sitteth not down first, and counteth the cost, whether he have sufficient to finish it?" (Luke 14:28).

This verse, spoken in a parable, holds much practical wisdom that can be extracted. Jesus is preparing His disciples for great persecution, all the while still being expected to faithfully serve Him. Christ is a mighty foundation to build upon. Nonetheless, the question is not, "Is it worth it?" We have His guarantee that it is (1 Corinthians 2:9; Ephesians 3:20). The question is, "Have you counted the cost?"

When you are in the middle of life and the heat is increased and the pressure is surmounting, what have you invested in the bank of your soul to get you through? Take time and count it. There is today to learn and tomorrow to grow.

> The reason many people fail is not for lack of vision but for lack of resolve and resolve is born out of counting the cost. (Robert H. Goddard)

194

Thankful for Righteousness

I will praise the Lord according to His righteousness: and will sing praise to the name of the Lord most high.
—Psalm 7:17

Thankfulness to God is expected and to Christians is understood. God is good to us and good, period. We have much to praise God for. Examples are: His providence, His love for us, and importantly, His grace provided through the work of His Son (1 Corinthians 15:3–4).

Nonetheless, recently I have acknowledged a failure to praise Him with thanksgiving for being simply who He is. Righteous. God is righteous. He is light. In Him there is no darkness (1 John 1:5). He invites humanity to be partakers of this righteousness (Romans 4:22–25).

As seasons come and seasons go, let us not neglect thankfulness, first and foremost, for a God who is righteous. And perfect. He is holy. Who is all righteous and looks to us, all depraved, and offers us the chance to take part in Him through the effort of His Son, Jesus Christ. With this in mind, praise the Lord according to who He is. According to His righteousness and sing praise to the name of the Lord most high! Praising His righteousness never carries empty praise.

195

Mistaken Vanities

Society has many varying divisions. These fissures include: money, looks, position, family name, and so forth, so forth. Sometimes, how others are elevated should make the common man (I say this to make a point) laugh. All of humanity's dignities are superficial, yet esteemed as immortal.

In our mortal flesh, we are bound to trouble, bound to sickness, and restrained to the chamber of our mind. You get the point. Still, yet, we find favor in the eyes of God. We find grace by His Son.

At one point, even Jesus could relate to the fragility of humanity, being "made a little lower than the angels for the suffering of death, crowned with glory and honour; that He by the grace of God should taste death for every man" (Hebrews 2:9). Now be careful not to run away with this Scripture as Charlie did with a golden ticket. Christ is not "lower" than angels as in ranking, but as in that He could taste death. Still, yet, He conquered death, and now we can taste death no more.

Nonetheless, in this verse and others within Hebrews 2, we see a reality about humanity. We are mortal—until we are not. But here, not glorified, no amount of hairstyles, muscles built, and money accumulated can raise our stature above that of fellow brethren and sisters.

Perhaps that is why Paul states, "Let nothing be done through strife or vainglory; but in lowliness of mind let each esteem other better than themselves" (Philippians 2:3). Currently, all of us are lower than the angels. We will taste death, until we don't.

> For this corruptible must put on incorruption, and this mortal must put on immortality. (1 Corinthians 15:53)

Therefore, love each other as Christ has loved you (John 15:12). Love each other as fellow passengers to the grave and from there, fellow heirs to glory. Put off mistaken vanity. Put on sincere love.

196

I'm Probably Gonna' Ruin This Song for You

Go to any Southern gospel revival and you will likely, in some form or another, hear the gospel praise song, "I Saw the Light." Although this song has been covered by a nearly innumerable number of artists, it originally rang from the lips of country music Hall of Famer, Hank Williams Senior.

But this song was not written in some incredible period of spiritual enlightenment. Rather, far from it. Recently, as Hank Williams and I yodeled alone in my kitchen, I became curious as to where exactly he had received such inspiration for this beautiful song. I learned this.

Williams, a notorious alcoholic, had this lyrical epiphany while returning from a show in Fort Deposit, Alabama. His mother was driving the sleeping, inebriated Hank Williams and his band back to Montgomery when she spotted the lights of Montgomery Airport. She woke the drunken Hank up and exclaimed, "I just saw the light!" This simple exclamation forms the basis of the song, which later received scriptural allusions.

This shocking backstory may surprise you, as it did me. But still, yet, I found inspiration in it. As a Christian, we carry a powerful light everywhere we go. You never know what those around you are going to pick up from us in our day-to-day encounters.

The apostle Paul tells his son in the faith, Timothy, to "Preach the word; be instant in season, out of season; reprove, rebuke, exhort with all long suffering and doctrine" (2 Timothy 4:2). Be faithful to the teaching of the Word and testimony of Christ. We never know what will stick and God will use to raise up a generation of men and women who, like you, have seen the light (John 1:5). Just point their tired eyes on high.

197

Follow Peace, Pursue Holiness

Follow peace with all men, and holiness, without
which no man shall see the Lord.
—Hebrews 12:14

As Christians, there are things we know are readily available at request from our heavenly Father. These include joy, love, grace, acceptance, and so much more. But what of peace? We often see peace as something that follows something. Not often do we see peace as something we must follow ourselves, as something elusive.

But on more than one occasion, various biblical authors describe peace as something that must be followed and captured! In Romans 14:19, the apostle Paul teaches the Church to "therefore follow after the things which make for peace, and things wherewith one may edify another."

When following something or someone, the key is to never let that entity get out of sight. When you lose sight of something, it may be hard to find it again. To an extent, we may just need to "be careful for nothing" and pray with thanksgiving (Philippians 4:6–7). The Word tells us this is one way to rope in peace, which God readily offers in seeking.

But we know that praying in struggle is not always an easy task. Paul must have understood this as he earlier said in Romans, "If it be possible, as much as lieth in you, live peaceably with all men." The phrase "if it be possible" indicates the possibility it may not be possible sometimes. This should not deter the Christian from following, however.

Our pursuit of holy living should never be an ending pursuit. The Word instructs us to, "Depart from evil, and do good; seek peace, and pursue it" (Psalm 34:14).

198

Chemistry in the Bible 3: Sulfur

When talking about chemistry discussed within the Bible, it is almost impossible to avoid a conversation about the element sulfur. Sulfur has an atomic number of 16 and can be found within the chalcogens, making it very likely to bond with other elements.

When discussing sulfur, I would love to talk about how brilliant of a material it is and how it is a crucial element for many living things. It would be nice to discuss how beautiful a yellow hue it holds and how familiar a smell it may put off when heat is applied. Nonetheless, when discussed in the Bible, it is not an element that one would want to come in contact with. Unless, of course, we refer to the wine mentioned in the Bible, which, in the process of oxidation, produces compounds known as sulfites that help preserve the drink (e.g., Isaiah 55:1; John 2:1–11).

Whenever the Bible specifically mentions sulfur, or as the ancients called it, brimstone (literally rendered "burning stone"), judgment was afoot. An obvious example could be of God's judgment over the twin cities of Sodom and Gomorrah. This judgment was carried out by means of sulfur and fire from heaven. But not only here is sulfur used as a conduit in administering the judgment of God; there are many more references (e.g., Deuteronomy 29:23; Psalm 11:5–6; Revelation 14:9–11).

Nearly every reference to sulfur includes a reference or allusion to fire. The final, eternal residency of those who deny Christ's Gospel will ultimately be in a lake of sulfur (Revelation 20:10). God has provided a means of grace and a means to pour out His wrath. To focus on God's love but ignore the wrath in His character, which results from humanity's assaults on His holiness, is to fabricate another god.

Some references to sulfur even mention wine. One reference pertains to the Mark of the Beast in Revelation. Once again, it discusses the wrath of God:

> And the third angel followed them, saying with a loud voice, If any man worship the beast and his image, and receive his mark in his forehead, or in his hand,
>
> The same shall drink of the wine of the wrath of God, which is poured out without mixture into the cup of his indignation; and he shall be tormented with fire and brimstone in the presence of the holy angels, and in the presence of the Lamb:
>
> And the smoke of their torment ascendeth up for ever and ever: and they have no rest day nor night, who worship the beast and his image, and whosoever receiveth the mark of his name. (Revelation 14:9–11)

This should not shock you, however. God is the God of science, and He absolutely knows the chemical structures of the food and drink we ingest. Despite God's fearful use of sulfur, we do not have to anticipate such an interaction with it. As a matter of fact, sulfur often interacts with various chemicals and makes incredibly useful salts. That is my goal today. To use sulfur to help "your speech be always with grace, seasoned with salt, that ye may know how ye ought to answer every man" (Colossians 4:6).

There is a heaven and there is a hell. God offers heaven every day to the unbeliever abundantly through the work of His Son, Jesus Christ.

Today can be the day where you solidify your future, not with scents of rotten egg as sulfur produces with fire, but rather a sweet-smelling savor as that given by the sacrifice of Christ (Ephesians 5:2).

Be sure you know the chemistry of faith. You will understand the product of His love.

199

Wrestling

Wrestling. An ancient art and an even more ancient sport. I mean this quite literally. There are paintings dated over fifteen thousand years ago that are plastered on caves from ancient France. Furthermore, ancient Babylon and Egypt (both biblical locations, mind you) detail wrestling methods that are still adhered to, to this day.

Jacob, son of Isaac, son of Abraham, perhaps holds claim to the most infamous match ever recorded. The narrative tells us this riveting story:

> And Jacob was left alone; and there wrestled a man with him until the breaking of the day.
>
> And when he saw that he prevailed not against him, he touched the hollow of his thigh; and the hollow of Jacob's thigh was out of joint, as he wrestled with him.
>
> And he said, Let me go, for the day breaketh. And he said, I will not let thee go, except thou bless me.
>
> And he said unto him, What is thy name? And he said, Jacob.
>
> And he said, Thy name shall be called no more Jacob, but Israel: for as a prince hast

> thou power with God and with men, and hast prevailed.
>
> And Jacob asked him, and said, Tell me, I pray thee, thy name. And he said, Wherefore is it that thou dost ask after my name? And he blessed him there.
>
> And Jacob called the name of the place Peniel: for I have seen God face to face, and my life is preserved. (Genesis 32:24–30)

This story is a shocking one, to say the least. It begs the question, "Is it possible that a person can wrestle with God and live?" But to that question, the answer is always, "If the Lord wills it" (James 4:15).

By God's providence, we have the ability to fight. We can fight for God, fight against God, fight against flesh, and fight against Spirit. But only, and I mean only, by God's will are we preserved. Only by God's will, do we prevail.

Know this. It is God's will that we prevail. Paul tells us in Romans 8:37–39:

> Nay, in all these things we are more than conquerors through him that loved us.
>
> For I am persuaded, that neither death, nor life, nor angels, nor principalities, nor powers, nor things present, nor things to come,
>
> Nor height, nor depth, nor any other creature, shall be able to separate us from the love of God, which is in Christ Jesus our Lord.

As Christians, we will not only prevail. We will do more than prevail, and nothing can dethrone us from this heavenly place! No ankle picks from the Devil or Olympic headlocks from the flesh can throw or slam us hard enough to detach us from the salvation and peace we have in Jesus Christ.

The very same Jesus Christ fought the already defeated Satan, one day, two thousand years ago, and was too holy to have a hand raised. He was raised from the dead and then raised to heaven, a sign of ultimate victory.

The score is won, and the match has met an end.

200

Christmas Skepticism, Be Gone!

It's that time of year again. It is time to deck the halls, find the freshly stocked eggnog, and sing the same three songs over and over and over and over again. Likely the only time such repetition is accepted begins around Thanksgiving (sometimes sooner) and ends around the new year! As Americans, it seems we have little patience for any one thing, for any amount of time.

But every year, we seem to see conversations repeat as well, sometimes from Christians themselves! You have the grinch who prods:

- "Why would you celebrate Christmas? It's a pagan holiday!"
- "Jesus wasn't even born in December!"
- "You don't find a Christmas celebration in the Bible!"
- "We are free of the law; why add more religious holidays to tie us again?!"

Admittedly, the last one I am a bit guilty of thinking, if not occasionally suggesting. Nonetheless, for the sake of unity, I would like to see the man or woman of God stray away from such "straw man" arguments and genetic fallacies. These scrooges, once again as Paul said, "I am chief," take the origin of something and minimize what it is currently. Although it isn't always quite such a fair assessment, I admit.

This is done elsewhere in other religious fields too. It often results in a stereotype, not a valid conclusion. Calvinism is a very popular theological framework internationally now, but if Christians held the same vehement arguments as they do Christmas, we would hear questions such as:

- "Why would you believe Calvin? He was a murderer / serial killer who offed those who disagreed with him!" (For more information, look up the history of Calvin and Servetus)
- "John Calvin believed babies who died went to hell; you must believe the same thing!"

Or perhaps this is too much of an illustration. I'll lighten it a bit. Perhaps we discuss food? Would there be a sound argument in the following logic:

- "Milk has lactose, and some people are intolerant to it, so you shouldn't drink milk! It's evil; it hurts people!"

Unlikely.

But for Christmas's sake, this is heard around tables and in conversation all season. Nonetheless, evangelicals have no problem admitting this truth:

> Christ came to earth, conceived of a virgin, was born, lived, and died for all transgressions of humanity.

Have a day. Have a month. Have a full year. Reflect on Christ's glory that began one holy night. A night made holy not because of a chronological calendar, date, or Christmas Spirit. It may be deemed holy because of who arrived—His name is Emmanuel, God with Us, Jesus the Christ.

Reflect on that. Not lofty ideas or uber-commercial traditions (2 Corinthians 10:5). Because the origins of Christmas did not come from a pagan holiday or a Catholic mass. It began one night in Bethlehem long before, and "God with Us" has no end (Luke 1–2). He is eternally ours, and we are eternally His.

Merry Christmas, friends.

201

Forget Logic, Try Common Sense!

For we are his workmanship, created in Christ Jesus unto good works, which God hath before ordained that we should walk in them.

—Ephesians 2:10

For the invisible things of him from the creation of the world are clearly seen, being understood by the things that are made, even his eternal power and Godhead; so that they are without excuse.

—Romans 1:20

The heavens declare the glory of God; and the firmament sheweth his handywork.

—Psalm 19:1

Every day I stand amazed at the hand and work of God. Sometimes I am blindsided as His providence works over the ins and outs of my life and the lives of those around me. Other times, I see the world that only a righteous, intelligent (understatement, I know) God as ours could make, and I regret any doubt I ever had.

Look in the mirror. Even within the corrupt shell we call our bodies, God's handiwork and intricate design are on display! Our bodies and the world around us are made of systems and substances that work so brilliantly to keep us nourished, moving, and seeking equilibrium. An indescribable number of atoms self-organize, and *everything* is, therefore, the result.

Even though everything natural (and unnatural in a contrasting way) points to the existence and glory of God, the trend nowadays in an increasingly self-glorifying world is to discredit; well, frankly, the obvious. This world, although depraved, has an origin, and it has an Eye over it.

> The lot is cast into the lap; but the whole disposing thereof is of the Lord. (Proverbs 16:33)

In the mainstream, if this idea is even thought, like clockwork, you can expect to hear something similar to the following: "Well, not everyone thinks like you" or "I prefer to think about life logically."

Dale Carnegie once said the following about logic:

> When dealing with people, remember you are not dealing with creatures of logic, but with creatures bristling with prejudice and motivated by pride and vanity.

You see, even logic has its limits. Logic is often considered the study of correct reasoning. Whatever train of thought you have on a topic will never arrive at the right station if you aren't even on the right track.

That is where common sense comes in. Good sense and sound judgment, often times, is an art much better than logic. God is the way and the only One capable of making a way. Making a way for the life you live now and the life you live in eternity (Psalm 139:13–16; 1 Corinthians 15:3–4).

Have some common sense about you.

202

Hell Bad, Heaven Good

Recently, I came across a theology page on Facebook as I normally do. It was in this page that some were debating the essence of hell. In this discussion, someone asked, felicitously might I add, the question, "Is hell bad?" In suit, there came a number of defenses saying that hell is not bad necessarily; it is only bad because it is a place our loved ones are sent. To this I respond, and I dare say, the only thing bad is unrepentant ignorance.

A physical location where there is no hope of drawing near the holiness of God and being eternally separated from the Father has apparently become a place that is not "bad." I was frightened to send a message and ask my burning question: If hell isn't bad, then is heaven good? People want to get lost in semantics and wordplay, to fabricate a truth that they are right by, instead of calling good and evil what it truly is. In the words of the late R. C. Sproul, "What's wrong with you people?!"

This is one of the many reasons that the vain philosophies of men are called out by the apostle Paul in his letter to the Colossians in verse 2:8. These philosophies put people on a false pedestal and allow them to slyly suggest they know better than God. To all these individuals, my charge is this: The Word states they will spoil you. Cut the semantics, read the Word, and believe the Word. God isn't looking for theologians; He is looking for believers.

Some may argue that every believer is a theologian. To this I say, fair enough. But being a theologian does not equate to a bona fide Bible-believing Christian. There are atheists, agnostics, and deeply troubled theologians as exemplified in that comment section. The Word, if you would believe it, states that only by faith is it possible to please God (Hebrews 11:6). If you find difficulty in believing or struggle to rightly divide the Word of Truth and use it as an instruction for righteousness, then hear this: There is peace in believing (Romans 15:13).

And as for the great debate of the armchair theologians, I will put it simply: hell bad, heaven good. Seek the upward calling of Jesus Christ our Lord (Philippians 3:14).

203

Google Annoymous

I would like to admit something to you all: I am a Google addict.

From everything from how to air fry chicken to who is that particular person I recognize in a movie to, embarrassingly enough, how to open a Pantene pump bottle (which have I yet to do even after watching a YouTube video). I knew I had a problem.

I rarely use my brain or my brain or my own strength for that matter, which led me to have conviction about my Bible usage. This question shook me, "How often do I use my Bible as a resource?" "How often do I look up that particular person in the Bible that I could learn lessons from?"

If we utilized our Bibles as much as Google, YouTube, TikTok, and similar platforms, the question arises, "How much wiser and stronger would we be on matters of true importance. Now, I am not saying not to use Google. It is there to help.

Nonetheless, I am pointing to a resource of much greater aid. In Colossians 1:9–10, the apostle Paul presents a far better desire for Christians. He teaches, "For this cause we also, since the day we heard it, do not cease to pray for you, and to desire that ye might be filled with the knowledge of his will in all wisdom and spiritual understanding; That ye might walk worthy of the Lord unto all pleasing, being fruitful in every good work, and increasing in the knowledge of God."

In this year, I personally (and if you would join me) want to Google a little less and Bible a lotta' more.

204

Martin King Jr. Gets a Name Change

On January 15, 1929, a man was born named Martin. Not Martin Luther King—just Martin King Jr. He was not born the infamous Martin Luther King Jr. as we know him. But truthfully, I like the real story better.

Five years after the birth of his son, Martin King Senior took a bit of a pilgrimage, one might say. He traveled throughout Europe, explored the Mediterranean, and was able to experience the location of a radical reformation long before Martin Luther in Germany. He was near the work of the apostle Paul and his ministry to the Gentiles and eventually to what is often deemed the Holy Land, which at that time politically was called Palestine but ultimately, as history proved, is rightfully named Israel, which means "He retains God" or "God is upright."

Nevertheless, Martin King saw it all. On this trip, he went to Germany, the homeland of reformer Martin Luther, a man who, by the Word of God and similar methods to his son's eventual reforming acts, was accredited. Martin King, so impressed with the impact of Martin Luther for Christ's heavenly kingdom, decided to make an impactful decision himself. He made an official name change for himself and for his son, to which he wanted his legacy to move forward.

You see, God is in the name-changing business. Some more notable ones include:

- Abram to Abraham
- Sarai to Sarah
- Jacob to Israel
- Saul to Paul

But hear this and make no mistake. Everyone who names the Lord as their God has a name change. You are no longer "children of the devil" but rather "children of God" (1 John 3:10). A name change comes with an identity change.

As Martin Luther King Jr. pointed out, we all have had an identity change. In the kingdom of God, there is no longer black or white, male or female, free man or slave. The Word of God highlights that this wall has been broken long ago:

> There is neither Jew nor Greek, there is neither bond nor free, there is neither male nor female: for ye are all one in Christ Jesus. (Galatians 3:28)

And

> Where there is neither Greek nor Jew, circumcision nor uncircumcision, Barbarian, Scythian, bond nor free: but Christ is all, and in all. (Colossians 3:11).

Where once Gentiles were titled by words like *sinful*, *unclean*, and *uncircumcised*, now God calls all to be His "friends," "children," and "coheirs" with Him (1 Samuel 17:26 and Galatians 2:15 turns to Romans 8:16–17 and 2 Corinthians 6:18).

So yes, Martin Luther King had a dream. But only God can make it a true, authentic reality. Seek His truth, love others as Christ has loved you, and perhaps we too can see revolutionary name changes rising up to proclaim freedom from sin.

205

To Those Who Are Depressed

If you are depressed, if you are struggling, if you are in pain, if you are in a situation, and you have no assurance that tomorrow, the sun could rise again, read the following passage in its entirety, knowing that these are words of God in response to a man who has endured more than most have in the history of the earth.

> Where wast thou when I laid the foundations of the earth? declare, if thou hast understanding.
> Who hath laid the measures thereof, if thou knowest? or who hath stretched the line upon it?
> Whereupon are the foundations thereof fastened? or who laid the corn stone thereof;
> When the morning stars sang together, and all the sons of God shouted for joy?
> Or who shut up the sea with doors, when it brake forth, as if it had issued out of the womb?
> When I made the cloud the garment thereof, and thick darkness a swaddlingband for it,
> And brake up for it my decreed place, and set bars and doors,

And said, Hitherto shalt thou come, but no further: and here shall thy proud waves be stayed?
Hast thou commanded the morning since thy days; and caused the dayspring to know his place;
That it might take hold of the ends of the earth, that the wicked might be shaken out of it?
It is turned as clay to the seal; and they stand as a garment.
And from the wicked their light is withholden, and the high arm shall be broken.
Hast thou entered into the springs of the sea? or hast thou walked in the search of the depth?
Have the gates of death been opened unto thee? or hast thou seen the doors of the shadow of death?
Hast thou perceived the breadth of the earth? declare if thou knowest it all.
Where is the way where light dwelleth? and as for darkness, where is the place thereof,
That thou shouldest take it to the bound thereof, and that thou shouldest know the paths to the house thereof?
Knowest thou it, because thou wast then born? or because the number of thy days is great?
Hast thou entered into the treasures of the snow? or hast thou seen the treasures of the hail,
Which I have reserved against the time of trouble, against the day of battle and war?
By what way is the light parted, which scattereth the east wind upon the earth?
Who hath divided a watercourse for the overflowing of waters, or a way for the lightning of thunder;

To cause it to rain on the earth, where no man is; on the wilderness, wherein there is no man;
To satisfy the desolate and waste ground; and to cause the bud of the tender herb to spring forth?
Hath the rain a father? or who hath begotten the drops of dew?
Out of whose womb came the ice? and the hoary frost of heaven, who hath gendered it?
The waters are hid as with a stone, and the face of the deep is frozen.
Canst thou bind the sweet influences of Pleiades, or loose the bands of Orion?
Canst thou bring forth Mazzaroth in his season? or canst thou guide Arcturus with his sons?
Knowest thou the ordinances of heaven? canst thou set the dominion thereof in the earth?
Canst thou lift up thy voice to the clouds, that abundance of waters may cover thee?
Canst thou send lightnings, that they may go and say unto thee, Here we are?
Who hath put wisdom in the inward parts? or who hath given understanding to the heart?
Who can number the clouds in wisdom? or who can stay the bottles of heaven,
When the dust groweth into hardness, and the clods cleave fast together?
Wilt thou hunt the prey for the lion? or fill the appetite of the young lions,
When they couch in their dens, and abide in the covert to lie in wait?
Who provideth for the raven his food? when his young ones cry unto God, they wander for lack of meat.

Job character profile:

- Wealthy and righteous man; under assault by Satan in an attempt to get him to curse God
- God knew Job as blameless and allowed the course to move forward
- Through it all, Job:
- Lost his wealth
- His children
- His servants
- And developed a sickness
- It was so horrendous, it made him wish to die from birth (Job 3:11).
- Job was done evil by nature, people, and physical ailments yet… He kept his integrity and refused to curse God.

We find in Job 38 a climax, where God responds with assurance of who He is and all that is held together by His hand. This entire monologue seems to be crowned with the question, "Where were you?"

Often, we find ourselves in the reverse, asking the God of the universe, "Where were you when…?", instead of "God, where was I?" God does not ignore trouble; He works despite the darkness of the world.

In your moments of frailty, know that God is past, God is there, and God is waiting in the future for you with a brilliant inheritance and purpose for those who believe. Have faith and know that His grace is sufficient for the moments of infirmity (2 Corinthians 12:9).

Be still and know that He is God (Psalm 46:10).

206

Heaven's Calculator

For by grace are ye saved through faith; and that not of yourselves: it is the gift of God: Not of works, lest any man should boast.
—Ephesians 2:8–9

As a teacher, the use of calculators is commonplace. In the modern world, generally everyone understands conceptually how to use a calculator. At the very least, the function is obvious: to calculate. Calculating indicates assessment. As the old saying goes, "You put two and two together, and you've got your answer."

Recently, I have administered end-of-course exams to a number of classes. While watching these students apply their intelligence and manipulate their calculators to get the correct answers, I thought: How often do we try God this way?

It makes sense to us to say, "My faith plus works surely will elicit God's favor," or perhaps, "I pray with thanksgiving as the preacher man told me to do, therefore God has to grant my request," or [insert whatever situation you find yourself in]. I hear so often people say, "I'm a good person," yet time and time again we plug this equation into our day-to-day rhythms and the answer never comes out right. The problem is not only the variables inserted into the calculator, it is also how you work it. Faith is not worked left to right (e.g., a + b → c), it is only possible when worked right to left (e.g., c → a + b).

God's favor (grace) → Faith + Nothing

The answer precedes the problem. God identifies Himself as "the Alpha and the Omega," which is the beginning and the end (Revelation 1:8; Revelation 22:13). He provided the solution many years ago and knew the solution before the beginning of the world. Plug in faith and nothing else, and you have grace everlasting. Changing the formula will always lead to a wrong answer and confusion.

> Blessed be the God and Father of our Lord Jesus Christ, who hath blessed us with all spiritual blessings in heavenly places in Christ. (Ephesians 1:3)

> There is therefore now no condemnation to them which are in Christ Jesus, who walk not after the flesh, but after the Spirit. (Romans 8:1)

Do the math!

207

Keep Your Head Up!

I will lift up mine eyes unto the hills, from whence cometh my help.
My help cometh from the Lord, which made heaven and earth.
—Psalm 121:1–2

If you were to walk into a classroom, gym, office cubicle, or any facility that expects productivity, you likely would see something motivational. You may see cliché signs blaring "No pain, no gain!" "Hang in there!" or the classic, "Nothing worth having comes easy." Although likely overused and now defunct, these signs once served their purpose. They were hung up, then somebody got necessary energy from them, and then, as they lived their life, encouragement became a daily rhythm that no longer motivated them.

Let me put it another way. Maybe life feels more like a search for motivation than it does a resume of victories. I get that. Let me offer this advice which never gets old:

Keep your head up.

Your child gets cut from the football team? Keep your head up. Someone else got the position at work you wanted? Keep your head up. No matter how hard you try, your wife and you still can't seem to get along? Keep your head up. This advice seems like a cliché just as well as the others, but consider for a moment its significance.

Things change when you simply lift your head up.

I like to think in terms of sports. As a lifelong wrestler, I know when you put your head down, you are opening yourself up to be pinned. As a runner, when you put your head down, nine times out of ten, it ain't coming back up. You are gassed. In basketball, defenders do not stop stealing the ball just because you refuse to be aware of their presence. When boxing, even when you bob and weave, you keep your eyes up and your hands mobile.

Keep your head up.

Moses was a man of God, who lived for God's purpose. He led the Israelites out of slavery, governed them, and delivered God's holy law unto the people. Saying this, there was a time when, because of his disobedience, God forbid Moses from entering into the land promised to the Israelites. Nonetheless, Moses never stopped seeking and even died looking at it, knowing that his offspring would receive it (Deuteronomy 34). God did not take Moses to this site for him to look down rejected at the ground. This was a reminder of God's faithfulness and faithfully he lifted his head.

You see, the heroes of the Jewish and Christian faith were men and women who responded faithfully to the sacred nudge to "keep your head up" (Hebrews 11:13). The apostle Paul literally lost his head at the hands of the Romans, but even in the midst of a stark reality, he kept his eyes set on where the Gospel was needed—Spain (Romans 15:23–24). You may ask if he ever made it and the likely answer is no; however, the truth is that he kept moving by keeping his eyes set on where he had to go. Every time his head was down, he remembered to keep his head up, only bowing his head in sovereign reverence of his king, Jesus Christ.

Be the one to pray in the midst of adversity, "I will lift up mine eyes unto the hills, from whence cometh my help" (Psalm 121:1).

208

The Bones of the Gospel

The bones of the Gospel. It is a phrase not discoverable within the Word of God. Nowhere can it be stumbled upon, and nowhere can it be deciphered. It is not an acrostic or a lofty reference to an Old Testament Scripture. It is a phrase that waltzed into my train of focus as I prayed in the shower.

So do not mark it as Scripture, but hear me out: bones hold flesh, and bones bear structure. Bones show when the covering of dermal vanity is laid as waste. The same bones form the undeniable shape of life when the fluff is blown away like insulation in a twister of death and false hope. Bones are what is left when the beauty we nourished is no more. They lay barren and snow white, despite the filth that clings for dear life but never could quite hold on. Bones rest as fact, while flesh is a carbon trace.

Saying this, why do teachers teach on all else, except the unexchangeable importance of the absolute interior? The structure, the shape, the mold, and the whitest, purest truth that in the end will outlast the grime of humanly muck. Why not teach the bones of the Gospel so the Holy Spirit eternal be edified above sinful decompositions?

Ephesians 1:13–14 reads,

> In whom ye also trusted, after that ye heard the word of truth, the gospel of your salvation: in whom also after that ye believed, ye were sealed with that holy Spirit of promise,
>
> Which is the earnest of our inheritance until the redemption of the purchased possession, unto the praise of his glory.

Romans 8:6 continues,

> For to be carnally minded is death; but to be spiritually minded is life and peace.

So what are the bare bones?

> For I delivered unto you first of all that which I also received, how that Christ died for our sins according to the scriptures;
>
> And that he was buried, and that he rose again the third day according to the Scriptures. (1 Corinthians 15:3–4)

Jesus is the Word of Life. Unbreakable. Teach and seek the unbreakable.

> For these things were done, that the Scripture should be fulfilled, A bone of him shall not be broken. (John 19:36)

209

A Lesson from My Cat

As I fed my cat this morning, I looked at him and thought, *Why do we get pets?*

Sure, they make us happy, they do funny things, and they're nice to snuggle. However, think a little bit deeper. We are setting ourselves up for heartbreak. Humans have a life expectancy much longer than nearly all pets, and we still get them. We get pets knowing that we are setting ourselves up for heartbreak.

So why do it?

As I thought about this question, I pondered answers such as, perhaps humans have the affinity to love and to take care of others. It's a nice thought but absolutely wrong. The Word of God says that the human race has a heart that "is deceitful above all things, and desperately wicked: who can know it?" (Jeremiah 17:9).

Although this appears to be an intention, many pet owners outside of the Body of Christ cannot exhibit true love and have a deceitful heart. So surely there is more.

Or perhaps it is because we do not think of the heartbreak that is to come because we are living in the moment, which is far more likely a human response. Or maybe we just ignore it and count the time that we had with them as a victory.

Or still yet, perhaps pets point to something far greater. Perhaps they are a furry tool of God that shows humanity how we are to treat other people—with love, grace, and respect. Jesus explained to His Jewish congregation the two greatest commandments:

> Master, which is the great commandment in the law?
>
> Jesus said unto him, Thou shalt love the Lord thy God with all thy heart, and with all thy soul, and with all thy mind.
>
> This is the first and great commandment.
>
> And the second is like unto it, Thou shalt love thy neighbour as thyself.
>
> On these two commandments hang all the law and the prophets. (Matthew 22:36–40)

The apostle Paul often reiterated to the Roman Church many times over the importance of love, and practically every New Testament author did the same. Love does not come naturally for a wicked, depraved people. However, by God's Word, the Holy Spirit, and yes, even your loving cat, perhaps we can learn to love as Christ loved the church.

Have a paw-fect day!

210

Atomic Faith

In the beginning, God created the heaven and the earth.
—Genesis 1:1

Many people know how it goes. It is the first verse of the Bible, and I always get hung up on it. Some theologian, right? The cool thing is, we can look around and see that it is true. God created everything, and Genesis does not need "the science" to support it.

Still, I like to take a faith-first approach and look at science as a cool afterthought. As I thought about what to write, I often got overwhelmed as everything in my life pointed back to a very creative God—the creative God.

One example of this comes from my days as a chemistry teacher. Every day, I am amazed by how intricate a world God made, how it often self-organizes, and how it does not unravel into chaos—like honestly, it would without God. An illustration of His providence can be found in an atom.

Atoms are the building blocks of the entire world, and they are so fascinating. Chemistry has many things that one must understand in order to make chemistry "work." Chemists must understand exactly what an atom is. But the truth is—no one is really sure of anything.

For example, a common phrase in chemistry is: "Opposites attract."

You see, the Bible really does have the answer for everything, including some pressing chemistry questions (I wish my students would read more) such as, what is the world made out of? Well, Hebrews 11:3 says,

> Through faith we understand that the worlds were framed by the word of God, so that things which are seen were not made of things which do appear.

But yet, the middle of the atom is made of positive and neutral particles, which are not opposites. Chemists really don't know what makes up the middle of the atom (nucleus), so they just slap a cover-all term, "nuclear glue," on it and call it an answer.

As a Christian, I know a far better answer: God. I know this because Colossians 1:17 says that by Him, "all things consist." He is the glue that holds everything together!

So look around. Look up. Then look down. After that, look side to side. There is a wonderful God who made wonderful things. Do not fall prey to the vain philosophies and sciences of men; rather acknowledge the truth and beauty of a benevolent God!

211

Combat of Life

And *he* said unto me, My grace is sufficient for thee: for *my* strength is made perfect in weakness. Most gladly therefore will I rather glory in my infirmities, that the power of Christ may rest upon me.
—2 Corinthians 12:9

Recently, I have started training in the combat art of jiujitsu. And all I have to say is—I have a lot to learn.

One of the biggest things I need to learn is that, unlike my background in wrestling, jiujitsu has a lot to do with fighting from your back. As a wrestler, you are told your whole life not to go to your back. Nonetheless, in Jiu-Jitsu, it is openly accepted and sometimes favored.

As I reflected on the differences between these two arts, I also reflected on the differences in positions I have been in with my relationship with Jesus Christ. I think to the story of Jacob and how he wrestled with God. Despite his loss, he prevailed, and this was considered a victory (Genesis 32:24–32).

Saying this, I was eager to utilize some of my wrestling moves, unfortunately, only to be put flat on my back time and time and time again, perhaps with a chokehold in there too. This is a perfect description of the Christian faith.

When we rely on ourselves and our power, Satan and our wicked flesh will put us in a chokehold—every time. It is in times like these that maybe the best thing to do is to lay flat on your back and listen to God as He instructs you through your struggle. God will point out what leverage you do have and do not have, when to push, when to hang back, and ultimately, when to simply trust Him.

212

On the Verge

And some believed the things which were
spoken, and some believed not.

—Acts 28:24

Late in Acts 28, we find a tired and imprisoned Paul, who in the last years of his life lived in Rome under house arrest. Paul, although still accompanied by a guard, had the ability to still minister. To the Jews in Rome, Paul informs them that he has been wrongly accused, and it appears they believe him, as well, they cannot find anything wrong with him.

He invited these very Jews to his home, where he spoke all that he knew of Christ and His Gospel, and what was their response?

> Some believed the things which were spoken, and some believed not. (Acts 28:24)

As a ministry, we are getting ready to embark on a new journey. We have a new opportunity. We have left a difficult time in our ministry, and now we are planting ourselves on the verge of a godly commission. We are to follow God, "who will have all men to be saved, and to come unto the knowledge of the truth" (1 Timothy 2:4).

But spoiler alert. In this ministry you are a part of, you will find some that will believe and some that will not, like Paul who pursued to the very end. Regardless, we have a goal and we know the Lord's intentions, so let us use this blessing and pursue it. Knowing that we cannot save the world and that we cannot save even one. But Christ can. And we are the hands and feet of the Body. So let us use this opportunity to not only be the Body but also act like the Body.

In unison, we are to live up to standards of peace, joy, grace, and lift up the name and finished work of our Lord and Savior, Jesus Christ.

213

Warning: This Will Make You Happy!

Here is a little story about happiness. Recently, I got stuck behind an Amazon van. The back and side of this van read the following:

Warning: contents of van may cause happiness.

I read it once. I read it twice. I read it a third time. And I thought, *That's it? That is what causes happiness? That is what feeds the American consumer's soul? The contents of a package?*

I thought of the likely thousands of Amazon packages my wife has ordered and how from none of those packages came forth happiness—at least any that wasn't fleeting. But then, I thought of a package that can. A packet of flesh—flesh purely intertwined with the Spirit of God, 100 percent man, 100 percent God.

This package was opened by Roman oppressors, a brutal whip, and a spear. Not so that we can be happy. But even more so that our joy may be made complete (1 John 1:4). And we as Christians say that by His stripes we are healed (1 Peter 2:24). We are made happy. And by His resurrection, we may have joy. Which is a sense of peace not swayed by circumstance and acknowledgment that we do not have to be happy; nonetheless, we must learn to be content. So I reckon there is such a package that can bring endless joy when opened.

214

Invite

Invitation is usually thought of as a kind gesture. It is an allowance to participate in something. We often invite others to participate in recreational events, ceremonial occasions, and yes, the Christian is quite familiar with inviting to church.

But we live in a day where it often seems hopeless. For someone to come to church and hear the Word? It is almost as stressful as having teeth pulled.

However, maybe inviting will be easier when we stop inviting people to an event, a concert, or an ear-tickling "moment with God" purposed to help someone feel better. Invitations must start with the most important truth: That all people have already been invited to encounter the living God. He has made it possible. Not only to encounter but to become a member of His family by believing in the death, burial, and resurrection of Jesus Christ.

The Holy Word says that,

> Now therefore ye are no more strangers and foreigners, but fellowcitizens with the saints, and of the household of God;
>
> And are built upon the foundation of the apostles and prophets, Jesus Christ himself being the chief corner stone;

> In whom all the building fitly framed together groweth unto an holy temple in the Lord:
>
> In whom ye also are builded together for an habitation of God through the Spirit. (Ephesians 2:19–22)

So as you invite, don't offer a new invitation. Rather, extend an invitation that has been waiting thousands of years to accept. Offered thousands of years ago, as a Savior with no breath, became a Savior with full breath, that was able to remove heavy stone from a hopeless grave. Relay the invite—believe (1 Corinthians 15:3–4).

215

Buying Stocks in Christianity

Christians are excellent at buying stocks. Buying as in bartering for something. Stocks as in a claim to a piece of something.

The true Christian is a member of the Body of Christ. The Body of Christ is those who believe in the Gospel of Jesus Christ and have been adopted into the family of God. Plain and simple.

What is amazing, however, is how readily we accept someone's claim to Christianity but then may abhor or treat differently those of a certain denomination, different theology, or "flavor" of Christianity (1 Corinthians 1:10; Titus 2:1).

At this point, the Christian has begun buying up stocks. The Baptist buys their stock, seeking to get a majority share of the Body of Christ, the Pentecostals buy their stock, seeking to get a majority share of the Christian organization. Or, "Oh no, the United Methodist Church has split their share with one half favoring one view, while the other the next!"

At this point, the Body of Christ is a far cry from unified and rather mimics a spiritual Wall Street. We need unity; nonetheless, unity will never come if we pretend unity is a constant exchange of stock or continue to preach Christ as if He is just another stock opportunity in the cesspool of world religion.

We need unity in this. Christ died, was buried, and rose again (1 Corinthians 15:3–4). We are baptized into one Body (1 Corinthians

12:12–13). And He is the only way (John 14:6). Why waste stocks? We are better together. Better when we operate with Christ as our CEO and we, the workers. Not the other way around (Ephesians 1:22). Do not buy stocks in Christianity.

216

Chemistry in the Bible 4: What's the Matter?

The earth is composed of two things. Just two. Energy and matter.

World religions have typically, if not always, been in consensus. Polytheistic religions state that their "gods" come from earth, water, the sun, and numerous other material sources. This is a common trend, passed down through history.

Regardless of their origin, there is only one account that reads,

> In the beginning—God. (Genesis 1:1)

Before matter. Before energy. There was God.

Verse 1 of the Holy Bible reads, "God created the heavens and the earth." He created matter, energy, and the rhythms that govern them. Our God claims preeminence over everything. Literally, everything. Matter and energy. The two things that make up things. No other religion has quite that bold of a claim and definitely not an ounce of inerrancy to back it up. All power and glory belong to the author of creation.

217

Beauty Is Skin Deep

> Beauty is only skin deep, but ugly goes clean to the bone.
> —Dorothy Parker

The above quote is rather convincing, but an astute Christian may notice that this quote allows for an additional element:

> Beauty is only skin deep, but ugly goes clean to the bone [and sin constricts the soul].

Christians are often pegged as pessimists for claiming humanity is born into sin and born (to put it lightly) "not good." To that, I say, what an understatement! People have such strong opinions of what is beautiful and may share them, a bit too openly.

You will hear individuals claim that people, nature, poetry, etc. are truly beautiful. But then comes the Christian to spoil it all by suggesting that there is not one thing on this earth that sin has not tainted, including people. And yes, this includes "the beautiful people."

> Beauty is only skin deep…

Moreover, the wise Solomon may prefer the adjective "vain" (Proverbs 31:30). Yet God's hand is not shortened, and He is working all things to the good of those who love Him and are called according to His purpose (Romans 8:28).

True beauty is found within the Body of Christ. Only here, is beauty beyond the skin. Those within the Body are clothed in a beautiful robe of righteousness, imputed to them by the beautiful display of love by Jesus on the cross and consequently—the empty tomb (Philippians 3:9; 1 Corinthians 15:3–4).

Only Christ's might is great enough to excavate the rotten spirit and arrogant flesh and refine our inner being as a polished geode fit to good works and His glory (Ephesians 2:10). I write all to suggest,

> Beauty is soul deep when the love of God has shone. (Romans 5:5)

218

How to Prepare for Easter

Easter is a beautiful time of year. April showers are busy bringing May flowers. Kids are getting out of school on spring break, so, like it or not, you gotta spend time with them. And there is an explosion of crosses, eggs, and bunnies plastered upon businesses, homes, and nearly every local entity.

It appears the theme of new life and growth permeates all culture, even those that, for all intents and purposes, are not Christian. Nonetheless, I cannot rag on those who are not Christians because, at times, I remember that many Christians hardly speak of the work of Christ's resurrection except for a three-day period in March and or April (whatever date it falls on).

At times, even I have been guilty of constantly reaffirming the blood and death of Christ, but hardly preach Him as a living God. God forgive me.

As we move into the Easter season (and out of it, this message works all the same) I am determined to share a bit of learned guidance.

1. Decide to Take Part in Easter

I refuse to inch into this portion of the message. Resurrection Sunday is a done deal and a free gift from God to you. It is not just a halfway mark for Christmas, where we are reminded to have goodwill to all men. Resurrection Sunday is a historical fact written within the fabric of the earth's and the cosmos' textbook.

Jesus Christ really did come to earth. He really was brutally and utterly inhumanly slaughtered by the very nature God painted on earth—a tree (Isaiah 53:7). Then, He really was buried, shrugged off death three days later, and rode water vapor to heaven (Acts 1:9). He really did pay our ransom and made all who believe, right with God (1 Timothy 2:6). This act really is all for His glory and really is a gift.

Yes, a gift. Like what you are given for your birthday. You cannot pay for it. Just believe and therefore accept. Now you take part in the Easter celebration. That's step 1.

2. Resolve not to Worship Easter

Now, worship Jesus, not Easter. Jesus is the One who died. He is the One who rose. His accomplishment is the significance, not the day. Nor the Easter concert at church. Neither, any other distraction that Satan may cover in gift wrapping (2 Corinthians 11:14). This day is about Christ and what He has done to offer humanity peace with God.

3. Agree to Take Easter with You

And this Good News, is not restricted to a day. It is written,

> But for us also, to whom it shall be imputed, if we believe on him that raised up Jesus our Lord from the dead;
>
> Who was delivered for our offences, and was raised again for our justification. (Romans 4:24–25)

We see an odd bit of grammar here. Christ was "raised" (past tense; therefore, is done) for our "justification" (present tense; therefore, continues). We see a past tense verb that justifies a present tense action. Christ's work continuously justifies us and makes us righteous. Not just Easter. Nor just Easter weekend. Not just during Lent. Christmas either. We are alive in Christ daily, because of Christ.

Therefore,

> Let no man therefore judge you in meat, or in drink, or in respect of an holyday, or of the new moon, or of the sabbath days. (Colossians 2:16)

We are to wake up daily preaching as the apostle Paul did,

> Christ crucified, unto the Jews a stumblingblock, and unto the Greeks foolishness;
>
> But unto them which are called, both Jews and Greeks, *Christ the power of God, and the wisdom of God.*
>
> *Because the foolishness of God is wiser than men; and the weakness of God is stronger than men.* (1 Corinthians 1:23–25)

219

Fishing, Wishing

I enjoy fishing. It is a pastime, like many others can relate, I never have enough time to enjoy. Nonetheless, my wife Hallie and I recently were looking to indulge in some fishing time as we vacationed at the beach. Unfortunately, however, out of all the things I was likely to forget when leaving, I left my rod and tackle box.

So as we entered the pier bait shop, I asked if they rented rods, and they only sold. So as any fisherman would know, fishing requires quite a few things. It demands a rod, lures, hooks, pliers, a fillet knife, bait, and (for sea fishing) it wouldn't be a bad idea to get some gloves.

Needless to say, this fishing outing was a pricey expedition. And as I sat for an hour or two, I discovered it was a bitter one too. I caught nothing. Zilch. Nada. Zero fish. This is the first time I have never caught at least one thing from this pier. And forgive the pun—I was salty.

But assuredly, God works all things to the good of those who love Him and are called according to His purpose (Romans 8:28). Forgive me if you find this verse a bit out of context. But as I later thought on this experience, my mind migrated to the uncanny similarity between people and their affinity for depravity.

All humanity is born into sin. It is not as if they forgot their fishing rod, or righteousness in this case, they truly never had it. So what does the world do? They buy more and more useless wickedness with their time and effort, catching nothing good, storing up wrath for themselves. But what do you do in these cases?

The simple answer is: change locations. More specifically, change positions (1 Corinthians 12:27). In birth, we are positioned within a position of slavery to Satan. But Jesus Christ has paid our ransom and freed us to live fully (1 Timothy 2:6). Believe His Gospel and you are positioned within grace and the Body of Christ. Full life awaits with a new purpose. No more frivolous fishing trips, your efforts are preblessed and we know that God Himself will go before us making every trip fruitful. Let's get fishing!

220

Worship Him!

When I worship, I would rather my heart be without words than my words be without heart.

—Lamar Boschman

Worship. Worship has always been a topic of debate within Christian circles. Yes. Always! How sad? Something God expects unceasingly, we mortals prefer to argue about it unceasingly.

Is worship in hymns? Perhaps it is contemporary in nature? Or what if worship does not only apply to music and or the arts? Could worship be the reading of The Word, a simple prayer, and or a life of dedication to God Almighty?

Ask yourself, "What is worship?"

In our humanistic day and age, worship rarely gets away from the arena of music. Many go to church and hear, "The sermon follows worship." To this and similar statements, I cringe. It is almost as if we expect God to transition with us from accepting our worship to leaning forward on the throne of heaven and listening in on what the pastor has to say. God makes no distinction.

Now I do not claim to be an expert on when God notices us engaged in worship, but I do know that worship has to do with our soul's posture. In John 4:24, Jesus teaches, "God is a Spirit: and they that worship Him must worship Him in spirit and in truth."

Scripture teaches that God is a Spirit, so therefore worship must be in the same rite. God is truth, so worship must be done in the same way. Worship is not inherently the strumming of vocal cords or the raising of hands, but more so the submissive bowing of the heart to the Lord. The words for worship in Scripture almost always describe a kneeling or faithful kiss. As a matter of fact, God addressed Israel and rejects their sweet songs, because their hearts were far and lacking of truth. The truth they clung to was man-made, therefore flawed.

He proclaims, "Forasmuch as this people draw near Me with their mouth, and with their lips do honour Me, but have removed their heart far from Me, and their fear toward Me is taught by the precept of men" (Isaiah 29:13).

This is where we should show caution in our musical tracks. What do the words of music reflect of God? Truth or ungodly persuasion? Is there a bowing of heart or a prideful rise to acclaim? Is worship all-inclusive—a life lived as a living sacrifice, being renewed in the process? Or a scheduled sing-along for a happy heart?

Worship is much more than what we often present it to be and important because of Who we worship desires our praise.

221

Finding Christ in Jane Eyre

It is weak and silly to say you cannot bear what
it is your fate to be required to bear.
—Charlotte Brontë

I have recently found myself working my way through the incredible literary masterpiece, *Jane Eyre*. This book is mournfully sad, yet, time and time again, you find characters who seem to lift your and Jane Eyre's spirit.

Jane Eyre was a fiery, abused young woman, rightfully struggling with forgiveness for those who have neglected her. Nonetheless, time and time again, she meets those who humbly remind her that God has expectations and a purpose for her, despite her sad past and frightening future.

Through numerous allusions and references to hell, heaven, and Christian duty, we see a truthful reality: The world will crumble at times around us, and the pressure will be immense, but we are not immune to these struggles.

Above, we find a quote from a friend, whom Eyre briefly knew until her shocking death. She reminds Eyre that her trials of faith are required of her to face (James 1:3). This quote took my mind to these places in Scripture:

> Yea, and all that will live godly in Christ Jesus shall suffer persecution. (2 Timothy 3:12)

and

> There hath no temptation taken you but such as is common to man: but God is faithful, who will not suffer you to be tempted above that ye are able; but will with the temptation also make a way to escape, that ye may be able to bear it. (1 Corinthians 10:13)

All Christians will suffer persecution, and God is faithful to guard your hearts through trial, temptation, and affliction, even though our earthly ailments relocate our eyes from our heavenly inheritance. We all have strife to bear, but we have a Christ strong enough to take it from us as well. There is Jesus who gives you joy to smile when it is not time for the trial to end. You have a spiritual nametag of (more than) *overcomer* that Satan will see and tremble, knowing that you are Christ's and He is yours.

So put off that which is weak and silly; there is much ahead with much behind.

222

The Wounded Heart

Whenever anyone has offended me, I try to raise my soul so high that the offense cannot reach it.

—Rene Descartes

We live in an offended world. Offense is taken in small things and large things. Nonetheless, I am not just a youngster knocking the volatile tendencies of others. It has always been this way! Name a century and name a year. There is a war somewhere in the world occurring. Name a country. You will find a land where much blood has been shed in an attempt to right a wrong. Name a person, you can find an overreaction.

Offense is a part of life. Sometimes it is entirely unwarranted. But there are times when it is wholly understandable. Christians worldwide suffer persecution. I will belittle no Christian's plight. Whether physical, spiritual, or mental abuses, we will be tried. We will be offended. Our offense is heard by our Father, but His answer is already delivered.

He has overcome the world; we are to benefit from His work and bless them which persecute you: bless, and curse not (Romans 12:14).

No matter how much God has given us (and believe me, "a lot" is an understatement), at times, my prayers turn primitive and ask

God, "How can you ask such a thing of me? Bless those who persecute me? Surely, God, you know I am a weak man."

And God does. I know He does. The apostle Paul affirms,

> And he said unto me, My grace is sufficient for thee: for my strength is made perfect in weakness. Most gladly therefore will I rather glory in my infirmities, that the power of Christ may rest upon me.
>
> Therefore I take pleasure in infirmities, in reproaches, in necessities, in persecutions, in distresses for Christ's sake: for when I am weak, then am I strong. (2 Corinthians 12:9–11)

When we are weak, God stands strong in our place. His grace is sufficient. We are rich, and those who persecute, without Christ, are poor. They definitely are in need of a blessing. And we, being so rich, how can we not offer it?

But plot twist: we really can't bless anyone. The word for bless here is a summoning or request from us to the Author of blessings upon those who curse us. Having a rich relationship with Christ, we have the ability to pray for intercession for others.

We have such a great power, but it comes in a task that is so difficult. Hand in hand, blessings and pain group. To be blessed (made happy), one must first be in torment, as is the case of the persecutors. Therefore, I pray for strength. For all who read this: the strength to endure trials, strength to pray, and a heart that does not question God but loves every answer He has given. This is my prayer.

Selah.

223

Lessons from Calf Feeding

Let me introduce you to a young calf beginning on milk. I thought giving her a slice of bread would make her stronger and healthier, faster. Unfortunately, I was wrong. She began to gag and was not quite ready for the rich bread. I then thought of 1 Corinthians 3:2, which states,

> I have fed you with milk, and not with meat: for hitherto ye were not able to bear it, neither yet now are ye able.

We must learn the fundamentals and build from the foundation first, which is Christ (1 Timothy 1:16). We are to study the Word (2 Timothy 2:15). This same concept is addressed in Hebrews 5:12–14.

We as a Church leave out tracts as they aid in offering an invitation to hear the Word of God rightly divided and depict how to be complete in Christ (Colossians 2:9–10). It is a simple thing to do, although sometimes I see tracts that can confuse more than explain. This often comes from giving meat before milk.

Some operate ignorant of the mystery truth—meat. In our key verse, 1 Corinthians 3:2, the Corinthians were unskillful in the Word, and when you keep reading, you will see they compare man with man. They were babes, not comparing spiritual things with spiritual things (Philippians 3:2).

On top of this, remember, God always gives the increase in time. So let us not gag someone with the Word, like the calf I spoke of earlier. People will reject the Word as the calf did the bread (Hebrews 5:13–14).

224

When Up Close

Have you ever done something that, when up close, seems so right? But when you step back, you wonder how you can be so wrong?

If you would, travel back in time with me to a memory I am sure is true but now feels so much like a fever dream I question it. My brother and I were young, very young at that. My mother had taken us to our grandfather's home, where to this day, our families still congregate and catch up. It is a quaint, beautiful small home, but due to the climate of its neighborhood, it may or may not require a privacy fence for the backyard. This fence has always been there. That is, as long as I have been alive.

Saying this, think of something that has been in your life so long you feel the urge to shake things up and break it. Could it be a rule at work? Perhaps some type of eyesore that surrounds your home?

My brother and I saw a fence. A nice fence, with strikingly thin boards. For this portion of the story, I believe my brother initiated it; however, since I am the storyteller, I feel obligated to take the blame. As we stood before this fence, an aggressor to our adventure, I raised my foot and kicked it. Following, we heard an exaggerated crack, and my brother and I peered through the hole that remained. You would expect us to feel instant shame and back away from the fence. You know what? I would expect this too.

But being so close to the damage, we felt powerful. Adrenaline pulsed through our sixty- and eighty-pound frames; therefore, we got busy kicking in every board in sight. But as everything in life, there came the last board. We kicked it in and then stepped back from our masterpiece, sure it would get hung up in the Louvre.

Nonetheless, we felt no pride. The emotion we felt was fear. We were literally scared, and we wanted to die. I could relate to Adam and Eve, who up close to the tree, found satisfaction in eating the one fruit they were forbidden to eat. But then, their eyes were opened, and fear gripped them with a mighty squeeze.

So we discussed it and decided to go tell our papa so our execution could be swift. When he stepped onto the porch, he asked one question. "Why would you do that?" To which we eloquently replied, "I don't know."

This situation also occurs biblically. Whenever God addresses the sin of man, in so many words, the only responses humanity ever has is "I don't know" or to deflect it altogether.

Adam murmured these words, "I heard thy voice in the garden, and I was afraid, because I was naked; and I hid myself" (Genesis 3:10). Cain tried to turn the question of murder on God, stating, "Am I my brother's keeper?" (Genesis 4:9).

Many years later, the apostle Paul wrote regarding the blinding of those closest to sin, the unbeliever. He writes in 2 Corinthians 4:4, "In whom the god of this world hath blinded the minds of them which believe not, lest the light of the glorious Gospel of Christ, who is the image of God, should shine unto them."

For the believer, we are positioned in grace. Yet sometimes our testimony causes second-hand grieving. Paul states in 1 Corinthians 15:9, "For I am the least of the apostles, that am not meet to be called an apostle, because I persecuted the church of God." Paul, the Apostle to the Gentiles, lived a life that seemed so right up close. But at a distance, it grieved him.

But like Paul, all must come to this next statement in verse 10:

> But by the grace of God, I am what I am.

Let that sink in. Then continue reading.

> And His grace which was bestowed upon me was not in vain; but I laboured more abundantly than they all: yet not I, but the grace of God which was with me.

That is the answer. Three words: "And His grace." Here we are, removed from the past. Only righteousness in our future by what Christ is imputing. Up close, it hurts. But now, step back, and we see the words, "And His grace." Grace, mercy, and peace are ours forevermore as we are seated in heavenly places.

225

A Good Thought

You ever have a random thought that seems silly but then progresses into a profound thought? Here is the most recent question or thought that popped into my mind: *How do animals first realize that water is necessary for their survival?* You may say, "They are thirsty, of course!" To that, I would reply, "Yes, they feel thirst." They know what thirst feels like, and they had gotten milk from their mother, but who told them they needed water to survive? How do animals know that is the key to survival and to pursue it?

Most of my life, I was told it was instinct. This is true. I also have been told it has to do with evolution. But the honest truth is, animals just know they need things. They know they need water. God gave them the ability to know. When they thirst, they seek.

The desire to pursue God is the same way. We are thirsty for something good, which in ourselves we have none (Romans 3:23). We have to find the source, a spring that will never run dry (John 4:13–15)! By the Gospel of Jesus Christ, we can be quenched, desire subdued, and grace abounds forevermore. Believe in His death, burial, and resurrection (1 Corinthians 15:3–4)! Making the real question, "Are you thirsty?"

And continue to pattern from instinct to thirst to Jesus Christ to relief.

226

A Good Carpenter Knows

A good carpenter knows the little details of the trade. The kind of details that only experience can teach and failures can reinforce. If you need work done around the house, get a good carpenter.

During my years in a trade school, we worked on a couple of projects, one of which was a 150-square-foot house that arose in the "tiny house" trend. Our school was making a home for a family who was suffering the effects of severe flooding.

Now there was a lot of money staked in resources. We had lumber, siding, roofing, appliances, insulation, and wiring. All these resources were entrusted in the hands of high school juniors, seniors, and one experienced teacher.

Now consider the following: with such a large amount of lumber in the hands of high schoolers, there were a few mistakes. Some students cut way too short, and other students cut way too much. But our teacher, a good carpenter, always cut the wood spot on at the right length. He often said, "You can always cut again, but you can't add any wood." He was saying, if you mess up, just make sure you cut too little and never too much. Saying this, he, as a good carpenter, always cut just right. He accounted for everything: tape measure flaws, the saw having an eighth of an inch width, and bows in the wood.

The scriptural equivalent of a "good carpenter" is an "unashamed workman" (2 Timothy 2:15). The apostle Paul states, "Study to shew thyself approved unto God, a workman that needeth not to be ashamed, rightly dividing the word of truth." You see, way too often, the Church settles for bad carpenters. These are the people who compromise the integrity of the Gospel, spread lies, follow the vain philosophies of men, and teach wrong doctrine (Colossians 2:8; 1 Timothy 6:3). The scary thing is, you find a lot of bad carpenters in churches, blinded by denominationalism, never acknowledging the pure grace of God.

God does not want us to cut short. He doesn't want us to cut too much. The Lord demands sound, healthy doctrine and a unified Body (Romans 16:17; Hebrews 13:9). We can be good carpenters without lengthy commentaries and eloquent teachers. The Church has the very words of God. It is our job to cut it right.

This means knowing who Scripture is talking to, who said it, and when they said it (Ephesians 3). Your Gospel is by grace through faith; just believe that Jesus Christ did all the work by dying on the Cross, being buried, and rising again. The apostle Paul is the Gentiles' apostle, teaching of the dispensation of the grace of God, and God operates today by grace, grace, oh sweet grace!

Be a good carpenter. Cut it right (Romans 16:25–27).

227

Faith of Mario

Most kids nowadays, as of the last thirty years, have played some variant of Super Mario Brothers. Recently, I had the nice experience of watching the new Mario movie with my wife. Following the movie, my philosophical mind kicked in, and I saw some interesting resemblance between Mario and the Christian.

At first, I thought of bashing the Christian prayer life that seeks power-ups as they pray. Many think of prayer time as a time of ascertaining a spiritual bonus. However, then I thought, what is so wrong with this? The Bible tells us to trust in God when we are weak, but then we trust God for strength, and religious authorities will bash you for being prideful (2 Corinthians 12:9).

Well, today I proclaim, let God be your power-up (1 Corinthians 6:14). We may not have Bowser in our universe, but we do have an adversary that is, in fact, much worse (Ephesians 6:10–18). But we have a God who is far greater and has won the victory (John 16:33)!

Fight the good fight, for you have a holy power-up! Then perhaps you'll have the faith of Mario!

228

What Came First?

Now I imagine a bunch of hands just went up saying, "I know! I know!" And still, some will say chicken, and others will say egg. But I'm not even asking about that. I am asking what came first in preaching the Gospel for those who follow. But first, you must define which gospel. The gospel of the kingdom or the Gospel by which you are saved today (1 Corinthians 15:3–4). This Gospel came to be preached first by Paul.

Now John the Baptist started the beginning of a gospel (Mark 1:1). Jesus had a gospel, but He first ministered to Israel. Then we have Peter and the twelve preaching the gospel of the kingdom (Luke 9:2). This is the same gospel that Peter preached at Pentecost. This is the message where Pentecostals begin and end.

But now we are left with Paul's Gospel in 1 Corinthians 15:3. Paul proclaims, "For I delivered unto you first of all that which I also received, how that Christ died for our sins." He was the first to preach the gospel of salvation as the glory of the cross (Galatians 6:14). Since Paul was the first to preach the Gospel, it follows that the Church must find its pattern (1 Timothy 1:16). That pattern can be found in the books of Romans through Philemon.

So the question is not as simple, but the plan and pattern for our lives are. Hopefully, the next time someone starts the riddle of what comes first, you will not automatically think of a chicken or an egg but of the Gospel that first came to you that can save your soul.

Selah.

229

Taking Care of Business

Business. That's the way it is, was, and will be. There was once an owner or builder of a very large company. He told his people, "If you come and work for me and do everything my CEO tells you to do, someday I will give you land plus all you need for the rest of your life."

However, it wasn't long until the workers started complaining, made themselves department heads, and despised the visitors who did hard manual labor.

So the owner of the company sent his CEO to tell them what needed to be done. But they wouldn't listen and, in turn, killed the CEO and took his shares of the company. Nonetheless, the owner still had more shares, so he sent his COO (chief operating officer) to speak to the department heads.

The unruly workers took him out to the back of the plant and beat him to death. The owner then proclaimed, "I have had enough! You can no longer run the company until I come back personally and build a new company in addition to land to live. But in the meantime, I will let the manual laborers run the company. They can go worldwide and tell everyone that they can come and be co-owners and coworkers of this great company."

The owner then sweetened the pot. He continued, "They will get to go to a whole new city, and everyone will get a new house to live with me nearby!" But the owner has not forgotten his first workers. He will still come back himself and start business back up with them. However, some will not want anything to do with him and will forever be unemployed. They will never have life, only death.

Now that was an allegory, but if you read in the Bible within the book of Ephesians chapter 2, the apostle sets forth the basic three-fold division: "times past" (verse 11–12), "but now" (verse 13), and the "ages to come" (verse 7). In times past, you have a division between Israel and the Gentiles.

But now the Gentiles are no longer on the bottom rung of the ladder (Ephesians 2:13) and no longer living under hard labor but under a time of free grace. Now in the age to come, God will bring His purposes to fruition (Ephesians 2:7). We can learn how all of the Bible is for us, but all of it was not written to or about us. So follow this timeline and you too can understand the Bible. Let the truth set you free today.

Selah.

230

Stand Strong, Move Quick

Any athlete who is serious about their sport knows in some shape or fashion the classic mantra, "Practice makes perfect." But practicing wrong can also do considerable damage if movements are practiced—well…wrong.

One thing often neglected by athletes is the importance of good footwork. If a football player only practices the broad logistics of a play, then the skills necessary to perform that play will suffer. If a boxer solely works on upper body rotation when punching, then the fighter will lose a good portion of energy generated in the legs.

While we are on this topic, consider the boxer Muhammad Ali. His footwork made his career more prolific than other boxers and had him stand out as likely the greatest boxer of all time.

Footwork gives you stability. It gives you power. Footwork gives you a foundation. But footwork only works when you put your feet in the right place.

So let me ask you, and let me ask myself while I am at it. Where is your foundation? Some may immediately respond, "Jesus!"

Let me ask another question and perhaps improve your foot placement. Who is your Jesus? Was He just a good man or Lord of all? Is He a God who expects us to work for His favor or a God who says, "It is finished!" (John 19:30)? What did your Jesus do? Did He die and stay dead? Or did He die and snicker at death's weight as He rose from the grave?

How's your footwork? This may be the same question as, "How is your foundation?" And we should know that "For other foundation can no man lay than that is laid, which is Jesus Christ" (1 Corinthians 3:11).

But while I am playing twenty-one questions, let me ask one more: You got a coach? Footwork is not something we often can correct with peer proprioception or self-infliction. Your internal change must come from external eyes. God cares for you, and He offers you instruction for righteousness. Instruction to build on top of that rock-solid foundation!

Cherish the great Coach and His Word!

> All scripture is given by inspiration of God, and is profitable for doctrine, for reproof, for correction, for instruction in righteousness. (2 Timothy 3:16)

231

What's Good for You Is Bad for Me!

All things are lawful unto me, but all things are not expedient: all things are lawful for me, but I will not be brought under the power of any.
—1 Corinthians 6:12

All things are lawful for me, but all things are not expedient: all things are lawful for me, but all things edify not.
—1 Corinthians 10:23

Take note of the word *expedient*. Now take hold of the word *grace*. Living in grace, we have spiritual freedom, and furthermore, we have physical freedom to do much while no longer being under the Law. But not everything is expedient or profitable. Profitable as in edifying. Edifying as in it will build you up.

For example, vigorous cardiorespiratory exercise may be extremely beneficial for me! To a recovering heart attack or stroke victim, maybe not so much. Adderall and similar medicines may be great for improving focus and concentration for someone with ADHD, but for those without ADHD, it can make someone dangerously overactive and hyperemotional. *Roe v. Wade* made abortion lawful in all fifty states of the United States for many years, but it sure didn't build up anybody. It just removed bodies and seared consciences.

Following Levitical Law was incredibly beneficial for Jewish Levite priests two thousand years ago, but for a Christian, it is best not to frustrate the grace of God.

> Knowing that a man is not justified by the works of the law, but by the faith of Jesus Christ, even we have believed in Jesus Christ, that we might be justified by the faith of Christ, and not by the works of the law: for by the works of the law shall no flesh be justified… I do not frustrate the grace of God: for if righteousness come by the law, then Christ is dead in vain. (Galatians 2:16, 21)

All things may be lawful, but not all things build you up. Not all things progress toward godliness; as a matter of fact, some things do the opposite. "The just shall live by faith. And the law is not of faith: but, The man that doeth them shall live in them" (Galatians 3:11–12).

Live in grace. Be graceful with yourself, be graceful with others, and most importantly, love the grace of God. For it is by His grace that you can live in grace. It comes full circle! Seek good things that build you up and uplift the grace of God (Philippians 4:8). And remember, what's good for you may be bad for me. Vice versa.

Praise God!

232

Cloudy with a Chance of Glory

Have you ever looked up at a beautiful clear sky and noticed a few painted clouds dotted across it? You ever just want to sleep on one? Or perhaps hop on Airbnb, rent a space within one, and just hang out for a while?

That upward longing may be instilled in the heart of the soul of the believer. We know that as Christ rose on one, so too shall He return (Acts 1:11). Clouds are pure water vapor. Nonetheless, they come from every water source, pure and not. This includes muddy waters, sewage, lakes, and salty oceans but when evaporated, they make pure fluff.

Similarly, we will rise from this earth (1 Thessalonians 4:17). We will be leaving the corruptible behind and putting on the incorruptible, glorified body (1 Corinthians 15:53–55). From there, we accumulate as a cloud of witnesses to Christ's goodness in heaven. And that, my friends, will be better than a cloud mattress!

233

I Need a Dentist!

Do you know what the hardest bone in your body is? Your mom would probably say that thick skull, which in motherly adoration is often referred to as "a hard head." But no, it isn't the hardest bone, nor is it the femur or the pelvis. It is your teeth. Specifically, the enamel of your teeth.

Recently, while caring for my daily hygiene, I had an internal revelation relating to this topic. I need a dentist. I have a few rough spots in my teeth that have eroded away from years of candy addiction. But then it occurred to me how this hardest bone of the body disappeared. It wasn't a clean break like that common of every other bone in the body. The hardest bone in the body eroded away over time. Little by little.

You know, the works of sin and plots of Satan work the same way to deter the power and vigor of your faith. Little by little, sin and things contrary to righteousness creep in under the door until the problem is even realized (Jude 1:4; 2 Timothy 3:1–7). But then it is too late, and you are ensnared (2 Timothy 2:15–18).

Perhaps you need more frequent dentist appointments (I'm preaching to the choir), more frequent brushing in Scripture and prayer. Maybe floss the Word of God a little bit more, looking for the tight places (Psalm 118:5–6). After all, we are called to be people whose spirit is pearly white and pure (1 Peter 1:22).

234

What Are You an Authority On?

At times, I look to Google and various sources to see what questions are trending and what writing prompts I should pursue. Recently, upon doing so, I noticed the question, "What are you an authority on?" A few things popped into my mind immediately. *I am an authority on many things!* Star Trek, *some obscure history topics, and other nerdy things!*

But then I think of some of the last words spoken by Jesus before His ascension into heaven that details a position He will have long after He comes back. "And Jesus came and spake unto them, saying, All power is given unto Me in heaven and in earth" (Matthew 28:18).

It's a powerful, comprehensive claim that time and time again, humanity thinks they can usurp in government positions and fancy degrees. But even the most elite of human positions are given that position from God as easily as a participation trophy is given to a child in last place. This does not mean defy these people or insult them. Romans 13:1 reads, "Let every soul be subject unto the higher powers. For there is no power but of God: the powers that be are ordained of God." Obviously, we still have an ear to give them as well. Nonetheless, it does mean our orders come first from

Christ and Christ alone. This echoes the affirmation of the apostles in Acts 5:29:

> We ought to obey God rather than men.

In a day where fact-checkers seem to collect authority into their hands, Christian, know this: the Bible is not outdated, antiquated, or flawed. The words of that Book are the words of authority from that God of authority whom we worship, to whom all authority is given. Live free in this truth today!

235

Make A Friend, Destroy an Enemy

Am I not destroying an enemy when I make a friend of him?
—Abraham Lincoln

The above quote was the response of America's sixteenth president following the Civil War. Lincoln was asked this because many Northerners were frustrated with Lincoln's kindness to the South. Relationships needed mending, but this could not be done at a distance. For Lincoln, this was likely more than a friendly gesture; it was intended to be a safety net.

Nonetheless, he was not given enough time to make many friends, as he was unfortunately murdered by an enemy named John Wilkes Booth. Proverbs, the biblical book of wisdom, teaches on many aspects of friendship, including that you want friends, but not too many close friends (Proverbs 18:24). Friends build each other up (Proverbs 27:17). Companions will act in their friends' best interests (Proverbs 17:17).

But this quoted truth goes much further than just earthly friendships. It is also an important component of our relationship with God. We were once enemies of God; however, by the work of Jesus Christ, we can draw nigh and be sons, daughters, and therefore friends of God! We no longer store up wrath against ourselves because God destroyed an enemy by making a friend.

But God commendeth his love toward us, in that, while we were yet sinners, Christ died for us. Much more then, being now justified by his blood, we shall be saved from wrath through him. For if, when we were enemies, we were reconciled to God by the death of his Son, much more, being reconciled, we shall be saved by his life. And not only so, but we also joy in God through our Lord Jesus Christ, by whom we have now received the atonement. Wherefore, as by one man sin entered into the world, and death by sin; and so death passed upon all men, for that all have sinned. (Romans 5:8–12)

236

Britain, America, and the Body of Christ

For our conversation is in heaven; from whence also we look for the Saviour, the Lord Jesus Christ: Who shall change our vile body, that it may be fashioned like unto his glorious body, according to the working whereby he is able even to subdue all things unto himself.
—Philippians 3:20–21

In July, there is a spark of patriotism that circulates around the Fourth of July. America, home of the brave, celebrates! It is also a point to remember an odd truth. At one point, America was essentially Britain, just across the Atlantic. We had the same government, accents, identities, and taxes. When the time came to separate violently, there was a pretty clean break.

In 1776, we took on an entirely different identity. The same people, buildings, and clothes remained, but we had become something entirely new. This didn't happen as a nation per se. It took thirteen individual states (practically small countries) to come together to achieve a common purpose. If you told an American in 1790 that they were just a sect or a part of Britain, you would likely get tarred and feathered.

This possibly could be an American way of teaching about the beauty of the Body of Christ, the Church, and how something so beautiful could come from something as rotten as our fleshly bodies. We have been rescued from vileness, although we are still waiting for the glory to come!

237

God-Instilled Father

> My son, despise not the chastening of the Lord; neither be weary of his correction: For whom the Lord loveth he correcteth; even as a father the son in whom he delighteth.
> —Proverbs 3:11–12

Think of a father—your father, a figure, the Holy Father. Now, think of something you have learned from them. How did you learn it?

I have had the blessing of having a few fatherly figures in my life—my "papa," my dad, and my step-dad Darrell. They all have a knack for cars, which is a knack that I still haven't picked up yet. Nonetheless, I have learned a lot about cars, mowers, and machinery from them. Recently, I was thinking about how they taught me and how one day I will teach others.

When something goes wrong (e.g., a car breaks down), I remember at first, I would look out the window and watch as they worked. Then I would end up on the porch watching. Then, I would be beside the car. And then, the next time, they would say, "Hold this," and hand me a ratchet. The next step was, "Hold this while I tighten this." It was only following this that the holy grail of father–son moments appears. They ask, "Hey, can you tighten that for me?"

It seems instilled in a father to progressively teach something to children. I asked myself, why is that? Probably because their father did the same thing. It is the ninth wonder of the world, the God-instilled father teaching method. The most beautiful of these moments is when a father figure teaches about God.

There is a story in the book of 1 Kings of a man named Jehonadab, dedicated to purifying Israel of idols (2 Kings 10:15–23). Implicitly, he births a family that many generations later is found adhering to the godly living modeled by Jehonadab (Jeremiah 35:6–19). God instills fathers with the desire to model life right. Godly fathers are expected to model holiness unto the Lord as well, and it does not take any complicated plans! Just follow the God-instilled teaching method for fathers.

238

Disagree Lovingly...

There are some things that all people need: water, food, and shelter. The fourth life need is often neglected: love. There are four types of love discussed in the Bible:

- *Agape*. Godly, all-encompassing love
- *Storge*. Familial love
- *Eros*. Romantic or sexual love

The last, I consider to be the least discussed in our culture:

- *Philia*. Friendly love and the love which unites the Body of Believers

Love is absolutely a necessity for life. The effect of love missing is drastic. There is a danger of breaking fellowship with other believers. Sometimes, we allow disagreements in ideas to bring disagreements in the love that two believers share with each other.

In Acts 15:36–41, there is a disagreement between the apostle Paul and John Mark. A disagreement so sharp that they departed to different ministry locations. This disagreement broke apart the physical relationship, but intact remained their love for each other. We know this scripturally, because in 2 Timothy 4:11, Paul's last letter before his martyrdom, he summons John Mark. Through it all, he calls John Mark "profitable."

Arguments and differences are a byproduct of human individualism. Love is a gift of God that does not have to be broken asunder and should not be. Keep the Gospel the main thing and seek unity in Spirit!

> Now I beseech you, brethren, by the name of our Lord Jesus Christ, that ye all speak the same thing, and that there be no divisions among you; but that ye be perfectly joined together in the same mind and in the same judgment. (1 Corinthians 1:10)

239

Run Behind Momma

In the 1990s, there was a show that many a momma adored titled *Kids Say the Darndest Things*. I have found this to be true in my young life. Children see the world through a lens quite different from that of an older, seasoned, and frankly bitter adult. I have also found, at least with relatives, that children can also be far more wrathful but more likely to get away with it too.

I'll tell you my secret childhood plot. Whenever I felt that a sibling was deserving of an attack (typically from being attacked myself), I would execute the attack only under certain conditions. Me being the younger sibling, my attack would only be carried out in proximity to my mother. I would swiftly swipe at my brother and then run behind my mother as my brother chased me. I would yell, "Momma, Wesley is trying to hit me!" and then peer from behind the safety of my mother. My brother and I would lock eyes, and his gaze would tell me, *Wait till she leaves.*

You are probably thinking this is pretty insidious, but don't you lie. I know you did it too. As my mom reads this, I'm sure she will smirk. As God reads my heart, He encourages this spiritually. Like God's edifying proclamation in Isaiah 41:10, He will strengthen us and uphold us. He has given us a shield against the fiery arrows of the enemy (Ephesians 6:16). This shield is faith! Leaning from behind God and peering at the evil spirits of this world, He even gives us the Sword of the Spirit to swing from behind the cover of His grace (Ephesians 6:17).

Behind God, you are wholly safe (2 Corinthians 12:9). When we are weak, He is strong. Run behind God!

240

Mean, Median, Mode

Nerd alert: This devotional contains math. Math that you may have seen at some point in your young academic careers. Math that may still haunt you to this very day when your children bring homework—scary, I know—home.

Mean. Median. Mode.

Now before I go any further, I know you are wondering, "What on earth do mean, median, and mode have to do with Jesus?" It may be complicated at the moment, but soon it will be easy as pi. Math jokes done. On we go.

Mean, median, and mode are what is called "measures of center." This means in statistics that these numbers become the center of your search for meaning.

On average, you may be most familiar with mean, which means the average of something. Nearly everything is averaged in modern society, including weather, income, government census, and a large variety of demographics. The mean of something is highly utilized in modern society!

Median also has many uses, although it is a little less focused on. The median of something is simply the middle of something. We use median a lot in statistics, showing median incomes and costs!

But then, you have mode. Mode shows frequency. Which typically is not anything really anybody cares about. For example, if you are trying to decide whether or not your child is on their phone too much, this is a genuine concern. So for a week, you write down their daily screen time. It is as follows, in hours:

2, 4, 4, 4, 8, 9, 15

On average, your child is on their phone 6.57 hours a day. Yes, almost a whole workday. Their median time is 6 hours. But their mode is much less at only 4 hours, being the most frequent.

Mode does not serve much purpose, at least not like this. What mode does show is important is things like which gender uses something more or showing what positions are most popular in a company. Mode answers questions that other methods just cannot answer!

So let me ask you this. "Do you ever feel like a mode?" Do you ever feel like you are missing your purpose? Like an outcast? Like the worst at your job or just so insignificant that if you fell off the face of the earth that no one would care? You may not be a mean. You may not be the median, but I promise you, you can be a mode and make a big change. You are still enough that Christ came to earth and died so you can be in the court of God as a coheir.

The apostle Paul testifies that, "This is a faithful saying, and worthy of all acceptation, that Christ Jesus came into the world to save sinners; of whom I am chief" (1 Timothy 1:15). Christ came, saves humanity, and on top of that, gives us purpose and inheritance. Your mode is to glorify God and point others to His glory, for He desires all men and women to be saved and come unto the knowledge of the Truth (1 Timothy 2:4). And not everyone has the same function as we are sent to live this purpose!

> For as we have many members in one body, and all members have not the same office: So we, being many, are one body in Christ, and every one members one of another. (Romans 12:4–5)

God's grace is sufficient to carry us when we fail, but know on average, your median is the mode of worship! Live frequently—no, eternally—glorifying God! Glorify God today in this truth that you are loved by the Creator!

241

Mega Millions

Mega Millions. The famed lottery is, as last I saw it, 1.25 billion. The fourth largest jackpot yet, which is pretty much a Mega Billion now. Although the chance is insanely low to win it, many are excited to get it. Just the very chance of winning such a ludicrous amount of cash thrills them. Just for the chance.

But there is actually a lottery with far more wealth that many care not a bit about, and it is sad. Scripture charges us to beware of uncertain riches and only to invest in the richness of God!

The First Epistle to Timothy 6:17–19 reads,

> Charge them that are rich in this world, that they be not highminded, nor trust in uncertain riches, but in the living God, who giveth us richly all things to enjoy;
>
> That they do good, that they be rich in good works, ready to distribute, willing to communicate;
>
> Laying up in store for themselves a good foundation against the time to come, that they may lay hold on eternal life.

I am not one who tells anyone not to gamble, but I am one to say if you do, at least have the insurance of godly riches to back your investment. He will take care of your every need (Philippians 4:19). You don't have to win the lottery; Christ has already paid the ticket, and the lottery of life is yours guaranteed (1 Corinthians 15:3–4).

242

Slow Down, Enjoy Life—It Gets Faster

The older you get, the more you appreciate things learned early in life. For example, when I was younger, I was studious but could never see how things applied to me. Older folk always said, "Slow down, enjoy life; it gets faster as you get older." I had no idea until someone hit the VCR fast-forward on my life. I didn't understand socks and underwear are amazing gifts. Nor did I understand love; now I get it every time I wake up and see my wife Hallie, sleeping peacefully.

I didn't understand that what you eat and drink *does* catch up to you. Younger me assumed it was a game of tag, and I'd always win. I didn't understand why people have to die (sometimes I still don't). But I know now that many people who have passed in my life are far better off than me now.

I didn't understand that your family (mom and dad) get older too. The first day I realized this, it crushed me. Nonetheless, on a lighter note, I didn't realize how I'd use a school education. The average American child spends 8,884 hours in school over nine years. That means that a child is in school for 8,884 hours over nine years. There are 78,840 hours in nine years. That's nearly 12 percent of their lives over a nine-year period. And the main goal that entire time is to learn. About 100 percent of that time, the child is wondering: "Where am I going to use this in real life?"

Now that I am older and a teacher myself, I know a little better. I love literature, but sometimes English class was the worst for me. It felt like someone was always criticizing little details of what I said (I am glad they did because words matter). Then one day we were discussing *synecdoches*.

> Definition: n. a figure of speech in which a part is made to represent the whole.

You hear them in the news all the time. For example, "We need boots on the ground" (need the army deployed); "America took home the gold!" (means a select group of athletes took home the gold); "Get your butt over here!" (angry parent says to kid).

Another example is that our very name is a synecdoche. You identify as your name, but your name labels your bodily character. You may wonder why I am rambling, but my questions today are Who do you represent? Who are you a smaller part of? Who is the bigger force that you take part in?

We the Church are known for many things. The Body of Christ, of which we are a part (1 Corinthians 12:12–31). The army of God, by which we stand proudly against the wiles of Satan (2 Timothy 2:4). I am Jacob, but this is now just a label for "a new creation" (2 Corinthians 5:17).

Life speeds up. The Psalms teach us, "to number our days, that we may apply our hearts unto wisdom" (Psalm 90:12). Therefore, redeem the time (Ephesians 5:15–17). Known by a label, living as someone who is truly alive. Know who you represent as an ambassador.

> Now then we are ambassadors for Christ, as though God did beseech you by us: we pray you in Christ's stead, be ye reconciled to God. (2 Corinthians 5:20)

243

Where Are You?

And the Lord God called unto Adam, and
said unto him, Where art thou?

—Genesis 3:9

In reading I had recently heard it suggested that in the garden of Eden (pardon me for not knowing from whom it came) that God did not ask Adam in the garden, "Where art thou?" because He didn't know. The Lord asked this of Adam because Adam did not know where he was at.

It seems so obvious when phrased this way. You think, "Of course God knew where Adam and Eve were! He's God!" But then you are left with the ageless question, "Why would He ask?"

This question echoes the rhetoric of Christ in responding to the Pharisees with His questions and once again you may think, "That makes sense! Jesus is God!" But once again, head knowledge cannot seem to answer the question, "Why would He ask?"

Questions serve the purpose of getting an answer. Nonetheless, when the inquisitor asks the question already knowing the answer, you must logically assume that the answer is for you to grasp, not the questioner. Saying this, I am not posed to pretend that I am God or that I am even further along in my spiritual journey than you.

But let me ask this. "Where art thou?" "Where are you?"

Are you still pretending that the very thought of death doesn't paralyzes you?

Perhaps, you're faith has been solid up to a recent cataclysmic event in your life?

Or maybe, you are a saved, justified, and sanctified believer, but like Adam you suddenly feel separated and exposed?

And for some, you are separated and exposed before a holy God and you need to know—you thirst to know, what right relationship looks like and where it begins.

Just answer out to God, *Here I am. Nude. Exposed. Needing you as my Savior. I know you came, you died, and you rose again so that I can be clothed with righteousness. Use me for Your purpose.*

When the question poised is "Where are you?" call out, "God, here I am."

244

Day at the Beach

You would be hard pressed to find someone who does not enjoy a good day at the beach. What would a beach day look like for you?

You see kids (and adults who act like children, such as myself) fighting waves. Beachgoers tanning. Sandcastles looming high over the masses. And people digging holes.

Yes. On the beach, digging holes takes a typically terrible time and makes it fun! But on the beach, with every shovel load, you combat the incoming waves which refill the hole just as fast as you dig it! And so it goes. Dig. Fill. Dig. Fill. Frustration. Quit digging.

You see, digging in sand is easier, but it never lasts.

Biblically, nothing much good comes from working in sand. For instance, Jesus taught a parable of the houses built on the sand. It was the house built on the rock which stood (Luke 6:48). As Christians, we understand that Jesus is our Rock and our chief Cornerstone on which we build.

> For other foundation can no man lay than that is laid, which is Jesus Christ. (1 Corinthians 3:11)

From a solid foundation, one can build. Any other foundation is sinking sand, being filled with the wrath of God. As you work to build, you sink deeper and deeper still. First and foremost, you must live from the solid ground of Jesus Christ.

Compare digging in a remote field away from the waves and the beach where water is constant. In comparison, you will see the importance of where you place your feet. You will see the importance of where you build your life!

245

Justice

Growing up, I idolized the iconic superhero, Batman. I wanted to be him, aside from the dead parents and deep, unending, introspective feelings of vengeance. I wanted to be "nice" Batman. One aspect that I have always admired about Batman is his love for justice. He was even on a wicked awesome team called the Justice League.

Living in a society where fictional superheroes are the ultimate unattainable view of justice sometimes blurs the line of what true, godly justice looks like. Try and prove me wrong. Recently, in an exposition of the book of Amos, I read over and over just how fed up God gets with injustice. In this entire nine-chapter book, there is little consolation to Israel, Judah, or any other nation that God promises to destroy for their negligence.

I thank God we live in an age of grace. It appears that within the last ten years, justice has been a topic that triumphs over all others. But this worldly sense of justice starts with what you do and then moves to try to fix the question of who you are. Perhaps Christopher Nolan's Batman highlighted popular perception best when grunting, "It's not who I am underneath, but what I do that defines me."

To God, justice and peripheral ideals do matter. To Israel, God spoke through the prophet Amos:

> Though ye offer me burnt offerings and your meat offerings, I will not accept them: neither will I regard the peace offerings of your fat beasts. Take thou away from me the noise of thy songs; for I will not hear the melody of thy viols. But let judgment run down as waters, and righteousness as a mighty stream. Have ye offered unto me sacrifices and offerings in the wilderness forty years, O house of Israel? (Amos 5:22–25)

The Israelites could do so much to appease God, but they would not get an inch closer to Him without first having a change of heart. But please, my friends, do not try to directly assimilate yourself into this verse.

"Why?" you ask. Because how we change is entirely different from the way Israel did. Their only hope of salvation here was faith in repentance. We, however, at the moment of faith, have the opportunity to be "new creatures." Or as some would have it, "new creations."

> Therefore if any man be in Christ, he is a new creature: old things are passed away; behold, all things are become new. (2 Corinthians 5:17)

Christ has become our righteousness. Christ and His Word have become the glasses by which we see the world, and justice comes alive. In Christ, your mind is renewed, and you understand that apart from God's grace, God's direction, and God's ultimate promise to bring justice, true justice is a mirage posed by unconverted hopefuls (Romans 12:1–2; Revelation 21).

For the places where justice has yet to illuminate, I pray justice to come quickly. But justice comes when, prayerfully, we shine the spotlight into the sky and see the only true superhero, Christ, come and save the souls of humanity who desperately need the Hero. It is here, empowered, we can move as the Body of Christ and make change.

Optimistically, I pray to see this soon.

246

The Knockout: Ministry 101

Fight the good fight of faith, lay hold on eternal life, whereunto thou art also called, and hast professed a good profession before many witnesses.

—1 Timothy 6:12

Boxing has historically been known as "the sweet science." It has this methodical, confectionary name because the sport of boxing requires an immense amount of skill, tact, and methodical combination to achieve desired success.

Boxing has a variety of possible strikes that are assembled in various orders called combos. Not every strike is designed for the anticipated knockout. For instance, a light punch called a jab is intended to wear opponents out and open them up for a bigger strike. Strikes to the body are designed to get opponents to drop their hands from their faces so that more punishment can be delivered. Uppercuts disorient opponents who lack a strong chin and typically end with a hook or an overhook to deliver the finishing blow.

I refuse to call ministry a sweet science too (this implies it is merely some kind of cold strategy); however, it does hold uncanny similarities to a primetime bout. How, you may ask? Ministry hurts. It's filled with disappointment. You see the lost and broken—well… lost and broken. You get fatigued often, and it feels like twelve rounds of a fight. And although you are always looking for God to score a knockout, not every encounter is a knockout.

Persistently, you seek out the lost. Jab. Persistently, you open yourself up for teaching moments. Cross. Persistently, you get rejected as you invite. Uppercut. Oof. You get hit back with financial turmoil. But don't worry, put your hands up, look to God in your corner, and go back at it. Till eventually, you see (or often don't see) the fruit of your labor, and someone believes the Gospel and has salvation evermore. Lead hook. Knockout (1 Corinthians 15:3–4).

This is the work. Persistent hope in the conditioning of Christ's Gospel, in the face of hard punches, we fight (Romans 5:3–4). Every strike isn't a knockout, but every action has the knockout in mind. Set it up and trust God's plan. Whether it is salvation, spiritual growth, or even just a new friend.

God, let our prayer be *"Blessed be the Lord my strength which teacheth my hands to war, and my fingers to fight"* (Psalm 144:1).

247

That Time of Year

Gearing up in America is a time of year defined by tailgates, reserved Fridays, and an excessive amount of chicken wing consumption. These three gleefully gluttonous events revolve around the yearly advent of football season. What a beautiful time of year it is. Even for those who have lived a full life and not once understood terminology other than "Touchdown!" continuous celebration is in order.

It takes me back to the years that I played football. I played for a decent program early in high school, but when I moved north to West Virginia, I joined a team that was, frankly, atrocious (to all my alums that read this, I apologize, but we all remember the days). We took many losses, yet to our parents, we were champions.

I think back sometimes to what caused such failures, and when comparing my North Carolina program with the West Virginia program, I am sure I know the answer. Fundamentals were lacking. Growing up, I knew that good football was founded on steady drilling. You drill footwork, tackling, passing, hip movement, reflexes, etc. Then when you have developed players, you drill plays while still drilling the fundamentals.

In West Virginia, this was a foreign concept. We learned plays and ran plays over and over again. Unfortunately, no one had the skill sets to pull off the plays. The team lacked the fundamentals; therefore, we lacked success.

Here, I insert my typical Christian application. As a Christian, if you lack the fundamentals or never grow in these, you will be an ineffective Christian. Period. For some, they may even see "salvations" but never see "touchdowns" because they taught a gospel founded on works. People will continue on an unhindered route to hell, meanwhile trying to work for their salvation and trying to be good enough for God. But none is good enough for God (Romans 3:23).

You need the fundamentals to cover you. You need to know that Jesus came to this earth, lived a perfect life, and died, was buried, and rose again for your salvation (1 Corinthians 15:3–4). This is salvation. You also need to know you are not alone. You are an individual member of a bigger family called the Body of Christ (Ephesians 3). Believe me, you will want to know that you are loved and saved by faith, not by works, and that nothing can separate you from the love that God has for you (Ephesians 2:9–10; Romans 8:35–39)!

Without the fundamentals, all the hotdog sales, charity donations, nice gestures, and good feelings mean nothing! It's like a ninety-nine-yard drive, but you fumble the ball every time.

> But we are all as an unclean thing, and all our righteousnesses are as filthy rags. (Isaiah 64:6)

Fundamentals make the game. Not minute details, happy feelings, or any other addition. Christ and Christ alone wins the game.

> I declare unto you the gospel which I preached unto you, which also ye have received, and wherein ye stand. (1 Corinthians 15:1)
>
> Jesus saith unto him, "I am the way, the truth, and the life: no man cometh unto the Father, but by me." (John 14:6)

248

Church Terms (Simple) 1: Conversion

You may sometimes hear the word *convert* or *conversion*. This English word comes from two Latin words that mean "turn around." It brings about ideas of tent revivals and services, but I want to stress that conversion is not the end result of believing the Gospel. God does not want you to "turn around"; He wants you to "become new" (2 Corinthians 5:17).

It brings about another church word you hear often: *saved*. Saved from yourself. Saved from wrath. Saved from turning around and still seeing the same old life. Don't turn around. Be transformed (Romans 12:1–2).

249

Bare, Bear, Bore

Who His own self bare our sins in His own body on the tree, that we, being dead to sins, should live unto righteousness: by whose stripes ye were healed.

—1 Peter 2:24

bare—(adj.) without the appropriate, usual, or natural cover.

bear—(verb) carry the weight of; support.

or

(noun) a large, heavy mammal that walks on the soles of its feet, having thick fur and a very short tail. Bears are related to the dog family, but most species are omnivorous.

bore (verb)—past tense: bear

or (verb) "make (a hole) in something, especially with a revolving tool" [or a lot more definitions that we are not going to list]

English is such a fascinating language. It is a language that borrows 80 percent of its content from 350 different other languages. It is a thief of a language. By this statistic alone, you can assume that at times, finding the right word is difficult. English has so many choices, and we still struggle to say what we need to say.

Recently, I came upon 1 Peter 2:24 in the King James Version but noticed something in the context of the verse that I had never picked up on. The verse reads, "Who His own self bare our sins in His own body on the tree." The Word says "bare," not "bear" or "bore" as I always had read it. When studying the word *bare*, I found that it nearly always denotes nakedness.

Its homophone *bear* is what I always inferred this verse meant. To bear something means essentially "to carry" or "hold." So I did what any theologian would do, and I found the original Greek word to describe it. It left me in much more confusion. The word is *anapherō*, and although it can be read as "to carry," it typically more so refers to "an offering," as in Jesus had offered His life on the tree or cross.

In confusion, I sat and wondered. Why would the translators of the King James Version (and other versions for that matter) use the word *bare*? So then I researched the Old English for the word *bare*, and what I found made me smile. The same word for "bare" or "naked" would have been *bær*, which holds the meaning "sheer, absolute" (c. 1200) and is from the notion of "complete in itself."

With that being said, read the verse again with that definition in mind.

> Who His own self bare our sins in His own body on the tree, that we, being dead to sins, should live unto righteousness: by whose stripes ye were healed. (1 Peter 2:24)

Now read it with the inserted definition.

> Who His own self [completed in Himself or offered absolution of] our sins in His own body on the tree, that we, being dead to sins, should live unto righteousness: by whose stripes ye were healed. (1 Peter 2:24)

The translators understood that Christ baring our sins meant only He who was complete in Himself could free us of "His own self," as the verse suggests. He didn't just carry or bear our sins. That verse would be incomplete then because it doesn't tell us where He dropped them off. If you carry something, eventually you will need to put it down. Jesus made us complete by absolutely doing away with our sin. He was the only person capable of doing so. The word here is not *bear*, *bore*, *carried*, or *offered*. The word is *bare*.

He gave absolution from our sins. And while we are in this conversation, one more definition couldn't hurt.

> *absolution*—(noun) formal release from guilt, obligation, or punishment

We are absolutely, entirely free because Christ "bare" our sins on the Cross.

And as Scripture preaches, "Christ hath redeemed us from the curse of the law, being made a curse for us: for it is written, Cursed is every one that hangeth on a tree:" (Galatians 3:13).

250

The Forces of This World

And it came to pass, when men began to multiply on the face of the earth, and daughters were born unto them… There were giants in the earth in those days; and also after that, when the sons of God came in unto the daughters of men, and they bare children to them, the same became mighty men which were of old, men of renown.

—Genesis 6:1–4

Earlier this year, I had a heartbreak. And I do not take this word lightly. *Heartbreak* is such a strong word.

heart—indicates the innermost of a person
break—indicates interruption or pause in continuity

Heartbreak is when your innermost yearning and being is paused as a result of something traumatic.

I had an unnamed heartbreak. This was the first one in a while that had me thinking of more physical heartbreaks. It had me thinking of a few things:

- Death
- Depression

- The spiritual realm

Yes, the spiritual realm. A real realm of influence. In America, where I write this, a survey came out recently by the Barna Group that claims 59 percent of American Christians, to some degree, do not believe that Satan is real. They believe he is just a symbol for evil. Eight percent said they just don't know. The same survey says that 58 percent to some degree do not believe the Holy Spirit is a real being; He just represents good. Nine percent were not sure. Surprisingly, though, 64 percent of Christians stated that they believe a person can be influenced by spiritual forces.

Do you find it surprising that the consensus is that Satan isn't real, the Holy Spirit isn't real, but demons likely are? With this logic, people can only give in to evil, but holiness will not prevail. This is where this logic leads. Therefore, no wonder pedophilia is rampant, drug overdoses kill so many, churches have become comedy bars, suicide is among the top killers of young people, and our nation's children are at an all-time high of suffering depression.

For problems to get solved, we have to believe they exist. In Matthew 24:37–39, we find Jesus teaching concerning the second coming of Christ. Jesus references a time when demonic influence causes an entire God-issued genocide. This was the age of Noah, or at least the time before the flood. It was evil, but still much like it is today. People did the same activities, such as eating, drinking, and giving in marriage. And who was a culprit then like now? Satan.

There is evil in the world sometimes deeper than the flesh and sin; there are dark influences. Our world is not the only world or realm, and I am not talking about aliens (Ephesians 6:12). There is the material world and the spiritual world, but they are both concrete and real. Look around you, and let me ask you, what has changed since the days of Noah? The flood killed the people but didn't kill the demons that influence the world to this day.

But flip the coin, and you also have holy influence.

> Ye are of God, little children, and have overcome them: because greater is He that is in you, than he that is in the world. (1 John 4:4)

There are literal forces opposing righteousness in the world, but the Christian doesn't have to fret. Christ has already overcome the world. Satan has forces; however, his allowed authority is bound by God's will, plan, and purposes.

Job 42:2, Job confesses God's sovereignty in stating, "I know that thou canst do every thing, and that no thought can be withholden from thee." As Christians, we are a possessed people—possessed by the Holy Spirit.

> *possession*—the state of having or owning something. (*Oxford Dictionary*)

When hearing the word *possessed*, we often think of horror movies and demon possession. But as a Christian, you fit the description of possessed.

Being possessed of the Spirit breaks the chains of darkness and essentially gives a chain of light (Acts 26:18). With light as our guide and light as our weapon, we can march on the dark forces of the world chanting,

> And the light shineth in darkness; and the darkness comprehended it not. (John 1:5)

251

Atomic Faith 2

And one cried unto another, and said, Holy, holy, holy, is
the Lord of hosts: the whole earth is full of his glory.
—Isaiah 6:3

A science teacher teaches about two things and two things only: matter and energy. The entire universe is made of these two things. Specifically, anything tangible is matter. Matter is made of atoms, the smallest identifiable piece of matter related to a chemical.

A science teacher often teaches about atoms and how atoms act. Different atoms have different personalities. Some examples include the following:

- Uranium-238 is radioactive and used for energy and weaponry.
- Potassium-32 is used to treat and detect cancer.
- Helium-4 is light and able to fill party balloons.

They are all able to do these things because of their structure. Atoms are made of subatomic particles (protons, neutrons, and electrons), and subatomic particles are made of more subatomic particles called quarks and so on. Every time you change the structure of an atom, you change its function. "Structure affects function."

God has a structure as well; this structure is called His attributes (a.k.a. personality; characteristics). In discussing His attributes, what better place to start than with His holiness? The *Oxford English Dictionary* defines an *attribute* as "a quality or character considered to belong to or be inherent in a person or thing; a characteristic quality."

The word you may often find in the Old Testament for holy is *qōḏeš* (*ko-desh*). This word is typically used when referring to sacredness and literally renders "apart" or "separate." God is apart, He is eternally pure, and He is not like any other being. In fact, He is so separate and holy that all other beings consist because He is holy (Colossians 1:16–17).

God is always wholly holy, and if man were to take holiness away from their view of God, then in their deceit, they redefine God. "Change the structure, you change the function." All of God's attributes are all in one, and one in all. You cannot regard God's holiness as greater than His love or His wrath, greater than His mercy, etc. All these depict God as He truly is, yet holiness encompasses all else.

He loves like no other. He is jealous like no other. He is good like no other. He is infinite like no other. Like with the atom, if you take one microscopic proton away from uranium, you have a whole other element with a different purpose. Protactinium has no known uses, but add one proton, and we use uranium for everything.

You may make God to be love, grace, and mercy, but if you do not regard Him as holy, you have the wrong god. He is separate, apart, and sacred. He is holy.

252

Sinners in the Hands of an Angry God?

For God hath not appointed us to wrath, but to obtain salvation by our Lord Jesus Christ, who died for us, that, whether we wake or sleep, we should live together with him.
—1 Thessalonians 5:9–10

In 1741, evangelist and pastor Jonathan Edwards preached a sermon twice within the New England area titled "Sinners in the Hands of an Angry God." This sermon literally scared the hell out of these congregations and sparked the First Great Awakening. This sermon emphasized one of the attributes of God that is important to understand—wrath. Tradition says Edwards was not even a designated preacher the days he preached.

Edwards had a deep understanding of God's holiness and his crowd. As he prepped the sermon, he knew he was addressing a vain and introverted crowd. Many of what history calls "revivals" began from the work of these fearful messages. A flavor of this sermon is in the following quotes:

> The bow of God's wrath is bent, and the arrow made ready on the string, and justice bends the arrow at your heart, and strains the bow, and it is nothing but the mere pleasure of God, and that

> of an angry God, without any promise or obligation at all, that keeps the arrow one moment from being made drunk with your blood.

Or

> The God that holds you over the pit of hell, much as one holds a spider or some loathsome insect over the fire, abhors you, and is dreadfully provoked; his wrath toward you burns like fire; he looks upon you as worthy of nothing else, but to be cast into the fire…you are ten thousand times so abominable in his eyes, as the most hateful and venomous serpent is in ours.

Is this how the world sees God today? What do you think? Is this why people hide in their homes on Sundays, with no hope? Is this the only God they know? As I write, I proclaim you can be 100 percent sure that you are saved within the fold of God. God does have wrath, yes (Nahum 1:2–6). But understanding, categorizing, and promoting an attribute above another provides believers and unbelievers with an inaccurate view of God.

Esteem wrath above all other attributes, and you see an angry God. Esteem love above all other attributes, and you see solely a loving God. We serve a holy God who is entirely capable of both perfectly and simultaneously.

Humanity is imperfect and cannot correctly model the attributes of God (Romans 12:19). The biblical word for this effort is *hamartia*; we better know it as sin. *Hamartia* means "to miss the mark," as in an archer shooting at a target. People are always in limbo and cannot balance it. Esteem love above all other attributes, and you see a loving God. Sounds good, right?

Until you see an angry God with no (or little) love or a loving God with no wrath (or little). But no, God is holy, wrathful, loving, omnipotent, peaceful, righteous, etc. All perfectly simultaneously. Scripture says we are storing up wrath (Romans 2:5). But what is wrath? In Scripture, it is reflected as *orgē* (*or-gay*), defined as "anger, agitation of the soul, typically leading to punishment." This is the God media passes on to the masses without ever consulting His Word.

But continue reading Romans 2:5 from verses 6 to 10. You'll see here that God is equally patient and peaceful. He is equally good and just to offer the Savior Jesus Christ, the only person righteous enough to cover our sins and appease God's wrath. It is not God's will that any experience His wrath. Want proof? Jesus.

God's holiness was assaulted by the filthiness of man, and He sent Jesus Christ to cover us with His righteousness. Only God's righteousness can atone for unrighteousness.

> Who will have all men to be saved, and to come unto the knowledge of the truth. (1 Timothy 2:4)

It is not God's will that any experience His wrath. But here's the catch: just because we are saved from wrath doesn't mean we should hate God's wrath. Think for a second of Christian music and then ask, "How many of them are praising the wrath of God?" Especially considering it is an attribute of God? Every attribute of God is holy and pure: loving, wrathful, infinite, omnipresent, etc. We should love God's wrath, as without it, there is no justice.

We live in an era of fighting for justice of all sorts—criminal, social, environmental, etc. But holistic justice is impossible apart from God. Philosopher Criss Jami writes in *Healology*, "God's judgment is not like man's judgment. It is not a suspension of His love but an extension of His love. His justice is always righteous, so His judgment is always love."

God loves justice; God is just. The best part of this news is that God is no respecter of persons! (Romans 2:11). His wrath is solely against wickedness, and He favors righteousness. God has appeased His wrath, offering us peace with Him. God has a plan for us to escape the coming wrath upon the earth by the Rapture. And there will be a day when there are no more tears, no death, no sorrow, no crying, no war, no light, and no darkness.

We have atonement for sin, but justice is on the way. Justice by way of wrath and life by way of grace and love. We are children of God in the arms of the Holy Father.

253

A Sickness

But shun profane and vain babblings: for they will increase unto more ungodliness. And their word will eat as doth a canker.
—2 Timothy 2:16–17

Upon the release of the Christopher Nolan film, *Oppenheimer*, many people wondered just who this man was. While many have heard of particular scientists like Thomas Edison and Albert Einstein, Oppenheimer had disappeared into obscurity until rediscovered by the masses with the new film. Oppenheimer led a legacy that, although admittedly he felt was right, drew the line when asked to repeat. The one piece of history that I can never understand in the legacy of Oppenheimer is how he got so far in life.

He was brilliant. Highly intelligent. Handsome. But he lived in the age of McCarthyism. For those not familiar with McCarthyism, it is also known as the Second Red Scare. This was primarily an American-led phenomenon headed by Wisconsin senator Joseph McCarthy. It was defined as a hair-trigger assault on Communist ideals and allowed ease of judicial action against Soviet-fueled ideology in the 1940s and 1950s.

Strikingly, despite US wariness against Communism, we had a Communist sympathizer heading one of the most cataclysmic government programs in US history: the Manhattan Project. This program was organized to assemble the first nuclear weaponry, which was soon to be unleashed on two cities in Japan, thus ending World War II. Although he never officially joined the Communist Party, it is known that he had attended meetings and paid dues. He knew what officially joining would cost him. Many alleged he was a Soviet informant. It eventually came to a head in 1954 when the Atomic Energy Commission revoked his membership, leaving him to be a collegiate lecturer for the rest of his life.

I give this brief history lesson to say this: within the church, do not compromise truth for intelligence. Sacredness for conformity. God-given plans for churchy business schemes. Do not compromise anything. "But shun profane and vain babblings: for they will increase unto more ungodliness." Do not colabor with ungodliness. Do not attack fellow laborers. What you build, do not let it be tainted. It is an infection that eats away at the church like gangrene or similar infections. Love all and fellowship with believers.

But perhaps the Word of God says it best:

> Be ye not unequally yoked together with unbelievers: for what fellowship hath righteousness with unrighteousness? and what communion hath light with darkness?
>
> And what concord hath Christ with Belial? or what part hath he that believeth with an infidel?
>
> And what agreement hath the temple of God with idols? for ye are the temple of the living God; as God hath said, I will dwell in them, and walk in them; and I will be their God, and they shall be my people.
>
> Wherefore come out from among them, and be ye separate, saith the Lord, and touch not the unclean thing; and I will receive you.
>
> And will be a Father unto you, and ye shall be my sons and daughters, saith the Lord Almighty. (2 Corinthians 6:14–18)

254

Here Comes the Sun

When leaving the house one morning recently, there was a beautiful sunrise that nearly took my breath away. It was not raining. Nearly one minute down the road, it was raining, but then—within another minute—the precipitation ceased.

But then I smiled. I had an epiphany. This is just like life. Our being is an ever-changing cycle of sunny and rainy days. In that moment I realized, it is the rain that makes you appreciate the sun for all its worth. Truly, sometimes you can't help but smile at the beauty and sound of rain, metaphorically and physically.

As you seek your destination of heaven, there are going to be times when it rains and when the sun shines. Sometimes, the rain will pop up in the middle of your sunny day. It is important in these moments to have faith in the sufficiency of God to hold on to you (2 Corinthians 12:9). To keep driving toward the light of heaven.

God is the God of rain (Hosea 6:3). He is the God of shine (Isaiah 60:1). God is the God of provision (Philippians 4:19). He is the God of salvation (1 Corinthians 15:3–4). He is God come rain or shine.

255

By Faith

By faith Abraham, when he was tried, offered up Isaac: and he that had received the promises offered up his only begotten son, Of whom it was said, That in Isaac shall thy seed be called: Accounting that God was able to raise him up, even from the dead; from whence also he received him in a figure.

—Hebrews 11:17–19

In Genesis 22, you find a unique story unlike any other in Scripture. Abraham, once Abram, was instructed to do an unthinkable task. A task that foreshadowed a sacrifice far greater by God Himself. God instructs Abraham to take his one and only son and sacrifice him.

No matter how firm your faith is, this story causes a knee-jerk "What?" reaction. What is even more shocking about this story is Abraham's response of obedience. He gets up, prepares transport, and takes his son to the mountains to do so. But right before he plunges the sacrificial knife into his son, God intervenes and forbids Abraham from doing so.

It is hard to imagine what was going through Abraham's head in these times, but 1,800 years later, believers get an answer from the book of Hebrews 11:17–19. Abraham held on to a promise. He believed in God's power, knowing He had the power to raise the dead.

Do we as Christians not do the same thing as we live our lives as a living sacrifice (Romans 12:1–2)? We go through our life with the hope of glory and faith that we too will rise toward heaven on the day of our judgment. We have faith in our resurrection and faith in the resurrection of Jesus Christ.

We believe. Therefore we sacrifice. And God has and will save us every time.

256

The Great Physician

> The good physician treats the disease; the great physician treats the patient who has the disease.
>
> —Sir William Osler

Sir William Osler, one of the Big Four founding professors of Johns Hopkins Hospital, explained the difference between a good doctor and a great doctor. As I pray, I often attribute the title of the Great Physician to God as I bring my needs before Him in prayer.

Many are familiar with the famous verse Philippians 4:6–7,

> Be careful for nothing; but in every thing by prayer and supplication with thanksgiving let your requests be made known unto God. And the peace of God, which passeth all understanding, shall keep your hearts and minds through Christ Jesus.

Knowing God is mighty capable of healing our physical needs, we must also recognize His ability to resolve our spiritual needs. Both have a spectrum of health that can easily be deviated from. Addressing these needs in prayer requires two things. One is to ask. The second must be paired with it: thanksgiving.

As we pray to God, the Great Physician who not only absolves the disease of sin and death but moreover renews the inner patient, loves to hear from those who are within His provision (Ephesians 1:7; Romans 8:26). He is the only one deserving of such an awe-inspiring title and capable of being what it describes—great. Praise Him today for His perfect practice!

257

Pizza Time

Which he wrought in Christ, when he raised him from the dead, and set him at his own right hand in the heavenly places, Far above all principality, and power, and might, and dominion, and every name that is named, not only in this world, but also in that which is to come.

—Ephesians 1:20–21

Most people have a place that takes them back to when they were a kid. For some, it is a child hood home. For some, it is a recreational facility. One of these places for me is Pizza Hut.

No, not the new, modern Pizza Hut. The old, authentic Pizza Hut. The one with a vintage aesthetic, a trapezoid top, and the iconic heaven-sent smell of fresh pizza.

But the one thing I remember the most is the clock—the Pizza Hut clock. An iconic, ever-spinning token of cheesy goodness, engraved within announcing, "It's Always Time for Pizza." It never stopped spinning as a reminder that it is always pizza time.

Likewise, we are always living on Jesus's time (Ephesians 5:16–17). Every minute and every second are for His glory. The Pizza Time clock did not stop spinning when I left Pizza Hut, and Christ's reign will not end when you, I, or anybody else leaves the earth.

The reign of Christ has been eternal. Jesus reigned before the earth was made, all throughout history, when He was on earth, after He took a seat at the right hand of the Father, and far after He steps back on to earth. Like Pizza Hut, His clock never stops (Psalm 115:3).

Forever He reigns. It's always Jesus time.

258

Moby Dick

> Talk not to me of blasphemy, man; I'd
> strike the sun if it insulted me.
> —Captain Ahab from *Moby Dick* by Herman Melville

Human wrath is a cunning and volatile phenomenon. Hate is repressed, shaped, molded, and loaded within the tongue like a cannonball moments from ignition (James 3:1–9).

There is a classic novel known to many titled *Moby Dick*. It is a novel told from the perspective of a sailor named Ishmael who boards a whaling ship under the command of a vengeful man named Captain Ahab. The tale follows Ahab's vengeful quest against a notorious whale who made a meal of his leg.

Following the tale, we find many morals within the story, but one shows the vanity of pursuing wrath. In the end, the pure in heart, Ishmael, survived; Ahab was consumed.

Unbridled and unrighteous anger leads to demise in the present and for the unbeliever can lead to the wrong side of eternity. For any injustice committed against you, know that vengeance is the Lord's and the Lord's only. Vengeance in the hands of humanity is a messy landslide.

Paul speaks to a culture permeated with glorified vengeance (the Romans) when he teaches:

> Dearly beloved, avenge not yourselves, but rather give place unto wrath: for it is written, Vengeance is mine; I will repay, saith the Lord.
>
> Therefore if thine enemy hunger, feed him; if he thirst, give him drink: for in so doing thou shalt heap coals of fire on his head.
>
> Be not overcome of evil, but overcome evil with good. (Romans 12:19–21)

Relinquish pride and the lust of the flesh and take hold of the fruit of the Spirit, which builds you up in righteousness. Do not carry a harpoon like Ahab, waiting for your ship to go down to throw it (Galatians 5). Allow the Spirit to take hold of you and live (1 John 4:13)!

259

Why Do I Even Need Church?

From whom the whole body fitly joined together and compacted by that which every joint supplieth, according to the effectual working in the measure of every part, maketh increase of the body unto the edifying of itself in love.
—Ephesians 4:16

We live in an age that increasingly finds belief in Jesus and church attendance to be incongruent. There are many reasons for this, and the infamous COVID lockdown of 2020 did not help.

You may hear people ask, "Why do I need a church? I got Jesus." Some have a more emphatic spin on this question, making it a statement. They state, "I do not need church. I do not need church to be close to Jesus." As the world becomes more independent, I reckon Christians do as well.

The independent Christian, however, will be a weak, inefficient, and targeted Christian. The Church (uppercase *C*) needs the churches (lowercase *c*) to build them up, support them, and grow alongside them in the knowledge of Jesus Christ.

I learned firsthand what independence gets you. When I was in eighth grade, I was on the wrestling team. I was invited to go to an off-season wrestling tournament. Long story short, I asked my mother if I could go, she said no, and therefore I did what any eighth-grade boy would do.

I told my friends she said yes, and I went to the tournament anyway at the local coliseum. I wrestled for the entire day and, losing one match, was wrestling for third place in a very prestigious tournament. In this last match, I was winning 8–0 when, off an illegal (dangerous) position by my opponent, I heard, *CRRRSH, CRAAACK, CRRSH!*

It didn't register right away, and I continued to wrestle. But when I saw my mangled arm wrap around my opponent like a seatbelt, I knew that something wasn't right. It was then I felt one of the worst pains in my life. This was an extensive injury that took place on my elbow joint, and it required a screw to pull my elbow back from three pieces to one.

Six weeks later, a humbled Jacob had this cast taken off, and I realized just how much I needed those around me. This included my parents, my friends, and Lord knows, my physical therapist. For over a week, I could not move my arm, and it was stuck in a right-angle even with the cast off.

I needed people to encourage me. I needed a physical therapist to help me move again. I needed my people. Whoever that was in my life at that time. Here, in this age of broken hearts and disappointments, nothing has changed for the Church (Psalm 34:18). We all need encouragement, we all need help moving better as the church, and we all need our people (1 Thessalonians 5:11–15).

Even the best life wrestlers can be—and will be—humbled. God created a beautiful family to be there when it happens and past when it happens (Galatians 6:10).

260

Thats's Cliché

For even when we were with you, this we commanded you,
that if any would not work, neither should he eat.
—2 Thessalonians 3:10

There is an old saying about old sayings called clichés. This saying goes, "Clichés are clichés because they are good."

I gotta say, sometimes that is true! But sometimes it is not.

Some good clichés could be the Christian yelling as you pass, "Have a blessed day!" Sometimes Christians are referred to as "On fire for God!" Or perhaps you hear after a sermon someone exclaim, "The pastor preached a powerful message. The pastor was filled with the Holy Ghost, and the Word of the Lord was anointed."

Wait. Does that one sound right? Shouldn't pastors (or all Christians, for that matter) be filled with the Holy Ghost, and isn't the Word of the Lord always anointed?

Or sometimes, you hear, "Let go and let God." Even this cliché can be widely misconstrued. There came a point when the Thessalonians let go a little bit too much waiting on the second coming of Christ and were warned by Paul that if they don't work, they shouldn't eat (by the way, that's not a cliché, check 2 Thessalonians 3).

There are numerous examples where clichés can become over-repeated, tone-deaf, and insensitive remarks that go on coffee mugs and T-shirts. Examples? "You can't outgive God!" as a pastor calls for a church member to give more. "If God brings you to it, He will bring you through it!" says the optimistic friend speaking to the young adult who just lost their parent to cancer. On that same note, "I guess God wanted them more" is not a good thing to mention when trying to encourage someone who suffered loss.

Now that I got your attention, I say all this to say: let us not be cliché Christians. Let us be biblical Christians because Scripture is always good (2 Timothy 3:16–17)!

> Thy word is a lamp unto my feet, and a light unto my path. (Psalm 119:105)

261

Prime Real Estate

Real estate cannot be lost or stolen, nor can it be carried away. Purchased with common sense, paid for in full, and managed with reasonable care, it is about the safest investment in the world.

—Franklin D. Roosevelt

Read the above statement. Then read it again. Now I want to ask, is Roosevelt talking about real estate investment or is this the current evangelical model for the church?

All too often, the contemporary church acts as real estate agents for heaven instead of ambassadors for heaven, although the God of Scripture favors unity over division (2 Corinthians 5:20). Unity is undermined often by two groups of people: "Good" Christians and false teachers. Either you have people who approach individuals in guile and deceit or well-intentioned Christians who attempt to win people to the Baptist, Methodist, Pentecostal, or Catholic side of heaven (2 Corinthians 11:12–15).

They walk the golden roads and proclaim, "Stay away from the poorer, uneducated suburbs of heaven. The best homes are reserved for the [insert Christian framework]!" or "The most crowns are for [insert denomination]." Christians may preach more about how much better the homes are for certain Christians instead of preaching the truth that "in due time Christ died for the ungodly" (Romans 5:6).

But no longer do I want to be in real estate! No longer do I want to see anyone homeless! I want everyone to know that heaven will be splendid for all for they are in the presence of our Savior, 24-7! Why sell when we have the capacity to tell others about the gift of grace provided by Jesus Christ by His death, burial, and resurrection (1 Corinthians 15:3–4).

Don't sell. Proclaim!

262

How to Keep Running (A Spiritual Guide) 2

> Ye did run well; who did hinder you that ye should not obey the truth?
>
> —Galatians 5:7

When writing to the Galatian church, Paul once was tasked with a church that joined the Body of Christ and lived fervently in His high calling. Yet with the arrival of "Judaizers" from Israel, they were taught (incorrectly) that in order to be true and complete Christians, they would have to submit to the Law of Moses and the circumcision of the Jews.

This heresy thus deemed Christ's finished work as insufficient for their salvation. Unfortunately, the Galatian church indulged in this teaching as promptly as they did the teaching of Paul. Such a turn of events incited Paul to beg the question:

> Ye did run well; who did hinder you that ye should not obey the truth? (Galatians 5:7)

He assured them that their persuasion was not of God. When we align ourselves with the faith, we all join the race. It is a road course leading to the grand prize. This grand prize is a matter of eternal glory in Christ Jesus. All who are sealed in Christ Jesus will see the finish through, and we should be encouraged that we are running sponsored by the Creator of the universe.

As our sponsor, He equips us with all the gear needed to grind through such an enduring race. We wear the shoes of the gospel of peace (Ephesians 6:15)! Nike, Adidas, New Balance, etc., have nothing that can even compare.

Which brings me to my point: If we are so properly equipped with the Word of God and intimately supported and sponsored by Jesus Christ, shouldn't our performance be an easy race? If it weren't for the many obstacles, perhaps it would be. But no other person has the tread or comfort that we have to endure the trials.

263

How to Keep Running (A Spiritual Guide) 3

He maketh my feet like hinds' feet, and
setteth me upon my high places.

—Psalm 18:33

Being properly equipped and properly trained does not make for an easy race. It should give assurance that you can finish the race well, but it does not eliminate the many obstacles that a race brings: fatigue, inclement weather, tough road conditions, and competitors.

Interestingly enough, these are all realistic things that the Christian runner must endure. This world is a nasty road course that often will turn up the heat and possibly make the Christian runner sweat and feel tired or worn. Yet by the Holy Spirit, we can have peace (Philippians 4:7) and are instilled with a spirit of power, love, and a sound mind to steady ourselves past the hurt.

Nonetheless, much like the Galatian church had rivals to the Gospel over two thousand years ago, the Gospel has competitors today as well. Just know, in this race, the world does not hate you. It hates the truth which you carry.

Look to John 15:18–27, where Jesus taught the nation of Israel about the intention behind the hate His followers will endure. Christ teaches,

> If the world hate you, ye know that it hated Me before it hated you. If ye were of the world, the world would love his own: but because ye are not of the world, but I have chosen you out of the world, therefore the world hateth you. Remember the word that I said unto you, The servant is not greater than his lord. If they have persecuted Me, they will also persecute you; if they have kept My saying, they will keep yours also. But all these things will they do unto you for My name's sake, because they know not Him that sent Me.

So do not run uncertainly. Be certain that the God who has already overcome the world abides in you and you in Him (John 16:33; Galatians 2:20). He will see you through to the prize (1 Corinthians 9:24–26). Stand firm in the face of internal and external opposition. This is why Paul kept himself in subjection (1 Corinthians 9:27), practicing (spiritually) the keys that make an athlete capable of finishing the race: commitment (to Christ), discipline (study of the Word), and hard work (preaching the Gospel).

Lay aside each weight that holds you back from putting one foot in front of the other for the Gospel's sake (Hebrews 12:1). Put off the sin and flesh which clog the arteries of the soul and put on the new man (Ephesians 4:24). And run with patience, looking to Jesus Christ, the finisher of our faith (Hebrews 12:2).

In this, we can stand firm like Paul, who boldly looked into the face of death and confidently spoke the words,

> I have fought a good fight, I have finished my course, I have kept the faith. (2 Timothy 4:7)

264

The Good Book

For whatsoever things were written aforetime were
written for our learning, that we through patience
and comfort of the Scriptures might have hope.
—Romans 15:4

In the above Scripture, the apostle Paul is addressing the responsibilities that Christians share with each other. God's Word has much to offer in the lives of Christians. One of these roles is comfort. We are comforted by the hope that He offers. We can have hope because Christ, the God of the universe, resides within us; and because He resides and we in Him, we have the promise of an eternal future (Colossians 1:27) with Him. This is included in the riches of His glory! And we are partaking of that!

So I want to encourage you, the reader, this week to take time to find comfort in the Scriptures. Read about the blessed hope that is your inheritance in Christ Jesus. Be comforted by this hope.

265

Happy Leif Erikson Day!

October 9 commemorates a holiday that not many people outside of Nordic communities know or recognize. It is a day known as Leif Erikson Day. It is a fascinating holiday that gets overshadowed by Columbus Day, which comes just a few days later (sometimes on the same day) or, as many now recognize it, Indigenous Peoples' Day.

Despite this, Leif Erikson Day is acknowledged by Nordic communities as the day that Leif Erikson led the first European expedition to America, hundreds of years before Columbus, who often gets that title. It is another holiday commemorating land, people, and ideas "found." You have Leif Erikson Day and Columbus Day set aside for this purpose, but no one ever considers Christ, who knew us before the world ever began, or how Christ, two thousand years ago, journeyed to a broken world to save it from a sinful demise.

> For ye were sometimes darkness, but now are ye light in the Lord: walk as children of light. (Ephesians 5:8)

We were once lost, but now we are found. Christ has found us. Jesus has saved us. And God is not interested in a holiday; He is interested in a holy life (Colossians 2:16–17). He made us capable of leading a holy life through Christ, who knew us before the foundation of the world (Ephesians 1:4).

So no, we may not be wearing horned helmets or stylish furs, but we have a heart to have others found too. We are to be a people who discover the truth and live unto that truth (2 Timothy 3:16). We once were lost, but now we are found.

Happy Leif Erikson Day!

266

The Christian Curse Word: Halloween

He that hateth dissembleth with his lips, and layeth up deceit within him… A lying tongue hateth those that are afflicted by it; and a flattering mouth worketh ruin.

—Proverbs 26:24–28

Around late September to early October, there is a certain unease that begins to stir inside some Christians, while a certain excitement stirs in others. Many Christians hate Halloween, and for some, it has become something of a naughty word for other Christians to acknowledge. Still, some Christians get excited and call it a ministry opportunity and organize "trunk or treats" at church, or for the sake of niceness, call it a Fall Fest or something of the like.

I am not here to debate whether Halloween is right or wrong. I have my own convictions, yes, but they don't matter. I have another axe to grind.

It is difficult to argue from a historical perspective. Halloween derives from two different faith traditions: Pagan Celtic and Catholic. The Pagan Celtic tradition known as Samhain commemorated the harvest at the end of the farming season, and masks were worn to keep evil spirits away. In the eighth century, Pope Gregory III instituted All Saints Day as a day of veneration for those who have passed on to heaven, with the day before being known as All Hallows' Eve (you are probably beginning to see the contemporary semblance). With the rise of the Christian faith, the holidays began to share qualities with each other.

With Halloween looming, there is only one point that I found necessary to reiterate. Evil spirits are not a holiday occurrence. They do not vacation in the halls of earth or the spirits of men. They are a constant, present, and real force continually in the world. Masks will not save you from them; masks aid only them (Proverbs 26:24–28). The only thing capable of covering you from their influence is the blanket of Christ's righteousness (Romans 4:6). The Holy Spirit seeks to indwell within you and fill every crevice of your heart so that there is no room for another spirit (Romans 8:9). With Christ, you do not have to hide; you are armored and equipped to stand your ground and fight in Jesus's name (Ephesians 6).

So no matter what you do this Halloween, do nothing outside the wisdom and discretion of the Holy Spirit (Ephesians 5:15–17). Spirits lurk on October 31 and July 31 all the same.

267

Come and See

And Nathanael said unto him, Can there any good thing come out of Nazareth? Philip saith unto him, Come and see.

—John 1:46

In John 1:43–51, we find a story of Jesus assembling the twelve disciples. In this particular instance, Jesus seeks Philip, who accepts His invitation to follow Him. In turn, Philip follows Christ and showcases his faith by seeking out Nathanael. The great thinker Godet writes, "One torch serves to light another torch."

When Philip invites Nathanael to see Jesus, Nathanael responds with a Jewish stigma of that day. He asks if anything good could possibly come from Nazareth, a place that many regarded with some sense of filth. On top of this, Nathanael was from Cana, another Galilean town, and it was common to have a rivalry.

Philip retorts with the same thing Jesus had said earlier to the disciples: "Come and see."

It turns out Jesus already knew Nathanael intimately. He speaks of the fig tree, which in Jewish culture usually refers to peace. Jesus addresses Nathanael as a peaceful person. Many Jews prayed under fig trees for shade, peace, and to be hidden as they communed with God.

Jesus knew Nathanael's deepest thoughts, and many regarded Nathanael as an ideal Jewish figure historically. Does it surprise you that Jesus Himself is telling someone to "come and see" Him? It seems so counterintuitive to how we as Christians think; we are raised on verses such as 2 Corinthians 5:17 and John 20:29, which emphasize faith oversight.

But a relationship with God has not always operated and or been available this way. Throughout Scripture, people have walked with God, literally (Adam and Eve; Enoch). Many people were guided by the laying of eyes on a pillar of smoke, which guided them (the Israelites). Early believers, despite being under the Law, had faith because they saw Jesus, and the early Church saw many miracles.

But when grace was poured out and the signs, sights, and supporting pieces concluded, the Christian no longer walked according to "come and see"; the Christian lives by "walk by faith and not by sight" (2 Corinthians 5:17). We walk with God, but it is not in the cool of the day like Adam and Eve. It is in the thick and thin. We don't follow a pillar of smoke; we follow Scripture. We don't need signs, because it is finished.

That which is perfect has come, and God's grace is sufficient for all that we see. All that we don't see. For all our needs.

Grace is sufficient (2 Corinthians 12:9).

268

An Unbaptized Hand

History is full of odd, nearly unbelievable stories. I once heard one of these stories when looking into the life of the infamous emperor Charlemagne. Charlemagne was a renowned king who desired his entire empire to be Christian. In this desire, he continued his military conquests, seeking to win "Christians" by force.

It is reported that Charlemagne would instruct his forces to go into the nearest river to be baptized with a mass baptism. The story goes that he would have his soldiers fully submerge under the water, but a hand holding a sword had to remain out of the water because their bodies were God's, but he would let them know that their fighting hand was his.

Whether this is true or not, no one really knows where the record began. But I do know that it is very believable, seeing the condition of the Church. We live freely in the liberty that Christ has given us, with justification as our living room, but sanctification as an ideal that isn't worth pursuing.

Like the soldiers who submerged themselves but held their hand high knowing just what they would do with it on their crusades and that God just wouldn't approve, we may think Sunday is an ideal time to "be good," but Tuesday just wouldn't be convenient this week.

But no, Scripture claims, "For we are his workmanship, created in Christ Jesus unto good works, which God hath before ordained that we should walk in them" (Ephesians 2:10). Scripture beseeches, "Present your bodies a living sacrifice, holy, acceptable unto God, which is your reasonable service" (Romans 12:1). God's Word states we can, "Now may the God of peace himself sanctify you *completely*, and may your *whole* spirit and soul and body be kept blameless at the coming of our Lord Jesus Christ" (1 Thessalonians 5:23).

There is nothing partial about God, nor does anything God do partially. The Lord God is one, and being baptized into His body, be completely submerged (1 Corinthians 12:13)! Drop the sword!

269

Oh, the Humanity!

One afternoon on May 6, 1937, over the horizon, many onlookers gazed at a large mass steadily piercing the air and approaching. It was a hydrogen-powered airship, the LZ 129 *Hindenburg*. As it approached an airfield in New Jersey in an effort to dock, it ignited without warning, killing thirty-five of the ninety-seven people on board and one person on the ground. Thirty-six people were killed within a ninety-second hydrogen fire.

To this day, no one truly knows what started this. Many remember footage of the event, with the announcement made by prominent radio broadcaster and pilot Herbert Morrison exclaiming, "Oh, the humanity!"

And indeed, oh, the humanity that was lost. In ninety seconds. Thirty-six lives lost.

There are many estimates of how many people have lived on earth throughout all history. Many say nearly 117 billion people have lived on earth throughout all of earth's history.

How many have been lost in the microscopic amount of time earth has existed? How many are perishing each second? Oh, the humanity!

How many can be saved today? Well actually, I know the answer to that one. Every single one (John 3:16; 1 Timothy 2:4). Not everyone will be saved. But everyone can be saved. Jesus Christ has provided a way to grace for all humanity no matter how depraved and wrongful they live. One drop of Jesus Christ's blood is just that powerful. His resurrection stands as testimony.

Christ has provided a Church to take the message of grace to all humanity (Ephesians 3; Romans 6:23). Oh, the humanity!

270

Multiplication Madness

For which cause we faint not; but though our outward man perish, yet the inward man is renewed day by day.
—2 Corinthians 4:16

When I was in fifth grade, I was training for competition. I mean seriously training. Day after day, I put in reps. Week after week, I did sets. Sets of multiplication problems. And boy, was I good.

This was years before I got into competitive sports. But multiplication madness was the deal. I was the real deal.

Multiplication Madness was a county-wide competition where one class from each school met in a central location and had a showdown to see who could recite, at random, their multiplication tables the quickest. We didn't really think. We just regurgitated. The same things we saw and heard every day.

And that is just like so many other things I have worked on in my life, including ministry. Before I looked more critically at my set of beliefs, I said what I heard at church, I ministered how I was taught to minister, I tithed what I had because I heard 10 percent was God's magic number. That He would love me more if I gave more. That more people would be saved if I just did so-and-so seven-step ministry plan.

But no, my prayer is that ministers move away from earthly and fleshly spiritual business models and move to giving the Gospel unadulterated. That is, Jesus Christ died, was buried, and rose again—for you (Romans 5:8). Because He loves you (John 15:13). This isn't something regurgitated. It is a constantly new message that makes constantly renewed people, who love lost people (2 Corinthians 4:16), who relate to lost people knowing that there is a God who loves them.

271

363 Days

Put on therefore, as the elect of God, holy and beloved, bowels of mercies, kindness, humbleness of mind, meekness, longsuffering; forbearing one another, and forgiving one another, if any man have a quarrel against any: even as Christ forgave you, so also do ye. And above all these things put on charity, which is the bond of perfectness.
—Colossians 3:12–14

Three hundred sixty-three days. This is typically the number of days that adults get to choose who they are around. For 363 days, you can choose where you go, what you do, and really why you do it. There are two days out of the calendar that many know you are bound to be around a certain group of people. A certain group of people whom you cannot choose.

Those days are Thanksgiving and Christmas. The certain people are family. You can't choose family. Especially during the holidays. On these days, there are large gatherings of family, and for some, this is a struggle. For some, the holidays are a practice session for the art and biblical instruction of "bearing with one another."

For those who dread the coming together of family, I do not have a magic message to fix the fears. But I can say that gratitude and thanksgiving will go a long way. For those who love to spend time with family over the holidays, as do I, just know that still, gratitude and thanksgiving will go a long way.

> In every thing give thanks: for this is the will of God in Christ Jesus concerning you. (1 Thessalonians 5:18)

As a matter of fact, the key to forbearance is gratitude for the blessing of communion and fellowship. Read on a few verses in Colossians 3, and verse 17 indicates, "And whatsoever ye do in word or deed, do all in the name of the Lord Jesus, giving thanks to God and the Father by him."

Life is so precious, and God gives it abundantly. Spiritually and physically, we have life that God intends for us to cherish. Gratefulness transcends past, present, and future and subdues frustration under the wonder of blessing. We are entering a season of great holidays. Cherish those around you and seek the wonder of thanksgiving. After all, you can't choose family.

272

The Berean Hour

Most of the evil in this world is done by
people with good intentions.

—T. S. Eliot

Hell is paved with good intentions.

—Samuel Johnson

Modern culture is filled with the desire to be good; unfortunately, people are very bad at it. So bad, in fact, that many of society's greatest moral vices are renamed as something good. Abortion is considered women's health. Pornography is considered sexual liberation. Universalism is titled inclusivity. Humans are just bad at being good.

There is a narrative within the book of Acts that highlights a group's desire to be good (Acts 17:10–15). The Scripture tells us that the apostle Paul goes into the Jewish synagogues of Thessalonica, where many of the Jews, believing that the Law has not yet been fulfilled by Jesus, start a riot to quiet apostolic preaching. They thought they were doing God's will, but instead, they were actually aligned entirely contrary to it. They were living in emotions and past experiences, and living in past experiences will cripple you with new fear. Truthfully, sometimes what once was good is harmful to those who can't tell when the good things have passed.

Or more accurately, fulfilled. Do not let good intentions keep you from faith in Christ. Do not let emotions hold you from truth. Please do not let experiences keep you from making new ones.

In this story, there was a group of people from Berea (the Bereans) who moved from emotional living and searched Scripture daily to see if what Paul was saying was true. Stepping outside their feelings, they stepped into truth and life. They had good intentions and effective action.

Two things that can only be found in pure form through the Word of God, the Author of truth.

273

What the Gospel Is, What the Gospel Isn't

> The Word was made flesh, and dwelt among us, (and we beheld his glory, the glory as of the only begotten of the Father,) full of grace and truth.
>
> —John 1:14

The Gospel is often described as beautiful and simple. Well, it should be simple. But it is described in so many ways.

It has been described as music: "The music of the Gospel leads us home" (Frederick Faber).

It has been described as a social program, as in the case of Charles Oliver Brown and his "social gospel." It has been described as something you work for.

These all sound good and nice, but the Bible, rightly divided, describes the Gospel as belief in Christ's death, burial, and resurrection (1 Corinthians 15:3–4; 2 Timothy 2:15).

The Gospel is not just a sweet song. We can't work a version of the Gospel to earn favor with God. The work is already done. Humanity was in need of a real-world superhero in a world where no hero could make them right with God. Except for God.

So no, we are not the heroes of our own story, and no, we cannot play God like a heavenly harp. We can only say, “God, I believe.” We can only say, “God, thank you.”

It was all God. No other. By His Son, Jesus Christ, we have a true, authentic, and truly simple Gospel.

274

The Veil Is Gone

But even unto this day, when Moses is
read, the veil is upon their heart.
Nevertheless when it shall turn to the Lord,
the veil shall be taken away.
Now the Lord is that Spirit: and where the
Spirit of the Lord is, there is liberty.
—2 Corinthians 3:15–17

As a teacher, I strive to make complicated things simple. This is the role of a teacher, simply put. As students grow up, from preschool all the way to graduation, teachers take an idea and build, build, build until all of a sudden, students gain clarity.

For example, kindergarteners begin learning their animals. Moving on, in comes fifth grade, and then students learn about cells, tissues, and maybe some organs like the brain and the heart. Then, in seventh grade, the topic gets narrower, and students learn about organelles. Still yet, here comes high school, and the students learn about what the organelles do, and on, on, and on it goes till eventually.

The student understands. The student understands what makes life. The student knows how it works. And the truth is beautiful.

Life is beautiful.

In the same way, for so long, Jews sought to work their way to God by keeping the Law. They worked, tried to keep the Law, added their own touches to the Law, muddled the Law, and were so deceived that when Jesus Christ fulfilled the Law, they couldn't even tell. Their sight was veiled. Everything they learned, they had not pulled together.

The Word of God reads,

> Wherefore the law was our schoolmaster to bring us unto Christ, that we might be justified by faith.
>
> But after that faith is come, we are no longer under a schoolmaster.
>
> For ye are all the children of God by faith in Christ Jesus.
>
> For as many of you as have been baptized into Christ have put on Christ. (Galatians 3:24–27)

But for those who believe on and in the Gospel of Jesus Christ, everything changes. The schoolmaster, the Law, brings you to Christ and shows your need for Christ. It is all the preliminary lessons. But then by grace, we are justified. We have clarity, peace, and above all, liberty. And where the Spirit of the Lord is, there is liberty forevermore (2 Corinthians 3:15–17).

275

Chemistry in the Bible 5: Carbon

Carbon is an element that is simple in composition, but functionally, it is complicated and very interesting. Even though it is simple in structure, there is nothing basic about carbon.

Although not one of the most prominent elements in the Earth's crust, it is the second most abundant element in the human body behind oxygen and is in every living thing on Earth. Yes, every living thing. There has not been a single living organism found without carbon.

There are many reasons for this, but to simplify, its abundance and ability to form numerous bonds make it very important.

In chemistry, there are things known as allotropes. Allotropes are forms that a certain element can take. Although carbon is typically manifested as black, one beautiful form of pure carbon is diamond. In fact, it is the only mineral made of one distinct element on Earth!

It also plays an interesting role in the Bible. Diamonds signify splendor on earth and heavenly splendor (Exodus 28:18). Similar to today, the toughness of diamonds is on display when described as an engraving utensil (Jeremiah 17:1). Diamond is the pinnacle of natural beauty that can be ascertained and the only entirely pure mineral. This is how it is portrayed in Scripture as well.

In other forms, carbon bonds with other elements and makes wonderfully useful things. One example of this formation is coal. We see coal written as a tool for purification and appeasement to God for the sins of Israel (Leviticus 16:12; Psalm 18:13). In Isaiah 6:7–8, we see Isaiah have his sins forgiven following the touching of his lips with a hot coal.

God knew the world initially when He made it and made the elements as manipulative for the good of those whom He loves—humanity. Carbon in the Bible introduces a standard—a standard of God's righteousness.

Diamonds are created by heat and pressure. Christians are refined and strengthened by the heat of trials and the pressure of the world. In the face of it, by God's grace, we grow. Today, God does not have angels descend upon us and purge our sins with hot coal, but for our sake, Christ endured the heat of suffering. He hung on a tree in the heat of the day, died a death we deserved to purge our sins, and descended to hell to pay our ransom, rising again to the cool of heaven.

Carbon is tough and grows tougher with trials. Heat it up, and it only grows stronger. As our hearts burn for God and we struggle, turn to Scripture and grow through it all, exemplifying God's splendor, glory, and power to forgive all sins.

> Therefore being justified by faith, we have peace with God through our Lord Jesus Christ:
>
> By whom also we have access by faith into this grace wherein we stand, and rejoice in hope of the glory of God.
>
> And not only so, but we glory in tribulations also: knowing that tribulation worketh patience;
>
> And patience, experience; and experience, hope:
>
> And hope maketh not ashamed; because the love of God is shed abroad in our hearts by the Holy Ghost which is given unto us.
>
> For when we were yet without strength, in due time Christ died for the ungodly. (Romans 5:1–6)

276

Inspiring Love

But just as you abound in everything, in faith and utterance and knowledge and in all earnestness and in the love we inspired in you, see that you abound in this gracious work also.
—2 Corinthians 8:7

In 2015 and 2016, a social media phenomenon emerged following the Supreme Court ruling of *Obergefell v. Hodges*. This court case essentially redefined the American sociopolitical view of marriage, and in the midst of it, the saying "Love wins" emerged. To this day, many years later, this saying lives on as a mantra of the LGBTQ+ community.

The biggest problem is that it is incorrect. "Love wins" indicates a future tense of love's final victory. The correct phrase should be "Love won," and it has nothing to do with homosexuality and everything to do with the all-encompassing, selfless act of Jesus on the cross two thousand years ago. On the third day following His crucifixion, when He rose from the grave, love won.

And the honest truth is, because love won, we have victory and can inspire love in others.

The order goes: He loved us, we love Him, we love others (1 John 4:19; Romans 13:10). Love won.

And as we see from 2 Corinthians 8:7, inspiring others in the love of God moves them to abound in the gracious work of God as well (Ephesians 2:10).

Therefore, inspire others to love with an inspiring love!

277

Homecoming

Looking for that blessed hope, and the glorious appearing of the great God and our Saviour Jesus Christ.

—Titus 2:13

Yearly in America, schools gear up for a special time called homecoming. Hallways are decorated, a king and queen are voted for, and alumni attend the Friday night football games. Churches typically welcome homecoming with music, special guest preachers, and welcome back members who have moved away or attend other churches at that time. Homecoming is a time to reminisce about the good ol' days and examine the legacy left behind.

But the Church? I mean the church with an uppercase *C*. No such thing is necessary. Our homecoming hails at the end of our time on earth and isn't a time to remember who is gone but a welcoming event to a home we never knew but then will know intimately for all eternity (Philippians 3:20). No one is coming back; we are all there to stay. We will not reminisce about the "good ol' days" but glory in the best of days for all eternity in the presence of our Savior.

There will be no decorations taken down after a week. Rather, treasure which never grows old and never fades away (1 Corinthians 2:9). Homecoming. Our blessed hope (Titus 2:13). Forevermore.

If I never get a chance to meet you, the reader, do not fret, I'll see you one day at homecoming (1 Thessalonians 5:9–10).

278

Equity

There is neither Jew nor Greek, there is neither bond nor free, there is neither male nor female: for ye are all one in Christ Jesus.
—Galatians 3:28

There is a recent phenomenon that is being seen in recent culture but is indistinguishable from another phenomenon that has been the goal for many years. That phenomenon is the idea of equity.

In recent years, equity has been a word that only bankers and businesspeople saw; nonetheless, with many of the political movements of the day, so many people have mentioned equity alongside equality.

Simply put, in sociology, equality is the final product where two or more human differences have been made equal through a change in heart, social policy, or thinking. In America, many think of the changed America following the Civil Rights Act of 1964. This law claims all men are created equal and legally prohibits discrimination based on race, color, religion, sex, and national origin.

Equity is something distinctly different. Equity is the process by which equality is seeded. This idea is usually discussed when showing the different locations, circumstances, and ideas that set two or more people apart.

On a large scale, all men are equitable from the moment they are born in that they are born into a sinful and depraved condition. All people are equal. From here, people are born into different circumstances, socioeconomic backgrounds, genders, and so forth. For thousands of years, people were born into two groups, and only one of them could be saved. The Jews were God's people, and everyone else was considered dogs. There was a chasm between the Jews and the Gentiles, and then something changed. Christ came and bridged the chasm in the ultimate act of equity and made all equal at the foot of the Cross by the power of His resurrection. There was no longer male, female, slave, free person, Jew, or Gentile (Colossians 3:11).

The mystery had been revealed, and all were made equal by the fellowship of the mystery (Ephesians 3:9). Humanity had achieved equality by the equity of Christ's sacrifice. The most equalizing event in human and heavenly history, Christ performed and finished.

Now we live justified, sealed, and coheirs with Jesus! By the equity of Christ's blood, we have all been made equal (Proverbs 22:2; Romans 2:11).

279

Bedrock

For by him were all things created, that are in heaven,
and that are in earth, visible and invisible, whether they
be thrones, or dominions, or principalities, or powers:
all things were created by him, and for him:
And he is before all things, and by him all things consist.
—Colossians 1:16–17

Forget about all the trouble of the world. For a moment, empty all the thoughts of war, poverty, pestilence, and other unpleasant things that reside on earth. Take it all away.

Now think of the most beautiful place on earth. Let your mind dwell on the natural beauty of mountains, open fields, natural landmarks, and the open seas. The world is gorgeous. But why should we ever be surprised by this? The world was created by our incredible God, who set space into motion to perfectly sustain the world. On top of a nickel and iron core and molten rock, we find the foundations of the earth—bedrock.

Bedrock is the foundational stone upon which all earth's beauty sits, dirt piles up, and the beauty we see stands (1 Corinthians 3:11). Without the bedrock, the world around us would have nothing to lay on, and nothing in the world would consist.

In much the same way, Christ is the bedrock of our world and of our faith.

By this I mean, without Jesus, the world would spin into chaos. Or more accurately, it would never exist.

Without Jesus, our faith would be meaningless and misplaced.

Christ is the bedrock of everything, and by Him the world exists (Isaiah 28:16; Ephesians 2:20). Without Him, nothing would exist. Nothing could be held.

Include Him when life gets difficult. When we can't find beauty in the world. But because Christ is our bedrock, we can be held—always. Forever and ever.

280

Wish! Temu!

For if he that cometh preacheth another Jesus, whom
we have not preached, or if ye receive another spirit,
which ye have not received, or another gospel, which ye
have not accepted, ye might well bear with him.

—2 Corinthians 11:4

With the advent of Internet shopping over the past years, there have been some interesting phenomena that have emerged. There have been really expensive luxury sites and moderately priced vast retail sites such as Amazon. But then, there are some sites that offer "luxury" at a significantly lower price.

Yes—I am referring to Wish. For clothes, I am referring to Sheen. I am referring to Temu. We know the sites!

You may get insanely affordable products with these sites, but theirs is no promise it isn't made with ethically questionable practices and or if you will get actual name brand. You may order an Xbox, only to open the box and a brand new Ybox! You may order an iPhone, open the box and surprisingly find a uPhone!

The price is great, but often, you may find that the quality is low. Over and over, things break because the honest truth is, they were never meant to stand the test of time. So you buy from Spiritual

Temu, over and over until not only are the products broke, but so is your wallet.

The cost was more than you had imagined. Do not settle for knock off Jesus (Galatians 1:8). Do not look for replacements for the one quality Jesus.

The best part of this deal is that although Jesus cost everything (1 Corinthians 15:3–4), He also paid everything so that you could afford Him by belief. He is a gift (Ephesians 2:8–10). And with Him we reside evermore, undeserving.

281

A Comeback

Now then we are ambassadors for Christ, as
though God did beseech you by us: we pray you
in Christ's stead, be ye reconciled to God.
—2 Corinthians 5:20

Ahead of his 2011 season with the Colts, Peyton Manning, underwent spinal fusion surgery. Come 2012, with Manning healing, the Colts had a failure of season ending with 2 wins and 14 losses.

There are not many athletes who can be injured severely, heal, and then come back better before. But Peyton Manning did just that.

Come 2013, Manning being cut from the Colts in favor of Andrew Luck, went with the Denver Broncos with all eyes on him and if he would ever play the way he once did.

Coming back from his injury, his first year he once again a top passer and the following year he set offensive milestones by throwing for 5,477 yards and 55 touchdowns. Then finishing his already stellar career, he led his team to a 2016 Super Bowl win.

Christianity is a faith of healing and reconciliation (2 Corinthians 5:11–21). To a people once injured and enslaved by sin, a new life with incredible healing is offered by the work of Jesus Christ. By the work of Christ, we can have an incredible "comeback" from where we once started. But all too often, following their healing, believers don't lead the charts for Christ, rather they prefer to ride the bench and stay safe.

At full health, vigor, and by the power of Scripture and the Holy Spirit, we have the opportunity to get in the game and preach the Gospel (2 Timothy 2:15)! Do not stay down, when you are all too healthy (Colossians 3:16)! Get in the game, proclaim, and win them souls as ambassadors for Christ (2 Corinthians 5:20). A great comeback!

282

Put It All Together

But for us also, to whom it shall be imputed, if we believe on him that raised up Jesus our Lord from the dead; Who was delivered for our offences, and was raised again for our justification.

—Romans 4:24–25

Life. It seems that most people have a different definition of it. Some people see life as far as a heart beating and a brain thinking, while others argue that you can be living, but not alive. Regardless, I see life as a privilege to live.

Every person on this earth who breathes a breath is bound to a certain set of characteristics that make life. An organism must have organization, development, the ability to reproduce, energy use, homeostasis, and the ability to adapt. If something lacks even one of these attributes, it is not considered alive.

Under the category of reproduction falls the molecule of life—DNA. DNA, which stands for "deoxyribonucleic acid," defines what an organism will be. In one human cell, there is nearly six feet of DNA containing nearly three billion letters that code for your proteins. That is enough letters to fill a thousand two-hundred-page books.

But here is the thing. If there were just these three billion letters in each cell, you would cease to exist. DNA is made of these bases (letters), phosphates, and sugars. It is only when all three crucial parts of DNA are together that life can happen.

This is much like the life we have as Christians. The Gospel consists of three parts that lead to one full life. Jesus Christ, our source of life

1. died,
2. was buried,
3. rose again.

These three things put together hold an innumerable amount of power and transform the identity of those who believe. You cannot live without these three actions completed and gifted to you by God's abundant plan.

Remember, miss one characteristic, and you are not alive. A dead God = a dead person (1 Corinthians 15:15–19). Christ was buried, proving His humanity. Jesus rose, proving that as He left death behind, so can you (Romans 4:24–25). Therefore, go and live.

283

Stay Off the Ice!

What shall we say then? Shall we continue in sin,
that grace may abound? God forbid. How shall we,
that are dead to sin, live any longer therein?
—Romans 6:1–2

There is a large variety of cultural differences in America that depend on your location. If you live in Florida, you could expect conversations about things such as a fast-paced life, football, and Disney World. But if you were to move northward, you'd begin to see large cities become further spread out, agricultural fields, and a slower way of life. What you would not hear about until maybe Northern West Virginia (if you were on the East Coast like me), is kids skating on ponds and lakes.

Come late fall and winter, many Northern states begin to see their freshwater sources transform into thick sheets of ice. Kids can go out on skates, put up hockey goals (something else you don't hear about in the South much), and have a bit of seasonal fun. Most of the time, the ice is thick enough that there is not a care in the world, but at times, there have been stories of people not being that fortunate.

At one point in my life, I heard a Northern friend speak of his own experiences skating on the ice. He told me that the weather was warming, but looking to make use of the family pond for a few more days, he headed out onto the ice despite his mother's warning to "stay off the ice." The story goes that he skated and shot goals for a long while before deciding to call it a day. So he skated back to the same location he had entered the lake but suddenly found himself in the water.

Unexpectedly, the ice had broken. Now, obviously, if he was telling this story, he made it out, but he described it as a near-death experience. He said that his body began almost instantly shutting down in the presence of the frigid temperatures. Although he managed to escape, thinking back on the story, I think of the similarities to the lives of Christians today.

We often hear sermons about how works do not define our relationship with Christ, and amen for that! Nonetheless, some feelingly overexcited in their newfound freedom use it as a license to sin, even though Scripture warns us to "stay off the ice" (2 Timothy 2:16). Grace was not given as a free gift for us to try and get a few more good days of debauchery out of the ice we skate. Grace was given to glorify God and as a means of living unto good works (Ephesians 2:8–10).

Our heavenly Father wants better for us and does not want us to skate on His love until we eventually fall in, grasping for His gracious hand (Matthew 14:30). He wants you to be transformed and live in the new, warmer seasons of life on solid ground (Romans 12:1–2). So stay off the ice.

284

How Can These Things Be?

Rabbi, we know that thou art a teacher come from God: for no man can do these miracles that thou doest, except God be with him.
—John 3:2

In high school, I participated in the student organization, the Fellowship of Christian Athletes. At times, I was outgoing in my faith, and I had a teacher with whom I would introduce biblical topics. Although I quickly realized that these conversations appeared spiritually fruitless because he believed that he already knew everything needed to know about Jesus.

He knew Jesus was:

1. a Middle Eastern carpenter,
2. a Jewish rabbi,
3. a good man

In fact, this man knew the Scriptures inside and out; although, it was obvious to see that this man did not know Jesus. He knew *of* Jesus. There is a massive difference between the two. In a biblical context, "knowing" someone meant one of two things, and both were of an intimate nature. Knowing indicated either a sexual love or intimate knowledge of someone. As Christians, we possess the latter.

This is completely contrary to what I, a Southern American, am raised to understand. In the South, we are often asked and align ourselves with whom we know. We are asked if "we know so and so." This typically means whether or not you know who someone is. We do not want this mentality in our faith. We want to know Christ deeply, as the Bible indicates.

In John 3, we find a Jewish leader by the name of Nicodemus, who in the night came wanting to know of Jesus, but likely left understanding Jesus and His purpose on a much more intimate level. Jesus answered his questions much deeper than even Nicodemus had intended. This crash course in spirituality conspired by asking the right questions.

One such question is, "How can these things be?" (John 3:9). You see, if you ask for clarity, God will and has provided it in His Word. If you want to know Christ intimately and of His love for you, look no further than His Word, which affirms that you can be as close as a son and as near as a coheir (Romans 8:17; Galatians 6:10). Ask the right questions, and you get the right answers.

285

Wine About It

You only live once—so drink great wine.
—Anonymous

For my adult readers, whether you enjoy wine or not, the Bible has much to say about the beverage. It holds special significance in particular portions of Scripture, but many people have no idea how it is even made. It is filled with the following steps, which often can become complicated and convoluted depending on the taste you are seeking.

Wine Recipe

1. Harvest
2. Destem
3. Crush
4. Fermentation/maceration ("new wine")
5. Malolactic fermentation
6. Clarification

This is an age-old process, and it is important to understand that nothing comes from nothing. Some people know this as the law of conservation of mass. Every action is intentional. But God is the only one who can circumnavigate all and make new, good wine from nothing.

In John 2, the well-known narrative of Christ's intervention in a wedding running low on wine stands as a testimony to the power of God. Looking deeper into this story, you may find a connection between the new wine that Christ made and the new covenant that Christ makes with the nation of Israel.

Wine typically represented blessing throughout the Bible, and the withdrawal of wine represented wrath (Haggai 1:11). This trend is found many times throughout Scripture. This is significant as it indicates a time when the Jews will return to God (2 Peter 3:8–18). Right now, they have no interest in seeking Christ, but when the pressures prophecy indicates arrive, and Israel is pressed, they will return to God.

God will make wine again. Once again, I say this is significant because God gives an opportunity for all people to come and experience His saving grace. This includes Jews, Gentiles, reprobates, legalists, children, elderly, women, men, Black, and White (Ephesians 2:13–17). God is not solely just and fair; He is additionally merciful. He is grace.

God desires to "have all men to be saved, and to come unto the knowledge of the truth" (1 Timothy 2:4). Taste and see that He is good. Jesus is the author of good things (Psalm 34:8).

286

I Need to Shave!

Why is it I always get my best ideas while shaving?
—Albert Einstein

Throughout my life, I have taken on many different images. In high school, I grew out my hair (oh, the awkward stages). In my college running career, I grew out a beard to assimilate to the sophistication of the collegiate crowd. I graduated, got a job in the local school system, shaved my beard, got a slick haircut, and now I live unto the professional life. And as I write this, I need to shave once again to be who I need to be to my students.

We are ordained to bring the Gospel to a lost and dying world. A lost and dying world is full of people in different places at different times with varying needs. But one need remains the same—the need for the salvation provided by the finished work of Jesus Christ. But the question is, how do you reach people for this uniform purpose with their many different needs? You become many things to many people.

Saying this, let me clarify. This does not mean fake it till you make it. It means to meet people where they are. Be graceful and understanding of your differences, but faithful to the convictions of Scripture. Not becoming a different person, but allowing yourself to be trusted in their circles so that Christ be glorified.

The apostle Paul had numerous citizenships, ministered to numerous ethnicities, and proclaims,

> For though I be free from all men, yet have I made myself servant unto all, that I might gain the more… I am made all things to all men, that I might by all means save some. And this I do for the gospel's sake, that I might be partaker thereof with you. (1 Corinthians 9:19, 22–23)

This passage stresses the priority of Scripture, and Paul gives a model of what it means to take the Gospel to the world. It does not mean change identity, but it may just mean to shave a little. I need to learn this lesson myself sometimes.

287

Why Can You Do It and I Can't?

For before that certain came from James, he did eat with the Gentiles: but when they were come, he withdrew and separated himself, fearing them which were of the circumcision.
—Galatians 2:14

And unto the Jews I became as a Jew, that I might gain the Jews; to them that are under the law, as under the law, that I might gain them that are under the law; to them that are without law, as without law, (being not without law to God, but under the law to Christ,) that I might gain them that are without law.
—1 Corinthians 9:20–21

There were times as a child when I noticed what at the time I considered favoritism by my mother. Now I know, favoritism generally meant that my mom was just tired and didn't notice something. Maybe my brother got to go out with friends and I couldn't. I'd ask my mom, "How come Wesley can do that and I can't?" Maybe my sister got to watch what she wanted on TV and I couldn't. I'd ask, "How come she can watch what she wants?"

I can imagine the apostle Peter asking this question as the apostle Paul called him out for withdrawing from the Gentiles whenever the Jews came around, as described in Galatians 2. Paul pointed out how Peter, in withdrawing from the Gentiles, "But when I saw that they walked not uprightly according to the Truth of the Gospel" (Galatians 2:14).

Some people may find this evaluation of character hypocritical since Paul later states, to the Jews he became as a Jew and to Gentiles he became as a Gentile (1 Corinthians 9:20–21). The difference couldn't be more significant. One story was of a man who walked in the truth of the Gospel, and the other didn't at the time. We can pretend intentions do not matter in ministry, but they absolutely do. Furthermore, one example showed a withdrawal from fellowship, and the other, Paul, showed an attraction toward fellowship.

Although similar actions, the placement of the heart was entirely different and speaks volumes to how we minister as we go into the world. Does your walk reflect the truth of the Gospel, or does it reflect fear of identity with Christ? Only one is righteous in the eyes of the Lord, and it is important to choose wisely in ministry. If the question becomes, "Why can so and so do it and I can't?" there needs to be a moment of reflection and redirect this question to "How can I more effectively live my life for the Gospel of Jesus Christ?"

> All things are lawful for me, but all things are not expedient: all things are lawful for me, but all things edify not. (1 Corinthians 10:23)

288

Aloe Me to Show You Something

Till we all come in the unity of the faith, and of the knowledge of the Son of God, unto a perfect man, unto the measure of the stature of the fulness of Christ.

—Ephesians 4:13

Aloe vera is a fascinating succulent that is known for its beautiful exterior, easygoing nature, and beneficial interior chemical nature. Aloe vera is used in moisturizers, ointments, sunscreen, sunburn relief, exfoliators, make-up, make-up removers, and so much more. Despite the benefits, only a limited number of aloe plants can offer such wonderful benefits. That is, the mature plants. Young aloe plants produce a much less efficient substance and are generally unfavorable for those harvesting it.

Another problem with this truth is that aloe vera is known for its slow maturation cycles. The plants grow from "pups" and take many years, often as long as three to four years, to produce anything beneficial. Oftentimes, the best things take a while to prepare. Saying this, I beg you as a Christian to give grace to those who are experiencing God's grace new and afresh. I am indeed talking about new Christians. All too often, they find salvation, and older Christians immediately expect them to change every little detail about their life in a matter of weeks.

But no, Scripture is beautiful in that God's Word offers grace, and we go through the process of renewal and transformation (Romans 12:1–2). God's grace bears with us as we grow, and there is no condemnation for those in Christ Jesus (Romans 8:1; 2 Peter 3:18). Have grace and offer help! It may take a while to see the benefits and power of their transformation, but just like aloe, know that it can take a while. But the process of sanctification is just as beautiful for you to watch as it is for the believer who is changing (2 Timothy 2:21). Be a sweet relief greater than any aloe to these people as Christ is to you! Give grace!

289

Faith of a Daredevil

I have always had an affinity for comic books and superheroes. I grew up enjoying Batman, Wolverine, and Spiderman; however, one superhero always piqued my interest. This superhero is Daredevil, also known as the Man Without Fear.

Daredevil, who suffered a chemical eye injury when younger, is a lawyer during the day and a vigilante by night. But instead of allowing this disability to restrain him, he soon learns it actually enhanced his ability to deliver justice. As a lawyer, he could hear heartbeats and clues. Additionally, as a superhero, he had increased agility, abilities, and proprioception.

There is science backing this. When one sense is lost, the brain rewires in order to enhance other senses so that individuals can still be efficient and thrive. The brain is considered plastic. It is always changing, developing pathways, and improvising. This phenomenon is known as supersensory.

Daredevil could not see, but he was far from blind. Perhaps Christians have much to learn from Daredevil. "Walking by faith, not by sight" does not mean having blind faith or continuously making a leap of faith.

Growing up, I was always taught that Christianity is one continuous cycle of ordered leaps of faith. You must have blind faith in spiritual leaders and decisions. In a sense, it is no better than "name it, claim it" theology.

The term *leap of faith* was originally coined by a Danish philosopher named Søren Kierkegaard, although it was originally titled a "qualitative step of faith." He defined it as, "to believe in something or someone based on faith rather than evidence; an attempt to achieve something that has little chance of success."

It traveled fast in Christian circles, and the problem is, people began interpreting Scripture off a human idea, instead of Scripture itself. Another issue is that it was convenient to build churches, press big decisions, and for relationship advice.

But walking by faith is not blind. If it were blind, we'd be in the right mind to worship any and everything, including nature, Buddha, Muhammed, etc. Blind faith is watered-down universalism.

God has given us ample evidence. He has given us nature, His Law, mercy, grace, the Bible, and most importantly, His Son incarnate, Jesus Christ. Lack of sight does not mean blind. We must depend on more than what we see, and start depending on what the ear has heard. As a matter of fact, "Faith comes by hearing, not by sight."

Romans 10:14–17 reads,

> How then shall they call on Him in whom they have not believed? and how shall they believe in Him of whom they have not heard? and how shall they hear without a preacher? And how shall they preach, except they be sent? as it is written, How beautiful are the feet of them that preach the gospel of peace, and bring glad tidings of good things! But they have not all obeyed the gospel. For Esaias saith, Lord, who hath believed our report? So then faith cometh by hearing, and hearing by the word of God.

The Word of God is our evidence. As a matter of fact, we are Christians because of the evidence. The Apostles preached by accounts of what they had seen and known to be true. Many biblical letters began by discussing what was seen (e.g., 1 John 1).

Paul encourages a search for that which is real, according to scriptural standards of course: "Prove all things; hold fast that which is good" (1 Thessalonians 5:21). In the Bible, accusations were not to be made by blind faith; the Bible always required at least two to three witnesses before verdicts were passed. Hopefully, our court systems function in the same way.

Deuteronomy 19:15 states, "One witness shall not rise up against a man for any iniquity, or for any sin, in any sin that he sinneth: at the mouth of two witnesses, or at the mouth of three witnesses, shall the matter be established."

But biblical evidence shows that Jesus died, was buried, and rose again. We live by evidence of a changed life, and faith has evidence (Hebrews 11:1). But it is also evidence of two things: the substance of things hoped for and the evidence of things not seen. Both of these things are well evidenced in God's Word.

So you too can trust what you hear and live with the faith of daredevils.

290

Noticing the Unnoticed

Did you know that 43 percent of the Bible is narrative/stories? Despite this, not many know how to read them. The characters in narratives do not always reflect Jewish or Gentile proper conduct. This is a big thing to consider, as misreading narratives is often the only argument atheists have against the Bible.

We see inbreeding, polygamous marriage, and sexual immorality in prominent biblical characters' lives. The Bible doesn't justify their actions, but it does record them. Saying that, there is much to learn about the attributes of God and the heart of man in narratives.

One example of these interesting narratives is the friendship between King David and King Saul's son, Jonathan. They were great friends!

As the two grew up, Jonathan had a son named Mephibosheth. When Mephibosheth was five years old, his dad, Jonathan, died in battle (2 Samuel 4:4). To save the boy, Mephibosheth's nurse fled with the five-year-old but in a hurry dropped him and permanently injured his feet/legs. Simply put, Mephibosheth could not walk. He had a disability.

When reading 2 Samuel 9, we find years later that David's enemies have been defeated. In turn, David looks for Jonathan's family (2 Samuel 9:1). After this long, exhaustive war, you may wonder why he looks for Jonathan's family. 2 Samuel indicates he did this so he can show them kindness.

Have y'all ever tried to look for somebody just so you can be kind to them? David does, finds Mephibosheth, and brings him to his palace.

Mephibosheth, in response, felt unworthy, and he calls himself a "dead dog." This was his view of self-worth. David lets Mephibosheth know that he is valuable. He restores all his inheritance lost with his father's death and allows him and his child to live in the palace the rest of their lives and be treated like his own children.

The amazing truth behind this story is that God always notices the unnoticed. Prior to Christ's Gospel unveiling the mystery through Paul, there was a divide between the Jew and the Gentile. There was only a gospel of the circumcision; there was no good news for the uncircumcised, non-Jews. Yet that all changed (Galatians 2:7).

And just because God's plan for them had not been unveiled, this doesn't mean God didn't notice them. God knows all and judges all! (Psalm 147:5; 1 Corinthians 2:10–11).

Christ's sacrifice broke down the wall of partition. And now, we can see how God sees us. There are a lot of people who go unnoticed in the world. If David did not look for Mephibosheth, he would have gone unnoticed the rest of his life. A lot of people do not know their worth. Everyone is valuable to God and is made right by His blood (John 3:16). They will not know their worth until the Body of Christ notices them and tells them. We can all make a difference and share the love of Jesus. At the end of the day, we all must know, "we can love the unnoticed."

291

Need an Air Freshener

The Lord give mercy unto the house of Onesiphorus; for he oft refreshed me, and was not ashamed of my chain.
—2 Timothy 1:16

A few weeks ago, I had plans to get to work early and begin my day on the right track and prepare my classroom for my students to come in and have an interesting lesson. I got ready, I headed out the door, and I got in my car, and my smelt one of the most repulsive smells I have ever smelled in my life. I looked over and I realized I had accidentally spilled some of my latte from the morning before, which contained milk, and it had spoiled. And it was in my car, stuck. And I had to go. I could not go and grab soap and clean, so I reached into the glove compartment, opened up an air freshener, and hung that bad boy up.

That sweet-smelling air freshener didn't clean up the spoiled milk. The air freshener did not shoo the stink out the window. The air freshener made the car bearable. The car still had particles of disgusting milk in the air, but I could get through it, drive to work, and not cringe the whole time because the air freshener had changed the atmosphere.

In 2 Timothy, the apostle Paul was awaiting his judgment and execution for his ministry ordained by God, but he reflects on someone who no matter what, was there and remained unashamed to the end of his friendship with Paul. This man's name was Onesiphorus, and he is an incredible example of how we as Christians should live.

I once heard we as the Body of Christ should be thermostats, not thermometers. We need to be a people who live for change. But oftentimes, change comes from those who refresh others.

Being someone who shares the truth of the Gospel and encourages others rarely ever changes the circumstances

(Isaiah 40:31). Very rarely do they ever clean up the sour milk in their lives, and the circumstances they drive through life in may stink. But the Body of Christ is an outlet to help make the world around others bearable. We should be a sweet-smelling, Pillar of Truth who brings a message of change to a broken world (1 Timothy 3:15).

And we must realize that it is okay if we don't change circumstances. But we can be a vessel of edification and refreshment to those in need.

You can be an air freshener by the grace and righteousness of God. You too can be an Onesiphorus!

292

Oxymoron

oxymoron: a figure of speech that combines two usually contradictory terms in a compressed paradox.

Language is such a beautiful thing. It is filled with an organized code of symbols that help us to better understand the world around us, record what we know, and tell others what we want to know. God foresaw that this is how humans would communicate, and "holy men of God spake as they were moved by the Holy Ghost" (2 Peter 1:21).

God even masterfully manipulated words so that humanity could understand the full breadth of what it is He wanted to say. Sometimes He did this in similes, parables, and other forms of language. One form of literary device that God uses is oxymorons.

An oxymoron is when two seemingly contradictory terms, when put together, make something make so much more sense. One example of this is when something is "bittersweet." Bitter doesn't do this feeling justice, and neither does sweetness. Only when the two contradictions are put together, do we see the beauty and reality of such a strong feeling.

One biblical oxymoron my mind drifts off to can be found in Isaiah 43:19 when God promises a work in Israel so amazing that there will be "rivers in the desert." God states that He has redeemed

His people, Israel, and that with God on their side, they should have no fear.

Saying this, I pray the power of God never becomes a topic cliché in the lives of believers. God is a redeemer. The Lord is holy. And yes, all that is spoken by God will come to pass. That means that a desolate land, which is eager to kill, will bring forth water that makes life able to be lived.

As Christians, we were once defined by the direction of our dry, desolate hearts until rivers of grace and life flowed through, irrigating the barren wasteland (John 7:38). We live now in the fertile crescent of righteousness and have overflow available for those interested in having the same (Philippians 1:6–7).

Only God can do such an amazing work and bring it to completion. Yes, I mean Him making rivers of the deserts of your heart.

Therefore, live life as an oxymoron.

293

Delegation

If you want to do a few small things right, do them yourself. If you want to do great things and make a big impact, learn to delegate.
—John C. Maxwell

Delegation is a beautiful thing. When one delegates, they focus on the biggest responsibilities manageable for one person, and all else, they give others around them the ability to solve and make their own way. Good bosses are good delegates. Knowing what to assign for a greater effect is crucial to living unto a unified purpose.

You know, this is true of the business world, but God also has a knack for delegation. After all, we are created unto good works (Ephesians 2:10). In every dispensation (the dispensation of law, grace, etc.), God gave authority to a spiritual leader, and that leader, by direction of the Holy Spirit, delegated roles to others.

In the dispensation of law, Moses received commandments from God, and Moses delegated down the roles of Levite priests and the civil crowd. For the dispensation of the grace of God, God delegated the message of the Gospel to the apostle Paul, who then instructed the Body of Christ to live as ambassadors unto the ministry of reconciliation (2 Corinthians 5:18–20).

So indeed, God delegated! Now do not get it confused, God giving Paul authority did not subtract any authority from Himself, but it did tell the Body of Christ that there are words that they are to particularly esteem (Ephesians 2:20). The Words now make our Scripture.

You have a role to play in this delegation, however. Your role is to heed instruction and take the Gospel with you everywhere you go (1 Corinthians 15:3–4). To make known the mystery of godliness and live according to the Word (1 Timothy 3:16).

Delegate every chance you can in life, but never delegate away your purpose. Keep the main thing the main thing, and share the grace of God!

294

Good Communication

If ye then be risen with Christ, seek those things which are above, where Christ sitteth on the right hand of God.
—Colossians 3:1

The Bible records that communication consisted of one single language that usually is broken apart within the story often titled, "The Tower of Babel." Scientists since then have found this to be true, although they sadly don't credit Scripture with having said it first.

Communication for nearly all of the human race is a local phenomenon. The mailing system was once only a group of couriers who took long periods to relay any messages. The first modern mailing system wasn't created until 1505, which is recent history relatively speaking.

Then, a man by the name of Antonio Meucci created the first basic telephone in 1849, and the rotary dial telephone was created by Alexander Graham Bell in 1876.

Even here, communication was still local and required mediums known as switchboard operators to transmit messages. In 1989, the World Wide Web was created by Al Gore (kidding) and publicly released in 1993, which made communication instantaneous.

We've seen the advent of the World Wide Web revolutionize communication recently with smartphones, laptops, etc.

At one point in biblical history, worship came about in a physical place with very specific mediums, but now in the dispensation of grace, we worship in spirit and truth, which is available to us anywhere, anytime. Worship is no longer about location, and it no longer needs a temple, for our bodies are a temple (1 Corinthians 6:19–20)! Nonetheless, it still has to do with position: You must be positioned within Christ.

Dwelling with Him in heavenly places by the Spirit. Worshiping in spirit and truth, available any place and all the time.

It is by the Spirit that we can communicate with God, by which we are saved, and Christ intercedes for us (Romans 8:26). It is by the Spirit and by truth, we worship God as the Body of Christ.

295

A Questions for Pastors About Pastors

> For there are certain men crept in unawares, who were before of old ordained to this condemnation, ungodly men, turning the grace of our God into lasciviousness, and denying the only Lord God, and our Lord Jesus Christ.
>
> —Jude 1:4

As a pastor and a writer, I am always looking for inspiration in my writings. I read books, I watch TV, and I am always looking for a lesson in everything. On one blog, the question was asked, "What is the most important thing you've learned from a TV preacher?" So I thought of as many TV preachers as I could think of, and I realized they were all horrible people. Now, now. I know that "all have sinned, and come short of the glory of God" (Romans 3:23). Whenever I address the flaws of others, I usually get this reprimand from other Christians.

"Judge not lest you be judged!"

"All have sinned!"

"You're not perfect!"

But along with the mountain of biblical evidence supporting reproval of brethren for their betterment, allow me to say, pastors are called to be blameless (1 Timothy 3:1–3). As I thought about what

I have learned from many TV pastors, I realized that they help teach by experience what I do not need to be as a pastor.

I should not be humanistic, greedy, self-absorbed, and I should never get caught saying the following true conversation by a number of famous TV pastors:

> Paul Crouch: "I am a little god. I have His name. I am one with Him. I'm in covenant relationship. I am a little god. Critics be gone!"
>
> Kenneth Copeland: "You are anything that He is."
>
> Creflo Dollar: "You are gods [little *g*]."

We are called to be blameless pastors and laypeople. Blameless. When people look at us, only pure grace and truth must be reflected.

Kenneth Copeland once said, "I am a billionaire, because the assignment that the Lord gave me, He said, 'I want you to begin to confess the billion flow.'"

What TV pastor have I learned the most from? Name them, and I have learned a lot. I've learned this is not my calling. My calling is to preach the mystery of Christ openly, proclaiming that Christ came to die, be buried, and rise again so that we too will rise again when that day comes (1 Corinthians 15:3–4; Ephesians 3). If it puts you or me on TV, don't compromise. If it puts you in the streets, don't compromise. If it gets you killed, don't compromise.

What have I learned from TV preachers? The way of this world is filth, and the Gospel is much more valuable than Jesse Duplantis's private jets.

Get your wisdom from the fountain of life, Jesus Christ, as dictated by Scripture.

296

Everyone Is a Theologian

Everyone is a theologian, even those who have stains on their souls.
—Basil the Great

When in college, I pursued a double track. I pursued ministry and I pursued exercise science. I remember being enrolled in one of my ministry courses and reading through a book titled *A Little Book for New Theologians* by Kelly Kapic. I read it and was constantly told that everybody is a theologian. I was told that because everyone had an understanding of God, everyone was a theologian.

R. C. Sproul once wrote a book titled *Everyone's a Theologian: An Introduction to Systematic Theology.* It discussed how everyone is a theologian and how the lens of the world must be filtered through how we understand God. It got preached to me that everything you do, you do by theology.

But still yet, nobody who preached this message actually believed it. I remember having a conversation one time with a teacher and hearing that I would make an excellent theologian if I continued through school to get my doctorate. I was insulted.

This comment told me that the only way I would be a theologian and have anybody respect my work in the Scriptures was if I went through seminary and was indoctrinated by religion. Reading

Scripture wasn't enough. Understanding the Scriptures wasn't enough. I needed a title.

I wrote an essay at one point and quoted particular pastors who had incredible insight into the Scriptures and the topic I was studying. They were considered unscholarly and not real theologians.

An inspiration to me has always been C. S. Lewis. In conversation with a teacher at one particular time, they said he was a good writer, but not a theologian, and if he was, he was just a "lay theologian."

On top of this, everyone who ever preached to me that "everyone" is a theologian would always deny being a theologian. *Theology* literally means "God's [*theos*] word [*logos*]." A theologian is someone who studies the nature of God, but everyone does this whether they realize it or not.

It is not, nor should it be, a term hijacked by the religion, spiritual aristocrats, and fabricated doctorates. Here I am, affirming you now. You are a theologian. No ifs, ands, or buts.

My question is, don't you want to be a "good" theologian? That requires the best tactics to know and understand God deeper. To grow in knowledge. The theologian's main tactic is to rightly divide.

> Study to shew thyself approved unto God, a workman that needeth not to be ashamed, rightly dividing the word of truth. (2 Timothy 2:15)

This esteems the study of God's Word as our highest action and making sound decisions regarding Scriptures by knowing where we are in Scripture, who is speaking, and to whom that person is speaking. People forget these basic principles of scriptural reading and esteem religion higher than Scripture. Religion hurts. God's Word brings reconciliation and healing.

Everybody does theology.

297

Unity of Religion

God requireth not a uniformity of religion.
—Roger Williams

Roger Williams was famous for creating the plantations that later became the colony of Rhode Island and eventually the state of Rhode Island. He gave the above quote knowing that the Christian faith was not about religion. Roger Williams is famous for detesting some of the ethical dilemmas of the Puritans, knew that the best thing to do was move away from Puritans, and was eventually described as a Baptist.

Scripture does not call the Christian to uniformity of religion. As a matter of fact, religion is detestable. It, particularly as we see and live it, enslaves, while a pure faith resides under the cloak of grace. Religion has the world chasing a man-made, fabricated standard of holiness.

But as believers, we are no longer bound to law or sin, but live freely in the unmerited favor provided by the finished Gospel of Jesus Christ (Romans 6:14).

Scripture calls us to unity in a number of things. Christ desires the Body of Christ to be unified in mind and judgment (1 Corinthians 1:10; Philippians 2:2). We are to be united in Spirit and maintain a strong bond of peace (Ephesians 4:3). We need unity in faith by the power of the Gospel, but religion? We don't need that. God doesn't require that. He doesn't want that. And I know that because, as the old song sings, the Bible tells me so.

> Let your religion be less of a theory and more of a love affair. (G. K. Chesterton)

298

The Jacket of Charity

Fall is a beautiful time of the year. The colors change. Holidays are ushered in. And seasonal drinks galore are advertised. But it can also be a confusing time. Sometimes, summer sticks around a bit longer than expected, and the climate remains hot and humid much longer than expected. Then again, sometimes, the world around us transforms quickly and the leaves change colors, fall, and then the weather crisps before we even change out our wardrobe.

When autumn arrives, it is the first time we even consider a jacket since the prior winter. But we also prepare our hearts for the seasons, which focus on thanksgiving, peace, and joy. The problem is, life moves quickly and all too often, we can't seem to equip these wonderful attributes.

My advice is to put on the jacket of charity. Wear the jacket of love.

In Colossians 3:12–14, the apostle Paul urges the Church to

> put on therefore, as the elect of God, holy and beloved, bowels of mercies, kindness, humbleness of mind, meekness, longsuffering; Forbearing one another, and forgiving one another, if any man have a quarrel against any: even as Christ forgave

> you, so also do ye. And above all these things put on charity, which is the bond of perfectness.

As believers in the Gospel of Jesus Christ, we are called to be kind, humble, meek, patient, forbearing, and forgiving. But above all these things, put on charity. God's Word very literally tells us to put on charity, like a jacket for the cold days ahead.

Before you leave each morning, put on charity. Don't just put on love. It is inadequate for the cold days ahead. Put on charity. Charity is a graceful representation of love that includes all of the above attributes that we are called to, and for the days when the weather of life is too nippy, God's charity is the only thing that insulates the heart adequately. Therefore, put on charity.

Enjoy the season. Edify those around you. And be charitable in all things, for this is the will of Christ Jesus!

299

Designed Superhero

The best way to find yourself is to lose
yourself in the service of others.
—Captain America

There is an assignment that I often assign to my chemistry classes that requires them to design their own superhero based on the attributes of that element. For instance, if they make a hero with an alkali metal, this superhero will be reactive, explosive, and easily provoked. If you were to choose a transition metal, you would be looking at a hero with hard skin and the ability to withstand a lot of energy.

Often, as I watch my students pour into their heroes, I sit and wonder, *If I were to make my own hero, what would he or she look like?* or *What would their backstory be?*

I design a hero who is strong, capable, has incredible powers, and an amazing backstory that has the hero likely falling into a pit of chemicals or [enter dramatic story of transformation].

Even as a Christian, this has been my perception of a hero. Never do I think of a hero as a lowly, Middle Eastern carpenter without a penny to His name, who is crucified and crushed without even putting up a fight. But the truth is, Jesus Christ, whom I describe, is the greatest hero in all history.

His backstory is that Jesus Christ humbled Himself, came from heaven, and lived a sinless but hard life (Philippians 2:8). He was crucified and killed by the people He came to save, buried, but rose again, fully manifesting His power and enabling others to have the same power which rose Him (John 3:17; Romans 4:25; 1 Corinthians 15:3–4).

Jesus isn't a designer hero. He is the holy Hero. Showcasing love, power, and might, He sits at the right hand of God (Colossians 3:1). Our hero.

300

Coffee Break!

Coffee is always a good idea.

—Unknown

Three in four Americans drink coffee every day. It is the second most consumed beverage in America behind water. The coffee industry is worth 80 billion dollars. Coffee tastes good, is moderately affordable, and it makes us feel good. But how does it do that?

The short answer that many Americans immediately know is caffeine. Duh!

But how does caffeine do it? Well, the simple answer is that it blocks the molecule in your brain that lets you get tired! Everyone has something called adenosine receptors that throughout the day collect adenosine and make you sleepy. Caffeine, however, fills the place that allows adenosine to do its job; therefore, caffeine keeps you from ever getting tired!

In the same right, there is a God in heaven who gave everything so that we can be sealed in His Holy Spirit (Ephesians 1:13). He gave everything so that no matter what the world throws, we do not have to lose hope or joy because we have the Holy Spirit acting as our caffeine (Romans 15:13). He energizes, strengthens, and encourages us when the rest of the world only sees defeat (Colossians 1:28–29).

When the world throws adenosine, and we should be getting bogged down, we can look to Christ for our renewal and restoration. Yes, much like a spiritual coffee break.

301

The Everlasting God

And Abraham planted a grove in Beersheba, and called there on the name of the Lord, the everlasting God.
—Genesis 21:33

In the Old Testament, and the New Testament for the fact of the matter, God is known by many names. Of course, God attributes to Himself the name of Yahweh. But there are times when in our finite flesh, humanity is just so astounded by the beautiful nature and works of God that they describe Him in as accurate terms as can be mustered.

There is a story in Scripture where God promises the patriarch Abraham that he will have a son. When this promise was made, Abraham was seventy-five years old. At the age of one hundred and after much anguish in waiting, this promise was finally fulfilled. Abraham's heir, Isaac, was born. Abraham was a hundred years old and Sarah was ninety.

As you can imagine, this was an amazing spectacle that occurred, and it only occurred by God's will. Do not be mistaken. Following this incredible miracle, we also see a treaty form between two men of power, Abimelech and Abraham, and Abraham being given the land where he was to dwell "many days," likely indicating the rest of his life (Genesis 21:34). Abraham had much to rejoice over. He had a long-awaited child and land, which was very valuable, and the rest of his life ahead of him.

In an overflow of joy, Abraham called upon "the name of the Lord, the everlasting God" (Genesis 21:33). The name for the everlasting God is El Olam, which indicated that God is unending. That means He has no beginning and no end. God is eternal. An eternal God has an infinitely better understanding of what is better for those who love Him and are called according to His purpose (Romans 8:28).

In Abraham's case, a righteous man who exemplifies his righteousness by faith ascertained physical prosperity (Romans 4:3–5). In our dispensation, or age, we do not need physical prosperity. I mean, it would be nice, right? But is it any better than the wealth of heaven (Ephesians 1:3)? Of joy (Philippians 4:4)? Surely all the physical prosperity the world can offer brings happiness, but the Word of God assures us that no amount of material wealth can offer joy (Matthew 6:19–21).

Joy comes from the spiritual betterment provided by an everlasting God, who offers everlasting peace (2 Thessalonians 3:16). That is our God, El Olam. He is unending. Never beginning. Eternal. Powerful. He is our God.

302

Chicken-Nugget Faith

But his delight is in the law of the Lord; and in
his law doth he meditate day and night.

—Psalm 1:2

Chicken nuggets. They are bite-sized bits of chicken goodness. They are a well-portioned chunk of delectable goodness! It doesn't make the full chicken breast, leg, or wing any less delicious. Chicken nuggets just make chicken more manageable and snack-sized.

There isn't much meat to this message I am giving to you today. Kinda like a chicken nugget. But this devotional is just a practical tip. Not a chicken breast. I am suggesting a way to snack on Scripture.

Don't read massive volumes of Scripture a day (Acts 17:11). That's a whole chicken. Don't eat too fast. That's heartburn. Snack on Scripture. Read a little bit and meditate on it (Psalm 1:2). Savor it (Psalm 119:11). Enjoy it. Dip it in the barbecue sauce of prayer (Romans 8:26).

Live your life on a chicken-nugget faith. Read small, sit, and savor.

303

Drawing Pictures

Wherefore comfort yourselves together, and
edify one another, even as also ye do.
—1 Thessalonians 5:11

Nearly every parent, kindergarten teacher, and daycare worker has been in the situation where they are approached by a child with an absolutely horrendous work of art and asked the question, "Do you liiike it?" Holding back an emphatic "No! It's awful!" they rather reply, "It's beautiful!" knowing that this is the appropriate response to such a representation of a house, parent, or car.

Why do we do the things we do not wish to do? Maybe in this way, we are relating to Paul as he laments in Romans 7.

Or perhaps we have an innate feeling that tells us, *That is a child. Watch your mouth. That is the best that they can do, so encourage them.*

But as that child grows up and begins to see the world in a more accurate light and develop perception, the drawings in art class get better and better. As they get better, however, the more they are scrutinized. If an older teenager draws an ugly picture, they are much more likely to be criticized than the cute-as-a-button kindergartener.

Much in the same way, we as Christians should be building each other up. This means encouraging those who need encouragement and sharpening the axe of those who need to be sharpened. The Word of God tells us that, "Him that is weak in the faith receive ye, but not to doubtful disputations" (Romans 14:1).

God is who makes us stand and by whom we should lean (Romans 14:4). Be fully persuaded in your own mind and bear with others who have another (Romans 14:5; Colossians 3:13). This is called grace. Having grace with one another is a practice we all too often neglect, although we should all too rather remember.

Just like a child who draws ugly pictures. They will develop. Sometimes this just requires a little, "Good job!" and a kind word of advice. When they grow and understand the fuller things of Christ, learn to share openly with them and push them in the right direction, but remember that only God and His Word can do a work in their heart.

> When I was a child, I spake as a child, I understood as a child, I thought as a child: but when I became a man, I put away childish things. For now we see through a glass, darkly; but then face to face: now I know in part; but then shall I know even as also I am known. (1 Corinthians 13:12–13)

304

Only the Church

The Christian army is the only army that
shoots and buries its wounded.
—Dr. Freddie Gage

This quote by Southern Baptist evangelist Freddie Gage does well to play into the shock factor that appalls the Church, but just enough to cause them to stop and think. Although truly shocking as a quote, I only partially agree with it.

Yes, the Body of Christ is an army. I wouldn't dispute this portion of the quote. This is biblical (2 Timothy 2:4; Psalm 144:1). Is it true that the Christian army shoots and buries its wounded? Sure. Look around and you see it all the time. Religion suffocates the grace out of fellowship (1 Corinthians 6:12). It drives people away, affirms their sin when it shouldn't be affirmed, and criticizes others who are struggling when they only need to be encouraged (1 Thessalonians 5:11).

Yes, the Church shoots its own and buries the wounded (Romans 14:12–13; 1 Corinthians 4:5). Christ doesn't though. This is an entirely humanistic development and offshoot of authentic Christianity. Where this quote is wrong and entirely overgeneralized is when it uses the powerful word *only*. The Christian Church is by far not the only entity that does this, as people are fleshly and entirely self-centered. Truly, the Church should be the only entity that doesn't shoot its wounded and bury them.

Be different. Live sanctified, which means to be set aside. Live different. Be a medic in the army of Christ—as you charge onto the battlefield, seeing those already wounded, stay and be the hand that helps them heal (2 Corinthians 5:18–21). Never leave a soldier behind.

305

Friendsgiving

There is nothing I would not do for those who are really my friends. I have no notion of loving people by halves; it is not my nature.

—Jane Austen

Greater love hath no man than this, that a man lay down his life for his friends.

—John 15:13

Friends. As a pastor, I firmly believe that we will never value them as much as we should. I am almost afraid to say that in many regards, the Church as a whole would rather call each other brother and sister than friend. Calling someone a friend indicates that you are fond of them.

But there is a new phenomenon that has begun to pop up around the same time as Thanksgiving called Friendsgiving. Much like Thanksgiving, this is a get-together but solely with the intention of cherishing and showing thankfulness for good friends.

No one really knows where this phenomenon came from, but some attribute it to the hit show, *Friends*. Others attribute Friendsgiving to a 2007 tweet, while others bought into the image dreamed up by a 2011 liquor commercial.

Wherever your vision for Friendsgiving lies, here is a message encouraging you to evaluate your friendships. Would you give your life for them? Are your only friends those who you are related to? Are your friends people who build you up as Scripture commends (1 Corinthians 15:33)?

Good friends will make you better and are definitely a treasure worth celebrating. Find reasons to get together and fellowship in the Holy Spirit, and be thankful for good friends!

> He that walketh with wise men shall be wise: but a companion of fools shall be destroyed. (Proverbs 13:20)

306

Protector of Sins

He that becomes protector of sin shall surely become its prisoner.
—Saint Augustine

Depravity. The word *depravity* describes a deep, moral corruption that has resided in the hearts of humanity since the original sin of Adam and Eve. There is nothing on this earth that depravity has not tainted, including the moral understanding of humanity. Many times within Scripture, God makes His disgust with the depravity of humanity known. Additionally, He indicates what happens as humanity continues to live in this illness without ever ascertaining a remedy.

Some biblical examples include the following:

> Woe unto them that call evil good, and good evil; that put darkness for light, and light for darkness; that put bitter for sweet, and sweet for bitter! (Isaiah 5:20)

> He that justifieth the wicked, and he that condemneth the just, even they both are abomination to the Lord. (Proverbs 17:15)

> This know also, that in the last days perilous times shall come. For men shall be lovers of their own selves, covetous, boasters, proud, blasphemers, disobedient to parents, unthankful, unholy, without natural affection, trucebreakers, false accusers, incontinent, fierce, despisers of those that are good, traitors, heady, high-minded, lovers of pleasures more than lovers of God; having a form of godliness, but denying the power thereof: from such turn away. (2 Timothy 3:1–5)

Hell has an overcrowded population. The world has an immense population of seared minds (Jeremiah 17:9). But what a good God, who looks at such a dismal and backward world, which constantly calls the good things of God evil and the evil things godly, and says, "I still love them. I still love these people so much that I am willing to save people from their disease."

And not only does God restore the fallen nature of humanity, He uplifts us and raises our status. This goes to the extent of having us be coheirs with Christ (Romans 8:17)!

Christ's work saves the seared. God's work saves those who are near Him. God's work saves the saved. God's work saves. It all just takes a move to stop protecting sin and relinquish it to the sacrificial act of Jesus Christ.

It really is as easy as admitting, "Jesus, I believe You came to die, be buried, and rise again, so that I can be saved. This is what was required. This is what I believe. Amen" (1 Corinthians 15:3–4).

Then no longer do you protect your sins. Christ protects you from your sins with His blanket of righteousness.

What a good God!

307

Getting Started

> The secret of getting ahead is getting started.
>
> —Mark Twain

Bible study is a labor of love. A labor of love for our Lord and Savior Jesus Christ. For the Christian, reading your Bible is almost instinctual, and failure to do so has an effect. If you read your Bible, you feel good. If you don't read your Bible, you feel guilty.

If you find some world-changing information in your scriptural study, you feel overjoyed as if you are closer to God! If you are trudging through Leviticus and you are struggling to understand the Scriptures, you feel disappointed, isolated, and estranged from God.

Oftentimes, new Christians' first questions include "Where do I start?" "What now?" "What book of the Bible should I read first?"

Does this sound familiar? I offered many scenarios to relate to.

But sometimes, the best pastoral advice I can give is to just get started! It may be extrabiblical advice, but I love the quote by Dropbox's CEO, Drew Houston. He states,

> If you have a dream, you can spend a lifetime studying, planning, and getting ready for it. What you should be doing is getting started.

The Christian faith is not a faith of complacency. It is not a SWAT-force faith, where you have to approach everything with special weapons and tactics. Just start.

Scripture is a book breathed out by God and is wholly edifying (Romans 15:4; 2 Timothy 3:16). Do not fear it, at least in regards that your eternal confidence is shaken by whether you pick it up or not. Just get started. If you want pastoral advice on where to start, whether younger or older Christian, go to Romans.

But truly, just get started. Fall in love with the Word which speaks of the purest love, the love of God (Romans 5:8). Just get started.

308

Sixty-Six-Book Love Letter

My bounty is as boundless as the sea,
My love as deep; the more I give to thee,
The more I have, for both are infinite.
—*Romeo and Juliet*

For men, it is generally frowned upon for them to say they love a good romance. "Bros" never discuss movies like *The Notebook*, *Pretty Woman*, and *Pretty in Pink*. An increasingly small minority prefer romance books over romance movies.

But perhaps one of the most timeless and purest expressions of love is the classic love letter. Nothing rivals them. Few things can melt the heart of a loved one more than putting into writing the expression of the things you can't quite verbalize. They mean the most. Their words endure.

Even more special is to watch how love letters develop and blossom as the love grows between two.

And even more unique is when the God of the universe manifests His love for humanity and pens His love for us in a flawless letter (Hebrews 4:12). God details His entire relationship with humanity from beginning, Genesis, to the end, Revelation. Between these two love letters, God shows how even though we try and escape the breadth of His love, He will pursue relentlessly and make a way for us to love Him back for eternity.

Scripture truly is a sixty-six-book love letter. Unrivaled and unmatched by Shakespeare and Nicholas Sparks. God never failed to pen a right word, His diction is flawless, and the very grammar is holy and awe-inspiring (Psalm 136:26). The love of God is sweeter than all other loves (Psalm 3:3).

> Charity never faileth. (1 Corinthians 13:8)

309

The Canon Made the Church

When I was in college, studying within a biblical course, I remember being asked the question, "If the Church decided what went into the Bible, what keeps the Church from adding to the Bible today? What keeps the Church from removing Scripture today? I mean, look at Martin Luther. He called the epistle of James an 'epistle of straw'!"

Even then, I shook my head at this question, and if I recall correctly, I replied, "People did not make the Scriptures, if that is what you are implying." And indeed, that is what was being implied, even if an evangelical Christian wouldn't flat-out say it.

Additionally, Martin Luther did not believe James should be removed from Scripture, but rather generated two tiers to Scripture. He said some things were for the Church and some things were for the Jews, or not as applicable because of context. But this is not my point.

In this devotional, I want to make a point abundantly clear. The Church is made by the canon of Scripture, the canon of Scripture is not made by the Church. And biblical "scholars"—note my quotation marks for sarcasm—argue, "Well, no. The canon was made by the Council of Rome in 382 CE!"

To this, I reply, no. They organized it. They shuffled the scriptural deck. They gave it some numbers.

God's Word is eternal (Psalm 119:89). God's Word spoke the universe into existence (Genesis 1:1). God's Word spoke the Church into existence. And by God's Word, which became flesh, died, and was your Sacrifice, God's Word made you eternal too (1 Corinthians 15:3–4).

The Church did not make the canon. The canon made the Church, and every book that is in the canon is there by God's will.

310

Perichoresis!

If you can't explain it simply, you don't understand it well enough.
—Albert Einstein

Have you ever been in an intriguing conversation and, right when you are about to drop some mind-blowing truth, you just don't quite know how to explain it? Albert Einstein would suggest that this is simply a lack of understanding of which you speak. And truthfully, I agree. Knowing something and truly understanding it are two completely different things. Knowing something well means that you can translate it into an understandable quotation of some sort.

An example of this type of conversation would be any discussion on the Trinity of God. The Bible speaks much of the Trinity, but in our finite human minds, there is only so much we can understand about it. Saint Patrick describes the Trinity as a three-leaf clover, but no, that's not quite right. That means there are three versions of God on one stem. God is wholly three in one, not segmented.

Another popular illustration you may hear at times is, "God is like an egg. You've got the yolk, the white, and the shell." But even then, God cannot be segmented into parts. He is wholly inseparable. Still, some will say, "God is like the three states of matter! Solid, liquid, and gas. They may all be God, just in different ways." But to that, I say, "That's polytheism!"

God is three in one. Fused together, but also individuals in a way that we cannot describe in words. Jesus Christ states, "I and My Father are one" (John 10:30). Or when you see the Holy Spirit descend upon Jesus at His baptism as the Father watches, you may raise the question, how are they all the same God, but also individuals in this moment (Luke 3:22). They aren't different modes or people. They are all God, at the same time!

Now I, as a pastor, am not one to lean on the wisdom of the early Church fathers, because if you look at their theology, it was often very flawed. But they did derive a very good explanation of the Holy Trinity in a manner that defends the Triune capability of God. This idea is called perichoresis. This word, literally rendered, means "holy dance." By "holy dance," they showed God as three individual beings that dance and are tied together in perfect unity as one person. It is not a perfect illustration, as previously stated, but it does show the unbroken nature of God, the Holy Trinity.

How you understand God to be affects how you understand the world to work. How you understand God affects how your view of salvation works. For instance, did God merely send a sacrifice to die for our justification while the Holy Spirit and the Father kicked back and watched, or did God Himself decide to die on our behalf; therefore, fully understanding what it means to "pour Himself out" (Philippians 2:7–8)?

Ponder this today and be sure to thank God for truths we can't fully grasp. Thank God for His perfect being and perfect will for our salvation (1 Timothy 2:4). For He is great.

311

Four Corners

G-O-D. Great Omnipresent Divinity.
—Stanley Paskavich

The United States of America is a spectacular place. The USA means so much to so many people. This amazing country has an incredible variety of biomes from deserts to rainforests. There are too many dialects to count. They may differ from city to city, county to county, state to state, region to region. America rightly deserves the title of "the Beautiful."

But there is one interesting place with a unique claim to fame within America known by a few names, but it is often called the Four Corners Monument. It is known as the Four Corners because it is the only place in America where you can stand within four states at one time. At this monument, you can stand within Utah, Colorado, New Mexico, and Arizona. All at once, you are in three unique locations while still being in one place solely. Yes, you would be in New Mexico, but you could also be in Colorado.

This is similar to how God interacts with the world. Many Christians understand God to be omnipresent. God is in heaven, and God is on earth. The striking feature of this statement is that He is both at the same time (John 1:1; Hebrews 1:3). God is all-powerful, holy, wholly different, and is able to manifest the glory of heaven on earth simultaneously. Among this truth, He has ambassadors, in whom He indwells by the Holy Spirit, who carry out His will on earth (2 Corinthians 5:20).

No matter where you go, you cannot escape His eye. So as the Body of Christ, allow what He sees in your life to be reflective of His majesty. After all, He won't miss a thing as He stands on the corner of heaven and earth (Psalm 139:7).

312

Saint and Sinner

Simul Justus et Peccator.

—Martin Luther

I grew up in a religious tradition that believed that in this life, we can completely beat sin and live an entirely holy life. For years, I was fed this doctrine until I came to the realization that our reward is a heavenly one and that it is not God's ultimate goal for our life to make such an earthly goal. Sure, to try is a standard, but not a rule.

My goal is not to go into a lengthy negation of this idea, but rather to explain the truth I find, firstly in the Word of God, and secondly, in the wisdom of Martin Luther, who pronounces, "Simul Justus et Peccator!"

Martin Luther, originally a devout Roman Catholic monk, knew well the once-universal language of Latin when announcing that humanity is "at once justified and a sinner." Luther homes in on the beautiful truth that at the moment of conversion, you are justified and made right with God, although the unending battle of the flesh rages on. Simply put? You have grace for sinful nature, and by grace, you are justified (Romans 5:1).

Like a child with a warm blanket afraid of monsters, when you equip Christ's Gospel and cover your head with His righteousness, the monster of death is no longer able to devour you (Romans

4:22–25). When God looks down at you, He sees Christ, and by His stripes, you are healed. You are a fleshly sinner, walking by the Spirit, covered by the imputed righteousness of God (2 Corinthians 5:21).

This message repulses some, and I reckon, once being deceived myself, I understand. But functionally, it is the key to grace. You mustn't become haughty and high-minded like the Pharisees and see yourself without and criticize those who live "worse." You must see yourself as you are. Rotten. Rotten and forgiven (Romans 8:6). Sinner and saint. Awaiting the redemption of your body in heaven (Romans 8:23).

Have grace!

313

Work Out

For bodily exercise profiteth little: but godliness is profitable unto all things, having promise of the life that now is, and of that which is to come.

—1 Timothy 4:8

Any gym rat knows the feeling of disappointment when they work out hard, design a good schedule, and just can't seem to "get their weight up." Any gym rat knows the gratification of getting their weight up and completing a hard set or reaching a max rep.

As a pastor, I often compare faith to a race, a sport, or a workout, but let's talk about our condition to get to that point. If you can, think of a time when you were struggling to get to that next goal in your routine, whatever routines you have.

It takes work, persistence, and oftentimes a little bit of resistance. When I tell you to work out with God today, I am encouraging you to lie on the bench of grace, which holds us up as we prepare to gain strength by benching the breadth and weight of Scripture. Each side of the barbell holds all that is needed to grow. But only those who take a hold of the bar can lift these weights.

The bar in this metaphor is the Holy Spirit. You cannot pick up weights without a handle (2 Timothy 2:15). The Holy Spirit makes this possible (1 Corinthians 2:14). The bench of grace holds you up (2 Corinthians 12:9).

There will be times when we can't get the weight up. The world can make you sore. But through persistence and vigor in your study of the Word, you will grow (Romans 5:1–5). You will make milestones. Most importantly, though, you will be a strong man or woman of God.

Get in the habit of working out your soul.

314

The Fruit of the Spirit

But the fruit of the Spirit is love, joy, peace, longsuffering,
gentleness, goodness, faith, meekness, temperance:
against such there is no law. And they that are Christ's
have crucified the flesh with the affections and lusts. If
we live in the Spirit, let us also walk in the Spirit.
—Galatians 5:22–25

Fruit is a very important food globally when considering the health benefits of eating such foods, the flavors they provide for so many things, and the symbols they elicit for so many. For example, consider the fruit from the tree of the knowledge of good and evil. This fruit, often depicted as an apple, although likely a fig or pomegranate, represents temptation to so many.

But fruit, in its purest form, represents the offspring of something. Therefore, when referring to the fruit of the Spirit, it is the offspring of spiritual life.

Only, it doesn't read as *fruits*. Galatians 5:22 uses the term *fruit*. This word is singular in English and in the original Greek word, *karpos*. Now this may not mean much to you at the moment, but it is very important in correctly understanding what the Spirit brings.

The fruit of the Spirit is not a good-feeling, mixed bag of wonderful emotions. It is one fruit, consisting of all nine attributes. It is not nine fruits, consisting of one attribute each. The Spirit is transformative and instills all nine of these fruits in those who love God and are justified by His Gospel.

So live by the Spirit, expecting to see the fruit. If you are seeing fruits individually, perhaps recognize that fruit takes time to grow, and there is no better fertilizer to achieve healthy fruit than the unadulterated Word of God. Knowing that those who are in the flesh cannot please God (Romans 8).

315

Friends for Reasons

A friend is someone who knows all about you and still loves you.
—Elbert Hubbard

As a teacher, I recently had an upgrade in my classroom. From the classic whiteboard, I was provided with a new active board. I could write on this board with a dry erase marker, a digital marker, or even with my finger!

But the day I got the board, I made a mistake. I went to write something on the board for my students, and when I wrote the first line, I realized my mistake. I had written one long line on the board with a permanent marker.

This was a grave mistake, and my heart sank. My entire class gasped. I stopped my lesson and stared at the board. Then I went to work with concentrated alcohol (a benefit of being a chemistry teacher) and cleared the board of this mortal sin.

But it made me think of something. It made me think of what is permanent in life and what is temporary (Ecclesiastes 3:1). Like friendships. Sometimes, you have friends for seasons. They are like a dry erase marker on a whiteboard. They serve their purpose in your life, and in that regard, they will always be your friend.

Then, you have your friends for life. These are like the things written on a whiteboard with a permanent marker. Sometimes, you do not even realize how long they impact you, but oh, it is beautiful. I find it hard to consider one a friend until they are willing to bear adversity with you. Up until this point, they are an associate.

A lifelong friend will stick closer than a brother or sister (Proverbs 17:17; 18:24).

> Friendship … is born at the moment when one man says to another, "What! You too? I thought that no one but myself." (C. S. Lewis)

316

Chemistry in the Bible 6: Bonds

Forbearing one another, and forgiving one another,
if any man have a quarrel against any: even as Christ
forgave you, so also do ye. And above all these things
put on charity, which is the bond of perfectness.
—Colossians 3:13–14

Chemistry is a beautiful science. The scientific definition of chemistry is the science that studies the interaction between matter and energy. I think of chemistry more so as the study of how God keeps the world unsyncopated and orderly.

One of the ways that the universe around us is held together is by bonds. The term *bond* always indicates a closeness, an agreement, or being joined together. A bond is what ties the world together. It makes individual atoms build into the complex structures and things that we need to live and the people that we love. Bonds make everything.

In the Body of Christ, we have a bond that ties us together. It is the Holy Spirit. The Holy Spirit, as an individual member of the Triune Godhead, is love (1 John 4:16). A graceful love known as charity, which we must choose to put on every day, as charity is a holy lifestyle that edifies the Body of Christ.

Fellowship between believers is a criterion of the Church. We are to forbear with one another, equip charity, and prefer one another. This looks like kind affection and obedience to what we know as the Golden Rule, "Do unto others as you would have them do unto you." We see this rule showcased in Luke 6:31.

Yes, love is a rule for the Christian, not the exception, and love is the bond that ties us together perfectly. This is true regardless of what age we live in Christian history. Like in chemistry, when a bond is made, energy is released. When a bond is broken, energy is released.

No matter how we deal love, there is a powerful energy that is being harnessed, and we need to be sure we are using it as God intends and for His glory. Therefore, put on charity and increase your chemistry with the Body of Christ and your faith in Jesus Christ, who resides in you (Ephesians 5:18).

> You've gotta dance like there's nobody watching,
> Love like you'll never be hurt,
> Sing like there's nobody listening,
> And live like it's heaven on earth. (William W. Purkey)

317

Longsuffering > Patience

There are many reasons why, as a pastor, I prefer and advocate for the use of the King James Version Bible. These reasons include the literalness of interpretation, the sources of documents utilized, the origins of these documents, the inclusion of Scriptures other sources remove, and many more.

But frankly, one of the best defenses of the King James Version is the rich, descriptive, and comprehensive language that coincides with the richness of the languages from which it was interpreted. One example of this is the Bible's multiple uses of the word *makrothymia*. This word is translated in the King James Version as *longsuffering*. All contemporary illustrations use a much shallower version of the term, such as *patience*. But even in the contemporary context, this word is insufficient for the term *makrothymia*. *Makrothymia* is a term that indicates endurance, forbearance, and an unmovable nature. It very literally means to "suffer long."

Christians should not be unfamiliar with suffering as the Word of God states that, "Yea, and all that will live godly in Christ Jesus shall suffer persecution" (2 Timothy 3:12). If you are living godly, you will suffer persecution, thus indicated by the word *all*.

Additionally, patience does very little but help you keep your cool in frustrating situations. Longsuffering offers moments of introspection and growth that are unattainable in times of no suffering

(Romans 5:1–5). Longsuffering is harder than patience but indeed superior.

It is additionally a part of the collective fruit of the Spirit. It is part of the fruit of godly living! It doesn't come immediately, but be patient, suffer long, and be ready for what this brings in your faith, whether good or "bad," knowing that nothing godly can ever be deemed bad. For

> we know that all things work together for good to them that love God, to them who are the called according to his purpose. (Romans 8:28)

318

Another Coat

Painting calmed the chaos that shook my soul.
—Niki de St. Phalle

Unlike the above quote, painting does not calm my soul. I hate painting. I am not someone who enjoys the tediousness of it, and I especially do not like having to apply second coats when painting homes. I hate working so hard only to have to do it again as soon as it dries. This would be when the whole choir shouts, "Amen!"

But this action is necessary. Every coat of paint laid onto the wall covers a prior layer of filth and varying color. The beautiful truth is, though, that every day our outward man is perishing, yet as believers, our inner man is renewed day by day (2 Corinthians 4:14–16). The undercoat will never fade away. It will never grow filthy. It will never get beyond repair. Because Christ, like the diligent painter, renews the walls of our hearts daily (Romans 12:1–2). This means we are made new every day we open our eyes. This pattern continues into eternity (2 Corinthians 4:14).

Coat after coat, our hearts are renewed by the loving blood of Christ, which is shed abroad in our hearts (Romans 5:5). Aren't you glad God never gets tired of making a new creation (2 Corinthians 5:17)?

319

Sound Doctrine, Part 1

What we believe is important. It has a bearing on our lives. So what should we believe and what should be taught? Simply, the answer is sound doctrine. As Christians, we must believe sound doctrine, at the head of which is Christ crucified, buried, and resurrected. From the Gospel, we are imputed the righteousness of Jesus Himself (1 Corinthians 1:30). In His righteousness comes the authority to teach sound doctrine within the broken realm of humanity and within the Church, for its edification (Titus 2:15).

So what is sound doctrine? Paul utilizes the Greek word *hygiainō*. *Hygiainō*, if you would notice, looks a lot like the word *hygiene*. *Hygiene* derives from *hygiainō* and likewise derives a powerful application. Hygiene is something heavily focused upon in American culture because many people rightly carry the understanding that better hygiene leads to better health.

Sound doctrine should carry the same understanding. The word *sound* means to be in good health. Sound doctrine is untainted by the virus of sin and promoted in fellowship with Jesus Christ. Spiritually, good health comes from believing good doctrine. Sound doctrine endures and is maintained consistent with the Word of God. Sound doctrine has a function. If sound doctrine is taught and the church ingests it, then it acts as a multivitamin for the souls of believers. It keeps the body healthy and keeps disease far from it. It provides instruction and rebukes those who try and contradict it (Titus 1:9). It reproves (reprimands), rebukes (admonishes), and exhorts (encourages). Sound doctrine heals and grows its adherents.

320

Sound Doctrine, Part 2

Sound doctrine is much like a daily multivitamin; Christians forget and refuse to take it. When this negligence is taken and sound doctrine is not believed, no matter how sincere we may be, we suffer a deficiency of faith and love. Spiritual deficiency makes for an ineffective Christian. No matter what spiritual gifts or talents we possess, they are going to waste. This is because the salvation and spiritual edification of man rely on the pure, untainted, and healthy Word of God.

Contrary to sound doctrine, all facets of our spiritual health degrade. One example of these facets is the fervor and effectiveness of a Christian's unique love. In 1 John 4:16, John the Beloved states,

> And we have known and believed the love that God hath to us. God is love; and he that dwelleth in love dwelleth in God, and God in him.

This is an example of sound doctrine living in (and out of) the believer. I want every believer on a mission, believing the Word of God (with sincerity), and taking it into their world as an effective vessel of the Gospel. After all, although I disagree with Charles Schulz's position on belief, I have a mutual consensus with him when he suggests, "There is no heavier burden than an unfulfilled potential." I share this consensus because every individual has the potential to be saved and come to the knowledge of the truth. Truth that is only unveiled within the display of sound doctrine (1 Timothy 2:4).

321

Just Another Message About Unity, Part 1

Here I am, writing once again about unity. Yes, this is just another message about unity. Everybody of every background, belief system, and opinion is talking about it, and I was deterred from writing this article in fear of feeding a cliché. Nonetheless, my conviction is my conviction. I am sure this is what God has called me to write about right now, and I will pursue it.

On October 7, 2021, an article was released by *The New Yorker* titled, "What American Christians Hear at Church." Allow me to note that this magazine is not a Christian magazine, although it is apparent that they culturally feel inclined to comment on their external position on the church. Why is this?

The answer, I believe, was unconsciously yet clearly stated within author Casey Cep's writing when he notes, "This is regrettable, since many more Americans attend church than subscribe to a newspaper." Hallelujah.

But nonetheless, I was intrigued by this article for a plethora of reasons. One of the most disconcerting reasons being that in evaluating the church on Sunday mornings, it was noted numerous times that there is a harsh line drawn between sermon presentations.

Read this quote:

> This country is filled with preaching on all sides of every political or social movement, with sermons on any given Sunday praying for the President or calling him illegitimate, arguing for reproductive freedom or against abortion, praising social welfare or condemning it, decrying socialism or explaining how Jesus practiced it. The fissures of our society are evident in our churches, as they have always been, and although the hope is that the divisions of the secular world can be erased there, all too often they are reinforced instead.

Once again I state, this is not a Christian magazine. I am not asking anyone (especially pastors) to put aside their political opinions; however, I am asking them (for who applies) to preach the Word and stop preaching themselves. If we honestly think that fleshly conversations from the pulpit are of God, then we are in a worse position than I thought.

Preach the Word, rightly divided (2 Timothy 2:15). The Gospel should be the unifying factor of the church, and it should promote unity. Paul addresses such division in 1 Corinthians. Let me introduce exhibit A, which is 1 Corinthians 1:10: "Now I beseech you, brethren, by the name of our Lord Jesus Christ, that ye all speak the same thing, and that there be no divisions among you; but that ye be perfectly joined together in the same mind and in the same judgment."

These phrases are glossed over as if they are optional:

- "Speak the same thing."
- "Be no divisions among you."
- "Perfectly joined together."
- "Same mind."
- "Same judgment."

This is what God wants for the church. It is not a leisurely suggestion that God will be happy with whether we heed His word or not. Unity is sound doctrine. Sound doctrine being "healthy" doctrine. False teachers (many of which the author affirmed as legitimate pastors) are not the only people fissuring an external and internal view of the church.

Biblically "sound" pastors are not doing the Body any favors either by teaching secondary opinions and giving more encouraging stories than the encouraging Word of God. The content of what is preached is essential to the calling of a pastor and in validating who is a pastor. Test the spirits and weigh whether the messages you hear are more Scripture or frivolous stories which glean no enduring truth.

322

Just Another Message About Unity, Part 2

God is unity, but always works in variety.
—Ralph Waldo Emerson

Following the previous devotional, "Just Another Message About Unity," there is an emphasis that needs to be met in the nature of those who proclaim God's Word. We must preach the Word; otherwise, we are merely paying lip service to God when we claim to be "Gospel-centered."

Let our foundation and like-mindedness be in that Christ died, was buried, and rose for our justification (1 Corinthians 15:3–4). Spiritual maturation is not learning long theological words or anything of our own righteousness. It is abiding in this truth and continuing to esteem Christ as the head of the Body of Christ.

Check out Paul's teaching in Ephesians 4:13–15 when he urges,

> Till we all come in the unity of the faith, and of the knowledge of the Son of God, unto a perfect man, unto the measure of the stature of the fulness of Christ:

> That we henceforth be no more children, tossed to and fro, and carried about with every wind of doctrine, by the sleight of men, and cunning craftiness, whereby they lie in wait to deceive;
>
> But speaking the truth in love, may grow up into him in all things, which is the head, even Christ.

By Paul's definition of unity, it never departed from the Gospel as the origin. He never reinstated unity as reorganizing a church, social programs, fleshly love, or anything else that we try and band-aid hurt with. It is the Gospel that bonds us into a perfect man and woman. Only Christ can do it.

When we depart from it and preach the secondary or chase other doctrines, we are bound to be deceived and further the fissures that the secular world is obviously seeing. Speak truth (Gospel-centered) in love and grow in Christ. Grow in unity.

So yes, as the title suggested, this is just another message about unity to pile on top of the thousands published these past couple of years. Yet if this one sticks for just one person, my heart will sincerely be glad. Because after all, a body doesn't function if dismembered, and it doesn't move without a head. If the Church confesses that Jesus is Lord and head of the Church, then we must be moved as one!

323

To Enrich

If you saw it, you'd likely not know it. If you held it, you'd likely not feel it. If you were a rock collector, you'd likely mistake it for something else. I am talking about uranium. Humanity often regards it as the future of energy and the epitomic resource of mass destruction. But man, you likely wouldn't be able to tell it apart from some of the gravel in a driveway.

So what makes it so valuable? To impatiently answer my own question, uranium must be enriched to be valuable. Or efficiently valuable, that is. Throw some uranium ore into a reactor, and it wouldn't do much. But refine it by a laser, excite the electrons of uranium, and you get something that some people would kill for. It is an incredible source of energy and is so valuable.

Humanity, when birthed, is raw, ugly, common, and sinful. We are not born good despite common perception. But there was a cataclysmic event in human, and moreover heavenly, history that offered enrichment. It offered purpose. This event changed the ores.

This event is the death, burial, and resurrection of Jesus Christ (1 Corinthians 15:3–4). By His life, we too can live by simply believing that He did so on our behalf (Ephesians 5:2). From here, you can grow daily in the knowledge of Jesus Christ, who gave Himself for you (2 Peter 3:18). As the days pass and you draw closer, you are enriched (2 Corinthians 9:8–11). Your purpose remains, but your effectiveness is magnified by the truth of Scripture. Therefore, seek enrichment by the Word of God!

324

Vines at Stake

As an American Southerner, I can testify to the things considered delicacies to a Southerner. Southerners like their chicken fried, sweet tea, and many a Southerner loves tomatoes (colloquially, these are *'maters*).

Many people grow tomatoes because there is the timeless belief that they are better when you grow them yourself. Saying this, every Southerner knows that in order to make tomatoes grow and survive, they need a stake for the vine to grow up. If there is no stake, the plant will fall over and get eaten by slugs and bugs until there is nothing left for a 'mater sandwich.

As Christians, we are offshoots of the true vine by which we get our sustenance and salvation, Jesus Christ (1 Corinthians 3:11). But know if you do not stake yourself to that vine and if you refuse to cling to it, you will slump, and your fruit will suffer. Your faith will get eaten quickly. And on that day, when you stand before God, your heavenly reward may suffer as a result.

We do not live this life for an earthly prize, but a heavenly one. We seek a day where God looks to us and shakes away all the fluff and only sees the righteousness brought about by the work of His Son, Jesus Christ (1 Corinthians 3:13–15). Cling to the stake. Hold fast. Look and move upward. Do not move out. Move up the stake (Philippians 3:12–14).

325

The Margin of Error

On what basis can a righteous God justify the ungodly? It is entirely and all of grace.

—Allistar Begg

Often, as a pastor, I write about the unity of the Church. It is a topic near and dear to me, as I desire to see greater unity in the Church as God desires. But I am one to admit that I believe there are levels to unity. By this, I mean that variation within the Church is beautiful. We all have quirks, personalities, and attributes that make us entirely unique and valuable in our efforts for the Gospel.

There is a scale to the margin of error applicable, and there are some things that cannot be excused. In study, I have found three categories that can be laid out in many ways; however, they need to be in this order: essentials, debatables, and opinions. In discussion, if a person moves from left to right, their allowable margin of error widens. But as people move right to left, the margin of error slims.

In essentials, there must be unity in the Body of Christ; otherwise, the consequences can be as grave as not being in the Body of Christ (Psalm 133:1; Philippians 2:2). This used to be called a poser. But in your opinions, you can be entirely valid as long as your opinions do not encroach on the essentials, which allow for no error. Primarily, these essentials have to do with the personhood and deity of Jesus Christ and the truth of His death, burial, and resurrection for our salvation (1 Corinthians 15:3–4). Debate this, and your margin of error is shattered. You are wrong.

But if you were to discuss whether or not Adam was made from the dirt with an incredible six-pack and bulging muscles (Genesis 1–2), I say, have at it! God is truly the artist. Considering this scale can help you stay out of hot water, but also help you identify the things that really matter in the faith.

And

> if it be possible, as much as lieth in you, live peaceably with all men. (Romans 12:18)

326

What Do You See in Me?

As in water face answereth to face, so the heart of man to man.
—Proverbs 27:19

Have you ever been around someone that entirely unnerves you? You do not know what causes it, still yet, there is an energy that is off-putting. In all truthfulness, the most unexplainably uncomfortable I have ever been around someone was around a pastor.

Saying this, have you ever been around someone that makes you feel glee, gladness, happiness, or joy? Isn't it strange how some people have the power to change your mood in the snap of a finger? People reflect people. People reflect what is inside them. They show their spirit. People show their filth. People exemplify their joy. Folks who live by the Spirit have people see the Spirit.

Humanity is a social race, yet most of what humans see in others is not verbal. It is a reflection of who they are, which is the nonverbal. People see it! Never be so self-conceited to think that you go unnoticed (Proverbs 3:7). God surely does, and there are many among you who are capable of seeing the goodness of Christ or the depravity of Satan.

How muddy is the water? Are you living blamelessly, exposing the beautiful fruit of the Spirit (Ephesians 5)? It is a good introspective question to ask because, "As in water face answereth to face, so the heart of man to man" (Proverbs 27:19).

Look in the water and what do you see?

327

The Intercession Quadrilateral

As a science teacher, writer, pastor, and anxiety-driven spazz, I need to admit: I like order. I love that our Lord is an orderly God (1 Corinthians 14:33, 40). I love that our Lord is an orderly God who loves me (John 3:16). Nonetheless, some things growing up never quite made sense to me until I put them in a chart. A nice, organized chart. I love them.

This one chart I devised was called the "intercession quadrilateral." The quadrilateral didn't really have a start and truly doesn't have an end, but for the sake of the illustration, it goes like this: A person intercedes on another's behalf (1 Timothy 2:1). The Holy Spirit, who indwells within us, intercedes up to Christ (Romans 8:26). Christ, as the right hand of God, intercedes horizontally to the Father (Romans 8:34). The Father intercedes down to those who were prayed for and who prayed (Romans 8:28).

Of course, this model has its flaws. Perhaps, intercession is not so linear; I admit that. What the intercession quadrilateral does account for, however, is that intercession is an unbroken chain that always is answered with a "yes," "no," or "not now" (2 Corinthians 1:20).

A good old-fashioned chart comes in handy sometimes!

328

I'm Getting Older Too

Well, I've been afraid of changin'
'Cause I've built my life around you
But time makes you bolder
Even children get older
And I'm getting older too.

—Fleetwood Mac

As children age, many times we neglect the fact that those around us also age. Perhaps the saddest realization on earth is looking across the room at your mother and seeing that she has aged. She isn't as young as she once was. She looks a little more tired than you remember.

But the worst part is that you didn't even notice her change. She was young once and then, in the blink of an eye, she isn't. This realization makes you feel scared and vulnerable because you realize how little you control. But God has provided His Word of comfort for those who are in the midst of aging.

Perhaps, the first thing to do is acknowledge that God is outside of time and that time exists because of Him. This is the God in whom you put your trust:

> But, beloved, be not ignorant of this one thing, that one day is with the Lord as a thousand

> years, and a thousand years as one day. (2 Peter 3:8)

Next, address why the fear of seeing your parents grow old makes you feel vulnerable. You feel a looming existential threat of aging, and for many, it is because you realize that one day, those you love will pass away. When they pass, you fear loneliness and the horror of no longer making memories with them. This fear is entirely rational, and I do not want to provide you with a philosophical pill to mask your fear. But I do want to encourage you that God resides through every step of life and that those in Christ will not see death. Jesus has defeated death, thus conquering it forever. Death will become an illusion and a brief passing (1 Thessalonians 5:13–18).

This promise is so amazing that Scripture titles it our "blessed hope" (Titus 2:13)! Begin immersing yourself in hope, and you will develop a hopeful endurance that will help you treasure those closest to you. God will sustain you in your greatest fears (2 Timothy 1:7).

329

The Seven Stages of Man, Part 1: Play Your Part

In the Shakespearean play *As You Like It*, there is a character who delivers a riveting and infamous dialogue addressing the origins, presence, and death of man. This monologue has been coined as "The Seven Stages of Man" and states that humans play many parts throughout their lives.

In biblical narratives, we see these parts time and time again, and typically, we find a trend of increasing maturity. I mean this both physically and spiritually, as the apostle Paul writes, "When I was a child, I spake as a child, I understood as a child, I thought as a child: but when I became a man, I put away childish things" (1 Corinthians 13:11). But even our spiritual heroes grow old and decrepit, as even the biblical hero David needed a companion to keep him warm as he lay awaiting his death (1 Kings 1:1–2).

So what do you do in these varying stages of life? Well, eventually, you learn to expect the unexpected and to trust the things that can be expected, which is solely God's faithfulness—every time (2 Thessalonians 3:3).

> All the world's a stage,
> And all the men and women merely players;

They have their exits and their entrances,
And one man in his time plays many parts.

It is of the Lord's mercies that we are not consumed, because his compassions fail not. They are new every morning: great is thy faithfulness. (Lamentations 3:22–23)

330

The Seven Stages of Man, Part 2: The Infant

His acts being seven ages. At first, the infant,
Mewling and puking in the nurse's arms.

Ah, the wonders of a child. So pure they come into the world. You often hear messages about how even the most innocent of children are born into sin, but you hold nothing against them when they smile. Regardless of their condition, God considers them "a heritage of [Himself]: and the fruit of the womb is His reward" (Psalm 127:3–5).

They are a true gift, and the Lord cares for them. Jesus provides strong caution against those who would harm a child, especially considering that one day a child will grow up into a godly adult who bears more children (Genesis 1:28; Luke 17:2). Christ's warning in Luke 17 speaks to the helpless nature of a babe and moreover, speaks to the adult's responsibility to sustain and care for them.

For Jesus loves the little children. Therefore, so should you as you desire the things that He desires (Romans 12:1–2). This is the first stage of man, innocence.

331

The Seven Stages of Man, Part 3: The Schoolboy (Preteen)

And then the whining schoolboy, with his satchel
And shining morning face, creeping like snail
Unwillingly to school.

But then the babe grows, learns, and is held accountable to the moral law written on his heart (Romans 2:12–16). Eventually, in this stage, the conviction of the law written on the heart of humanity shows the adolescent that they are to be held accountable for their transgressions against God.

But at this age, they also learn that Christ provided a way to wipe their slate clean forevermore, and they have a heavenly Father who loves them beyond comprehension (Romans 5:6–11). God loves them despite their whining, pride, and failure to heed warnings. This is a beautiful age of discovery.

They may make the decision here to believe in the Gospel, but sometimes, lessons are learned here that bring people to their knees in the next stage of life.

332

The Seven Stages of Man, Part 4: The Lover (Teenager)

And then the lover,
Sighing like furnace, with a woeful ballad
Made to his mistress' eyebrow.

The teenage years can be some of the most confusing years in a human's life. You want to be an adult, with adult responsibilities. You don't want to be considered a kid, but you want to have fun. You have a budding sexuality that arrives with the onset of puberty, but instilled guilt for pursuing it in an ungodly manner (1 Corinthians 10:13). On top of all these factors, there is a wild influx of hormones and influences that make you question who you are.

God gets it. But these experiences that you have purpose. As the world changes around the teenager, God offers the most stable lifeline to hold onto—Himself. Youthfulness is the root of maturity. To be mature, you first must experience what it is to be young and dumb (Ecclesiastes 11:9).

But it is those who find and believe in God young that live full lives and gain extended maturity as they flee youthful passions and gain godly experience. The teenage years are the metaphoric boot camp years of life that prepare the person of God for soldiership (Titus 2:6). It is the years where we become experienced in love and hate, which are powerful forces.

333

The Seven Stages of Man, Part 5: The Soldier (Young Adult)

Then a soldier,
Full of strange oaths, and bearded like the pard,
Jealous in honor, sudden and quick in quarrel,
Seeking the bubble reputation
Even in the cannon's mouth.

Past the teenage years, where you proverbially "get your feet wet" in life, the battle has merely just begun. The teenage years offer time to experience life but in a much more sheltered way, comparatively even for those who grew up harder than others. The young adult is released into the battlefield of life, where they begin to make their own way.

Traditionally, this was signified by the cleaving together of a husband and wife. But not all experience this, especially in the post-modern age we live in. But the Christian adult lives differently. A Christian adult does not get entangled in the normal life of a young adult, which is mundane and purposeless. The Christian adult, a soldier of God, does not get "entangleth himself with the affairs of this life; that he may please him who hath chosen him to be a soldier" (2 Timothy 2:4).

The soldier of God learns to be quiet, to the business they are called to, and take care of those who need to be taken care of (1 Thessalonians 4:9–11). Soldiers, young adults, need purpose. God gives purpose, and He loves seeing soldiers live unto that purpose (1 Timothy 2:4)!

334

The Seven Stages of Man, Part 6: The Justice (Middle-Aged)

And then the justice,
In fair round belly with good capon lined,
With eyes severe and beard of formal cut,
Full of wise saws and modern instances;
And so he plays his part.

As a young man, here I lose ethos. My credibility may suffer in terms of experience. But Scripture holds rich reminders for those who feel like kingdoms that they built are crumbling and that they are becoming distant from who they once were. Weight is gained, different things excite you, and hormones don't quite energize you like they once did.

In times like these, it is important to remember that although we change, our position in Christ does not. You are justified, sanctified, and sealed unto that faithful day when our bodies are redeemed. Christ, who began a good work in you, will see it through, and it is okay to adapt to life and continue to grow into older age (Philippians 1:4–6).

There is nothing on earth or beyond that will separate you from the love of God and the good purpose He called you unto (Romans 8:35–39; Ephesians 2:8–10).

335

The Seven Stages of Man, Part 7: The Slippered Pantaloon (Old Man)

Last scene of all,
That ends this strange eventful history,
Is second childishness and mere oblivion,
Sans teeth, sans eyes, sans taste, sans everything

In the Seven Stages of Man, individuals begin to devolve once again into a stage much like infancy. The life of a man and woman is much like a parabola or a curve. It has a point of origin (infancy), it has a climax (the thrill of adulthood), and it is a decline back into deficiency (end point).

Scripture indicates that "the hoary head is a crown of glory, if it be found in the way of righteousness" (Proverbs 16:31). The aged person can sit back, enjoy the life they have lived, and answer the question of what things were worth living for. Some people reflect and find a fulfilled life. Some reflect and ask, "Why did I waste so much of my life?" Even for those who feel this way, it is never too late to realize that your position is in Christ and that God still has purpose for you, even when you can't take care of yourself.

When you are weak, Christ is strong (2 Corinthians 12:9). Self-worth should not be viewed through your own introspective lenses.

This will leave you disappointed, particularly when you focus on what you can't do instead of what you can do. I am not advocating for the power of positive thinking, but I am advocating for you to seek things that are above when life has you down (Colossians 3:1–4).

336

The Seven Stages of Man, Part 8: Once Again a Babe (Near-Death)

Last scene of all,
That ends this strange eventful history,
Is second childishness and mere oblivion,
Sans teeth, sans eyes, sans taste, sans everything.

In the last moments of life, Shakespeare describes this as a "second childishness and mere oblivion." Like an infant, life is frail here, and there is a proverbial return to innocence. The mind slips, the body fails, but Christ is faithful. Sometimes there is a bedside salvation.

So be it. Praise God. Too many people discredit these occurrences. Religion and pride cloud their judgment. But regardless, at the moment the body passes this realm, the individual has a blessed hope. They have the promise of life forever, where there is no more pain or suffering, and they live as coheirs with Christ (Romans 8:17).

I was once asked, as a pastor, what my funeral sermons look like. I'll first tell you what they don't do. I don't lie. I don't tickle ears. But what I do is preach hope. I preach the redemption of our bodies in heaven (Ephesians 1:7). I preach an unyielding God who promises resurrection and sent His Son to provide it (1 Thessalonians 4:14). A fitting way to end the seven stages of man and to begin the one unending stage of eternity.

337

Stop Making a Theory of God! A Message to Myself

For the invisible things of Him from the creation of the world are clearly seen, being understood by the things that are made, even His eternal power and Godhead; so that they are without excuse.
—Romans 1:20

As a science teacher and a Christian, I have found myself guilty many times over of giving what I deem unsatisfactory answers to questions that kids have asked, or heck, I have asked myself.

One example of this is when in chemistry, I talk about how the world is made of atoms, and atoms are made of opposite charges such as electrons and protons. But then when I, or a student, ask deeper questions such as what holds together the heart of the atom, the nucleus, scientists have a name for the force called the "nuclear glue." But no one knows how it works. There are theories, but that's all they really are. Therefore, I say, "That's just the way it is." I guess that is all I am allowed to say in a public school. But I know the answer. I need to guard my thoughts.

That strange nuclear glue is the providence of God, which holds the universe together and keeps the world from falling apart. We don't understand it because it isn't our creation to understand.

In biology, how do embryonic stem cells choose what they are going to divide into? How do they know what is needed? Sure, we can have shallow answers like "The DNA activates, so it changes." But how does it know what to change into?

People can act like they know, but no one knows how life truly comes about. Well, actually, we do. God does it (Colossians 1:16). He knits together life (Psalm 139:13–16).

We, as people of reason, need to stop leaving the beauty of creation to chance. We need to stop making a theory of God and give Him His due credit and glory for His wondrous works. This is a lesson much more to myself than any other person, but if the shoe fits for you too, wear it! We'll share that shoe! The works of God are not a theory!

338

Can You Lose Your Salvation?

> When God offers a man life, God offers a man only one kind of life, and that is eternal life. Eternal life is the life of God, and as God's life could never be terminated by death, so the life of God, given to the child of God, could never be terminated.
>
> —J. Dwight Pentecost

As a pastor, I am often asked the infamous question, "Can you lose your salvation?" I know many of you are holding your breath as you read my answer to this question. This question may become a heated debate within Christianity. But my answer is this: You can by no means lose your salvation; however, you can lose your faith. There is a difference. Allow me to explain.

When you accept the Gospel of Jesus Christ, a number of things happen. There is an acronym that covers the breadth of the Holy Spirit's work at the moment of your belief. It is called CRIBS, and each letter has a strong biblical precedent. You are

- circumcised (Romans 2:25–29),
- regenerated (Titus 3:5),
- indwelt (Romans 8:9),
- baptized (1 Corinthians 12:13),
- sealed (Ephesians 4:30).

These are all very firm actions with various purposes, many of which are permanent. Not to get graphic, but there is no way to "uncircumcise" yourself or degenerate yourself when you have been regenerated. That is likened to a caterpillar who has been regenerated into a butterfly proclaiming, "This flying stuff is too hard! I am going to be a caterpillar again."

Allow me to place emphasis on the sealing aspect of the Spirit's role. We are sealed until the day of our redemption (Ephesians 1:13–14; 4:30). That is otherwise known as our glorification when we reach our heavenly destination. I am not preaching to live however you want from salvation on, but we must realize that our Christian duties forward are repaid by a heavenly reward (1 Corinthians 3:12–14; 2 Timothy 2:19–20). If there is nothing we can do to ascertain our salvation (as it is a gift), what could we possibly do to unseal the work of the Holy Spirit?

Nonetheless, there are examples of men in the Bible who have erred from the faith. One example of this can be found in 1 Timothy 1:19–20. There is an account of two men who had "shipwrecked" their faith, yet Paul delivered them unto Satan (a form of excommunication), so that they can learn and be restored. There are numerous cases of Paul doing such, yet it was for the restorative purposes of their faith, not their eternal salvation.

339

A Good God? Part 1

Sin is cosmic treason. Sin is treason against
a perfectly pure Sovereign.

—R. C. Sproul

I was recently asked a question that many atheists and agnostics have prompted as a defense of a dead or nonexistent God. Many believe that the question, "How can God send someone to hell if He sent His Son into the world to bear our iniquities?" or "How could a good God send anyone to hell?"

This is a classic question, often phrased in a number of ways. I once heard it explained this way: "God does not send people to hell. They simply decline His offer to come home." Since then, I have heard this explanation offered up in different ways, and it almost seems too simple to be true. Metaphors can only go so far, but the point is this: God is holy. In order to ascertain a holy eternal residency, one must be holy. Imagine this: someone wants to live in a multimillion-dollar mansion. So they go to a real estate agency and tell the agent which house they picked out. When the agent ultimately asks the person how they intend to pay for it, they reply, "Well, I can't. I am broke." It would not make sense. You cannot live above your means. In the same way, it is the pride of a human to say, I want to live somewhere holy, but they are depraved or sinful.

Now let us reimagine the above situation. The poor man goes to the real estate agent and says he wants to live in the mansion, and the real estate agent exclaims, "Great! We actually have a very rich and powerful person who gave everything up so that you can live there! The cost is paid!"

At this point, you have two options:

- Humbly accept this free gift.
- In pride, deny it and work for something you will never be able to grasp.

This is the same situation as the question asked, but metaphorical. Hell is a real place, instituted by separation from God. It is contrary to His holiness and what we deserve. But when Christ died for us and was buried, He rose again in victory so that we may also have victory in death. When you are saved, Christ's righteousness makes you holy, and you are deemed acceptable. The only requirement to accept His holiness is to believe this message.

340

A Good God? Part 2

Can God love and hate me if I sin at the same time? Does He separate the sinner from the sin or hate both?

Once again, I want to examine a question that requires us to look at the nature of humanity in light of the nature of God. There is a common folk theology that states that God does not hate sinners, but only their sin. This is not accurate biblical theology. I can provide ample biblical evidence that shows God does hate sinners (Psalm 5:4–5; Proverbs 6:16–19; Malachi 1:3).

Many attempt to do biblical gymnastics with these verses, but the truth is, even if there were not countless verses to defend this fact, only one verse is needed. One verse is enough. We truly need to ask ourselves some hard questions about God's character if we cannot believe the Scriptures for what they say. Wrath and righteous vengeance are attributes of God, just as much as His love is.

Yet even with His strong disdain for the sinfulness of man's being, the attribute of His love still presides, and He opens the doors for a right relationship with Him. The two inherently do not seem to jive, but God is the ultimate anomaly. This is why we should never overlook verses such as 2 Corinthians 5:17, where in Christ, we become new creations. God does not and will not tolerate painted-over sin; He desires a new and totally acceptable creation provided by Jesus Christ's righteousness.

341

Free Will

There's too much tendency to attribute to God
the evils that man does of his own free will.
—Agatha Christie

Free will. Churches have split and systems of theology have been written all revolving around the question of free will. But may I suggest this question: "Why wouldn't God allow someone to choose their own path?"

God, in creating humanity, intended a relationship with humanity and, through a number of dispensations, offered ways by which a relationship could be ascertained. Once hinging on the covenant of works, we now live in an age of grace by which an intimate relationship with the Father is possible by the Gospel of Jesus Christ through the indwelling of the Spirit.

It is often (possibly oversimplified) said that God did not create us as robots; rather, He created us in original form to desire a relationship with Him, yet sin soiled this original nature. But before that ever happened, God had a plan to restore us to the right relationship and call us to Himself (Ephesians 1:3–6). Christ fulfilled this plan.

342

Have No Fear!

Ah, but a man's reach should exceed his
grasp, or what's a heaven for?
—Robert Browning

Have you ever been gripped by fear as you asked yourself the question, "What happens after death?"

Although this becomes a sad thought as we think of loved ones and people who have not believed in the Gospel of Christ, it is still an amazing thing to say that what happens after death is your choice.

The two sides of the coin are this: eternal life in heaven or eternal damnation in hell.

There is much discussion among theologians as to exactly what this transition to either state looks like, whether there is an intermediate state while awaiting a new heaven and new earth, and so on, and so on. But let me offer you a few of the definite.

Both places are real (Matthew 10:28; John 3:13). Heaven is unspeakably wonderful (1 Corinthians 2:9). Hell is unimaginably torturous (2 Thessalonians 1:9). Your spirit will be translated to one of these places, but as for those in heaven, there will be a bodily resurrection in which you will receive a glorified body (1 Corinthians 15:50–58).

If you have not made heaven your eternal residency, do not wait. Understand your current situation of depravity and sinfulness, and believe that Jesus Christ came to earth, died on the Cross, was buried, and rose again to save you from that state of being and has offered you a heavenly inheritance (Romans 3:23; 1 Corinthians 15:3–4; Ephesians 1:11–14). Here, there will be no more suffering or anguish, but life everlasting (John 3:16; 2 Corinthians 5:1)!

343

A Demon-Possessed Christian? No, I Think Not

I have heard the question asked before, "Can Christians be demon-possessed?" To this, I simply reply, "Oh, what a contradiction!"

But to answer this question in depth, we need to address two preliminary matters. First of all, one must understand what a demon is. Second, one must understand what possession is. Once we understand those two matters, we can understand what our standing in Christ has to do with both of these matters.

A demon is an angel who followed Satan in his prideful revolt against God (Luke 10:17–18; 2 Peter 2:4). This celestial event may bring up other discussions about free will and what angels can and cannot do, but what is important for this discussion is this: demons, like angels, are spirits.

Saying this, spirits have a number of capabilities that humans in this mortal state do not. One of these is indeed to fill the empty crevices of human souls. This is what is referred to as possession. The Bible records many instances of demon-possessed individuals, and it is worth noting that individuals could have more than one demon residing within them (Luke 8:30).

Now contrast this kind of possession to when we receive the Holy Ghost. The Holy Spirit also resides within the soul of humanity, but in this case, there can only be one Spirit. The implication of the biblical truth "once saved, always saved" is applicable in this conversation as well. When an individual is saved, they are sealed until the day of redemption (Ephesians 4:30). Demons no longer have access to drive the soul and body of a human. You are possessed by the Holy Spirit and therefore slaves to Christ, as Paul depicts in Romans 1:1.

But I should offer this warning. No longer can a Christian be possessed; however, understand that there will continue to be demonic influences. These influences are something that we will wrestle with for the remainder of our lives while we are still in our flesh, but we can remain strong in our faith by equipping the armor of God (Ephesians 6:10–17).

344

Bad Christians

Don't let your lips and your lives preach two different messages.
—Anonymous

As a Christian, have you ever felt guilty for not living up to the expectations you believe God has for you? Have you ever thrown your hands up and exclaimed, "Why do I even try? I am such a bad Christian!"

You may know that there is no one good, not even one (Romans 3:10, 12). Many in the faith repeat this verse like a scratched and broken record. So in that regard, yes, you may be a bad Christian. But you may also know that Christ imputes His righteousness on us so that we are seen as righteous by Him. So in that regard, no.

Still, we are storing up rewards in heaven (2 Corinthians 5:10; 2 Timothy 2:20–21). This is made clear, so the obvious answer would be that some have "done better," but a Christian is not "bad" if made "good" by Christ. Perhaps the question needs to be better defined. Maybe a better question is, "Are you an efficient Christian?"

345

God, Give Me a Sign!

The purpose of life is a life of purpose.

—Robert Bryne

I once had a friend confide in me about a deep-seated issue they were having. In confiding in me, they additionally asked me, "How do you tell what God wants you to do?"

Continuing on, they said they were looking for signs and confirmations. Every billboard they drove by, they paid close attention. They were looking for a sign. For every sermon they heard, they looked for direct correlations to them to confirm the decisions they were making. But everything they did, they felt unsure of.

I explained to them that God's will is like a funnel. A lot of times we treat God's purpose for us as a funnel, but an upside-down one. We want to know the specifics of purpose before we get the bigger picture. But purpose-wise, we need to treat our purpose like a funnel as it is intended. We have our broad, and then we find the details as they trickle down (1 Timothy 2:4). Then the Lord fulfills His purpose for you (Psalm 138:8).

Regardless, instruction from that point on is the Word of God and led by the Holy Spirit within you (2 Timothy 3:16–17).

346

I'm Stuck

At the heart of Christian faith is the story
of Jesus' death and resurrection.

—John Ortberg

There are hundreds of books written by Christians about Christian discipline. As Christians, we want to constantly know what to do in order to be our best, and sometimes, this thought is a burden to our faith because we feed into the lie that God will love us less if we mess up. Then, you feel stuck.

But there is good news! There is the Good News! The Gospel of Jesus Christ states that Jesus was born, died, was buried, and rose again to seal you in the Body of Christ!

My understanding of Scripture is that in our dispensation or age, being a Christian has much more to do with what you believe than what you do. Belief directs the direction of your discipline. Our faith is not of works (Ephesians 2:8–9), but we are created unto good works (Ephesians 2:10). Discipline's origin is observance and study of the Word. When truth is accepted, pursue action and grow.

347

Position over Condition

> The devil knows he cannot touch our position,
> so he attacks our condition.
>
> —Anonymous

Only God can identify with true perfection (2 Corinthians 5:17). Christ is the head of all principalities and is King of all (Colossians 2:10). Do not be deceived into thinking that Satan does not know the power of Christ to seal you for all eternity. He doesn't attack your position; he attacks your state and condition.

When I use the word *principalities*, I do not want you to only think of the Church, but know that Christ is Lord over all evil principalities as well. God is holy. God is sovereign. We cannot attain perfection; we can only respond to His (Romans 3:24; 1 Corinthians 15:3–4).

Saying this, we have the privilege to walk in and with Christ, and here in this condition, we should desire, individually and collectively: fullness, growth, increase, and maturity. This means no longer being babes in Christ, and faith is a catalyst that actualizes this maturity. From this point, what we practically increase in are

- patience,
- experience,
- hope,

- assurance,
- faith,
- love,
- knowledge,
- understanding,
- wisdom,
- judgment,
- thankfulness,
- strength.

This increase ultimately leads to our part in living in God's will: salvation and growth in all things (1 Timothy 2:4; Philippians 1:9–10). And lastly, with this, in everything, give thanks (1 Thessalonians 5:18).

348

NASCAR Theology

For as we have many members in one body, and all
members have not the same office: So we,
being many, are one body in Christ, and
every one members one of another.
—Romans 12:4–5

I recently listened to a series of NASCAR interviews following a tightly contested race. They sounded like typical NASCAR interviews; however, I recognized something that I had never thought of before.

During the interview, none of the five drivers who were racing referred to themselves—not once. They didn't say, "I did something" or "I did this." They said "we" every time they spoke of something accomplished. This shows that driving is only a small part of NASCAR, although it is the only part that is recognized. The *we* includes sponsors, a pit crew, a radio team, and some even regard the team's fan base.

Oh, if the Body of Christ were to follow in this example and refer to the big *we* instead of the shallow *I*—some would be the drivers, some would be radioing the calls, and some Christians would just stand as a spiritual health pit crew (1 Corinthians 12:12–27)—what part of the team are you?

349

Rejoice, Pray, Give Thanks (Part 1)

Rejoice evermore.

—1 Thessalonians 5:16

As Christians, we have many tools at our disposal to help better our lives physically and, more importantly, spiritually. Our God is a God of comfort, and He desires you to keep at your disposal Scripture for comfort. Our salvation is to be at the top of this "comfort toolbox."

Comfort toolbox is a term I coined that describes an inventory of things we can take comfort in. But as for comfort, there is no comfort without salvation and justification. I think all too often the book of James is incorrectly described as the Proverbs of the New Testament. Even more applicable are the "proverbs" found in 1 Thessalonians 5. These proverbs extend to every realm of life in one way or another.

When reading the book of 1 Thessalonians 5, particularly the verse of 1 Thessalonians 5:16–18, the reaction should be to rejoice. Jesus is alive, Jesus is King, and Jesus has made a way. He is the way. If you are in Christ, rejoice.

350

Rejoice, Pray, Give Thanks (Part 2)

Pray without ceasing.

—1 Thessalonians 5:17

The best commentary on the Bible is the Bible. As you look at the 1 Thessalonians 5:17 proverb of "pray[ing] without ceasing," the wording is critical. It does not say make a "habit of prayer"; it says "pray without ceasing."

> Prayer is to be the accompaniment of our whole life. (Cambridge Bible)

Prayer is not only the bending of the knee but, even more so, the bowing of the heart. To pray without ceasing elicits the will of God before your own; therefore, you address Him in reverence, knowing that He is wholly capable of fulfilling His own will. It's not elegant words that God adores; it's humble hearts yearning for Him (Matthew 15:7–8, 18–20).

You may wonder why you pray, knowing that God is all-knowing and already knows what you need. But prayer is not about what you pray for but who you pray to. Bow your heart and acknowledge He is able. Live a lifestyle of unending prayer.

351

Rejoice, Pray, Give Thanks (Part 3)

In everything give thanks: for this is the will of
God in Christ Jesus concerning you.
—1 Thessalonians 5:18

The First Letter to the Thessalonians 5:16–18 gives a holy trifecta of wisdom: rejoice, pray, give thanks. All three of this trifecta are the will of God, and the way Paul lists them suggests attention to the chronological order. Rejoice! Do not pray without the joy of the Lord (this is not the same thing as being happy). And give thanks knowing that God our Father hears every request and prayer.

But why give thanks? I think the above reasons are sufficient, but amazingly, the Lord always exceeds our expectations. We should first give thanks because it is the will of Christ Jesus. A thankful, prayerful heart has plenty of reason to rejoice evermore because of our salvation. When we pray for our needs, it must be accompanied with thanksgiving. This is a good practical bit of information to enhance your prayer life. Rejoice. Pray. Give thanks. And

> the grace of our Lord Jesus Christ be with you. Amen. (1 Thessalonians 5:28)

352

The Next Generation

The Cold War was a state of hostility between US-led and Soviet-led countries. It began following the use of the atomic bomb in 1945 and officially ended with the collapse of the USSR in 1991. But it was more than a conflict between weaponry and power. It was a war for the mind, ideals, and way of living.

Before Ronald Reagan was president, he addressed California, saying the following in his inaugural speech as governor:

> Perhaps you and I have lived too long with this miracle to properly be appreciative. Freedom is a fragile thing, and it's never more than one generation away from extinction. It is not ours by way of inheritance; it must be fought for and defended constantly by each generation, for it comes only once to a people. And those in world history who have known freedom and then lost it have never known it again.

But this isn't a message necessarily of American patriotism. It is an announcement that the victory is already won (John 16:33; 1 Corinthians 15:57).

Take heart, I have overcome the world.

As members of this generation, we are made complete in knowing this truth. But with freedom and victory in Christ, the world still reaches for the silver lining of truth. This is just like the slaves in Galveston, Texas, who hadn't heard the news that the Civil War had ended and their salvation was coming soon. The war between death and life is won.

But being isolated from Jesus Christ (the way, the truth, and the life), anything they are being told is a lie! So what can we do? The answer is simple: pass it on! Whenever you get the chance, pass it on. Let us verbally open our mouths and tell people, "The war is over, Christ is victorious, and He is offering you a chance to join the winning side."

To the next generation, "passing truth on" is becoming more difficult. A wise man once said that with the "freedom of speech comes the freedom to listen." As Christians, the freedom to listen is our friend and enemy. This is because of the truth of Romans 10:17:

> So then faith cometh by hearing, and hearing by the word of God.

If someone doesn't first stop and listen, they won't hear. At the same time, this is one of the beautiful things about the Gospel. God did not create robots to love Him, and in His perfect compassion, He allowed the choice to love Him. Jesus Himself submitted His will to the Father (John 7:17). This submission to Truth pleased God. Today's generation is listening to a lot of voices, some of which God allows. In every dispensation and age, God gives the choice of life and allows the alternative.

> See, I have set before thee this day life and good, and death and evil. (Deuteronomy 30:15)

Silence is not worth the eternal consequences to the unbeliever. Pass on the message of hope to this and the next generation!

353

Here to Help

Grace be unto you, and peace, from God our
Father, and the Lord Jesus Christ.
—1 Thessalonians 1:1

Paul's purpose for this letter is to encourage. He does so by teaching God's grace (unmerited favor) and salvation (soul assurance) (Ephesians 2:8–9; Philippians 4:6). Both are a blessing. *Merriam-Webster* dictionary insufficiently describes a blessing as "something conducive to happiness."

We are conduits and reflections of grace, with God as the source. Perhaps this is why our speech should always be with grace (Colossians 4:6)! And as conduits of His grace, we are bearers of His purpose. Our ultimate purpose and reason for creation is to glorify God (Isaiah 43:7).

Perhaps, being a creation of Glory, we must also praise Him who made us. Praise redirects our attention to His holy character and how He provides and has provided for us. Therefore, allow this to be a reminder of who we are in Christ and to live as vessels of blessing and praise for others.

354

Christmas Scaries

Many adults develop something known as the "Sunday scaries" every Sunday following a nice relaxing weekend. It is a feeling of dread. Dreading work or real life, we get to feeling down and scared. Many a teacher gets this feeling as they prepare each week for Monday.

This may be a familiar experience as well to something many of us have experienced. You may have the "Christmas scaries" too. We invest so much time, money, and planning all for the sake of one day, and then it is all over within hours. Then many people dread the return to normal life, where there are no more gifts, no more unending family interaction, and you realize how much money you spent on that day when the new year rolls around.

I understand the fears that you hold; but remember these words by Romanticist author Jean Baptiste Alphonse Karr, "We can complain because rose bushes have thorns, or rejoice because thorns have roses." Perspective is important; nonetheless, we are not to get lost in a day. Each day is a chance to recenter and remember why Christmas matters.

Every day is new: "It is of the Lord's mercies that we are not consumed, because his compassions fail not. They are new every morning: great is thy faithfulness" (Lamentations 3:22–23).

> Birth Becomes Significant in Death, Death Becomes Significant in Life. (Jacob Harris)

Whew, it feels good but also very narcissistic to quote myself, but I think the quote makes my point. Christ was born to die, which by His death, we can die to ourselves and live life to the fullest.

The life of humanity is not linear; it is a crooked parabola (a *U*). You are born, you die, you live again (or die again depending on a very important choice). Christmas matters because the Son of God came to ultimately die. But with His death, He rose again and ushered in more life for those who believe (1 Corinthians 15:7–8). If He didn't rise, your faith would be in vain (Romans 4:25).

Therefore, have no fear. Because Christmas has begun a long journey back around. Allow Christ and His wonderful promise of life to encourage you and alleviate the Christmas scaries.

355

Mercy and Grace

In the King James Version of the Bible, there are 170 uses of the word *grace*. Of the 170 references, 131 of these references are in the New Testament. This leaves only 39 references to grace in the Old Testament. That is about 23 percent of the references in the Old Testament.

The word *mercy* is used 274 times in the King James Version of the Bible. This is significantly more than grace. Mercy can be found 149 times in the Old Testament and 125 times in the New Testament. Here the Old Testament wins out with mentions of the concept of mercy.

The Old Testament in many regards appears much more familiar with the term mercy than grace. There are many possible reasons for this, but I want to suggest one. God is a God of mercy and grace. Nonetheless, the sacrifices God allowed to happen so that His wrath was not poured out was mercy (James 2:13). Ever since I was young, I have heard that mercy is not getting something you deserve.

But then, God gave us something we didn't deserve. He gave His Son, Jesus Christ, perfectly exemplifying grace as getting something you don't deserve (Ephesians 2:8–9). This is God's unmerited favor and the riches of heaven. Here is where you see the impact of a dispensation. God deals with humanity differently through different times (Ephesians 3). Where once mercy was God's main conduit of salvation by faith, grace was greater with the death, burial, and resurrection of His beloved Son. Grace and mercy.

356

Buffer

Look not every man on his own things, but
every man also on the things of others.
—Philippians 2:4

Divorce is a big problem in the United States. In the US, nearly 50 percent of marriages end in divorce. The number skyrockets for remarriages. But this message, unlike many Christian messages, is not going to be one that assaults the minds of those who have undergone divorce.

I empathize with those who have experienced divorce and have been affected by it. And that is who this message is for. It is for those who have firsthand experience with the devastation divorce causes.

When I was in college, as a child of divorced parents, I studied what it would take for the United States to see a decrease in the harmful effects that divorce caused, such as repeating the cycle, high school dropouts, etc. I carried out this study by looking at the success stories. The people who made it through the tough times they experienced from their parents became objectively successful. Almost all these case studies had something in common. They had a buffer.

They had a parent who would unrelentingly give love and attention to the child at the same time their life was falling apart as if it wasn't falling apart. As a pastor, I would never advocate for "faking it till you make it." But I do advocate for loving like Jesus. Sacrificial love is the goal (Romans 12:1–2). As a parent, remember that your children are a heritage of the Lord, and they will turn out how you raise them.

If at all possible, do not raise them to be victims, angry, and scared. Raise them as fearless and cheerfully joyful human beings (Proverbs 22:6). Buffer them from the depraved effects of the world (Ephesians 6:4).

357

Jesus, You Confuse Me

This is a prayer for when you are overwhelmed by the love of God.

Jesus, You confuse me. I feel off even admitting it. I try to understand, but alas! I do not.

God, with no pressure, I confidently say I would lay my life down. Nonetheless, Lord, hear me out. Living life knowing that I would lay my life down is terrifying. Therefore, I worship You, who cracks not under pressure. Rather, You mend under pressure (2 Timothy 4:8). You reconcile (Ephesians 4:2).

Jesus, You confuse me. But I will not doubt You because You made Your point known. You love me. This confuses me. But that's alright. I would rather live in the confusion of Your love than the knowledge of fools who know it not (1 Corinthians 1:25–31).

In the name of the Holy Trinity, amen.

358

Center Me

This is a prayer for when you are anxious and in need.

Lord, center my mind. I want this; however, I need that. My anxiety is crippling, but You are restoring. Center my mind therefore in and on You.

Center my mind. In meditation, I am not going to empty my mind. I will fill it with Your truth (Psalm 119:15). But center me in the correct posture of the Spirit. Show me what to glean and what to reject (1 Thessalonians 5:22).

Center me in righteousness where I belong as a child of You (Psalm 106:3). Center me, God, away from the misalignments of the world; and from my lips eternally you shall hear amen and amen.

359

Extend Your Arm!

This is a prayer for when you are desiring authentic faith over the superficial.

Lord, extend Your arm and hold me back when I seek the superficial elements of the world over the breadth of Your truth.

Dear Lord, I know that entire churches and entities are founded on subjects that mean nothing (Colossians 2:8). I do not want to waste time. I want to redeem it because the days are evil (Ephesians 5:15–17). Redeemed times will bring redeemed souls, and I want to be a needle on the clock that ticks.

Please, God, center me as a dial that does not unhinge. Guard me from the superficial and bring me to the authentic. I only desire the richness of Your Word (2 Timothy 3:16).

Amen.

360

Prayer When Life Is Unfair

This is a prayer for when you desire justice but see none on the horizon.

Father, life is unfair at times. I know You are a God who loves justice. I will not pray for You to make Your justice known. You have already done this with the great protest of sin at and on the Cross. Praise You!

Grant me the perseverance to sustain. To be faithful amid cold winters and blazing summers. Give me discernment to seek justice (Isaiah 1:17). But love still yearns when justice is not met. God, lead my thoughts as they provoke my action (2 Timothy 1:7). And I will not fail to give You the thanks, honor, and glory (Isaiah 43:7).

Amen!

361

The Lucky Ones

Thems that die'll be the lucky ones.
—Robert Louis Stevenson, *Treasure Island*

My favorite fiction story of all time is *Treasure Island*. It is an incredible story of men who seek treasure but show the ultimate futility of the search. It also shows the truth that good men are rewarded for their deeds and bad men will receive just recompense.

With some maneuvering, this story reflects an interesting scriptural truth that in Christ, there is an ultimate reward for those who seek goodness, and although the wicked do well in life initially, their effort is in vain. The godly will win out in the end as the Body of Christ has been granted the greatest of rewards—heavenly inheritance as coheirs with Christ (Ephesians 1:3)!

With this truth, we can relate to the apostle Paul, who states confidently, "For to me to live is Christ, and to die is gain" (Philippians 1:21). We have assurance of life in this life and the next. We have already ascertained the treasure provided by the Gospel of Jesus Christ and believe in it. Therefore, have no fear (2 Timothy 1:7)! Live confidently (Proverbs 3:26)!

362

Carnal Christians

If a Christian remains in a carnal condition long after experiencing new birth, he hinders God's salvation from realizing its full potential and manifestation. Only when he is growing in grace, constantly governed by the spirit, can salvation be wrought in him.
—Watchman Nee

I recently heard a story about a young man who lived like a double side of a coin. He would do all kinds of wickedness throughout the week, but around certain individuals, he would act as if what he did was not wrong. One day, a friend asked, "Hey man, why do you do what you do? Don't you profess to be a Christian?"

The young man replied, "Yes, I am a Christian. Just a carnal one."

This story, whether true or not, exemplifies a group of individuals who I have no doubt are saved by the Gospel of Jesus Christ (1 Corinthians 3:3). But their fault is a misconception of grace. People may experience the grace of God but only feel it most intimately when they sin and are feeling as if they need more of it.

It becomes an obsession, like a drug addiction. Mentally, grace registers as something that is only given when we act "bad." However, we have grace regardless of our shortcomings. We are insured by grace 24-7 because that is how comprehensive the work of Christ was two thousand years ago. Sin is defeated and death is usurped, but it is not a license to sin (Romans 6:1–2). Therefore, grow beyond the name tag of "carnal Christian" and desire the name tag of "mature Christian" (1 Corinthians 14:20). Build upon your heavenly reward by heavenly renewal!

363

Discern Me

This is a prayer for when you want to need guidance and multiple decisions plague you.

Father, I come before You this day, seeking discernment. I am in a season of life that when one situation is presented, another immediately follows suit.

I need discernment. You know all things and You know what is appropriate. Even if both choices are okay, I desire the choice that reflects Your glory most. Give me discernment, but first, discern my heart and see that all I want is Your will to be done. If this is not my desire, renew me from my innermost bowels to the skin that every person sees.

Discern me and I discern the world (Hebrews 5:14). Remind me that fear of You is the beginning of wisdom (Proverbs 9:10). Above all, let my words and actions lift Your holy name high above the highest mountains, but leave it low enough to where all on earth can see (1 Corinthians 10:31).

Jesus, I love You (1 John 4:19). Discern me first.

364

Desire and Thanks

Father, this is a prayer of thanksgiving.

I desire to make this known. I ask nothing of You now because I am overwhelmed by the truth that You have already given everything. At times, I forget this, but God, here and now, I recognize—You are good and the only one deserving of the title, "awesome" (Psalm 100:4). Keep my lips from vainly speaking this word. I am in awe of You and the Holy Trinity.

The awe I am in is far beyond appreciation, and thanksgiving is such a mediocre word for what You deserve (1 Thessalonians 5:18). Yet at this time, language is so finite, and You are infinite, so I acknowledge the disconnect (Colossians 3:15). Nonetheless, You know what I need without me even saying a word. Therefore, Father, take this prayer as a sacrifice of what I could ask for and rather, what I want. That is to glorify You.

365

Living Enriching Grace

This is a prayer for when you want to live more in the realm of enriching grace.

Lord, our ministry embodies enriching grace. But do I?

Lord, allow me to be a testimony to the grace that enriches. This is a grace that transforms and transcends, not merely makes something "better" (Romans 8:6–7). God, I desire transformation by Your Word and by Your Spirit (Romans 12:1–2). Enrichment does not make better; it is the result of something made new (2 Corinthians 5:17).

Use me as a constantly new creation that is renewed day by day. I am Yours. A vessel of enriching grace is what I desire to be (John 1:16; Romans 3:24).

Amen.

About the Author

Jacob Harris is a young North Carolina native, bivocational pastor, and high school teacher who has had a lot of living in his years. Harris has worked a number of odd jobs, was a track-and-field runner in college, is a coach, and has been wed to his forever bride, Hallie. Together they spend much of their time seeking God's will in how to further the Gospel through their lives and church, Enriching Grace Church. In his off-time, Harris would describe himself as an avid reader and family man.

Printed in the USA
CPSIA information can be obtained
at www.ICGtesting.com
CBHW031807221124
17856CB00010B/62